OCTOBER SURPRISE

OCTOBER SURPRISE
BARBARA HONEGGER

Tudor Publishing Company
New York and Los Angeles

DEDICATION

To the 52 Americans
Held Hostage 444 Days in the U.S. Embassy in Tehran
November 4, 1979–January 20, 1981

The Truth Will Set You Free

Thomas Ahern

William Belk

Robert Blucker

Donald Cooke

Max Copeland

William Daugherty

Robert Englemann

William Gallegos

Bruce German

Duane Gillette

Allan Golacinski

John Graves

Joseph Hall

Kevin Hermening

Donald Hohman

Leland Holland

Michael Howland

James Hughes

Charles Jones

Malcom Kalp

Moorehead Kennedy, Jr.

William Keough, Jr.

Steve Kirtley

Kathryn Koob

Frederick Kupke

L. Bruce Laingen

Steven Lauterbach

Gary Lee

Paul Lewis

John Limbert

James Lopez

Johnny McKeel, Jr.

Michael Metrinko

Bert Moore

Richard Moorefield

Paul Needham

Robert Ode

Gregory Persinger

Jerry Plotkin

Regis Ragan

David Roeder

Barry Rosen

William Royer, Jr.

Thomas Schaefer

Charles Scott

Rodney Sickmann

Joseph Subic, Jr.

Elizabeth Ann Swift

Victor Tomseth

Phillip Ward

ACKNOWLEDGMENTS

I would like to acknowledge these people of faith and courage
who made this book possible:

To my Parents,
Who taught me to think for myself.

To Mae Brussell,
Who taught me to seek truth for its own sake.

To Martin Anderson,
Who taught me to act on the truth.

To Sarah McClendon,
Who taught me to stand up to get the truth heard.

To Dr. Margaret Brenman-Gibson,
Who taught me the true meaning of vigilance.

To David McMichael,
Who was there when it mattered most.

To Martin Kilian,
Who really cared about the story:
Take it from here.

To Mansur Rafizadeh,
Who had the courage to kill the lie.

To President Carter,
Who kept the faith.

Thank you.

Contents

Introduction		1
I	The October Surprise	7
II	Quiet Diplomacy	54
III	The PLO Connection	106
IV	In Like A Burglar	120
V	Once Upon A Perfect Timing	129
VI	The Smoking Guns	147
VII	A Neat Idea	170
VIII	Project Democracy	186
IX	The Name of the Rose	229
X	The Sound of Silence	245
Epilog		283
References		293

INTRODUCTION

"A democracy cannot be both ignorant and free."
—Thomas Jefferson

My motive for writing this book is straightforward. I believe that truth and justice really are the American way and that, with information, vigilance, and the determination of "ordinary" citizens, truth and justice can and will be achieved. For three years I worked in an administration, that of Ronald Reagan and George Bush, whose guiding principles were that loyalty to a royalist vision of the United States presidency was more important than the Constitution, and that truth was a "problem" to be solved. I worked in an administration, also, which held the cornerstones of democracy, an informed electorate and the rule of law, in open contempt. I saw firsthand how this attitude began to eat at the moral fiber first of the President's own appointees and then of the nation, and determined to do something about it. In 1983 I made the honorable, but personally costly, decision to resign and, in August of that year, became the first resignation of conscience from the Reagan-Bush Administration. Shortly before I did, President Reagan's chief domestic policy adviser signed a photograph of himself with these words: "To Barbara Honegger, the conscience of the (White House) Office of Policy Development." That parting message is one of my proudest possessions.

This has not been an easy book to write. Its main thesis—that the 1980 Reagan-Bush campaign cut a secret arms-for-no-hostage-release agreement

1

with the Khomeini regime in October 1980—is not one that I wish to be true. During my nearly four years as a political appointee in the Reagan-Bush national campaign, transition team, White House, and Department of Justice, I grew not only to like, but to love Ronald Reagan as an individual. The very idea that he could have done what I believe the facts force one to conclude *was* done, is deeply and personally painful. After much soul-searching, I made the decision not to publish the results of seven years of research on the "October Surprise" story until after Mr. Reagan left office. This decision was made for a fundamental reason. I worked unceasingly for Mr. Reagan in his 1980 campaign for the White House because I believed then, as I do now, that he was the right personality at the right time, needed to heal the nation. After twenty-five years of assassinations and assassination attempts on our political leaders, it was vital that the next president serve out his elected term in office with as much good will as the American people could muster. It was as if, in a coming-to-life of *Parsifal*, the great underlying myth of Western civilization, Ronald Reagan became the wounded "king" upon whose healing the fate of the nation, and the world, depended. That healing achieved, a full accounting of history now becomes the imperative.

I will never forget what Ronald Reagan said one afternoon in the Roosevelt Room of the White House when asked the secret of his "Teflon coating." "I may be wrong," he laughed, "but I'm never in doubt." Though I may often have wished for such blind certainty, I do not share it. I still doubt the reliability of some of the self-proclaimed witnesses and informants whose testimony is contained in these pages. Unlike most journalists in the status-conscious world of the establishment media, however, I decided not to wait for the gold-plated eyewitness with a smoldering gun to appear on *Nightline* before informing the public of what was known thus far. Perfect proof may happen in Ronald Reagan's Hollywood, but it is rare in real life. As an independent journalist, I believe profoundly in the right of the American public to hear from all parties who claim to have information on charges as serious as that an arms-for-hostage-delay deal was made between the Reagan-Bush campaign and Iran. Parties offering information should not be pre-screened for "credibility." Such "credibility control" is nothing more than a subtle and insidious form of censorship. The American people have the right to hear from *every* witness, and to know their backgrounds, before making up their own minds about a matter of such overriding importance.

Some of the witnesses and informants who have added their voices to the "October Surprise" chronicle in these pages are not sterling characters. Neither, however, were the radical Iranians with whom Mr. Reagan, Mr. Bush, and Mr. Casey dealt for years under the cloak of secrecy. Neither was Manucher Gorbanifar, the Reagan-Bush Administration's "first channel" to radicals in the Khomeini regime, who repeatedly failed the CIA's own lie detector tests. Such failures did not prevent Mr. Casey from continuing to use him as the key middleman in the 1985–86 arms-for-hostages dealings.

The Reagan-Bush officials who have denied that the "October Surprise" story is true—former national security adviser Richard Allen, former national security adviser Robert McFarlane, former attorney general Ed Meese, former White House spokesman Larry Speakes, and those of the ilk of Oliver North—have no shining records of their own. Richard Allen, a longtime consultant to Japanese corporations, left the White House in 1981 under a cloud of charges that he accepted a bribe from Japanese businessmen. He had already reportedly accepted payments of $10,000 a month from an associate of fugitive financier Robert Vesco.[1] Robert McFarlane failed his own administration's lie-detector tests and has pled guilty to four counts of withholding information from Congress about events in the Iran/Contra scandal.[2] Ed Meese, the former attorney general and Ronald Reagan's chief of staff in the 1980 presidential campaign, left government enmeshed in a web of revelations of misconduct if not outright illegal actions. Larry Speakes has admitted to lying about what the President of the United States said, euphemistically called "making up quotes." And Oliver North's altering of documents, destruction of documents, and insistence that he had a "right to lie," are simply overt manifestations of the underlying attitude of the entire Reagan-Bush Administration, which placed affirmative value on deceiving the American public, the Congress, and the national media. President Ronald Reagan himself is known to have invented and embellished "facts," to have changed his testimony to Iran/Contra investigators at least three times, and essentially to have lived in a world of make-believe. And Mr. Reagan's Vice-President, George Bush, directed the Central Intelligence Agency, which perceives one of its primary functions to be to lie, to mislead and to spin carefully constructed webs of "plausible deniability." As my former supervisor and mentor, President Reagan's first domestic policy adviser, Dr. Martin Anderson, ever stressed, "It's always compared to *what*?" Compared to the record of veracity of the officials in the Reagan-Bush administration who have said that there is "nothing to" the "October Surprise" story, the testimonies of those who insist it is true deserve at least an equal hearing. Unlike the now-exposed liars from the covert layers of the

Reagan-Bush government, they may not always be socially "reputable." One has even been charged with a crime, which he is appealing. Some claim to have worked with the CIA, but will not identify themselves; and others who have identified themselves have been spurned by CIA spokesmen. But truth, like politics, makes strange bedfellows. We have no choice but to take it where we find it.

Some of the claims and charges contained in this book could be classified as rumors. But just because information begins as a rumor does not mean that it isn't true. A perfect example is from national security aide Oliver North's own White House files. In a June 3, 1985 memorandum, North wrote with obvious irritation,

> "For several weeks now there have been rumors of stories being prepared which allege an NSC [National Security Council] connection to private funding and other support to the Nicaraguan resistance. The rumors originally surfaced with a reporter, Alfonso Chardi [*sic:* Chardy] . . . At my request [name censored] went to Chardi . . . and told Chardi . . . that if he printed any derogatory comments about the FDN or its funding sources that Chardi would never again be allowed to visit FDN bases or travel with their units."[3]

We now know why Mr. North did not want these "rumors" to be circulated, especially by Pulitzer-prize-winning reporter Alfonso Chardy. Other so-called "rumor mongerers" of the "October Surprise" story, according to the only article on the subject published by the *Washington Post*, are former President of the United States Jimmy Carter and former President of Iran Abolhassan Bani Sadr.[4] When "rumors" reach such levels, they deserve to be paid attention to and treated with utmost seriousness.

Good history, like good science, begins with a theory, and the goal of both is to articulate a broad framework for events, one which fits as many of the known facts as possible. Though I personally wish it were not the case, the "October Surprise" theory does just that. It explains the timing of the release of the hostages held in Iran, only minutes after Ronald Reagan's inauguration. It explains why the Reagan-Bush Administration risked political suicide by shipping arms to the Khomeini regime at all. It explains the timing of the flow of U.S. armaments to Iran, which began, not in 1985, but immediately after Mr. Reagan and Mr. Bush gained power in 1981. It explains why these weapons, which are the real "smoking guns," of the "October Surprise" story, were delivered to the Khomeini regime when there were *no* U.S. hostages in Iran and fully three years *before* the first American hostage was taken captive in Lebanon. It explains the secret U.S. arms shipments to Iran in 1985 as a simple extension of the earlier deliveries, in keeping with a pre-1980-election agreement, and why they continued regardless of whether American captives were released, tortured, killed, or seized anew in Lebanon. It explains why U.S. arms shipments to Iran continued even after Iran's culpability in the bombing of the U.S. Marine barracks and U.S. embassies in Beirut and Kuwait had been clearly demonstrated. It explains why U.S. arms shipments to Iran continued even after the revelations of the Iran/Contra scandal, despite administration claims to the contrary, until at least as late as June 1988[5]—simple blackmail. It explains why President Reagan told a shocked Senator Dole that "we" would have continued the Iran arms operation "even if no [U.S.] hostages existed" in Lebanon at all.[6] It explains why the Reagan-Bush Administration insisted on dealing with often inept and thoroughly disreputable middlemen in 1985–86: they had been involved in the original negotiations before the 1980 election and the 1981–83 arms deliveries that stemmed from them. It explains the appointment in 1981 of officials knowledgeable about the pre-election "October Surprise" negotiations to exactly those positions in the new administration responsible for authorizing and overseeing arms deliveries to Iran. It explains the "mysterious" deaths of numerous individuals who, it is now claimed, were eyewitnesses to or knowledgeable about the pre-1980-election negotiations with Iran. It explains why the Reagan-Bush administration went out of its way to divert attention from the center of terrorist training and indoctrination, Iran, to a carefully crafted scapegoat, Libya. It explains the palpable fear of top Reagan-Bush officials of the congressional investigation into the theft of President Carter's debate briefing books, a dread which was completely out of proportion if all that they were afraid would be uncovered was the source of a few pilfered memoranda. That investigation focused attention on October 1980, where the terrible secret lay. It explains the great lengths that administration went to, to limit the Tower Commission, Congressional Iran/Contra Committee, and Iran/Contra special prosecutor's investigations to only the later 1984–86 period, using the literal diversion of alleged arms sales proceeds to the Contras to refocus their "mandates" away from the danger zone.

When a theory explains so many acknowledged and otherwise inexplicable facts, it deserves to be classed as a fact itself. This is now particularly true in light of the Supreme Court's recent ruling that legal "findings of fact" include "conclusions by way of reasonable inference from the evidence."[7]

On December 19, 1986, President Reagan called for "all the facts [in the Iran/Contra affair] to come before the American people." And on January 11, 1989, just before leaving office, he said, "An informed patriotism is what we want." This book is the author's wholehearted attempt to respond to both calls. As Senator Edmund Muskie once told his staff, "There is only one reason to be in politics. It is to stand out there all alone and to have yourself proven right." It is even more difficult to be willing to stand out there all alone knowing that you might be proven wrong. But this is a risk that I gladly accept. For if new witnesses come forward, or off-the-record informants become willing to speak on the record, or an open congressional hearing is finally held, or under-oath testimony is finally taken, or subpoena power is finally obtained, or a special prosecutor's investigation is finally undertaken, or some of the former U.S. hostages decide to bring legal action—or if even a single new critical fact is smoked out that moves the story closer to the truth one way or the other, this book will have served its purpose.

I

THE OCTOBER SURPRISE

**"Someday when the team is up against it,
and the breaks are beating the boys,
ask 'em to go in there with all they've got,
and win just one for the Gipper."**

**Ronald Reagan as George Gipp of Notre Dame, in
*Knute Rockne, All American***

For the top echelons of the 1980 Reagan-Bush campaign, everything depended on preventing the "October Surprise." If an "October Surprise" happened, President Carter would keep the White House. If it didn't, Ronald Reagan and George Bush would take the reins of the most powerful nation on earth. It was that simple. But what *was* this all-important "October Surprise"?

"October Surprise" was the name that the Reagan-Bush campaign gave to the single event that stood between Ronald Reagan and the White House—an eleventh-hour release of the U.S. hostages held captive in Iran, which they knew could sweep President Carter to an almost certain victory. As Reagan's top aide, Michael Deaver, put it, "One of the things we had concluded early on was that a Reagan victory would be nearly impossible if the hostages were released before the election. . . . There is no doubt in my mind that the euphoria of a hostage release would have rolled over the land like a tidal wave. Carter would have been a hero, and many of the complaints against him forgotten. He would have won."[1]

In the spring of 1980, the Reagan-Bush campaign's pollster, Richard Wirthlin, and his computer-ace assistant, Richard Beal, made an astonishing and frightening discovery. The Political Information System (PINS) they had created, which combined a sophisticated program projecting

7

relative votes for Reagan and Carter on election day, the mainframe computer at Brigham Young University in Utah, and the input of three hundred highly-trained telephone interviewers, predicted that President Carter would receive a stunning 10 percentage-point boost in the polls if he brought the fifty-two U.S. hostages home from Iran during a critical "window of vulnerability" which lasted only one week in October. It opened, PINS showed, on October 18th, two weeks before the November 4th election, and closed a week later, on October 25th.[2] As PINS had also predicted that Reagan would otherwise maintain a steady 5 to 7 percentage-point lead over the President, preventing a hostage release during that critical week, which would put Carter 3 points in the lead, became a do-or-die goal for the inner circles of the Reagan-Bush campaign. When Richard Wirthlin learned of the projection from Beal in August in 1980, he recognized instantly that preventing an "October Surprise" was an absolute condition for victory. "Rich," he ordered Beal, "better tell Bill Casey we should start working up a counter strategy right away. Ten percent could sink us. We have to come up with tactics which will whittle that down, making the worst-case assumption that Carter could do something in that week of the 18th to the 25th."[3]

The same month that Beal revealed the critical "window of vulnerability," halfway around the world, in Iran, top Iranian officials decided that the American hostages had lost their domestic political value to cement the Islamic revolution and started talking about negotiations for their release. In August, at a meeting of Iran's Revolutionary Council, the Ayatollah Khomeini's son Ahmed and Ayatollah Mohammed Beheshti, Iran's top religious leader under Khomeini, put pressure on President Abolhassan Bani Sadr, their political rival, to sign a "waiver" saying that he would agree to whatever resolution of the hostage crisis they decided upon. Bani Sadr, who was then commander-in-chief of Iran's military and therefore also the official who would receive any U.S. arms as part of a negotiation for release of the hostages, refused to sign. This refusal set the stage for what was to become a battle between Bani Sadr's attempts to obtain an early release of the hostages with President Carter and efforts by his rivals to delay their release to the benefit of the Reagan-Bush campaign."[4]

The "Bill Casey" whom Wirthlin had asked Beal to warn of the pending "October Surprise" window of vulnerability was William Casey, Ronald Reagan's 1980 campaign manager. A wily Irishman, he had been in charge of European special operations for the Office of Strategic Security (O.S.S.), the predecessor to the CIA, in the latter part of World War II[5], and if ever there was a real-life Wizard of O.S.S., it was Casey. He was the perfect spy, the author thought upon first meeting the lanky ex-spook; his incurable mumbling ensured that he would never have to use a scramble phone. The second thought that occurred to the author was that between Casey's speech impediment and Ronald Reagan's hearing problem, almost any hairbrained scheme could wind up getting approved in a future Reagan-Bush administration.

With a campaign manager who had been responsible for clandestine operations inside Hitler's Germany and a vice-presidential candidate, George Bush, who had been director of the Central Intelligence Agency when it intervened to affect the outcome of national elections[6], it was perhaps inevitable that the Reagan-Bush campaign, upon hearing about the "window of vulnerability," would be tempted to apply the covert methods it had used to interfere with the political processes of other nations, at home. Between them, Casey and Bush had intimate ties to the CIA, the majority of whose officers and agents wanted desperately to see a Republican victory[7] and many of whom thought George Bush "walked on water."[8] Casey also had intimate ties with Iran. He was a partner in the law firm, Rogers and Wells, which represented the Pahlavi Foundation of New York, the American branch of the family trust of the former Shah of Iran,[9] whose admission to the United States had triggered the storming of the U.S. embassy in Tehran and the taking of the hostages in the first place.

In addition to Casey and Bush, the Republican campaign had access to a number of high-level former and active intelligence officials, on its payroll and working quietly in the background. One top Bush aide, Stephan Halper, who had been in charge of foreign policy for presidential candidate George Bush before Bush joined Reagan's campaign in July, was the son-in-law of Ray Cline, a former deputy director of the CIA and a member of the Executive Board of the Veterans of the O.S.S., which reportedly "ran" the CIA from behind the scenes.[10] One of the senior watch officers in the campaign's communications headquarters, called the Operations Center, was a former director of internal security for the CIA, Robert Gambino, who had also been a Bush bodyguard. Acting as functionaries in the campaign's correspondence office and nearby shops were former CIA agents from the Bush side of the campaign who maintained close ties with the Agency and with a large, angry community of former CIA covert operatives who had been fired or demoted by President Carter's CIA director, Stansfield Turner. The Reagan-Bush campaign had active-duty intelligence officers as moles inside the Carter bureaucracy. Senate Intelligence Committee aid Angelo Codevilla, who was in communication with Reagan's campaign foreign policy adviser, Richard Allen, told the congressional committee investigating the theft of Carter's debate briefing books that active intelligence agents were working on behalf of the Reagan-Bush campaign.[11]

According to a former graduate student of deputy Reagan-Bush campaign pollster Richard Beal, the CIA may even have funded the critical "October Surprise" computer study itself. In March of 1980, the same month that Beal's PINS program projected the October 18–25 "window of vulnerability," Brigham Young University graduate student Pierre Blai was told by Beal, who was one of his professors in the Department of Government, that the Agency had funded another study he was working on at the time, on political redistricting.[12]

Reagan-Bush campaign manager, William Casey, wasted no time putting together teams to develop and put into action "counter strategies" to neutralize an "October Surprise" by President Carter. In July 1980, he used the term "intelligence operation" for the first time to refer to one of these groups in a breakfast meeting with reporters on the second day of the Republican National Convention.[13] Inside the campaign's national headquarters in Arlington, Virginia, however, the "intelligence operations" were known as the "October Surprise" Groups.

One of the "October Surprise" Groups that met regularly was headed by Reagan's top foreign policy adviser and future White House national security adviser, Richard Allen, whose mission was to monitor Carter's moves to release the hostages and preserve Reagan's lead in the polls.[14] His group consisted of some ten foreign policy experts, including Dr. Fred Ikle, who became President Reagan's undersecretary of defense for policy; John Lehman who became secretary of the Navy; and Admiral Thomas Moore.[15] Later, during the first year of the Reagan Administration, it would be Lehman and Allen who would bring a little-known Marine major, Oliver North, onto the White House National Security Council staff as Marine Corps liaison after only one year at the Naval War College, in August 1981.[16] (North was promoted to Lt. Colonel in 1983). According to Professor Ray Tanter, a campaign adviser on Lebanon and the Middle East who participated in Allen's "October Surprise" Group, they were sometimes joined by Robert McFarlane, then an aide to Senator John Tower on the minority staff of the Senate Armed Services Committee.[17] As President Reagan's third national security adviser, McFarlane would later be instrumental in the genesis of the Administration's secret arms-for-hostages deals with Iran, which became known as "Irangate." As we shall see shortly, he also reportedly endorsed a strikingly similar arms-for-hostages proposal to Allen to solve the "October Surprise" dilemma of the 1980 Reagan-Bush campaign.

Richard Allen estimated that as many as 120 foreign policy and national security advisers worked with the Reagan-Bush campaign, a number of them with military and intelligence backgrounds. In addition to this wealth of "consultants," Allen's team was supplemented by yet another network of active and retired CIA and FBI agents overseen by campaign manager William Casey himself, according to the FBI report to the congressional committee which investigated the theft of President Carter's debate briefing books. By October 1980, according to the congressional "Debategate" report, the Reagan-Bush campaign had informants in the CIA, the Defense Intelligence Agency (DIA), the National Security Council (NSC), and even the President's own White House situation room.

A second Reagan-Bush campaign "October Surprise" Group was headed by Admiral Robert Garrick, a retired Navy reserve admiral, high-powered public relations executive, and the head of the Office of Policy Development and Research, where the author worked.[18] Garrick was later described by one of his own co-workers, Stephan Halper, as being "paranoid" that an "October Surprise" would happen. After learning of the October 18–25 "window of vulnerability" from Beal, campaign manager Casey ordered Garrick, who reported to chief of staff Edwin Meese III, to set up an "intelligence operation" to monitor military bases across the United States where arms and spare parts might be readied for shipment to Iran in exchange for a release of the hostages. "Dick Wirthlin says that bringing the hostages back from Iran could mean a 10 percent swing to Carter," Casey told Garrick. "We want you to monitor every d--- thing Carter is doing about Iran. It's a hostage watch. . . . Use all your military contacts to keep an eye on movements of aircraft, such as the big C-5A transporters on the East Coast. . . . You can use some of our staff here to check the tail numbers of the planes—some first-rate people with CIA training. They came across with [James] Baker and Bush when they joined our campaign.[19]

Garrick was quick to comply with Casey's request. Each morning at 6:00 A.M., Garrick, campaign manager Casey, campaign chief of staff Meese, campaign ad man Peter Dailey, and pollster Richard Wirthlin met in an apartment at Skyline House in Falls Church, Virginia, to go over the latest "October Surprise" intelligence and to devise counter strategies.[20] Under Garrick's operation at campaign headquarters was the coordinator for veterans affairs, Jack Kelly, who was put to work pulling together a network of active and retired military and intelligence personnel to keep tabs on supply depots and military bases across the country.[21] In particular, they were to watch Tinker Air Force Base in Oklahoma, Andrews Air Force Base near Washington, D.C., McGuire Air Force Base in New Jersey, where Iran had built a facility during the reign of the Shah to house its stocks of U.S.-made weapons and spare parts, and Norton and March Air Force Bases in California. Also recruited into the operation were twenty-seven military public affairs officers who had served under Garrick when he was Navy reserve admiral. To assist his network in monitoring suspicious movements of spare parts, Garrick had obtained a list of all the U.S. military equipment that Iran had already paid for under the Shah and that might be expected to be exchanged as part of a hostage swap.[22] He also gathered intelligence from John Coale, the attorney representing the minority and female hostages who had been released early from the U.S. embassy in Tehran in late November 1979.[23] Coale later told the Scripps-Howard News Service that he had passed Carter-State-Department documents classified "Secret-Eyes Only" to Garrick, beginning in August 1980, to be used in case of a pending "October Surprise."

Although Garrick told the Congressional Committee investigating the theft of President Carter's debate briefing books that he could "not recall" any of the names of his network of informants,[24] many of the "first-rate people with CIA training" Casey had recommended to Garrick were in fact working with former deputy CIA director Ray Cline's son-in-law, Stephan Halper. Halper had been in charge of foreign policy issues for George Bush's presidential campaign, before it joined the Reagan camp after the Republican convention in July, and was the Reagan-Bush campaign's policy coordinator. One campaign aide told *The New York Times* that Halper's network "kept track of things inside the government, mostly in relation to the "October Surprise." According to the campaign's Iran expert, Mickey Smith, it was Halper who, in about mid-September 1980, ordered Bush's aides to come up with a list of counter strategies to defeat the dreaded "October Surprise."[25] The report of the congressional committee that investigated "Debategate" concluded that Halper ran a "highly secretive" operation "involving a number of retired CIA officials" whose mission was to collect inside information from President Carter's foreign policy team, particularly with relation to Iran and the hostages.[26] Halper's operation, which included former CIA officials who worked near the campaign's Operations Center, was known to be highly sensitive to everyone on the second floor of Reagan-Bush headquarters, where the author worked. Though Stephan Halper nominally worked for Admiral Robert Garrick, his "intelligence operation" soon took on a life of its own. In the wake of revelations in the "Debategate" scandal, Garrick accused Halper's network of having gotten out of control and of running its own spy operation. "The problem [with Halper]," Garrick told the Los Angeles *Times*, "was that he lied to me. . . . He was always slinking off someplace. . . . I couldn't keep track of him. . . . Every time I turned around, his door was closed."

These reports are in keeping with the author's experience inside Reagan-Bush national campaign headquarters. Halper skulked around the second floor of the building with the almost comical demeanor of an agent out of a dimestore spy novel. On one wall in his office was a map of the Persian Gulf and Iran with arrows and pins, as if indicating some secretive operation, and his door, unlike others in the informal campaign headquarters, as Garrick noted, was almost always closed.

Halper requested in mid-September 1980 that members of his network come up with counter strategies to defeat an "October Surprise." The timing was significant, for it was also in mid-September that the Reagan-Bush campaign first learned that President Carter's chief hostage negotiator, Deputy Secretary of State Warren Christopher, had held a secret meeting in Bonn, West Germany, with a member of Khomeini's inner circle, Sadegh Tabatabai, to work out terms for a release of the hostages *before* the November 4th election.[27] On September 9th, Tabatabai, Khomeini's son Ahmed, and the new speaker of Iran's parliament Hashemi Rafsanjani had met to discuss ways to resolve the hostage crisis. The following day, September 10th, the Iranian parliament formally approved the fourteen-member cabinet of Prime Minister Mohammad Ali Rajai, a step which Khomeini had declared earlier to be necessary before Iran could negotiate terms for a hostage release with the United States. Also on the 10th, Tabatabai notified the Carter Administration, through West Germany's ambassador in Tehran, Gerhard Ritzel, that Khomeini was prepared to order a release of the hostages *before* the 1980 election and that they could be set free within only 48 hours of President Carter's agreeing to Iranian demands.[28]

A week later, on September 16th and 18th, U.S. negotiator Warren Christopher and Tabatabai met in Bonn with West Germany's foreign minister Hans-Dietrich Genscher to discuss Iran's offer. In his September 10th message, for the first time, Tabatabai had raised the issue of the delivery of U.S. arms and spare parts already owned by Iran but embargoed by President Carter shortly after the hostages were taken—the arms which Admiral Garrick's "intelligence operation" had been formed to monitor. Christopher had with him in Bonn a partial list of those arms, worth some $50 million (out of a total of $360–$400 million), which he said could be made available to Iran once the dispute over the hostages had been resolved.

Longtime Reagan adviser Peter Hannaford has reported that the Reagan-Bush campaign learned of President Carter's negotiations in September 1980, but he has not said how the campaign found out. The most likely sources for this leak were Captain Gary Sick, Carter's Iran expert on the NSC (codenamed "Navy Blue"), who often briefed Herbert Cohen of the Hoover Institution, who was in communication, in turn, with William Casey and Prescott Bush, George Bush's brother[29]; Donald Gregg, a CIA officer also then on President Carter's National Security Council, who later became Vice-President Bush's national security adviser; or Paul Henze, another Carter NSC aide who passed information to the Reagan-Bush camp.[30]

The Reagan-Bush campaign went into panic mode when it learned of Khomeini's offer to President Carter to release the hostages before the November 4th election. A release of the hostages before the election, as Iran was proposing, would be the long-dreaded "October Surprise," which could spell certain defeat for the Republicans. Though these mid-September meetings in Bonn were the last that Carter officials would hold with the Iranians until after the election, due to the outbreak of the Iran-Iraq war only a week later, on September 22nd,[31] the Reagan-Bush camp had no way of knowing this ahead of time and decided to act.

According to a former intelligence official, after the Bonn meeting in mid-September, Licio Gelli, the grandmaster of an outlawed Italian secret society called "P-2," which had high-level links to the Reagan-Bush campaign, and another P-2 member, Stephano della Chiaie, met with Iranian officials in Geneva, Switzerland, to discuss the idea of trading U.S. arms for hostages outside the framework of Carter Administration negotiations. According to former CNN reporter Kevin Sanders, George Bush had previously made Gelli and della Chiaie CIA "assets." At the inaugural ball on the night that the fifty-two U.S. hostages were released, Gelli was photographed in the place of honor at the official table next to Ronald Reagan. Beginning in 1981, shortly after the Republicans gained office, P-2 reportedly became a key broker for secret U.S. arms shipments to the Khomeini regime (See Chapter IX). According to a reporter for the Pittsburgh *Post Gazette*, Khomeini's hostage negotiator, Sadegh Tabatabai, also met in Geneva, in October 1980, with Iranian middleman Manucher Gorbanifar to further discuss the arms-for-hostages proposal.[32] Gorbanifar, Iran's chief arms buyer for Europe, would later be used by William Casey, once he had became CIA director, to facilitate secret arms-for-hostages deals in 1985 and 1986. When the author first asked Mansur Rafizadeh, the former U.S. chief of SAVAK (the former Shah's secret police) about reports that top Reagan-Bush campaign officials had met with Iranian agents in Paris before the 1980 election (see Chapter II), he responded, "Yes, and they had other meetings—in Geneva, in Zurich, and in the Middle East."[33]

A MODEST PROPOSAL

Shortly after these meetings in Geneva—according to an account given to professors at the University of California at Berkeley by former 1980 Reagan-Bush campaign Middle East adviser Ray Tanter—Robert McFarlane, then an aide to senator John Tower on the Senate Armed Services Committee, also proposed delivering arms to Iran in exchange for the release of the hostages during a Reagan-Bush campaign "October Surprise" Group meeting. The leader of the meeting, in all probability Reagan's chief foreign policy adviser Richard Allen, reportedly told McFarlane, "Don't talk about that here."[34] According to sources available to the former president of Iran, Abolhassan Bani Sadr, McFarlane had met in Zurich, Switzerland, this same month, September 1980, with a top arms procurement official of the Iranian Revolutionary Guards, Hamid Nagashian. As we shall see in the next chapter, Nagashian is reported to have met in Paris, France, the next month, in mid-October, with vice-presidential candidate George Bush, Reagan-Bush campaign manager William Casey, Richard Allen, Allen's campaign aide Dr. Fred Ikle, the minister of Iran's radical Revolutionary Guards Moshen Rafiq Dust, and future Iran/Contra middleman Albert Hakim to finalize an arms-for-hostage-delay with the Khomeini regime.

Though neither Tanter nor McFarlane are now willing to comment on McFarlane's purported proposal to the Reagan-Bush "October Surprise" Group, it is now well acknowledged that shortly thereafter, in early October 1980, McFarlane, Richard Allen, and Allen's campaign aide Laurence Silberman, soon to become William Casey's liaison to the CIA following the election, met at the L' Enfant Plaza Hotel in Washington, D.C., with an "Iranian emissary" who offered precisely what Mr. McFarlane had already allegedly proposed—an exchange of U.S. military equipment for the release of the American hostages to the Reagan-Bush campaign in such a way as to "ensure President Carter's defeat."[35] This "Iranian emissary" is now claimed to have been Iranian-American arms dealer Houshang Lavi who, according to reliable sources wishing to remain anonymous, showed up again in Paris on October 20, 1980, at a meeting with CIA contract agent and arms dealer Richard Brenneke, Iranian banker and middleman Cyrus Hashemi, Reagan-Bush campaign manager William Casey, President Carter's NSC aide Donald Gregg (soon to become Vice-President George Bush's national security adviser), French intelligence agents, and other Iranian officials to work out the logistics for post-inauguration U.S. arms shipments to Iran. Though McFarlane, Allen, Silberman, and "Iranian emissary" Houshang Lavi all acknowledge that this early October meeting in Washington, D.C., took place, their contra-dictory claims about whose idea it was, when it happened, what was discussed, and what became of Iran's offer made through Lavi make the question of what *did* happen at the L' Enfant Plaza Hotel one of the enduring mysteries of the "October Surprise" story.

In an interview with the author on June 14, 1988, Iranian-born arms dealer Houshang Lavi acknowledged for the first time that it was he who had met with Richard Allen, Laurence Silberman, and Robert McFarlane on or about October 2, 1980, at the L' Enfant Plaza Hotel. Mr. Lavi subsequently acknowledged having been the "Iranian emissary" at this meeting to the *Washington Post*, the *Boston Globe* and the *Oakland Tribune*.[36] In January 1989, Lavi provided the author with a copy of a note he made after the L' Enfant Plaza meeting with Reagan-Bush campaign officials. Based on interviews with the author and other journalists, and on this note of the meeting, the following summary of Mr. Lavi's version of events can be reconstructed.

Houshang Lavi's Story

Houshang Lavi claims to have initiated contact with the 1980 Reagan-Bush campaign in a series of telephone calls to vice-presidential candidate George Bush's top aide and former campaign manager, James Baker III. His note of the meeting, dated October 2, 1980, reads:

> "Foll[owing] telecon[versation] with J. Baker, to meet [Laurence] Silberman, [Richard] Allen, Bob McFar[lane], [take] 40 page document [regarding] F-14 parts already paid for [by Iran] in rtun [return] of [for] hostages. Swap in Karachi [Pakistan]. Charter 707 [plane]. Signed: Houshang Lavi."

The major condition that he placed on his arms-for-hostages offer, Lavi says, was that President Carter not receive credit for the hostages' freedom. Lavi also claims that he first offered to arrange for the U.S. hostages to be delivered to the Reagan-Bush camp in Karachi, Pakistan, before, not after, the election in exchange for the delivery of approximately $50 million worth of military equipment and spare parts for Iran's F-14 fighter jets. Lavi had been an agent for Grumman Corporation, which makes F-14's, in the 1970's, during the reign of the Shah, but could not collect on his final commission until the goods, which President Carter had impounded, or their equivalents were delivered. Interestingly, $50 million also is the value of the arms that President Carter's hostage negotiator, Warren Christopher, told Khomeini's negotiator, Sadegh Tabatabai, could be released by the U.S. upon a resolution of the hostage crisis at their mid-September meeting in Bonn. It was also the amount of U.S. military equipment, according to President Carter's NSC Iran expert Gary Sick, which his Administration had earlier agreed to release to Iran at a September 1979 meeting in New York with Iranian officials. But the taking of the hostages shortly thereafter, in November 1979, had prevented this early $50 million arms agreement from being consummated.[37] Significantly, $45 to $50 million is *also* the value of U.S. military equipment that the former president of Iran, Abolhassan Bani Sadr, estimates was delivered to the Khomeini regime between the spring of 1981, shortly after Reagan and Bush gained power, through the time that Mr. Bani Sadr was forced from office in June of 1981.[38] The similarity in amounts suggests that something indeed came of Mr. Lavi's contacts with the Reagan-Bush campaign, though Allen, Silberman, and McFarlane all insist that no arms-for-hostages offer was seriously considered at their meeting with him in October 1980.

Three additional lines of evidence suggest that the Reagan-Bush campaign did, in fact, seriously consider *and act on* an arms-for-hostages agreement with the Khomeini regime. First, sources available to the former President of Iran, Abolhassan Bani Sadr, have claimed that Mr. McFarlane met in Zurich, Switzerland, in September 1980, the month before McFarlane's Washington meeting with Lavi, with Hamid Nagashian, a top arms procurement official for the Iranian Revolutionary Guards and with another Iranian, a "Mr. Hakimi," whom the author believes to have been Iran/Contra middleman Albert Hakim. Second, sources who claim to have been present, but who wish to remain anonymous, have told the author and other reporters that Mr. Lavi met in Paris, France, on October 20, 1980, with Reagan-Bush campaign manager William Casey, NSC aide Donald Gregg, Iranian middlemen and Lavi's associates Manucher

Gorbanifar and Dr. Cyrus Hashemi, French intelligence agents, top Iranian arms procurement officials, and CIA contract agent and arms dealer Richard Brenneke to work out logistics for secret U.S. arms shipments to the Khomeini regime. Knowledgeable sources in West Germany have told *Der Spiegel* magazine that Mr. Lavi and U.S. arms dealer Richard Brenneke were later in ''constant'' contact in the 1980's. As we shall see in the next chapter, Mr. Brenneke acknowledges having personally met with Reagan-Bush campaign manager William Casey and Iranian officials, according to some sources including the deputy minister of Iran's radical Revolutionary Guards, Hamid Nagashian, at the above-mentioned October 20th Paris meeting two weeks after Lavi's Washington, D.C. meeting with McFarlane, Allen and Silberman in early October. Third, in April 1981 and again in October 1981, a company owned by Houshang Lavi's brothers, also New York arms dealers, began making arrangements to ship F-4 and F-14 parts, HAWK missiles, fuses, and other military equipment to the Khomeini regime—some of the same military equipment Mr. Lavi had proposed exchanging for the fifty-two hostages at his meeting with Robert McFarlane, Richard Allen, and Laurence Silberman in early October in Washington, D.C. According to Houshang Lavi, he himself worked directly with Israeli prime minister Menachem Begin, Israeli General Baram, and a Belgian company named ASCO in the early 1980's to deliver HAWK missiles and HAWK missile parts to Iran.[39] Though Baram was later indicted along with some sixteen other defendants in a $2.5 billion U.S. government ''sting'' operation in April 1986, neither Houshang Lavi nor his brothers have ever been charged with a crime; though it was then, and still is, illegal to export or conspire to export U.S. military equipment to Iran. Influential Swedish arms dealer Sven Klang told *ABC News'* European correspondent Pierre Salinger that the Reagan-Bush Administration secretly delivered F-4 fighter jet engines to Iran in 1981, shortly after they gained the White House, from NATO warehouses in Belgium, where ASCO, the company with which Lavi worked in the early 1980's, is headquartered.

Mr. Lavi claims that he was not alone on his trips to Washington, D.C. In an interview with the author on June 14, 1988, he said, ''Representatives of the Iranians came to New York and met with me and brought the list of F-14 [fighter jet] parts and said that they needed them, and they wanted them. These two Iranians, Mitchell Rogovin, and I went to Washington.'' Significantly, Mr. Rogovin, the man whom Lavi said accompanied him, not only was Lavi's personal attorney at the time but had been special counsel to George Bush when Bush was director of the CIA in

1976. Though Lavi at first said that he could not remember the names of the two Iranians who accompanied him to Washington, and later stated that he chose not to identify them, subsequent investigation led the author to deduce that they were most likely American-Iranian businessman Hadi Háeri and Iranian banker Dr. Cyrus Hashemi, whom Khomeini trusted to handle the financial arrangements for Iran's arms purchases. Dr. Hashemi was a close associate of Mr. Lavi's with whom he had worked on numerous projects, and was often in New York, from where Lavi had flown to Washington; and Háeri, according to author Amir Taheri in *Nest of Spies* also met with Allen, Silberman and McFarlane in Washington before the 1980 election. The former President of Iran, Mr. Bani Sadr, has reported that he was aware in October 1980 that his political rivals, Hashemi Rafsanjani and the Ayatollah Mohammed Beheshti, had sent envoys to the L' Enfant Plaza Hotel meeting.[40] Dr. Hashemi may well have been this representative of Rafsanjani to whom Mr. Bani Sadr referred, as he was Rafsanjani's cousin. Representatives of these same two Iranian officials, Rafsanjani and Beheshti, were soon to turn up again at reported October 19–20, 1980, meetings with Reagan-Bush campaign manager William Casey and vice-presidential candidate George Bush in Paris, France, to formalize the reported arms-for-hostage-delay agreement with the Khomeini regime. (See Chapter II).

Houshang Lavi also claims that he already knew Laurence Silberman, then an aide to Reagan-Bush campaign foreign policy adviser Richard Allen and a friend of Ronald Reagan's,[41] who attended the October 2, 1980, meeting at the L' Enfant Plaza Hotel. "I first worked with Mr. Silberman back in late 1978 or early 1979 when we got Phoenix missiles and sensitive radar tracking hardware out of Iran—out of Isfahan," Lavi told the author in June 1988. "We had many meetings together. Jacksonville, Florida. The Hilton Hotel in New York. . . . There were two Iranian generals who became CIA agents who worked with us to get the Phoenix missiles out of Iran before the hostages were taken."[42] This claim of Lavi's is consistent with a report by *The New York Times* in December 1979 that one purpose of U.S. General Robert E. Huyser's trip to Iran about this same time on behalf of President Carter was to "safeguard the U.S. planes and missiles that had been provided to the Shah but that appeared to be imperiled by a rising rebellion among Air Force technicians and cadets."[43]

According to Mr. Lavi, Mitchell Rogovin, who was Lavi's personal attorney and had been CIA Director George Bush's special CIA counsel in 1976, was then "still close to George Bush."[44] To complicate matters further, Rogovin was also general counsel to the 1980 presidential campaign of independent candidate John Anderson at the time, in October 1980. When it is added that Ronald Reagan's friend and campaign official Laurence Silberman, who was also at the L' Enfant Plaza meeting with Lavi, and "Bush's friend" Mitchell Rogovin were next-door neighbors, good friends, and boating partners[45], the incestuous nature of the October 2, 1980, meeting suddenly becomes apparent.

Though Reagan-Bush campaign officials Richard Allen and Laurence Silberman, as well as Robert McFarlane, insist that they rejected Lavi's offer out of hand, it is clear that the situation is not nearly so simple and that all three participants are worried that the true nature of the L 'Enfant Plaza meeting will become known. When one compares Lavi's documented version of events with those of the other participants, and his open sharing of information with their emotional finger-pointing, the picture becomes even more interesting.

Mitchell Rogovin's Story

Mitchell Rogovin—Bush's friend and former special counsel at the CIA, Lavi's personal attorney, and then general counsel to the John Anderson presidential campaign—has refused to identify Lavi as the "Khomeini emissary" who met with Allen, Silberman, and McFarlane in early October 1980. He has, however, acknowledged that the "emissary" is known to him and was "an Iranian and an international businessman who is now an American citizen" and, at the time of the meeting, had been a client of Rogovin's Washington law firm,[46] all of which fit the description of Lavi. Though Houshang Lavi also approached the John Anderson campaign with a similar arms-for-hostages offer, and Rogovin, being Anderson's campaign counsel, knew it, Rogovin told U.S. Representative John Conyers's aide, Frank Askin, that he "did not believe that the same Iranian who contacted the Anderson campaign also approached the Reagan camp," but noted that he was "not certain."[47] As Lavi himself has now admitted that he approached both campaigns, Rogovin's statement is curious. In fact, Houshang Lavi approached the Reagan-Bush and Anderson campaigns *and* the Carter Administration with his arms-for-hostages proposal in the same month: October 1980.

According to published accounts by the Anderson campaign's former director of policy planning, Alton Frye, in the *Los Angeles Times*[48], and its former campaign manager, Michael MacLeon, in the *Miami Herald*, a similar arms-for-hostages offer was made to the Anderson campaign by an unidentified "Iranian emissary," now claimed to be Lavi. Frye reported in the *Times* that the Iranian emissary who approached him also offered to exchange the hostages for U.S. military equipment in Pakistan. The proposal of Pakistan as the place for the exchange is confirmed by Lavi's notes' reference to Karachi, in western Pakistan. Frye reported that the offer was rejected as "immoral" and that he and Rogovin alerted President Carter's Assistant Secretary of State for Middle Eastern Affairs Harold Saunders of the approach in a personal meeting. Carter's State Department then asked the Anderson campaign officials to test the "emissary" to see whether his contacts with Iran were legitimate. They did, and reported they had no doubt that they were. Lavi communicated with Iran and produced a computerized list of military equipment and spare parts which, Carter officials agreed, could only have come from Iran's Air Force.

Assuming Mr. Lavi is telling the truth, and the author believes that he is, his own attorney, a longtime friend and colleague of George Bush, has gone out of his way to disguise Lavi's identity as the man who met with Bush's own campaign aides, Richard Allen and Laurence Silberman, and with Robert McFarlane, in Washington, D.C., a little over a month before the 1980 presidential election. In addition, if Mr. Lavi is telling the truth, Mr. Rogovin has further led reporters away from the story by suggesting that Mr. Lavi did not meet with both Anderson and Reagan-Bush campaign officials, when in fact he did. The question, of course, is *why*?

Richard Allen's Story

Though Ronald Reagan's chief foreign policy adviser in the 1980 presidential campaign, Richard Allen, has acknowledged his participation in the L'Enfant Plaza Hotel meeting, he claims not to recall the identity or the description of the "Iranian emissary" with whom he met. He also claims, not believably, that the meeting was, in effect, forced upon him, and that he participated "against my better judgment."[49] Allen claims that Robert McFarlane called him in late September 1980 and was "emphatic" and "incessant" that he meet with the "Iranian emissary." When McFarlane was informed of Allen's version of events, however, he implied that Allen was lying and exploded, "Mr. Allen is a fool. There was no pressure on Allen."[50] Richard Allen has also said that the Iranian proposed "an arrangement whereby the hostages could be released to the Reagan side at a date indeterminate."

Though Richard Allen has admitted that he wrote a memorandum recording the meeting, he now claims not to be able to find it. This probably has something to do with the fact that Allen told the congressional committee investigating the theft of President Carter's debate briefing books, which was also looking into the Reagan-Bush campaign's broader "October Surprise" "intelligence" operation, that he had "thinned" his campaign files prior to that "Debategate" inquiry. Mr. Allen has also said that he does not recall whether he gave a copy of the memo he wrote about the L' Enfant Plaza meeting to Reagan-Bush campaign manager William Casey.[51] Whether Casey received a copy or not, Allen almost certainly gave a copy of the report, or a verbal briefing, to vice-presidential candidate George Bush. The very next day, October 3, 1980, Bush announced publicly for the first time that the Reagan-Bush campaign was "predicting" an "October Surprise" move by President Carter. As we shall shortly see, the same day as the L' Enfant Plaza meeting summarized in Allen's disappearing memo, Houshang Lavi also met with an "undercover" CIA agent and with George Bush's old friend, Mitchell Rogovin. At the same time, in early October 1980, according to presidential biographer Theodore White, the Reagan-Bush campaign began "bringing George Bush into this [campaign strategy] more and more," including briefings by the CIA.[52] It must be asked whether any of these "CIA briefings" mentioned Mr. Lavi's approach to the Carter CIA on exactly the same day that he met with Richard Allen and Laurence Silberman of Mr. Bush's own campaign staff.

Like Robert McFarlane and Laurence Silberman, Richard Allen claims that the arms-for-hostages offer made by the "Iranian emissary" was rejected, even though *Newsday* has reported that Lavi and his arms-dealer brothers began making arrangements to sell U.S. military equipment to Iran shortly after Reagan and Bush gained office in 1981 and that the Reagan-Bush Administration did nothing to stop them. Furthermore, Houshang Lavi's own HAWK missile deals with Iran were negotiated in cooperation with the Israelis shortly after Richard Allen himself, in December 1980, gave what Israel's agent took as authorization to begin delivering U.S. arms and spare parts to Iran. (See Chapter VI)

Richard Allen also claims to have been "incredulous that McFarlane would have brought a guy like this to us [the Reagan-Bush campaign] with this kind of scheme,"[53] even though McFarlane had reportedly already raised a similar arms-for-hostages proposal prior to the L' Enfant Plaza meeting at one of Allen's own "October Surprise" Group sessions and had been warned "not to talk about that here" by the group's leader, almost certainly Allen himself. Though Allen's then aide Laurence Silberman claims that the "Iranian emissary" was told to deal with the Carter

Administration, Allen says that the contact by the "Iranian emissary" was *not* reported to the Carter government. He ought to know. Harold Saunders, President Carter's assistant secretary of state, who was in charge of the hostage crisis at the time, told *Newsday* and the *Los Angeles Times* that one of his duties was to brief Richard Allen, Edwin Meese, and William Casey on the status of the hostages, and that, though he talked with Allen "several times during October 1980," Allen never mentioned that the Reagan-Bush campaign had been approached with an arms-for-hostages offer[54] or that the campaign had allegedly suggested to Mr. Lavi that he contact the Carter Administration. Despite these numerous conversations with Saunders, Reagan-Bush campaign officials also maintained the public fiction that they refused official briefings on the hostage crisis to "avoid politicizing the issue."

It is clear that there is something about the L' Enfant Plaza Hotel meeting and the Reagan-Bush campaign's interaction with Mr. Houshang Lavi that Richard Allen does not wish the public to know.

Laurence Silberman's Story

Laurence Silberman, who, if Houshang Lavi is telling the truth, already knew Lavi when they met at the L' Enfant Plaza Hotel in early October 1980, gives quite a different story. He claims, first, that the meeting happened in late September 1980, not in "early October" as recalled by Allen and McFarlane or on October 2, 1980, as recorded on Lavi's note. More interestingly, Mr. Silberman told the *Miami Herald* that he did not know the identity of the man with whom they had met and, furthermore, thought that "he might have been a North African" rather than an Iranian, which Mr. Lavi most definitely is.[55] If what Lavi says is true, that they already knew one another, it must be asked why Mr. Silberman would go to such lengths to disguise the identity of someone with whom he had worked in the CIA. Curiously, Mr. Silberman later told *Newsday* that he was "sure" that the emissary was *not* Houshang Lavi.[56] How he could have been so certain unless he already knew Mr. Lavi, as Lavi himself insists, remains a mystery.

Curious as to how Mr. Silberman could have been "sure" that Mr. Lavi was not Mr. Lavi, the author read Lavi's record of the L' Enfant Plaza meeting to Mr. Silberman in a telephone interview. After hearing the text of Lavi's note and being informed of Lavi's claim that the two already knew one another in October 1980, Mr. Silberman then stated that he was only "virtually" certain that it had not been Houshang Lavi with whom he,

Allen, and McFarlane had discussed a proposal for releasing the hostages to the Reagan-Bush campaign. When the author informed Mr. Silberman that Mr. Lavi also claimed to have worked with him on a Phoenix missile project in late 1978 or early 1979, Mr. Silberman replied cryptically, "Look carefully into 1978–79. You may win a Pulitzer Prize."[57]

Mr. Silberman has acknowledged that the man with whom he, Allen, and McFarlane met in Washington did "purport to have contacts with Khomeini's subordinates and suggested the prospect of gaining release of the hostages if they could be released to representatives of candidate Ronald Reagan rather than President Jimmy Carter."[58] In the above-mentioned telephone interview with the author, Judge Silberman, however, denied that the "Khomeini emissary" had raised a quid pro quo of U.S. military equipment for the release of the hostages, as Lavi insists was the case and is well documented to have been Lavi's reason for attending the meeting.

When Ronald Reagan and George Bush won the 1980 presidential election, Laurence Silberman was appointed by William Casey to be the Reagan-Bush transition team's liaison to the CIA during the period between the election and Reagan's inauguration. In this post, he would almost certainly have been knowledgeable of, and in a position to participate in, the CIA's interaction with the Khomeini regime during that transition period. According to Mansur Rafizadeh, former U.S. chief of SAVAK, who had worked with the Agency for as long as eighteen years, during this same transition period while Silberman was the Reagan-Bush liaison to the CIA, Republican-loyal forces in the Agency briefed Iran's than foreign minister Sadegh Ghotbzadeh to persuade Khomeini to delay the release of the U.S. hostages until Reagan's inauguration.[59] Earlier, in mid-October, not long after the L'Enfant Plaza Hotel meeting, Reagan-Bush campaign manager William Casey had received a requested strategic analysis from Hoover Institution fellow Herbert Cohen proposing that very timing—a release of the hostages on Reagan's inauguration, which amounted to at least a 76-day delay.[60] Also during the transition period, according to *Washington Post* reporter Bob Woodward's book *Veil*, President Carter's CIA director, Stansfield Turner, reportedly gave a copy of a sensitive memorandum on the Agency to "a member of the Reagan-Bush transition team who was looking at the CIA for the new administration"[61]—in all probability, then Reagan-Bush CIA liaison Laurence Silberman.

When Ronald Reagan became President, he appointed Laurence Silberman to a judgeship on the U.S. Court of Appeals for the powerful District of Columbia Circuit in the nation's capitol. From that position, Mr. Silberman ruled that the federal law providing for special prosecutor Lawrence Walsh, who was investigating charges of criminal conspiracy in the Administration's secret arms-for-hostages dealings with Iran, was *unconstitutional*. Given his own participation in the L' Enfant Plaza Hotel meeting in early October 1980, where the first arms-for-hostages proposal was advanced at the behest of Robert McFarlane, who was also at the center of the later Iran/Contra scandal, there is reason to believe that Mr. Silberman should have considered disqualifying himself from the case. Luckily for the nation and the rule of law, the Supreme Court overruled Mr. Silberman in a 7-to-1 decision on July 29, 1988, allowing the special prosecutor's investigations and case to go forward.

Robert McFarlane's Story

Probably the most interesting and most important version of events is that of Robert McFarlane, who was then an aide to Senator John Tower on the Senate Armed Services Committee. In an interview on August 25, 1988, a journalist from a major news weekly informed the author that his magazine had been told by sources that the Iranian emissary who met with McFarlane, Allen, and Silberman in early October 1980 in Washington, D.C., had first approached Senator John Tower himself. If this is true, it would make sense of why Houshang Lavi says he flew from New York to Washington after first talking with James Baker, the top aide to then vice-presidential candidate George Bush. Senator Tower had been a personal friend and avid political supporter of George Bush for over twenty years. Tower had endorsed Bush in his congressional race in 1962, worked actively on behalf of his Senate bid in 1964, and publicly backed Bush in his contest for the 1980 Republican presidential nomination against Ronald Reagan when it was politically unpopular in their home state of Texas to do so.[62] According to the *San Francisco Chronicle:* "At critical junctures," Tower's friends and associates said, "Tower was there to help Bush."[63] If Lavi, or any other "Khomeini emissary," did first contact Senator Tower, it makes sense that Tower would have asked his aide Robert McFarlane to put the emissary in contact with James Baker, the aide to Tower's close friend George Bush, to set up a meeting with officials of the Reagan-Bush campaign. This, of course, is precisely what Houshang Lavi claims happened.

Mr. McFarlane, who has pled guilty to withholding information from Congress in the Iran/Contra affair, refused to respond to the author's telephoned and written inquiries about the reported Tower connection to the L' Enfant Plaza Hotel meeting. However, a number of reports about

McFarlane's participation in the meeting have appeared in the press. The first was by *Washington Post* reporters Bob Woodward and Walter Pincus in a front page article on November 29, 1986, which revealed that "Even before 1981, McFarlane proposed dramatic covert initiatives involving Iran. In 1980, while he was on the staff of the Senate Armed Services Committee, McFarlane approached the Reagan campaign's foreign policy adviser, Richard V. Allen, with an Iranian exile who proposed to deliver the American hostages then held in Iran to the Reagan camp prior to the November election."[64]

Even more so than Richard Allen or Laurence Silberman, Mr. McFarlane's claims not to be able to remember the identity of the "Iranian exile" with whom he personally arranged the L' Enfant Plaza Hotel meeting are simply not credible. All parties concerned acknowledge that Mr. McFarlane put together the meeting, and it is extremely unlikely that in his capacity as aide to a well known senator, he would not have thoroughly checked out the identity, background, and credentials of anyone he or Senator Tower recommended to the campaign of a man he hoped would become the next President of the United States. Still, McFarlane claims that he did little or nothing to pre-screen the Iranian or his proposal: "He was rather ambiguous, both as to whom he represented and what kind of proposal he wanted to make," McFarlane claimed. On this point, Mr. McFarlane is almost certainly misleading the press and the public, as he has already admitted to having done with Congress.

Richard Allen claims that the meeting with the "Iranian emissary" was Robert McFarlane's idea and that McFarlane was "emphatic" and "incessant" that he join them at the L' Enfant Plaza Hotel a little over a month before the 1980 election. As mentioned previously, however, when told of this claim of Allen's, McFarlane insisted he was "completely wrong" and exploded, "Mr. Allen is a fool. There was no pressure on Allen."

After Houshang Lavi acknowledged to the author and subsequently to other journalists that he had been the Iranian who attended the L' Enfant Plaza Hotel meeting after speaking with James Baker and Robert McFarlane, Washington journalist Brock Brower included the following assessment in a 1989 profile of McFarlane published in *The New York Times Magazine:*

> "Under Tower, McFarlane made his move in the Iran game. He brought Reagan campaign aides Richard V. Allen and Laurence Silberman together in October 1980 with a questionable emissary named Houshang Lavi, who claimed he could "achieve the release of the hostages."[66]

Though the identification of the emissary as Lavi in this article is not attributed directly to Mr. McFarlane, his attorney Leonard Garment wrote to the *Magazine*, not long after the publication of the piece containing the above excerpt, to critique other aspects of the article, but did not question this reference to Lavi. Presumably, therefore, Mr. McFarlane has now at least implicitly acknowledged that it *was* Lavi whom he, reportedly at Senator Tower's direction, put together with the man who would become President Reagan's first White House national security adviser, Richard Allen. If so, he and his attorney have changed their story, for Garment told *Newsday* in April 1988, again on McFarlane's behalf, that the "Iranian emissary" was not Houshang Lavi.[67] Mr. McFarlane himself later became President Reagan's third White House national security adviser and was at the center of the genesis of the 1985–86 arms-for-hostages deals with the Khomeini regime, which became known as the Iran/Contra affair.

After the Iran/Contra scandal broke, President Reagan appointed none other than Senator John Tower—McFarlane's boss at the time of the L' Enfant Plaza Hotel meeting where the first arms-for-hostages offer was proposed to Reagan-Bush officials—to head the Tower Commission charged with investigating McFarlane's complicity in the affair. Also on the Tower Commission was another former boss of McFarlane's, General Brent Scowcroft. McFarlane had served as Scowcroft's military aide in the Ford Administration when Scowcroft was President Ford's national security adviser. According to *Time*, McFarlane remained "close" to Scowcroft[68], as he had to Tower. The third man on the three-man Tower Commission was former Senator Edmund Muskie who, as secretary of state in the Carter Administration during the hostage crisis, was reported to have been the source for sensitive information relating to the hostages which reached Richard Allen, McFarlane's associate in the campaign's "October Surprise" Group.[69] McFarlane had also been personally close to Rhett Dawson, staff director and counsel of the Tower Commission, who also had worked for Tower on Capitol Hill.[70] Both McFarlane and Scowcroft had also worked directly with Henry Kissinger—McFarlane as Kissinger's military aide when Kissinger was Nixon's national security adviser, and Scowcroft as a partner in Kissinger's Washington, D.C., consulting firm—as had Alexander Haig, who reportedly authorized Israeli-mediated U.S. arms deliveries to Iran shortly after Reagan and Bush gained office in 1981[71], and Richard Allen. Not long after Reagan and Bush gained the White House, Houshang Lavi himself, whom McFarlane reportedly put together with the Reagan-Bush campaign in early October 1980, cooperated with the Israelis to broker huge U.S. arms shipments to the Khomeini regime at a time when McFarlane was Haig's liaison to Israel.[72]

Intriguingly, one of the Israeli arms dealers involved in the late 1985 U.S. arms deliveries to Iran, which Robert McFarlane was again instrumental in arranging, was Yaacav Nimrodi, who also reportedly began selling U.S. arms to Iran a mere sixty days after the L' Enfant Plaza Hotel meeting between McFarlane and Jewish-Iranian arms dealer Houshang Lavi.[73] (See Chapter VI). It should also be noted that the brother-in-law of Senator John Tower for whom McFarlane then worked, Sam Cummings, is one of the world's largest private arms dealers. Cummings reportedly used to work with the CIA and supplied arms to the right-wing Somoza dictatorship in Nicaragua, the country that formed the second leg of the Iran/Contra affair.

As with Richard Allen and Laurence Silberman, it is clear that there is something about the L' Enfant Plaza Hotel meeting that Robert McFarlane would prefer to remain unknown. If McFarlane's boss at the time, Senator Tower, did instruct him to set up the meeting between Lavi and the Reagan-Bush campaign officials, it would explain why the Tower Commission was packed with McFarlane's associates and why Tower might not have been as thorough in his investigation or reporting of the 1980 origins of the arms-for-hostages deals with Iran as he might otherwise have been. At the end of his 65-day investigation, in fact, Senator Tower stated that "the entire Iran/Contra affair is still an enigma. The whole matter cannot be fully explained." Whatever Mr. McFarlane, and perhaps also Senator Tower, did not wish revealed about the genesis of the arms-for-hostages dealings with the Khomeini regime was serious enough that Mr. McFarlane reportedly attempted to take his life with an overdose of Valium on February 9, 1987, the night before he was to testify to the Tower Commission. Given that press reports at the time noted that taking Valium is a notoriously unsuccessful way of committing suicide, it is interesting that CIA Director William Casey later boasted that a lie detector could be fooled "with Valium and a few tricks."[74]

Mickey Smith's Story

The Iran expert in the 1980 Reagan-Bush campaign was Michel Smith, known as "Mickey." Mickey Smith was one of four senior watch officers in the campaign's Operations Center communications headquarters and had served as the Iran desk officer for years at the Department of Commerce. He had also been stationed at the U.S. embassy in Tehran only a few years before its takeover in November of 1979. In interviews with the author and another journalist in the summer of 1988, Mr. Smith recalled having received a telephone call "in late September or early October 1980," in the Operations Center, from a former colleague who was then an assistant to Harold Saunders, assistant secretary of state for Middle Eastern affairs in charge of handling the hostage crisis for President Carter at the Department of State. The colleague asked Mr. Smith whether he had heard of "a Houshang Lavi," the Iranian arms dealer who reportedly met with Richard Allen, Laurence Silberman and Robert McFarlane at the L' Enfant Plaza Hotel on October 2, 1980. On the same day, October 2nd, Lavi and Bush's former CIA special counsel Mitchell Rogovin had also met with an undercover agent for President Carter's CIA who reported their meeting to the same man, Harold Saunders. Mickey recalled that, yes, he had heard the name Houshang Lavi mentioned in the campaign, probably from Stephan Halper, who worked with Admiral Robert Garrick, Bush campaign manager William Casey, and campaign chief of staff Edwin Meese on counter strategies to defeat an "October Surprise" hostage release.[75] According to Smith, Halper had also asked him to research U.S.-Algerian relations in early September 1980. This is significant because the Algerians did not become involved in discussions regarding the hostage crisis until mid-October, at the United Nations in New York, and did not become the official mediator between the United States and Iran until November 2, 1980, two days before the election—too late to help President Carter. Smith also claims that Halper asked him for background information on Sadegh Ghotbzadeh and Manucher Gorbanifar in October 1980. According to Mansur Rafizadeh, the former U.S. chief of SAVAK, elements in the CIA loyal to Halper's boss, George Bush, prevailed upon Ghotbzadeh to get Khomeini to agree to delay the release of the hostages until Reagan's inauguration.[76] Again, according to the congressional report on the theft of President Carter's debate briefing books, William Casey received a report from Herbert Cohen of the Hoover Institution following their meeting in New York of mid-October 1980, which also proposed a strategy for obtaining the release of the hostages on Reagan's inauguration.[77] And Manucher Gorbanifar, the other Iranian Halper asked Smith for background information about, the reader will recall, was the head of Iran's arms-buying and intelligence operations in Europe at the time, working directly for Iran's prime minister, Mir Houssein Mousavi.[78] If a secret Reagan-Bush arms-for-hostages deal was in the works, Gorbanifar would be one of the men the Reagan-Bush campaign would need to talk to.

THE TOWER OMISSION

Former senator John Tower headed the Tower Commission, which investi-
gated the legal arms-for-hostages deals of late 1985 and 1986. If Senator
Tower, whom Robert McFarlane worked for in October 1980 on the
Senate Armed Services Committee, was the official first approached by
Houshang Lavi offering an arms-for-hosage exchange, as sources told
Der Spiegel, Tower's failure to acknowledge that fact would constitute an
omission of the gravest magnitude.

In an interview on December 17, 1988, the author raised the *Der
Spiegel* report with Mr. Lavi. In response to the question as to whether he
had spoken with Senator Tower before the meeting at the L' Enfant Plaza
Hotel with McFarlane, Allen, and Silberman, he replied, "It's a possibility." He then stated that he preferred not to discuss the matter further over
the telephone, and agreed to meet with the author upon returning from
an upcoming trip to Europe. (Shortly after mailing the author a copy of his
note from the meeting at the L' Enfant Plaza Hotel, Mr. Lavi was
reportedly stricken by a heart attack while on a business trip in Munich,
West Germany.) Significantly, when the author asked Mr. Lavi a different
question in an earlier interview of June 14, 1988—whether he had been the
unnamed Iranian at the L' Enfant Plaza meeting—he had used the same
language: "It's a possibility." In subsequent interviews he then acknowledged that he had, in fact, been that "Iranian emissary." Presumably, then,
Mr. Lavi's statement that it was "a possibility" that he had contacted
Senator Tower to ask for his assistance in setting up the L' Enfant Plaza
Hotel meeting with Reagan-Bush campaign officials in early October 1980
may be equally pregnant with meaning. Interestingly, in the same interview Mr. Lavi told the author that an attempt had been made on his life.
"They tried," he said, after having just stated that another Iranian arms
dealer at the center of both the 1980 and 1985–86 arms-for-hostages
negotiations, Cyrus Hashemi, had been killed by "American agents" to
protect the October 1980 origins of the Reagan-Bush Administration's
Secret Iran initiative.[79] According to a source who claims to have been
present, but who wishes to remain anonymous, Mr. Lavi and Mr. Hashemi
had both participated in an October 20, 1980, meeting in Paris two and
one half weeks after the L' Enfant Plaza meeting, with Reagan-Bush
campaign manager William Casey, Carter NSC aide Donald Gregg, CIA
contract agent Richard Brenneke, French intelligence agents, and Iranian

arms procurement officials, including Hamid Nagashian of Khomeini's Revolutionary Guards, to formalize arrangements for arms shipments to Iran once the Republicans had gained the White House. (See also Chapter II). According to a long time associate of Nagashian's, former CIA contract agent William Herrmann, Nagashian told Herrmann in January 1981 that Robert McFarlane, Richard Allen, and Allen's campaign aide Dr. Fred Ikle had also participated in Paris meetings with Iranian officials, including Nagashian himself, at approximately this same time: mid-October 1980. These October Paris meetings referred to by Nagashian probably included the October 20, 1980, meeting in Paris reportedly attended by Mr. Hashemi and Mr. Lavi, who, if true, would then have met with Mr. McFarlane in Europe as well as in Washington shortly before the 1980 presidential election.

Mr. Lavi's heart attack in early 1989 occurred during the height of the FBI's highly publicized background investigation of former Senator and Secretary of Defense designee John Tower, who (Tower) happened to have been the political mentor of the man in charge of the inquiry, FBI Director William Sessions. Sessions reportedly received his first big political break through the intercession of Mr. Tower, who had helped him obtain an appointment in the Criminal Division of President Richard Nixon's Department of Justice.[80] On December 21, 1988, five days after the author's interview with Mr. Lavi, in which he first said that it was a "possibility" he had spoken with Senator Tower prior to the L'Enfant Plaza Hotel meeting, the author was contacted by the FBI requesting an interview, as part of its background investigation of Mr. Tower. Though the FBI had received information on the Tower-L'Enfant Plaza connection much earlier, its agents waited to contact the author until *after* releasing the initial report to president-elect George Bush, which alleged that no improprieties had been discovered in the former senator's background. Press coverage of this first FBI report stated that the Bureau, headed by Tower's protégé, Sessions, had "failed to document any glaring difficulties that could preclude Tower's confirmation.[81] Ironically, the same day as the author's interview with Mr. Lavi, December 17, 1988, U.S. newspapers carried headline stories that president-elect Bush claimed to be "completely satisfied" with the result of the FBI's "thorough" investigation of former Senator Tower.

Five days after the FBI released its report on Senator Tower, on December 21, 1988, the author was interviewed by FBI agent George Mozingo in Monterey, California. Two copies of a tape recording of that interview, which detailed reports of the Tower-L'Enfant Plaza connection and Mr. Lavi's response to questions about it, were sent to senior White House correspondent, Sarah McClendon. Ms. McClendon, in turn, personally delivered a copy of the tape to a top aide to Senator Sam Nunn, Chairman of the Senate Armed Services Committee, who was investigating Tower and who had taken a particularly keen interest in the results of the FBI's investigation. Tower had been minority leader of the same Senate Armed Services Committee at the time of the October 1980 L' Enfant Plaza Hotel meeting between Lavi and Reagan-Bush campaign aides, and had served as its chairman from 1981 to 1984, during President Reagan's first term in office. Following the author's and Ms. McClendon's interviews with the FBI, the Tower nomination process ran into difficulties, purportedly due to reports of the former senator's personal, as opposed to professional, improprieties.

In his remarks on the Senate floor on March 9, 1989, Senator Nunn noted that "a very thick part of the [final] FBI report" on Senator Tower's background investigation dealt with "whether Senator Tower was aware of an approach to the 1980 Reagan-Bush campaign through his staff [Robert McFarlane] by an alleged emissary from Iran who was talking at the time about making a deal with the campaign for the release of the hostages after the election." Though the FBI had reportedly resolved this question in Mr. Tower's favor, witnesses had not been questioned under oath, and President Bush refused to release the report to the public. Until this portion of the FBI report is made available, the public has no way of making up its own mind as to the validity of the report's conclusions.

In his remarks on the Senate floor of March 3, 1989, Senator Nunn acknowledged that the Senate took the word of the FBI on the question of Senator Tower's reported involvement in arranging the L' Enfant Plaza Hotel meeting: "Mr. President," he stated, "there were other allegations raising serious issues about Senator Tower's fitness . . . whether [he] was aware of an approach to the 1980 Reagan-Bush campaign, through his staff, by an alleged emissary from Iran who sought to make a deal with that campaign for the release of the hostages after the election. We could have called witnesses on these matters. There would have been days, if not weeks, of examination, cross-examination, and rebuttal. We did not do that. We relied instead on the FBI report and our informal inquiries for our determination that Senator Tower was not involved in these matters." Given the degree of inconsistency in the reports of participants in the L' Enfant Plaza Hotel meeting in question and the fact that Mr. Sessions owed a major political favor to Mr. Tower, the author proposes that the word of the FBI and the "informal" Senate inquiry may be insufficient grounds upon which to reach a meaningful conclusion.

HOUSHANG LAVI'S PARALLEL OFFER TO THE CARTER
ADMINISTRATION REJECTED

In numerous interviews with the author, Mr. Houshang Lavi claimed that he made not one, but fifty-three trips from New York to Washington, D.C. between 1979, shortly after the U.S. hostages were taken in Tehran in November of that year, and the October 1980 meetings with the Carter Administration, Reagan-Bush campaign, and Anderson campaign. These trips, he says, were attempts to assist the Carter Administration to get the hostages of Iran. Some fifty-two of Mr. Lavi's trips, therefore, were prior to the Washington, D.C., meetings of October 1980 and were for interactions with Carter Administration officials with whom, he said, "I never got anywhere."[82] Lavi also claims to have talked with President Carter's CIA Director, Stansfield Turner, who "wouldn't listen."

If what Lavi says is true, records should exist in U.S. government files documenting dozens of interactions with Carter Administration officials, dating back to at least late 1979. In April 1988, however, in response to requests from Congressman John Conyers's office for records pertaining to Lavi's contacts, the Reagan-Bush State Department, which then controlled documents from the Carter period, only declassified and made available memoranda covering the short period from October 2, 1980—the very day of Lavi's meeting with Reagan-Bush campaign officials at the L' Enfant Plaza Hotel—to October 29, 1980, when the Carter Administration formally rejected Lavi's arms-for-hostages offer. These now-declassified documents covering only the month of October 1980 were written by Carter Administration officials in response to the Anderson campaign's referral of Mr. Lavi to the Carter Administration.

The first declassified document shows that an unidentified undercover CIA agent met on October 2, 1980, with Lavi and with Lavi's attorney, Mitchell Rogovin, who had also been special CIA counsel to George Bush when Bush was CIA director in 1976. October 2, 1980 was the same day as the L' Enfant Plaza Hotel meeting with Reagan-Bush campaign officials and Robert McFarlane. The meeting with the CIA agent took place at a "law office"—in all likelihood Rogovin's own law offices in Washington, D.C. At that time, Rogovin was general counsel to the John Anderson presidential campaign as well as being Lavi's personal attorney.

A memo by the unidentified undercover agent, dated October 2nd, states that Mr. Lavi [name censored] "implied" that he was acting on behalf of then President of Iran, Abolhassan Bani Sadr, who shortly thereafter denied the claim. Mr. Bani Sadr, in fact, has reported that Lavi had been sent, not by himself, but by his political rivals Hashemi Rafsanjani and the Ayatollah Mohammed Beheshti.[83] Mr. Bani Sadr told journalist Leslie Cockburn that he had been aware of the Washington contact with the Reagan-Bush campaign and had warned Rafsanjani that it was "dangerous" to undercut Carter and deal instead with Reagan, and that he had also complained to Khomeini about the Reagan-Bush contact.[84] Mr. Bani Sadr is almost certainly telling the truth when he says that Mr. Lavi was not sent with his authorization. When pressed by the author in an interview, Mr. Lavi admitted that he had only spoken with Mr. Bani Sadr once on the telephone, long before the early October 1980 meeting, in December 1979 when he (Bani Sadr) was acting foreign minister of Iran.[85]

The October 2, 1980, memo by the undercover CIA agent who met with Mr. Lavi and Mr. Rogovin was transmitted the following day, October 3, to the Carter Administration's Deputy Assistant for National Security Affairs David Aaron. Working for Aaron at that time on the NSC was CIA officer Robert Gates[86], whose nomination for CIA Director was retracted by the Reagan-Bush Administration in the wake of questions about his participation in the secret 1985-86 arms-for-hostages deals with Iran which became known as the Iran/Contra affair. Gates could even have been the "undercover CIA officer" who met with Lavi and Rogovin, since he worked for Aaron at the time, as could have Donald Gregg, then CIA liaison to the Carter National Security Council and future national security adviser to then vice-presidential candidate George Bush. Gates had also previously worked for Henry Kissinger.

The October 3, 1980, memo to Mr. Aaron from the undercover CIA officer notes that Lavi is Jewish and that Lavi suggested that an Israeli plane escort the U.S. hostages to be freed in exchange for F-14 fighter jet parts under his proposal. Lavi's attorney Rogovin, a longtime friend and CIA colleague of George Bush, or the undercover CIA agent himself, may have alerted Bush to Lavi's October 2, 1980, approach to the Carter Administration, for on the same day as the CIA memo, October 3rd, Bush publicly "predicted" an "October Surprise" move by President Carter.[87]

Another now declassified Carter Administration memo is dated October 8, 1980. It notes that Lavi's attorney, Mitchell Rogovin, had been informed by an unnamed Carter Administration agency that Lavi had not yet provided sufficient information to enable the Administration to assess his arms-for-hostages proposal.

The next declassified document is a heavily censored memorandum dated October 9, 1980, from Assistant Secretary of State Harold Saunders to Deputy Secretary of State Warren Christopher, President Carter's designated negotiator in the hostage crisis with Iran. It states that Saunders had met with Mr. Lavi and with Mitchell Rogovin and Alton Frye of the John Anderson campaign to discuss Lavi's arms-for-hostages offer and that Saunders had informed them that the Carter Administration would need to check with Mr. Bani Sadr, the President of Iran, to see if Mr. Lavi's proposal indeed came from him. A list of "options," presumably on how to deal with the proposed arms-for-hostages proposal, covering an entire two pages, is deleted, as is another complete page of the document. This October 9th document is the only action memorandum in the series, which meant that the Carter Administration was taking the approach seriously and that some action or decision needed to be taken by President Carter's chief hostage negotiator. The same day as this Carter action memo, October 9th, Reagan-Bush campaign pollster Richard Wirthlin sent an urgent message to campaign manager William Casey and other top campaign officials, stating that Reagan-Bush then had no choice but to "neutralize" President Carter's building push towards an "October Surprise."[88]

Another declassified memorandum, dated October 10, 1980, is a follow-up communication from Alton Frye, director of policy planning for the John Anderson presidential campaign, to Mr. Saunders of Carter's State Department, requesting feedback from the earlier meeting with Iranian arms dealer Houshang Lavi. Released with this document was a memorandum to Warren Christopher from Saunders regarding Saunders's recent telephone conversation with Mr. Rogovin, in which Rogovin alleged that Lavi had spoken with the President of Iran, Mr. Bani Sadr, who had urged him, he claimed, to "get on with it." Mr. Saunders notes that he had once again stressed the importance of the Carter Administration's receiving its own assurances from Mr. Bani Sadr that the hostages would be released safely. Copied on this October 10th memorandum (marked "EYES ONLY") is Mr. Arnold Raphel, who was then a State Department official. Raphel later died in an explosion on board a plane with Pakistan President Mohammad Zia-ul-Haq while U.S. Ambassador to Pakistan in August 1988, shortly before the 1988 presidential election. It is interesting to note that Mr. Lavi's proposal to both the Reagan-Bush campaign and the Carter Administration entailed a swap of the hostages for military equipment to take place in Pakistan, the country to which Mr. Raphel was assigned as ambassador by the Reagan-Bush Administration. Mr. Lavi would therefore have been in communication with Pakistani officials, perhaps even with Mr. Zia himself, regarding the possibility of using his proposed landing site in Karachi, Pakistan, for the arms-for-hostages exchange. In this light, it is interesting to note that two men who were probably knowledgeable about the 1980 arms-for-hostages offers to the Reagan-Bush campaign and Carter Administration died in the same plane crash during the height of publicity on the "October Surprise" story, shortly before the 1988 presidential election. Press reports at the time of his death stated that Mr. Raphel had also been one of the few Reagan-Bush officials knowledgeable about details of the administration's later 1985–86 arms-for-hostages deals with Iran.

The next declassified memorandum, dated October 15, 1980, was classified "SECRET/SENSITIVE." It is by Mr. Harold Saunders for the record. It mentions a telephone conversation among Mr. Rogovin, Mr. Saunders, and a "Bob Owen" on October 14, 1980. Though this "Bob Owen" in all likelihood is Roberts Owen of the State Department, it is interesting to note that a "Bob Owen" also became an aide to then senator Dan Quayle and subsequently a courier for Lt. Col. Oliver North to the Nicaraguan Contras. Research by the author into the history of the Robert Owen who was North's courier and Quayle's legislative aide revealed that he was in the States at the time, having recently returned from overseas.

The October 15th Saunders memorandum also records an additional meeting among Saunders, Rogovin, and Lavi on the afternoon of October 15th, during which Lavi produced a new, updated list of F-4 and F-5E jet fighter parts to be added to the original list of F-14 equipment Lavi had originally claimed the Khomeini regime was willing to exchange for the hostages. Saunders also refers to Lavi's mention of "two Iranian officials from New York" who were prepared to meet with the administration to negotiate Khomeini's other demands. Mr. Saunders noted that he again stressed that the administration would wait until it had heard from Mr. Bani Sadr, Iran's President, and recorded that he would give Mr. Lavi's latest list of military equipment to Captain Gary Sick, President Carter's Iran expert on the White House National Security Council. Navy captain Sick was later identified as the "NSC source" codenamed "Navy Blue" who provided information to Reagan-Bush campaign foreign policy adviser Richard Allen through Herbert Cohen of the Hoover Institution.[89]

As neither Reagan-Bush foreign policy adviser Richard Allen nor Robert McFarlane (who had set up the October 2, 1980 meeting with Lavi at the L' Enfant Plaza Hotel) reported their contact with Lavi to the Carter Administration as the Anderson campaign had; and as Gary Sick (who received Lavi's lists and was kept apprised of his contacts with the Carter Administration) had been a channel for information to the Reagan-Bush camp through Cohen, it is probably no coincidence that the same day Saunders noted he would pass Lavi's list of military parts to Sick, October 15th, Richard Allen learned of an alleged Carter plan to exchange military parts for the hostages.[90]

On the same day that Richard Allen received this "intelligence," the Reagan-Bush campaign reportedly engineered a "leak" of the alleged imminent Carter arms-for-hostages exchange to the press. On October 15th, WLS-TV in Chicago, an ABC affiliate station, ran a story, instantly picked up by the national wire services, that President Carter was about to send five cargo planes loaded with military spare parts to Iran in exchange for the U.S. hostages. The story was clearly false, as the Carter Administration at the time was still awaiting word from Mr. Bani Sadr regarding the legitimacy of Lavi's offer, and Carter Administration officials had to vehemently deny the disinformation in the media. President Carter has also publicly denied that he ever sent, or contemplated sending, arms to Iran.[91] An unidentified witness later testified to the congressional committee investigating the theft of President Carter's debate briefing books that the source of the October 15, 1980, WLS-TV report was a high-level active U.S. intelligence officer linked to the Reagan-Bush camp, who wanted the information publicized to sabotage even a possible deal whereby President Carter might be able to bring the hostages home before the election. According to the congressional report, "The suggestion [from the witness] was that publicizing the secret hostage negotiations would have delayed a pre-election release of the U.S. hostages in Iran to the benefit of the Reagan-Bush campaign."[92]

The WLS-TV reporter who put out the fabricated story of a pending Carter arms-for-hostages swap on October 15th was Larry Moore. Moore was later reported to be angry at being "used" by the Reagan-Bush campaign. His "source" for the story, which WLS cited as "military reserve pilots," in all likelihood came from the network of reservists reporting to Admiral Robert Garrick's "October Surprise" intelligence operation inside the Reagan-Bush campaign.[93] Moore, who still refuses to name his source, went on to work for MacNeil-Lehrer. It was on that program, on November 7, 1986, that Richard Allen revealed that President Reagan had ordered him on January 21, 1981, Reagan's first full day in office, to warn Iran that "the deal's off" unless a fifty-third hostage, the wife of a friend of Allen's, was also released from captivity. She had been taken hostage in early May 1980 and had not been set free with the other hostages on the day of Reagan's inauguration.

As Houshang Lavi told the author that he himself had worked with the

CIA since at least early 1979, and as he claimed to have already known vice-presidential candidate George Bush's friend and colleague Laurence Silberman, who was then Allen's foreign policy co-chairman in the Reagan-Bush campaign, the possibility must be seriously entertained that Senator John Tower's then aide Robert McFarlane and the Reagan-Bush camp worked *with* Lavi to set up the Carter Administration for the fabricated October 15th arms-for-hostages "leak" as a "sting" operation. Mr. Lavi, after all, had a long history of working undercover with the CIA and the U.S. Customs Service on such operations. We know of at least three such "sting" operations in which he was centrally involved after Reagan and Bush gained office: two in 1982 and 1984 with Iranian arms dealer Cyrus Hashemi, and a third in late 1985 and 1986. The latter was a major operation against seventeen American, French, and Israeli businessmen and arms dealers "stung" for attempting to ship $2.5 billion worth of U.S. arms to Iran.

A memo for the record from Harold Saunders, returning to the now-declassified memoranda on Houshang Lavi's October 1980 approach to the Carter Administration, is dated October 21, 1980. It notes that Saunders finally informed Lavi's attorney, Mitchell Rogovin, on that day that "(Iranian President) Bani Sadr said Lavi has no authority to speak on Bani Sadr's behalf." In numerous interviews with the author and other journalists, Mr. Bani Sadr has since reconfirmed that he was not in contact with Mr. Lavi in October 1980 and that Lavi had no authority to negotiate on his behalf with the Carter Administration. Once it had determined that Lavi did not have the blessings of the President of Iran, the Carter Administration cut off its contacts with the arms dealer. According to one Carter Administration aide, "An arms swap, legitimate as it may have been, was tantamount to paying ransom to terrorists. Too risky, too unreliable. Carter had some real problems with it."[95]

As we have mentioned previously, Mr. Bani Sadr claims that Lavi and other intermediaries in meetings subsequent to the October 2, 1980 contact at the L' Enfant Plaza Hotel approached the Reagan-Bush campaign, not on his behalf, but on behalf of his political rivals Hashemi Rafsanjani and Mohammed Beheshti, who desired to remove him from power. Significantly, Mr. Saunders notes in his October 21st memo for the record that Mr. Rogovin told him during their telephone conversation of the same date:

> "Rogovin said he had heard that the Iranians were not going to make a negotiation with the Carter Administration. I [Saunders] said I had not heard that."

In Chapter II, we will see how significant the timing of this "tip" was, coming as it did in the middle of the October 18–25 "window of vulnerability" for an "October Surprise" so dreaded by the Reagan-Bush campaign.

The last declassified memorandum, dated October 29, 1980, is from Harold Saunders to Deputy Secretary of State Warren Christopher, President Carter's designated hostage negotiator. It notes that Houshang Lavi was still insisting on receiving a telegram from the Carter Administration stating that it was prepared to negotiate the proposed arms-for-hostages exchange with Iran. With such a telegram in hand, a "sting" operation could have been consummated. Mr. Saunders avoided making such a promise and notes that (though the Carter Administration did consider it):

> "We have never proposed a spares-for-hostages swap. The *only* way that issue has come to us has been through such channels as the one Mitch Regovin has been party to. Apart from the Lavi-Regovin channel, we have not had proposals from authoritative Iranians for any such limited [arms-for-hostages] deal. . . . The *only* time we have received a list [of military equipment desired by Iran] was through the Lavi-Regovin channel." [author's emphasis added]

In summary, Mr. Houshang Lavi, then an Iranian emigré of Jewish background with a long history of working with the CIA, the Customs Service, and the Israelis, in all probability worked secretly with the pro-Reagan-Bush CIA and the Reagan-Bush campaign to lock the Carter Administration into a political no-win situation in October 1980. If the Carter Administration rejected Lavi's offer outright, the Reagan-Bush camp, which was kept apprised through its CIA and White House moles, could "leak" the damaging story that Carter wasn't serious about freeing the hostages. On the other hand, if the Carter Administration accepted Lavi's offer, the Reagan-Bush camp could "leak" the equally if not more damaging story that Carter was cynically trying to bring the hostages home before the election for purely political reasons. In short, Mr. Bani Sadr's political rivals, Rafsanjani and Beheshti, and Mr. Carter's political rivals, Reagan and Bush, may have used Mr. Lavi to make the Carter Administration an offer they thought it couldn't refuse, but which it also couldn't accept.

Even if Mr. Lavi was not consciously working on behalf of the Republican camp, his efforts could easily have been turned to their advantage. The recommendation of the unidentified undercover CIA officer who first met with Lavi on October 2, 1980, purportedly on behalf of the Carter Administration, against pursuing his arms-for-hostages offer may have been

designed to discourage the Carter camp from following up a proposal that
the Reagan-Bush campaign could then take advantage of itself. As this
agent met with Lavi on the same day that Lavi met with Richard Allen,
Laurence Silberman, and Robert McFarlane of the Reagan-Bush camp,
and as the CIA at the time was strongly pro-Republican, the agent's
suggestion not to pursue the Lavi contact may have been intended to serve
the hidden agenda of the Republican campaign. In any case, the congressional committee that investigated the theft of President Carter's debate
briefing books determined that the source of Richard Allen's information
about Lavi's contacts with the Carter Administration was a "highly-placed
member of the U.S. intelligence community" somehow associated with
the Reagan-Bush campaign. That "highly-placed" intelligence source could
easily have been the undercover CIA agent himself, or even Mr. Lavi.

According to former Reagan-Bush campaign Iran expert Michel Smith,
Mr. Bani Sadr, and Mr. Lavi, Lavi's meeting at the L' Enfant Plaza Hotel
on October 2, 1980, with Allen, Silberman, and McFarlane was by no
means his last contact in Washington D.C. with the Republican campaign.
Mr. Lavi has told the author that he had numerous subsequent contacts
with Mr. Bush's top aide, James Baker. In the next chapter we will also
review reports, some from alleged eyewitnesses, that Mr. Casey, and
perhaps also Mr. Bush himself, held follow-up meetings to discuss the
more palatable proposal of a release of the hostages after, not before, the
November 4th presidential election in exchange for a promise of U.S. arms
through the Israelis, at least one of which was reportedly attended by Mr.
Lavi. President Carter himself became aware of such efforts by the Republican camp before the election. On June 15, 1988, in an interview on the
Larry King radio program, he revealed:

> "There were reports made to me before the election that this was going
> on—that the hostages would not be released [to me] and that [U.S.]
> weapon sales would be restored to Iran, either directly or through the
> Israelis."[96]

President Carter has not yet revealed, however, how he knew that "this
was going on." Perhaps the Democrats had a few "moles" of their own.

LIKE A PHOENIX RISING

Houshang Lavi has told both the author and *Playboy* magazine reporter Jonathan Silvers, in separate interviews in 1988, that he and George Bush's former CIA counsel Laurence Silberman, who was also Richard Allen's aide in the 1980 Reagan-Bush campaign, worked together in early 1979 on a secret Agency mission to remove F-14 Phoenix missiles and/or Phoenix subsystems, and sensitive Aug-9 radar tracking equipment from air force bases in Isfahan, Iran, so that they would not fall into the hands of the Iranian revolutionaries or the Soviets.[97] According to Lavi, he, Silberman, and two Iranian generals-turned-CIA-agents were "90 percent successful in getting the Phoenix missiles [and/or Phoenix missile parts] out of Iran." Lavi's claim is supported by a report in October 1980, in *The New York Times*. In that article, a spokesman for Sperry-Vickers was quoted as saying that, "When U.S. military technicians left Iran in early 1979, a special effort was made to remove essential parts from the Phoenix missiles."[98] The article also quoted an unidentified Pentagon spokesman, saying that these same Phoenix missile systems had been moved to the Philadelphia Navy yard just prior to the 1980 presidential election.[99] From the date of the story, October 30th, it can be inferred that the Phoenix parts, probably like those Lavi says he and Silberman removed from Iran in January 1979, were ordered transferred to the Philadelphia Navy yard on or around October 29th—the day that the Carter Administration rejected Lavi's arms-for-hostages offer. Two days later, on November 1, 1980, Evans and Novak put out a "special bonus column" also reporting that war materiel was being transferred from military warehouses to the same Philadelphia Navy yard for transfer to Iran.[100] Evans and Novak alleged that the planned shipment of Phoenix parts to Iran was part of a secret deal exchanging arms for the U.S. hostages. Could Houshang Lavi and Laurence Silberman of the Reagan-Bush campaign, both with long histories of working with the CIA,[101] have been involved in arrangements for the transfer to Iran of the very equipment they had reportedly removed from Iran two years earlier? If Lavi's story is true, they would certainly have been in a position to know precisely what Iran's air force needed, and why.

Immediately after Reagan's election victory and less than a week after these reports that the Phoenix missile equipment had been transferred to the Philadelphia Navy yard for shipment to Iran, Mr. Silberman was appointed liaison to the CIA for the Reagan-Bush transition team. In that position, he would have been able to ensure that the very equipment he had reportedly removed from Iran would be returned as part of a secret agreement for the future release of the U.S. hostages to the Reagan-Bush Administration.

In one of the strangest episodes of the entire campaign period, at about the same time that the Phoenix parts reportedly arrived in Philadelphia for supposed shipment to the Khomeini regime, a ship bound for Egypt was hijacked near Philadelphia and redirected to Iran in a bizarre plot allegedly involving the Gambino Mafia family of southern New Jersey.[102] Though press reports at the time stated that its cargo was 13,500 tons of corn, it is possible that the hijacked ship, which was named *The Poet,* was carrying something far more valuable than corn.

Houshang Lavi and his brothers began making arms deals with the Iranian government as soon as Ronald Reagan and George Bush gained the White House. Though they have been investigated by the State Department, the Customs Service, and the FBI for years, and though it was and remains illegal to export or conspire to export U.S. arms to Iran, none of the Lavis have never been charged with a crime.[103]

Houshang Lavi was interviewed by the Congressional Iran/Contra Committee in a closed-door session. Given the wildly contradictory stories and finger-pointing by the men with whom he claims to have met on October 2, 1980—Richard Allen, Laurence Silberman, and Robert McFarlane—it is certain that Mr. Lavi had much to enlighten the Committee about. Whether they asked him the right questions, however, is unknown, as the proceedings remain classified. Perhaps public pressure will now be brought to bear on Congress to finally bring what this "mystery man" had to say into the light.

WHERE'S THE BRIEF?

It is well known that President Carter's debate briefing books got into the hands of William Casey, James Baker, and other top-level officials of the 1980 Reagan-Bush campaign. In the summer of 1984, official Washington turned itself upside down to follow up a footnote in Laurence Barrett's book *Gambling With History,* which mentioned that the Reagan-Bush campaign had obtained a copy of President Carter's debate books. Suddenly, a literal footnote in history *became* history. Congressman Donald Albosta's House Subcommittee on Human Resources devoted six months of hearings and interviews to an attempt to discover how the "purloined papers" found their way into the Reagan-Bush camp. The scandal that ensued became known as "Debategate."

After six months of investigations, the Albosta "Debategate" committee concluded that the briefing books had entered the Reagan-Bush campaign through campaign manager William Casey, who in turn gave them to James H. Baker III, George Bush's former campaign manager and then the top aide in charge of debate preparations for the campaign. Despite reams of press coverage on the scandal and over two thousand pages of published testimony in the committee's two-volume final report, published in May 1984, three key facts about "Debategate" are still not widely appreciated by the general public—perhaps by design.

The first is that President Carter's debate briefing books were obtained by the Reagan-Bush campaign as a windfall of its larger "intelligence operation" designed to net much bigger fish—classified "inside" information on the Carter Administration's "October Surprise" negotiations for a pre-election hostage release. According to Frank Askin, counsel to Congressman John Conyers, who investigated the "October Surprise" story and its relationship to "Debategate" in 1987 and 1988, "William Casey set up a mammoth intelligence operation, including past and present members of the military and intelligence communities, to spy on Carter's negotiations with Iran. This is the network which obtained the Carter debate papers."[104]

The second fact not well understood about "Debategate" is that the definitive evidence that President Carter's debate briefing book was in fact stolen surfaced on the day *after* the Albosta subcommittee decided to "indefinitely postpone" its investigation, in mid-January 1984. The third little-appreciated fact about "Debategate" is that the Reagan-Bush campaign actually used one of President Carter's briefing books *during* President Reagan's debate rehearsals, in which former Congressman and former aide to then presidential candidate John Anderson, David Stockman, "played" President Carter. We will address the latter fact first.

Ronald Reagan took time out from his campaign on October 25, 26, and 27, 1980, to rehearse for the October 28, 1980 presidential debate. These debate rehearsals were held in the garage at "Wexford," the West Virginia estate where the Reagans stayed during the final months of the campaign. Photographs of the rehearsals taken inside the Wexford garage show that it had been fitted with stage lights, two podiums—Reagan's on the right and Stockman's on the left—and a row of tables for top campaign officials and consultants "playing" the panel of journalists who would ask questions of the candidates during the debate, or who just observed or made suggestions. At the back of the garage, opposite the podiums, was a video camera operated by Mr. William Caruthers.[105] The photographs include Reagan, Stockman, James Baker, debate team member Frank Hodsoll, communications expert David Gergen, economist Alan Greenspan, campaign chief of staff Edwin Meese, communications consultant Myles Martel, domestic policy adviser Martin Anderson, and other campaign officials. From his testimony to the Albosta subcommittee it is known that the campaign's foreign policy and defense adviser, Richard Allen, also participated in the Wexford rehearsals.

The most important and obvious place for President Carter's debate books to have been used would have been in the Wexford garage during these debate rehearsals. In fact, there is a large body of evidence that they were used there. In one photograph taken of the rehearsal sessions, a dark binder can be seen resting on Stockman's podium. The color of this binder is significant, because the congressional investigation revealed that President Carter's debate briefing books were in hardcover black binders. The Reagan debate briefing books, prepared by James Baker and Frank Hodsoll's team, were in red, light blue, and mixed-color binders. Stockman himself boasted in a public address in Cassopolis, Indiana, on October 28, 1980, the day of the debate, that he had used President Carter's debate books to coach Reagan in the rehearsals. As we shall see, he had been using them one day before, in a rehearsal in the Wexford garage. During the debate itself, according to the *Elkhart Truth*, President Carter "said almost word for word what Stockman predicted" at Cassopolis.

Richard Allen told the congressional committee investigating "Debategate" that, during the debate rehearsals, someone in the garage called out that the Reagan campaign had obtained Carter debate briefing materials.[106] It is unlikely that this would have happened unless the "materials" were being used in the garage during the rehearsals.

On October 26, 1980, the day of one of the rehearsals, Frank Hodsoll told Myles Martell, both of whom can be seen in the photographs of the debate rehearsals, that the campaign had obtained President Carter's debate briefing books.[107] A copy of President Carter's foreign policy debate book was later found in Frank Hodsoll's campaign files. A copy of the same foreign policy book was also found in the campaign files of David Gergen, who was also at the rehearsals in the Wexford garage.

Milton Graham, 1980 Reagan-Bush campaign photographer, told the author in an interview that he was present in the Wexford garage taking photographs from 1:00 to 5:00 p.m. on the afternoon of October 27th, the last of the three days of debate rehearsals. He described what he observed:

> "Stockman *had* to have been using Carter's debate briefing books. He had it down *word for word*. Stockman had memorized whole paragraphs from the debate books—*verbatim*. It was as if he were the embodiment of Carter. In fact, Reagan got really angry at how good he was. His temples would flare, almost like they were going to burst, he was so angry at how good Stockman was at being Carter."[108] [author's emphasis added]

After developing the photographs he took on October 27th, Graham kept thirteen or fourteen negatives and put the rest of the negatives and all of the seventy-two photographs in a filing cabinet in the campaign's press area. After the November 4th election, when he returned to check on them, all of the photographs showing Reagan-Bush campaign officials in the Wexford garage were missing. Only those showing Reagan and Stockman at the podiums, and in one case James Baker at the podium with Reagan, were still there. No one seemed to know who had removed the majority of the photographs, or why they wouldn't want it known who else was in the room. According to Graham, when the Iran/Contra affair began to break, the FBI threatened him if he talked to the press about what he knew.

Though the final Albosta report on "Debategate" claimed, in the introductory section, that it contained all testimony taken by the committee, key testimony was in fact left out of the report. In late August 1983, the author, whose office in Reagan-Bush campaign headquarters was next door to the debate preparation team, gave over 3 hours of tape-recorded testimony to the majority counsel for the Albosta subcommittee, at their request. This included an account of White House speechwriting aide Misty Church having told the author that Ann McGlinn—a secretary who worked in Room 208 of the Old Executive Office Building next to the White House during the Carter Administration—openly boasted of having leaked President Carter's debate briefing materials to the Reagan-Bush campaign. Not only was this testimony left out of the final congressional report on "Debategate," the report did not even mention that the author had given solicited testimony. When the author wrote to Congressman Donald Albosta pointing out the omission and requesting an explanation, he wrote back "explaining" that the testimony had been left out of the report in the interests of the author's security. Why the subcommittee chose not to apply the same criteria to the dozens of other witnesses, whose "security" interests were just as real and whose testimony they did include, remains a mystery.

Ann McGlinn, the Carter secretary who the author was told boasted about leaking debate materials, survived the "ruthless purge" of Carter Administration secretaries by Edwin Meese immediately after Reagan gained the White House. Jim Roland, another Carter White House staffer, testified to the Albosta subcommittee that he had left thirteen copies of President Carter's debate briefing books in Ms. McGlinn's office on the morning of October 24, 1980, the day before the first Reagan-Stockman debate rehearsal, where they were needed most.

Another Carter White House aide, Kathy Reid, who had direct access to President Carter's debate briefing books, also survived Meese's "purge." Reid had the final versions of the foreign policy and domestic policy briefing books in her possession as soon as they were first completed, at 2:30 A.M. on the morning of October 27th, at Camp David. Milton Graham heard David Stockman speaking "verbatim" from President Carter's debate books during the Reagan's third debate rehearsal later that same day.

A third Carter White House secretary who survived the Meese "purge" was Wilma Hall, the mother of Fawn Hall, who was Oliver North's secretary during the Iran/Contra operations. In October 1980, Wilma Hall was a night secretary to President Carter's national security adviser Zbigniew Brzezinski. She typed the foreign policy debate briefing book, a copy of which ended up in the campaign files of Reagan-Bush aides David Gergen and Frank Hodsoll. In a sworn affidavit to the congressional "Debategate" subcommittee, Mrs. Hall claimed that she had no knowledge of how President Carter's debate briefing books got into the Reagan-Bush campaign. Yet, in this same affidavit she states, astoundingly: "I have not *purposefully* withheld information from the Subcommittee on Human Resources that is relevant to its investigation of materials during the 1980 presidential campaign," and then *crossed out* and initialled the word "purposefully."[109] As Wilma Hall was the secretary to President Carter's national security adviser Zbigniew Brzezinski, it is interesting to note that the "Debategate" investigation also revealed that Reagan-Bush campaign foreign policy adviser Richard Allen obtained copies of Brzezinski's "sometimes extraordinarily sensitive" daily NSC staff reports prepared by his senior aides.[110] Mrs. Hall was also the secretary of national security adviser

Robert McFarlane at the time of the genesis of the secret arms sales to Iran in 1985.[111]

The final report of the Albosta Subcommittee, which investigated "Debategate," concluded that Reagan-Bush campaign manager William Casey received the debate briefing books at campaign headquarters from an "informant," who received $2,860 for his "services," and passed them to George Bush's former campaign manager and the debate team leader, James H. Baker III. Though Baker insisted that the debate books had been delivered to the Reagan team by Casey, Casey contradicted him, claiming that he had never seen any Carter debate materials during the campaign period.[112] Casey also castigated Baker in the open press after the scandal broke, saying that "He should have known better than to touch such political dynamite."[113] Despite the public disagreement, Mr. Baker's version of events is almost certainly the more accurate one. Casey later boasted that he was ready to challenge Baker to a "lie detector shootout" over who was telling the truth about how the debate papers entered the campaign because, he said, a polygraph could be beaten "with Valium and a few tricks."[114]

As noted earlier, the debate rehearsals in the Wexford garage were recorded on videotape. The audio portion of those three days of video-tapes, therefore, shows exactly what was said in the room. If the transcript of the audio portion of those tapes had been released, the public would have been able to compare it with the text and questions-and-answers from President Carter's debate briefing books to see for itself whether his debate books had been used in the rehearsals by the Reagan-Bush campaign. But no transcripts of the videotapes made it into the 2,413 pages of the allegedly "complete" final report of the congressional "Debategate" investigation.

The Federal Bureau of Investigation, which is under the auspices of the Department of Justice, reviewed the videotapes for the Congressional subcommittee. In 1987, a Freedom of Information Act request was filed requesting the tapes and/or the transcripts. The tapes were refused. When the transcripts were released by the Reagan-Bush Administration, 90 percent—almost all—of the text had been censored.[115] Even with the 10 percent remaining, however, it is clear that the FBI had made the 1980 Reagan-Bush campaign's "October Surprise" intelligence operation and William Casey's attempts to obtain classified information on President Carter's hostage plans a major focus of its "Debategate" investigation. Clearly, the final and "complete" report of the Albosta Subcommittee revealed only what was not important for an understanding of this massive breach of security, ethics, and the law.

After the congressional "Debategate" investigation was "indefinitely postponed" in mid-January 1984, Attorney General Edwin Meese, who had been in the Wexford garage during the debate rehearsals, came under scrutiny as the result of numerous charges of impropriety. An independent counsel, more popularly known as a "special prosecutor," was appointed under the Ethics in Government Act to investigate the charges, which included allegations of Mr. Meese's participation in "Debategate."

Shocked at what had been left out of the final report of the Albosta Subcommittee, the author wrote to the independent counsel, Mr. Stein, summarizing the evidence that President Carter's debate briefing books had been used during the rehearsals in the Wexford garage and urging him to compare the audio portion of the videotapes with the text of Carter's questions-and-answers from his debate briefing materials with that in mind. Yet Mr. Stein chose not to ask the FBI for this one piece of evidence which could definitively have proven, or disproven, that David Stockman had used the debate books during the rehearsals or in preparation for them. Instead, he merely accepted the "word" of the Federal Bureau of Investigation that there was allegedly "no reasonable parallel" between the transcript of the audio portion of the videotapes and President Carter's debate briefing materials.[116] If, in fact, there was no "reasonably clear parallel" between the two, it remains a mystery why the Reagan-Bush FBI felt it necessary to censor almost 100 percent of the transcript of the tapes before releasing them to the public under the Freedom of Information Act.

In correspondence with independent counsel Stein, the author also recommended that he investigate the nature of the debate briefing books, which are clearly visible in photographs of the debate rehearsals in the Wexford garage. In his final report, Mr. Stein analyzed the Reagan-Bush debate books on the tables where campaign aides were seated, but did not even mention *the key* dark-colored briefing book clearly visible on David Stockman's podium in some of the photographs, the only one that really mattered. Again, the section of the Stein report on "Debategate," like that of the congressional subcommittee, revealed only what was not important for the public to know.

On January 18, 1984, the Congressional Albosta Subcommittee ended its investigation with a recommendation that the attorney general appoint a special prosecutor to continue the inquiry under the Ethics in Government Act. That act requires the Attorney General, upon receipt of "specific and credible information'' showing possible wrongdoing by high officials, to promptly undertake an investigation and report the results to a special judicial body. Yet both outgoing Attorney General William French Smith and the new attorney general, Ed Meese, not surprisingly, chose to ignore the law. In March 1984, a federal judge ruled that the Justice Department had acted improperly. U.S. District Judge Harold Green determined that the attorney general should have conducted a ninety-day preliminary investigation, as required by law, based upon the more than "specific and credible information" compiled by the congressional "Debate" subcommittee over a period of six months. It should have reported its results to a special division of the U.S. Court of Appeals chosen by the Chief Justice of the Supreme Court to determine if an independent counsel should be appointed to pursue the case, as required by law.[117] The Reagan-Bush Justice Department, however, did nothing.

The most significant evidence that President Carter's debate briefing books were actually stolen surfaced—perhaps coincidentally, perhaps not—only one day after the Congressional "Debategate" subcommittee decided to "indefinitely postpone" its investigation. The congressional investigation closed down on January 18, 1984. That same day, an 8th grade schoolgirl, Kristin Preble, "rediscovered" what was soon to be identified as the original debate briefing book of President Carter's White House press secretary and top aide, Jody Powell. It was found in a closet in her home in Bradford Woods, Pennsylvania, a little town about 20 minutes by plane from Cleveland, Ohio, where the October 28, 1980, Carter-Reagan presidential debate was held.[118] According to Kristin's mother, Carol Preble, in an interview with the author, her daughter "found" the debate book, which had been in the closet for almost four years, and received her permission to take it to school to complete an assignment on U.S. presidential elections for her social studies class.

The next morning, January 19, 1984, the day after the congressional investigation closed down, Kristin Preble took Jody Powell's debate briefing book to her social studies teacher, Mr. James DeLisio, at the Ingomar Middle School just north of Pittsburgh, Pennsylvania. Mr. DeLisio had just finished an article in the local newspaper on the "indefinite postponement" of the "Debategate" investigation when she turned in her "assignment" about 8:00 a.m. that morning. When he saw the briefing book marked clearly with a large white label: "CARTER DEBATE" his eyes popped out. In his hands was not only an original of President Carter's debate briefing book in a hardcover black binder, but also an inch-and-a-half-thick stack of loose White House documents marked "CLASSIFIED"

"EXECUTIVE CLASSIFIED," and "ADMINISTRATIVELY CLASSI-
FIED."[120]

After school, Mr. DeLisio took the debate briefing book and the sheaf
of papers home to his residence in Sewickley, Pennsylvania. Though
DeLisio told the press, which came calling in droves, in January 1984, that
"I really didn't even look at them, and I especially didn't want to look at
the one that had something to do with Iran," he revealed quite a different
story to the author once the heat wore off. According to Mr. DeLisio, he
and his wife, Carol, read through the briefing book and papers from about
5:00 p.m. to 10:00 p.m. the night of January 19th. It was only by so
doing, he said, that he realized that the book and papers should be turned
over to the FBI.[121] Mr. DeLisio said that the loose Iran-related documents
showed without question that the Carter White House refused to deal with
the Ayatollah Khomeini to resolve the hostage crisis and was willing to
work only with Iranian President Bani Sadr and another Iranian official
who he said was identified in the papers by a code name. Mr. DeLisio also
remembered that one of the memoranda stated that President Carter's top
aides realized that it would "take a miracle" to win the election if the
hostages didn't come home in mid-October 1980. He also recalled that
most of the memos were to President Carter or to Jody Powell.

On the morning of January 20, 1984, Mr. James DeLisio called the
Federal Bureau of Investigation in Pittsburgh only to find that no one
would believe that he had either classified White House documents or
President Carter's debate briefing book. After speaking to a number of
agents, someone finally asked him to check the bottom of a document and
read off the "classification line." When he did, the agent barked, "*Freeze!
Don't move! We're coming for them!*" But DeLisio had to teach a class
that morning and left the briefing book and papers with the school's
principal, from whom they were picked up by the FBI. As part of the
FBI's subsequent investigation, President Carter's former White House
press secretary, Jody Powell, confirmed that the book was his original
copy.[122]

That is how an original of President Carter's debate briefing book got
into the hands of the FBI. What is more interesting by far is how it got into
the hands of Kristin Preble's father. According to Kristin's mother, Carol,
her husband, Alan Preble, "found" the briefing book and papers on his
bed at the Bonds Court Hotel in Cleveland, Ohio, where he was staying
while attending a conference during the time of the Carter-Reagan debate,
which was held in Cleveland on the night of October 28, 1980. The Bonds
Court Hotel happened to be where the Carter presidential party was

staying, beginning on the night of October 27th. Mr. Preble's room, his wife recalled, was in the same hotel and on the same floor as Jody Powell's.

According to press reports after Mr. DeLisio turned the papers over to the FBI, a "maid" had allegedly placed Mr. Powell's briefing book and classified papers on Mr. Preble's hotel-room bed, thinking that he was part of the presidential party.[123] Rather than turning them into the hotel desk, however, Mr. Preble took them home to his house in Bradford Woods, Pennsylvania. When Mrs. Preble asked her husband how he came by the documents, she recalled, he gave a story different from the one in the press. He told her that a maid had said that Jody Powell had handed her the debate briefing book and papers and had said to "Put them in that room." The maid, presumably, then put them in the "wrong" room.

If Mrs. Preble's memory is accurate, her husband's account is almost impossible to believe. President Carter's White House press secretary simply would not have handed a package of highly classified U.S. Government documents and his own incredibly sensitive debate briefing book to a stranger, let alone a hotel maid. There is also the question of why Mr. Preble was allowed to have a room in the same "secure" area as the President's party.

It is far more likely that the Bonds Court "maid" used her master key to *take* the briefing book and papers from Mr. Powell's locked hotel room sometime on October 27th in time to be used by the Reagan-Bush debate team in their final debate rehearsal of the same day. They could then have been returned to the "wrong" room on the 29th, the day after President Carter's party left, as Mrs. Preble recalled. By the time her husband found the materials on his hotel-room bed, she remembered his having told her, Mr. Powell and his colleagues had already checked out. Alternatively, of course, Mr. Preble, who was then a steel-marketing executive with National Intergroup Corporation, may have been acting as an agent of the Republican campaign himself. Unfortunately, personnel at the Bonds Court Hotel claim that their records have probably not been maintained back to 1984, and would be confidential in any case.

Also unfortunately, Mr. Alan Preble is not alive to clarify the situation. According to his wife, he died of a brain tumor—as did William Casey just before he was to testify to Congress—in the summer of 1983, just as the congressional investigation into how President Carter's debate briefing books found their way into the Reagan-Bush campaign was getting underway. According to Mrs. Preble, her husband read through the debate book and the classified papers after bringing them home from the Cleveland hotel.

Intriguingly, the Associated Press left one key fact out of its January 21, 1984, report of the "discovery" of Jody Powell's debate briefing book by schoolgirl Kristin Preble. The wire service, which is picked up by newspapers across the United States, reported only that Mr. Alan Preble had "found" President Carter's debate briefing book on his hotel-room bed in an "unspecified city." That "unspecified city," of course, was none other than Cleveland, Ohio, where the October 28, 1980, presidential debate between Ronald Reagan and President Carter took place—a mere minor detail.

When a colleague of the author's interviewed Mr. Jody Powell about his reaction to the "October Surprise" story, curiously he made no mention of the fact that his own debate briefing book had disappeared from the Bonds Court Hotel in Cleveland, Ohio, while he was there the day before the debate.[124] He did say that he believed that the real target of the Reagan-Bush campaign's "intelligence operation" had been information about President Carter's hostage negotiations and any last-minute rescue plans, which might have been discussed in classified memoranda. When asked for his reaction to the "October Surprise" allegations, according to the interviewer, Powell said that there should not only be a criminal investigation, but that "These guys should be hung out to dry."

"QUIET DIPLOMACY"

During the October 28, 1980, presidential debate between President Carter and Ronald Reagan, journalist Barbara Walters asked Mr. Carter to comment on reports that he might be negotiating a release of the hostages for weapons and spare parts. President Carter responded: "If the hostages are released safely, . . . we would make delivery on those items which Iran owns." The United States government at the time was holding some $240 million worth of military equipment which President Carter had embargoed shortly after the hostages were taken in November 1979, arms which were therefore formally "owned" by Iran. When Barbara Walters asked President Carter that question, Ronald Reagan must have been smiling. For, based on his campaign's "purloined" copies of the president's debate briefing books, Mr. Reagan already knew exactly what Mr. Carter was about to say. The 10 percent of the FBI report on the debate rehearsals that made it past the Reagan-Bush Administration's censors contains a reference to "Q [Question] #7 on 'Reagan Debate Practice Tape #2.' " The question was, "Would the candidate sell military spare parts to Iran in exchange for the hostages?" Though the question was not censored, the answer was.

During the October 28th debate, in response to a similar question from Ms. Walters as to how he would resolve the hostage crisis, Ronald Reagan had a far more interesting answer:

> "I have been accused lately of having a 'secret plan' with regard to the hostages. . . . My ideas require quiet diplomacy, where you don't say what it is you're thinking of doing."

In the next chapter, "Quiet Diplomacy," we will see what a group of self-proclaimed eyewitnesses have to say about the kind of "quiet diplomacy" Ronald Reagan may have had in mind.

II

QUIET DIPLOMACY

**"I am a man who sees life in terms of missions.
Missions defined, and missions completed."**

**Vice-President and Presidential Candidate George Bush
Republican National Convention, 1988**

As the October 18, 1980, opening of the "October Surprise" window of vulnerability drew near, fear among the leaders of the Reagan-Bush campaign rose perceptably. Press reports described the atmosphere inside national Reagan-Bush campaign headquarters as one of "trepidation bordering on paranoia."[1] *Time* magazine's poll put Carter ahead of Reagan 42 to 41 by mid-October. As of October 16, pollster Richard Wirthlin's more precise vote projection program, PINS, put Reagan ahead by 6 percentage points on election day,[2] but the lead could be wiped out in an instant by the 10 percentage point surge President Carter was expected to receive if he brought the hostages home between October 18th and 25th. Then, on precisely the 18th, the dreaded opening of the window of vulnerability, after Reagan's "trees cause pollution" gaffe and Carter's hard-hitting images of Reagan as a war mongerer, even media coverage turned against the Republican candidate.

Adding to the fear already raised by Wirthlin's absolutist warnings, the Reagan-Bush campaign had learned through its moles inside the Carter Administration that the Ayatollah Khomeini had decided that a Carter victory aided by a pre-election hostage release would be advantageous to the new Iranian revolution.[3] As a result, the head of Khomeini's secret police SAVAMA had just been to Washington meeting with CIA officials during the second week in October, only one week before the opening of the dreaded window of vulnerability. The Iranian official and Agency representatives discussed a plan to free the hostages before the November 4th election in conjunction with Iran's need for U.S. weapons and spare parts to fight the new war with Iraq, which had just begun on September 22nd.[4] A Carter official almost certainly involved in these negotiations, or intimately knowledgeable about them, was Donald Gregg, the CIA's liaison to President Carter's National Security Council, who would shortly become Vice-President George Bush's top national security adviser. The Reagan-Bush campaign's chief foreign policy adviser, Richard Allen, quickly learned of the CIA's negotiations with the Khomeini emissary. A memorandum in Allen's handwriting uncovered during the congressional investigation into the theft of President Carter's debate briefing books reads, "FCI [Fred C. Ikle, a member of Allen's "October Surprise" Group]—Partial Release of hostages for parts."

Within days of the SAVAMA chief's visit, President Carter sent an official message to the Khomeini regime, dated October 11th, offering $150 million in U.S. arms, including aircraft spare parts[5], an amount only $10 million less than the CIA and Khomeini's emissary had discussed, $160 million. At the same time, then President of Iran Abolhassan Bani Sadr confirms, an agreement between his government and the Carter Administration had been reached[6], and by October 15th the *Washington Post* was predicting a "break" in the hostage crisis based upon interviews with "senior U.S. [Carter] officials."[7]

As the window of vulnerability opened on October 18th, therefore, the long-feared "October Surprise" seemed imminent at Reagan-Bush national campaign headquarters where the time for counteraction had clearly come. Just as this decision was being forced upon the campaign's leadership, Iran's Prime Minister Mohammad Ali Rajai happened to visit the United Nations. Arriving on October 16th, Rajai, who had been appointed a member of Iran's hostage release policy committee, refused to meet with President Carter, Secretary of State Edmund Muskie, or any other Carter Administration official. As fate, or design, would have it, he was due to leave New York on the night of the opening of the "window of vulnerability," October 18th.

Between October 18th, the date that Rajai left New York, and October 20th, something of major significance happened to change Khomeini's mind about negotiating a pre-election hostage release with the Carter Administration. Unaccountably, the Iranian government decided to completely ignore President Carter's official offer of desperately needed arms and spare parts.[8] Iran did not even acknowledge having received the White House communication. As Rajai was visiting New York and refusing to talk with Carter Administration officials, Israeli Prime Minister Menachem Begin sent a "test" planeload of American military equipment to Tehran without having first obtained President Carter's permission.[9] (Begin would shortly meet with Houshang Lavi, the alleged Khomeini emissary who offered an arms-for-hostages proposal to Richard Allen and Robert McFarlane in early October.[10]) According to Iran's President Bani Sadr, then "everything [Iran's negotiations with Carter] stopped."[11]

On October 20, 1980, only two days into the period of greatest danger from a pre-election hostage release and two days after Iranian Prime Minister Rajai left New York, Reagan-Bush campaign manager William Casey suddenly was no longer worried about an "October Surprise."[12] Within only 24 hours of whatever had happened to give Casey his surge of confidence, Mitchell Rogovin, the man who had been vice-presidential candidate George Bush's special counsel at the CIA when Bush was director in 1976, told President Carter's assistant secretary of defense, Harold Saunders, that "he had heard that the Iranians were not going to make a negotiation with the Carter Administration [before the election]."[13] This was information so "inside" that even the official in charge of the hostage crisis at President Carter's State Department, Mr. Saunders, had not yet learned about it.[14] The same day as Rogovin's astonishing "tip" to Saunders, October 21st, presidential candidate Ronald Reagan made reference on the campaign trail, for the first time, to his "secret plan" to free the hostages.[15] Twenty-four hours later, on October 22nd, Prime Minister Rajai, having returned to Iran, announced officially what Rogovin had gained advance intelligence of: despite the recent invasion of its territory by Iraq, Iran was suddenly dropping all demands on the Carter Administration for U.S. arms and spare parts in its negotiations for release of the hostages.[16] The reason for the surprise switch, according to an Iranian journalist, was that the Khomeini regime had just been guaranteed another, better, source of arms.[17] "It was amazing," President Carter's then Iran expert on the National Security Council, Gary Sick, recalls. "They were at war, after all."[18] According to then Iranian President Abolhassan Bani Sadr, the Ayatollah Mohammed Beheshti, Khomeini's number-two man, told him at about this same time that "they" (according to Bani Sadr, Beheshti and Iran's parliamentary speaker Hashemi Rafsanjani) had received a better arms offer from the Reagan-Bush camp and no longer needed to deal with President Carter.[19]

"This better offer," received by Khomeini was no doubt the reason for an "abrupt" and "dramatic" change in his attitude and the behavior of the religious clerics around him in October 1980, observed by Iran's former ambassador to the United Nations, Mansur Farhang.[20] "There was a very dramatic change of mood among the Iranian clerics [religious leaders] in October 1980 towards the [Carter] negotiations to release the hostages," Farhang recalls. "I was completely dumbfounded, confused, incapable of making sense of it at the time. . . . We who claimed Iran would get a better deal with Carter were dismissed. They [Beheshti, Rafsanjani, and Khomeini's son Ahmed] said Iran would 'do better' with Reagan."[21] The way in which the American hostages were treated also shifted dramatically in October 1980. According to then hostage William Belk, in October "everything changed." He and other hostages were moved from Evin Prison and suddenly treated far better, as if their captors had learned that their year-long ordeal had finally produced a promise of future dividends.[22] "It's an interesting question why the [prospect of] promising meetings [with the Iranians] we had in September [1980] ended so abruptly," Warren Christopher, President Carter's designated hostage negotiator, told the *Los Angeles Times*.[23] Interesting, indeed.

After leaving New York on the night of October 18th, Iranian Prime Minister Mohammad Ali Rajai reportedly stopped off in Algiers on his way to Iran. Back in Tehran on October 22nd, he made the surprise announcement that Iran would refuse to consider arms and spare parts from the Carter Administration as part of a negotiated resolution to the hostage crisis. Something had happened between October 18th, the night that he had left the United States, and October 22nd to change Khomeini's mind about receiving arms from the Carter Administration to fight its new war with Iraq. Mr. Rajai, therefore, may have made other stops besides Algiers before returning home. After Rajai's return, Sadegh Ghotbzadeh, Iran's foreign minister at the time, and according to former SAVAK official Mansur Rafizadeh also a CIA agent, told then Iranian President Bani Sadr that "They [the Americans] have solved the 'problem' with Rajai."[24] As Rajai had refused to meet with President Carter, Secretary of State Muskie, or any other Carter Administration official, this "they" had to refer to some other group of "Americans" who had pressing reason to negotiate with Iran. According to Rafizadeh, it was also Ghotbzadeh who, on behalf of Bush-loyalists in the CIA, persuaded Khomeini to delay release of the American hostages until Ronald Reagan's inauguration, based upon meetings before the 1980 election.[25] Perhaps coincidentally, perhaps not, in "mid-October 1980," Reagan-Bush campaign manager William Casey had received a solicited plan from Hoover Institution fellow Herbert Cohen outlining a strategy for obtaining a hostage release on precisely this date, Reagan's inauguration.[26] According to the 1980 Reagan-Bush campaign's Iran expert, Michel Smith, who worked with CIA-linked "October Surprise" intelligence operation "rogue" Stephan Halper, Halper was asking about Ghotbzadeh at about this same time.[27] Then, on October 24th or 25th, an assistant to Stephan Halper's "October Surprise" intelligence operation echoed William Casey's newfound confidence, boasting to the author in the Operations Center where Smith worked that the campaign no longer needed to worry about an "October Surprise" because "Dick cut a deal." Richard ("Dick") Allen, the head of one of the campaign's "October Surprise" Groups, had recently met in Washington with a "Khomeini emissary," reportedly Iranian arms dealer Houshang Lavi, who had offered an arms-for-hostages deal with Iran. According to former CIA contract agent William Herrmann, who claims he was told by Iranian Revolutionary Guards officer Hamid Nagashian, Allen had also just returned from Paris where he, Nagashian, vice-presidential candidate George Bush, Allen's campaign foreign policy aide Dr. Fred Ikle, Reagan-Bush campaign manager William Casey, then aide to Senator Tower Robert McFarlane, soon-to-be Iran/Contra middleman Albert Hakim, and Iranian officials Ayatollah Mohammed Beheshti, Hashemi Rafsanjani, and Moshen Rafiq Dust (Nagashian's superior in the Revolutionary Guards) met in various combinations to formalize the Reagan-Bush campaign's "better" arms offer to the Khomeini regime.

The "they" whom Mr. Ghotbzadeh told Iranian president Bani Sadr had "solved the [hostage] problem" with Prime Minister Rajai was clearly not the Carter Administration but the 1980 Reagan-Bush campaign, in evident cooperation with Republican loyalists in the Central Intelligence Agency. And the meeting or meetings at which "they" had solved the "problem" had to have occurred between October 18th, the end of Rajai's three-day stay at the United Nations, and October 20th, the day that William Casey suddenly was no longer worried about an "October Surprise" (also the day that George Bush's friend and former special CIA counsel, Mitchell Rogovin, received "inside" information that Khomeini had changed his mind about dealing with the Carter Administration before the election). President Carter himself, in fact, has revealed that he received similar reports before the 1980 election that "the hostages would not be released [to me] and that [U.S.] weapon sales would be restored to Iran, either directly or through the Israelis."[15] It was Israel that had just infuriated President Carter by delivering an unauthorized planeload of American military equipment to the Khomeini regime.

What happened between October 18th, the opening of the "window of vulnerability," and October 20th to turn the situation for both Iran and the 1980 Reagan-Bush campaign so completely around?

According to the former President of Iran, Abolhassan Bani Sadr, Houshang Lavi had been sent to Washington to meet with Richard Allen and Robert McFarlane, in early October 1980, by Bani Sadr's political rivals in Iran, parliamentary speaker Hashemi Rafsanjani and radical Hezbollah founder Ayatollah Mohammed Beheshti.[28] Contrary to Richard Allen and Robert McFarlane's claims that they rejected Lavi's basic arms-for-hostages proposal, Mr. Bani Sadr insists that the Khomeini emissary, following his initial contact at the L' Enfant Plaza Hotel, held additional meetings with other Iranian representatives and at which the Reagan-Bush campaign agreed in principle that the hostages would be held until after the election and that, if elected, Reagan would provide significantly more arms than Carter had been offering.[29] The Reagan-Bush campaign, he said, "assured the Iranians that 'third parties'—independent arms merchants and "friendly" foreign governments, like Israel—would handle delivery of specific parts and weapons."

Then, at the point where the preliminary details of an agreement had been worked out, Mr. Bani Sadr revealed to *The New York Times,* a "final" meeting was arranged at the highest levels of the Khomeini regime and the Reagan-Bush campaign. "There was a meeting in Paris between a representative of Beheshti and a representative of the Reagan-Bush campaign," he told Paris correspondent for the *Times,* Flora Lewis.[30] In subsequent interviews, Mr. Bani Sadr became more specific regarding the identity of the "representative of the Reagan-Bush campaign" who met with Beheshti's emissary in Paris. "The first reports"—which he had said were from "military intelligence officials" in Iran "with access to government documents"—"stated that [George] Bush had met with a representative of Beheshti."[31] Putting together Mr. Bani Sadr's statements to *The New York Times* and to *Playboy*, the author inferred that the Bush/Beheshti-emissary meeting had in fact been the Paris meeting, which Mr. Bani Sadr said had happened in late October 1980, and wrote the former Iranian president for confirmation. He responded that in one of the communications he had received from Iran, "They inform me that Bush was in the discussions in Paris . . . that his name had been on the document. I have it in writing. As long as the present dictatorship is in power [in Iran], it [the communication] cannot be distributed. Not only the life of the writer would be threatened," he wrote, "but the lives of many [other] people would also fall into danger."[32] Given that the Ayatollah Khomeini has authorized the execution, depending on the report, of between one thousand and twelve thousand "opponents of the revolution" since the announcement of a cease-fire in the Iran-Iraq war in August 1988, Mr. Bani Sadr is no doubt accurate in his assessment.

Mr. Bani Sadr has also revealed that, as President of Iran, he wrote an official letter to the Ayatollah Khomeini on the day of the signing of the Algiers Accord in mid-January 1981.[33] The Algiers Accord formally ended the U.S.-Iran hostage crisis. This letter, which he says was based upon his conversations with the Iranian officials who had organized the Paris meeting(s) and the then Procurer General of arms for Iran's military, detailed what was then known about the meeting(s).[34] Mr. Bani Sadr says that he did not take a copy of this letter with him to Paris, where he is now in exile, but obviously the Ayatollah Khomeini, being its recipient, is in possession of the original. If true, this would be an unprecedented blackmail card to hold against two Presidents of the United States, both Ronald Reagan and his successor, George Bush.

The "document" referred to in the letter Mr. Bani Sadr claims to have received, mentioning George Bush's presence at a pre-election meeting in Paris, is almost certainly an arms contract. The former President of Iran has explained in numerous interviews that, as Commander-in-Chief of Iran's armed forces at the time, any contracts with foreign countries, including the United States and Israel, required his signature to be legally binding. Because Mr. Bani Sadr had refused to sign a waiver, allowing Mr. Rafsanjani and the Ayatollah Beheshti to set the terms for an arms-for-hostages agreement, and also the "document" produced at the Paris meeting, he says, on the day that Reagan and Bush were elected, November 4, 1980, these same Iranian political rivals sent a formal request to Rafsanjani's parliament asking Khomeini for his [Bani-Sadr's] banishment from Iran.[35] According to Mr. Bani Sadr, he had to be forced into exile so that the agreement made before the 1980 election could be signed by someone else and the arms could be received by Iran. Mohammad Ali Rajai, the man whom Ghotbzadeh said had "solved the problem" of the hostages with "them" before the U.S. election, became Iran's President after Bani Sadr was forced to flee Iran in July 1981.

Is it possible that Mr. Bani Sadr's sources inside Iran are correct, as former President Carter stated in a letter of February 24, 1988, that "such an agreement was made involving Bud [Robert] McFarlane, George Bush, and perhaps Bill Casey" before the 1980 presidential election? Is it possible that the "representative of the Reagan campaign" who attended the Paris meeting(s) that Mr. Bani Sadr was informed about was none other than Ronald Reagan's vice-presidential running mate, George Bush? Is it possible that the "mystery event" we are looking for—which would explain why Reagan's campaign manager, William Casey, was suddenly so certain on October 20th, just two days into the dreaded "window of vulnerability," that an "October Surprise" hostage release wouldn't happen after all—was, in fact, this very Paris meeting? Is it possible that William Casey could have been so sure because he was in Paris himself? Is it possible that the Ronald Reagan who "everyone knows" was incapable of harboring an unkind thought could have conceived, let alone acted upon, such a "secret plan": to conspire with the most radical fanatics of an enemy nation to interfere with the negotiations of a sitting U.S. President to subject fifty-two Americans to seventy-six days of unnecessary captivity in order to gain election victory?

Finally, is it possible that these men would run such a phenomenal risk and subject themselves to possibly as many as four presidential terms, twelve years, of blackmail by a medieval despot just to increase their chances of winning the White House? As we shall see, the answer to all of these questions is, astonishingly: Yes. As *Los Angeles Times* reporter Oswald Johnson put it, "Pressures inside a modern-day presidential campaign can become so great that individuals take risks that, from a calmer vantage point, they would not consider worth the candle." Politics, indeed, makes strange bedfellows and can produce even stranger sources. If what a motley crew of self-proclaimed eyewitnesses from the dark underbelly of the American, Israeli, and French intelligence communities say is true, Ronald Reagan, George Bush, and William Casey cut the deal of the century in the ten days before the 1980 election, knowing full well that the United States would be open to a decade or more of blackmail as a result.

HEINRICH RUPP'S STORY

Heinrich "Harry" Rupp is a U.S. citizen and a Swiss national. Trained in the Adolf Hitler School of Flight in the latter part of World War II, he claims to have begun flying for the CIA in the late 1950's for its proprietary airline Air America in Southeast Asia. He later flew for another Agency company, Tiger Air, and for the Saudi royal family. He also claims to have worked in the Middle East with former CIA Beirut station chief William Buckley, who, he says, was betrayed by the CIA.

Rupp's version of events is contained in a videotaped interview he gave to KUSA television (Channel 36) in Denver on October 5, 1988. He claims to have flown William Casey and five other V.I.P. passengers on a British BAC-1-11 jet from Washington, D.C., National Airport to Le Bourget Airport outside Paris, France, on the night of October 18, 1980, via Gander, Newfoundland, arriving approximately 10:00 a.m. Paris time the morning of the 19th. Though Rupp did not refer to a stop-over in New York during the interview with KUSA, an unnamed associate told the *Rocky Mountain News* that Rupp had said that he flew the plane to New York on the way to Paris.[36] A discrepancy between Rupp's account and that given by his attorney, Michael F. Scott of Denver, to *In These Times,* is that Rupp has said that he flew Casey and five other passengers to Paris on the night of October 18, 1980, while his attorney has stated that he flew Casey and only three additional V.I.P.'s.[37] This is not a serious discrepancy, however, as Mr. Rupp has never claimed to have seen his passengers while on board the plane, only on the tarmac in Paris, where his view from the cockpit could easily have been obstructed by the plane's wings.

Depending on which version is the more accurate one, Rupp's or his attorney's, Heinrich Rupp flew between four and six VIP's to Paris, France, on the night of October 18, 1980. This is an interesting number of passengers in light of the claims of former CIA contract agent, William Herrmann. Mr. Herrmann is a longtime associate of the deputy minister of the Iranian Revolutionary Guards, Hamid Nagashian. In a letter to the author dated March 29, 1989, Mr. Herrmann shared the following recollection from his conversation with Nagashian in January 1981 about five Reagan-Bush campaign "VIP's" whom Nagashian had said were in Paris in October 1980:

> "I can confirm the fact that Bush was in Paris in October 1980 and met with Iranian nationals to stop the release of the hostages held in Iran. I can further confirm that it was [Robert] McFarlane, [William] Casey and Dick Allen that were in Paris prior to the Bush meeting trying to make the deal with the Iranians. However, the Iranians did not want to commit themselves to the above and only wanted to deal with Reagan or Bush personally. Allen and McFarlane stayed in Paris and awaited the arrival of Bush, who showed up within a 24-hour period, bringing with him Dr. Fred Ikle for this meeting with the Iranians. From the Iranian side, the following people met, with Bush: Mohammed Beheshti, Rafsanjani, [Albert] Hakim, Moshen Rafiq Dust [Minister of the Revolutionary Guards], and Hamid Nagashian, his [Dust's] deputy."

According to Sue Lindsay, a *Rocky Mountain News* reporter, who interviewed Rupp, the former Nazi pilot stated that he is "100 percent certain" that he saw then Reagan-Bush campaign manager William Casey on the tarmac at Le Bourget Airport outside of Paris the morning of October 19, 1980. He also stated that he is "98 percent sure" that the "tall man with the crooked eyes" he saw on the same tarmac that morning was former CIA director George Bush.[38] Though Rupp did not know Casey at the time, he told KUSA that when he saw him testifying on television during the Iran/Contra investigation he instantly recognized him as the "Old Professor" whom he had flown to Paris in October 1980. In a separate interview, Rupp told the *Boston Globe* that he was also "99.9 percent sure it was Bush" whom he saw at Le Bourget Airport. "He was there . . . No if, ands, or in betweens," he said.[39]

Rupp told his attorney, Michael Scott of Denver, that he believed the "first officer" in the cockpit with him on the flight was Joseph Alto, a retired U.S. Air Force major. Alto co-owns a company in Washington, D.C., ONA, Inc., which reportedly coordinated Rupp's travel plans and those of other CIA missions. According to Scott, the second co-owner of ONA, Inc., is Khakil A. S. Othman. One of the two is also a general manager of a company called Saudi Wings, for which Rupp also flew. Scott has copies of Rupp's cancelled checks from ONA showing that he was paid by the company as a pilot.[40]

According to interviews by former CNN and WABC-TV reporter Kevin Sanders, Rupp claims that the Grumman Gulfstream II jet, which he says flew then vice-presidential candidate George Bush to Paris on the same night as Rupp's flight with Casey, October 18, 1980, was re-fueled at Le Bourget Airport on Adnan Khashoggi's credit card, and that Rupp had seen the same Gulfstream parked at Butler Aviation, either at Burbank or Van Nuys airports, in California.[41] According to Informant "Y" (see below), the Gulfstream that Bush took to Paris then belonged to Unocal (Union Oil Company of California) and arrangements for its use on October 18–19, 1980 had been made by a CIA agent and former "silent" business associate of Bush's from his days at Zapata Offshore Oil Company in the 1960's then associated with Unocal. The man's name, he recalled, was something like "Waddington." Although a spokesmen for Unocal's aviation office at Burbank Airport refused to confirm or deny this contention, and a check of Unocal's annual reports for 1980 and 1981 showed no "Waddington" either as a member of the board or as an executive officer, "Y" insisted that the man had been using Unocal at the time as an "Agency cover." A check of Federal Aviation Administration records did reveal that Unocal had two, if not three, Grumman Gulfstream II jets in October of 1980, all three based in California (other planes were in Texas), and that one, whose call sign was N-760U, was based at Burbank, near Van Nuys, at the time. The plane's chief pilot in 1977, the last year for which the FAA had records, was Charles C. Wheeler. A source who wishes to remain anonymous, however, told the author that the pilot of the Grumman Gulfstream II, which allegedly flew Bush to Paris on October 18, 1980, was Jack Tolliver, who, he said, was "Felix Rodriguez's favorite pilot." Rodriguez is a longtime CIA operative who had been a close associate of Bush's for years and who reportedly met at least seventeen times with Vice-President Bush's top national security staff during the period of the Iran/Contra operations.

Though the 1988 Bush presidential campaign heatedly denied Heinrich Rupp's claims, the day after Rupp's taped interview with KUSA television, on October 6, 1988, federal marshalls arrived to move him to an undisclosed location, which later turned out to be a prison in Oklahoma. Rupp was then transferred to the Bureau of Prisons Federal Medical Center in Rochester, Minnesota, where his lawyer was unable to speak with him. "I've spent as long as 35 minutes on the phone trying to get a message to him," attorney Michael Scott of Denver told *In These Times* shortly afterwards. "But people I talk to [at the prison] won't tell me who they are." Scott said that he had never, in his entire career, had "this big a problem" reaching a client.[43] An intelligence source told former CNN reporter Kevin Sanders that the Minnesota medical center had done "rehabilitation" research, using a drug called haloperidol, reportedly used by the Soviet KGB to destroy memory.[44]

At the time of his revelations in September and October 1988, Heinrich Rupp, who was also a gold dealer in Aurora, Colorado, had been convicted and sentenced to forty-one years in prison for loan fraud that had led to the collapse of the Aurora Bank in 1985. He had been charged with planning to use laundered money through his Swiss banking connections to purchase $9 million in Mafia funds, which never materialized. Rupp had already been tried and convicted on the same charges in December 1987, but had won a new trial when a co-defendant in the case, Faud Sam Jezzeny, filed a letter with the court saying that Rupp had been a victim of a plot to entrap him. Rupp claims that the Aurora scheme was sanctioned by the CIA for whom he was working at the time, as part of an Iran/Contra-related "national security operation." He says that federal agents asked him to pose as a money launderer and that he reported his actions to the Agency, but the jury didn't buy his story. Another self-proclaimed former

Agency operative told the author that the Agency 'routinely' laundered Mafia money to 'legitimate' it for the purchase of arms in the Iran/Contra operation.[45] Just before Rupp and Jezzeny's second trial in September 1988, Jezzeny jumped bond on Labor Day weekend and fled to Texas. A law enforcement official who was asked by Rupp's friend Richard Brenneke (see below) to locate Jezzeny checked his computer, which came up "FBI Priority 1." At the time, Jezzeny was reportedly being grilled by federal marshalls in a safe house in Texas before being returned to Colorado.[46] At the time of this writing, Rupp's sentence has been reduced from forty-one to two years.

After his conviction in the retrial on September 15, 1988, Rupp's attorney filed a motion for yet another trial. Rupp's friend Richard Brenneke claimed that the federal prosecutor in the case, Thomas O'Rourke, had conspired with the Reagan-Bush Administration to "put Rupp away" so that he couldn't talk about his October 18, 1980, mission to Paris. What Rupp knows about the "betrayal" of CIA Beirut station chief William Buckley is also, apparently, extremely sensitive.

Rupp's sentencing hearing with Judge James Carrigan suddenly turned into a courtroom scene from the Watergate-era film, *All the President's Men*. On September 23, 1988, Rupp's attorney, Michael Scott, asked to speak to the judge. Although reporters present could not hear him clearly, he was overheard to say "CIA," "George Bush," "NSC," "the hostages," "William Casey," and "Iran/Contra." Immediately following the bench conference, Judge Carrigan held a hearing in his private chambers to take the under-oath testimony of self-proclaimed former CIA operative Richard Brenneke. Brenneke told the judge that Rupp had been framed by the Reagan-Bush Administration in what had been a CIA operation. Because Rupp refused to violate his oath of silence with the Agency, Brenneke told the judge that he had decided to speak in his behalf at the sentencing hearing rather than see an old friend take the 'rap' for having followed the orders of his superiors.

RICHARD BRENNEKE'S STORY

Every good scandal needs a "mystery witness," and for the "October Surprise" story, Richard Brenneke is that witness. A quiet, bookish, self-effacing man in his late forties with a nervous demeanor and receding hairline, this real-life Walter Mitty hardly seems the international arms dealer and triple intelligence agent that he claims to be. An Oregon businessman, Brenneke has been an informant for the FBI and the U.S. Customs Service [47] and claims to have worked for eighteen years, from the late 1960's until 1985, as a contract agent for the CIA [48]—although he told *The New York Times* for thirteen years.[49] Richard Brenneke also gave key testimony to the Tower Commission and the Congressional Iran/Contra Committees, claiming in May 1988 that Vice-President George Bush's national security adviser, Donald Gregg, a career CIA officer, had been a White House contact for the illegal Contra arms supply operation bankrolled with drug money. Brenneke also testified to Senator John Kerry's Senate Subcommittee on Terrorism, Narcotics and International Communications in 1988 on the drug connection to the Contra operation, and he claimed to be knowledgeable because he himself had flown some guns-for-drugs flights for the Agency in Central America, in cooperation with the Israelis. Brenneke also was the source for the equally explosive revelation that President Reagan's national security adviser Admiral John Poindexter, who had been brought into the NSC by Reagan's 1980 campaign foreign policy adviser Richard Allen, had approved the hotly-contested December 1985 shipment of U.S. HAWK missiles by Israel to Iran.

Richard Brenneke, in sum, is a man who has "been there" and knows the details of the Iran/Contra operations from the inside. He knew, he said, because he had not only been a contract agent for the Central Intelligence Agency for eighteen years, but had also participated in Mossad (Israel's intelligence service) operations "on loan" from the Agency.[50] He also claimed to have worked with French intelligence as a "free lance" consultant.[51] The Israeli embassy in Washington, D.C., issued a statement that "Mr. Brenneke has never been employed by the Israeli government."[52] This assertion, however, is open to question. According to President Carter's NSC Iran expert, Captain Gary Sick, "When its [Israel's] arms salesmen do something that furthers their ideological or political objectives, they are officially certified Israeli agents. But when Israel wants to disassociate itself from them, these same dealers are suddenly 'independents.' "[53]

Richard Brenneke's Iran/Contra testimony created a minor political explosion in Washington, D.C., and was reported in detail by the major news media, including *The New York Times,* ABC TV's *World News Tonight,* and *Newsweek.* More importantly, it was proven to be accurate. One of Brenneke's major claims was substantiated by former consul to Panamanian dictator Manuel Noriega, Jose Blandon.[54] In a lame attempt to discredit Mr. Brenneke, White House press spokesman Marlin Fitzwater suggested that he had a criminal history. "Wasn't he on trial?" he asked rhetorically at a White House press briefing. "I challenge you to look up his court case in New York."[55] But this was all more red-white-and-blue smoke and mirrors. Brenneke had never been charged with a crime, and even Vice-President Bush soon conceded that the White House press secretary had been mistaken. What Mr. Brenneke had done was to provide key documentation in a major Iran/Contra-related "sting" operation case in New York, supporting claims by defendants in the case that they had been assured that their $2.5 billion arms deals with Iran in 1986 had the approval of none other than Vice President Bush himself. This case, in which Iran/Contra middleman Manucher Gorbanifar was also initially arrested in Europe, was dropped on January 4, 1988, shortly before Mr. Bush became President, because the federal prosecutor decided he would be losing a "headline case" if it went to trial.

In addition to the White House, the Reagan-Bush CIA went out of its way in an attempt to discredit Mr. Brenneke. The Agency, which normally neither confirms nor denies its association with individuals, took the extraordinary step of claiming that a letter on its own stationery, which Mr. Brenneke presented to Congress as evidence of his CIA background and which stated that he was "thorough, competent and trustworthy," was a "forgery" it had received from the Portland *Oregonian*. The *Oregonian*, however, denied ever having received such a letter, showing the "forgery" to be the agency's own.

Mr. Brenneke, in other words, has established a track record of having been on the right side of the truth. This, together with the fact that his most vocal detractors were the very individuals he was exposing to criticism, make what he has to say about the October 19–20, 1980, Paris meetings worth paying attention to.

Over a period of a little under a month, from August 25 to September 23, 1988, Richard Brenneke's version of events in the "October Surprise" story changed in detail, though not in broad outline. In an interview with the author in his office at the Washington, D.C., International Center for Development Policy, where he was a Senior Fellow, on August 22, 1988, Mr. Brenneke revealed for the first time that he was knowledgeable about the pre-1980-election Paris meetings. For details of this conversation, see Chapter VII. Until that August 22nd interview, he had revealed only a portion of what he knew in sealed testimony to various Iran/Contra investigators, but not to journalists. In response to a question from the author, Mr. Brenneke stated without hesitation that he had been in Paris at the time and had been told by "Iranian contacts," whom he "happened" to meet the day after the October 19, 1980, meeting, that then Reagan-Bush campaign manager William Casey, CIA-NSC liaison Donald Gregg, Iranian arms dealer Cyrus Hashemi, and Iranian arms buyer and European intelligence chief Manucher Gorbanifar had met at the Raphael Hotel the previous day, October 19, 1980. The author has since received information that Iranian arms dealer Houshang Lavi—the man who offered Richard Allen and Robert McFarlane an arms-for-hostages proposal in Washington, D.C., on October 2, 1980—was also at the October 20th meeting with Brenneke in Paris.

In his initial interview with the author, Mr. Brenneke did not mention the presence of then vice-presidential candidate George Bush. When asked about Mr. Bush's possible participation, as claimed by then President of Iran Abolhassan Bani Sadr, Mr. Brenneke stated that he would "make a few phone calls to see the 'lay of the land' " and discuss the matter with the author in a subsequent interview. In this meeting, Mr. Brenneke also made no claim to have been involved himself in any of the Paris meetings with officials of the 1980 Reagan-Bush campaign. He claimed instead to have learned about them "second hand" because of the "coincidence" that he happened to be in Paris from October 18–21, 1980. When asked how he had learned of the meetings "second hand," Mr. Brenneke stated that he had heard about them from Cyrus Hashemi and French intelligence agent Robert Benes. When asked the date of the meeting between Mr. Casey and the Iranian agents, he stated without hesitation in the initial August 22, 1988, interview that it had been "On the Sunday before the last full week in October 1980. I know, because my meeting with the Iranian who told me about it was at the Florida Hotel [in Paris] the following Monday or Tuesday." When asked who else could confirm the meetings, Mr. Brenneke said, "Will Northrop. He talked with Casey a lot." William Northrop, who is related to the military giant Northrop Corporation, has reported long ties both to the CIA and to the Israeli intelligence agency, Mossad.[56] Northrop has since confirmed his own belief, based upon discussions with Mr. Casey, that an agreement was struck between the 1980 Reagan-Bush campaign and Iran before the 1980 election.[57]

Three days after the initial interview with Mr. Brenneke, on August 25, 1988, the author held a press conference at the National Press Club in Washington, D.C., to bring reporters up to date on the evidence for the "October Surprise" story. Mr. Brenneke attended this press conference, although at the time he had an agreement with the author that his identity would not be revealed as a source for the allegations. Following the press conference, the author held numerous additional meetings with him, including one with a journalist from a major news weekly, in which he again insisted that he had only indirect knowledge of the October 1980 Paris meetings between Reagan-Bush campaign and Iranian officials.

Not long after the August 25th press conference, the author returned to California and received an unsolicited call from an informant who claimed to have been with the CIA for twenty years, until the mid 1980's. The caller claimed to have knowledge of the October 19–20, 1980, Paris meetings based upon a French intelligence report, which he at first said he had read in Agency files on the seventh floor of CIA headquarters in Langley, Virginia, in December 1980, two months after the events summarized in the report. The informant told the author, and subsequently told other journalists, that there had been not just one, but two days of meetings in Paris, on October 19th and 20th, 1980, and that Mr. Brenneke had been more directly involved than he had at first led the author to believe. It was only upon being confronted, in a telephone interview, with the considerable wealth of detail provided by the informant, that Mr. Brenneke then "fleshed out" his original story. He then acknowledged that he had told various congressional committees, including Senator John Kerry's investigation of the Contra arms-drugs connection, about the Paris meetings, but claimed that they had not wanted to pursue the matter. [58] "I made these statements to Kerry's committee and the U.S. Senate— again, under oath . . . they have found me to be accurate with my information . . . They have found it to be precise and detailed," he said.[59]

In subsequent telephone interviews with the author and other journalists in early to mid-September 1988, Mr. Brenneke acknowledged that there had in fact been three meetings in Paris, two on October 19, 1980, and one, which he had attended, on October 20, 1980. What he was doing in Paris on October 18th, the day he arrived, or on October 19th, the day of the key meeting allegedly attended by both Mr. Casey and Mr. Bush, he did not choose to reveal. It is the author's opinion that, if they occurred, Mr. Brenneke also attended these two earlier meetings.

According to Mr. Brenneke's second and "more complete" version of events, the first Paris meeting took place about noon on October 19, 1980, and was attended by (partial list) Mr. Bush, Mr. Casey, Mr. Gregg, Mr. Gorbanifar, and "two Iranian officials" whom he did not wish to identify for reasons of their safety. (Mr. Herrmann differs, claiming that Gorbanifar was not a participant.) Mr. Brenneke did not name Dr. Cyrus Hashemi as having been at the first meeting on October 19th at the Raphael Hotel. Mr. Brenneke stated that there had been a second, "follow-up" meeting later

on the 19th, in the afternoon, also at the Raphael, with the same participants as the morning session, but minus Mr. Bush. He also now acknowledged that the third meeting in the series was, in fact, that which he had
earlier referred to as his "happenstance" discussion with the Iranian
official on the 20th who had purportedly told him about the meeting the
day before on the 19th. This third meeting on the 20th, however, he now
characterized as a full-blown session at the Hotel Florida in Paris, attended
by himself, an Iranian representative of parliamentary speaker Hashemi
Rafsanjani whom he declined to identify, another Iranian government
official whom he also refused to name, Mr. Casey, Mr. Gregg, Cyrus
Hashemi, Manucher Gorbanifar, Major Robert Benes of French intelligence, a "woman" whom he did not name, and "perhaps also a German." Subsequent investigations revealed that the "woman" present was
in all likelihood either Madame Robert, a second French intelligence agent
who accompanied Benes to the meeting, or Jamie Frydel, an arms dealer
whose company reportedly shipped arms to Iran in the early 1980's. (The
former President of Iran, Abolhassan Bani Sadr, has provided the author
with copies of invoices covering Ms. Frydel's arms dealings with Iran, the
earliest dated March 8 and 9, 1981.) Former CIA contract agent and
businessman William Herrmann claims that the two Iranian officials who
attended one of the October 1980 Paris meetings with Brenneke whom he
refused to name were Hamid Nagashian, an arms procurement official for
the radical Iranian Revolutionary Guards, and Nagashian's superior, Moshen
Rafiq Dust. Sources available to the former President of Iran, Abolhassan
Bani Sadr, claim that Mr. Nagashian had already met the previous month,
in September 1980, with freelance Reagan-Bush campaign adviser Robert
McFarlane in Zurich, Switzerland.

When the author asked Mr. Brenneke why he had not originally mentioned Mr. Bush's presence at the Raphael Hotel meeting on the 19th, he
claimed that he did not have direct knowledge of his participation and had
not wished to make any statements without first checking with others who,
he recalled, had told him about it. The "few phone calls" he had said that
he would make before responding to the author's original question about
Mr. Bush's possible involvement were apparently to Mr. Benes and Mr.
Northrop, as Mr. Hashemi had died in July 1986. In any case, Mr.
Brenneke subsequently confirmed Mr. Bush's presence at the October 19,
1980, Paris meeting, and also claimed that he had earlier "checked with
Donald Gregg," who, he said, had confirmed in a telephone conversation
that Bush had been there. In a telephone interview with the author, Mr.
Gregg later denied ever having spoken with Mr. Brenneke on the phone,

though Mr. Gregg's own credibility is open to serious question, as will be discussed further below.

On September 23, 1988, Richard Brenneke appeared at Heinrich Rupp's sentencing hearing in Denver, Colorado. In the courtroom were Robert Parry of *Newsweek,* who had covered Brenneke's charges in the Iran/ Contra affair extensively in the past, and Martin Kilian of the West German news weekly *Der Spiegel.* In an under-oath deposition taken by Judge Carrigan in closed-door session, Mr. Brenneke testified that, "On the 19th of October, Mr. Rupp brought Mr. Bush, Mr. Casey, and a number of other people to Paris, France, from the U.S. for a meeting with Iranian representatives."[60] Mr. Brenneke subsequently told the author that he had "misspoken" in this deposition and had not intended to imply that Rupp had personally flown Mr. Bush to Paris, only that Mr. Bush had also been flown to the same meeting attended by Mr. Casey.

In his under-oath deposition in Rupp's case, Mr. Brenneke also recounted an October 20, 1980, follow-up meeting at the Florida Hotel, which he said he had personally attended. He stated that he had known Cyrus Hashemi and that Hashemi had told his family before his death in July 1986 that he had attended the pre-1980-election meeting. Mr. Brenneke stated that Donald Gregg had indicated to him that the Carter White House, for whom Gregg worked at the time on the National Security Council, had not been aware of his participation in the Paris meetings.[61] Brenneke also revealed to the judge that he had gone to Paris at the request of CIA officer Robert Kerritt. The Agency subsequently refused to acknowledge that a Robert Kerritt was one of its employees, but Informant "Y" (see below) later characterized Mr. Kerritt as being "close to Gregg," "a Bush man," and an expert in covert arms shipments who had also been involved in the CIA's Central America operations.[62]

Richard Brenneke testified under oath that the "purpose of the [Paris] meetings was to negotiate, not only for the release of the hostages then being held in the U.S. embassy in Tehran, but also to discuss, if the negotiations were successful, the means by which the terms that were agreed to would be dealt with, how we would go about satisfying everyone involved. As a consequence of that, the French were present, because they would become a major factor in satisfying the requests. In the end, agreement was reached, and the logistics of transferring $40 million for the purchase of weapons was worked out."[63] He continued, "As a result of this meeting, certain French individuals did go on and did purchase weapons; did, in the end, exchange those weapons for, or at least as part of the condition of, the release of the American hostages then being held in

Tehran."[64] Brenneke later told *In These Times* that "French foreign ministry types" expedited the arms-for-hostages deal.[65] "Some of the people doing the purchasing were French," he stated in his deposition, "Others were Iranian—Mr. Gorbanifar, for instance, who was present also part of that day [October 20, 1980]."[66] Later in the court transcript, Mr. Brenneke stated that he himself had played a role in purchasing the arms.[67]

Brenneke's testimony goes on to state: "The people involved in that meeting [of October 20, 1980]—there has been, in the course of the last eight years, a systematic attempt by the U.S. Government made to discredit these individuals, and, in my opinion, . . . to cause the death of some of these individuals. And, in my opinion, the reason for that is that they were privy to information that people didn't believe that they would keep quiet; that is, the principals involved in these meetings did not believe that individuals such as Harry Rupp and I would keep this quiet . . ."[68] He also revealed that, "I do have access to and can obtain for the court, copies of invoices and details that relate to the purchase and later reshipment of that—of those weapons." In addition to the individuals named thus far as having allegedly been involved in the October 19–20, 1980, Paris meetings, Richard Brenneke also mentioned a General Lafassi and Reagan's then campaign foreign policy adviser, Richard Allen. As we will see below, Mr. Allen appears to have an airtight alibi, which would preclude his having been personally present in Paris on October 19, 1980. But he may have been in Paris on a different date in October 1980, as claimed by former CIA contract agent William Herrmann. According to Informant "Y," General Lafassi had worked with the outlawed Italian secret society P-2 to assist Argentina in the purchase of French Exocet missiles in the early 1980's.[69] For a detailed discussion of P-2 and its relationship to the "October Surprise" story, see Chapter IX.

Mr. Brenneke's under-oath testimony in Harry Rupp's sentencing hearing, summarized above, was given with the understanding that it was under seal and would not be made public. It is therefore clear that he was not trying to influence the media, public opinion, or the 1988 election by what he had to say. The transcript of his testimony, however, was made public by Judge Carrigan on October 1, 1988, in response to a court order by the Denver-based *Rocky Mountain News*. The *News* and the Scripps-Howard News Service then carried a series of stories based upon Mr. Brenneke's unsealed deposition. The stories ran from September 24 through October 5, 1988.[70] These publications of his identity as a source in the "October Surprise" story released the author from an earlier non-disclosure agreement with Mr. Brenneke, made during the initial August 22, 1988, interview.

In interviews with the author following the publication of his under-oath testimony, Mr. Brenneke revealed many other significant details of the story. He claimed that he had collected intelligence for the CIA in the Middle East and, in the process, had developed a close working relationship with two officials in the Iranian government, who had attended the Paris meeting of October 20, 1980 in addition to Cyrus Hashemi.[71] In several memos sent to Reagan-Bush Administration officials between November 30, 1985, and February 25, 1986, Mr. Brenneke alluded to these "high-ranking Iranian officials" who, he claimed, would only deal through him in arms negotiations as part of "normalizing relations with the West."[72] Mr. Brenneke also claimed that he had the trust of two of the most powerful men in Iran, the speaker of Iran's parliament, Hashemi Rafsanjani, and Khomeini's relative-by-marriage Sadegh Tabatabai, who had been the Ayatollah's designated hostage negotiator with the Carter administration in 1980. Rafsanjani and Tabatabai, in fact, may be the "two high-ranking government officials" who Mr. Brenneke said attended the Paris meeting of October 20, 1980, but whom he refused to identify; alternatively they may be Revolutionary Guard officials Hamid Nagashian and Moshen Rafiq Dust. Brenneke claimed to have the personal telex number of Mr. Rafsanjani, and said that Mr. Rafsanjani's aides had told him that they would supply tape recordings of meetings with Reagan-Bush officials if he came to Tehran to get them.[73] The president of Iran at the time, Abolhassan Bani Sadr, says that he has reason to believe that one of the two "mid-level" Iranians at the Paris meeting, whom Mr. Brenneke declined to identify, was a Mr. Parvis Sabati.

Mr. Brenneke insisted to the author that he had learned of George Bush's presence at the Paris meeting of October 19, 1980, from four sources: 1) French intelligence agent and colleague Robert Benes who, he claims, "actually saw him [Bush]"; 2) Iranian arms dealer Cyrus Hashemi; 3) pilot Harry Rupp[74], who, he claims, told him about a month later, in November 1980, that he had seen Bush on the tarmac at Le Bourget Airport outside of Paris; and 4) Vice-President Bush's national security adviser, Donald Gregg, who, he claims, confirmed Bush's presence in Paris during a telephone call sometime later, he believed in 1983.[75]

Though former French intelligence agent Robert Benes has denied Mr. Brenneke's claims, there is evidence that he did so under considerable pressure from U.S. and perhaps also French government authorities. Mr. Brenneke insists that Benes does know about the Paris meetings but decided not to talk. He says that Benes had even told him that he has access to documents about the Paris meetings, which he would consider giving to Mr. Brenneke for use in Heinrich Rupp's retrial. In an interview with Los Angeles radio journalist Carol Hemingway, Mr. Brenneke revealed that, according to his discussions with Mr. Rupp, Donald Gregg may have been one of the V.I.P's besides Mr. Casey whom Rupp flew to Paris on October 18, 1980.[76] He later revealed that Gregg had also been "the note taker" at the Paris meetings.[77] At the time of this writing, Mr. Rupp has not been available to confirm these statements. Mr. Brenneke also told Hemingway that it was made clear at the October 20, 1980, meeting at the Hotel Florida in Paris that the U.S. hostages would not be released until Ronald Reagan's inauguration. Although the Iranians at the meeting appeared ready to release the hostages at "any time the U.S. wanted," he said, Mr. Casey fixed the timetable. "What was . . . made clear at the meeting I was present at was that the hostages would not be released until after Reagan was sworn in. That was a 'given'. . . . The bargain was basically, we were ransoming the hostages. . . . They [Casey and Gregg] were adamant that the arrangement would be that the people would be released in late January, in 1981 [i.e., on Reagan's inauguration]. It was a non-negotiable statement. Period."[78] When Mansur Rafizadeh, the former U.S. chief of the Shah of Iran's secret police, contacted a top Iranian official before the 1980 election, the official denied that the Republican-leaning CIA wanted the hostages released. "Maybe there's a government inside the [U.S.] government, or maybe they're lying to us, or they're lying to you, [but] that's not the demand," the official told Rafizadeh.[79]

According to Richard Brenneke, William Casey's role at the October 20, 1980, Paris meeting with Iranian officials was to "make sure the Iranians didn't fixate on the wrong things [arms]. . . . There was great concern by the Americans that what was sent [to Iran] was appropriate for the occasion."[80] Mr. Brenneke said that it was Mr. Casey who handled the $40 million, which would be used to purchase the arms agreed upon at the meeting, and none of which changed hands at the time, he said. He claimed that Casey had said that the money would be deposited in a number of accounts in European banks, including Bank Lambert in Brussels, Belgium. According to Informant "Y," some of the money was also deposited in Iran's bank account in Bank Leu in Zurich, Switzerland.

As for the specific arms that were to be purchased with the $40 million, Brenneke told the author that part of the money was to be used to buy F-14 and F-4 fighter jet parts and equipment.[82] He also told *In These Times* that the rest of the money went for the purchase of Czech-made AK-47 assault rifles, shoulder-fired anti-aircraft missiles, and rocket-propelled grenades made in the East Bloc, as well as sophisticated U.S.-made aircraft parts (i.e., for the F-14s and F-4s).[83] It was for precisely such parts for the F-14s that Houshang Lavi had first offered to arrange a hostage exchange with Reagan-Bush campaign foreign policy adviser Richard Allen, Senator Tower's aide Robert McFarlane, and Allen's aide Laurence Silberman at the L'Enfant Plaza Hotel in Washington on October 2, 1980, only a little over two weeks before the Paris meetings. According to two knowledgeable sources who wish to remain anonymous, Mr. Lavi himself was at the Paris meeting of October 20, 1980, with Mr. Brenneke, making arrangements for the shipment of the F-14 parts.

After the release of his under-oath testimony, Mr. Brenneke identified two other Iranian officials from the Hotel Florida meeting of October 20, 1980. They were, he said, Ahmed Heydari (a.k.a. Khudari), an arms procurement official who was acting on behalf of Iran's military chief of staff and who worked with the Israelis; and Colonel K. Deghan (a.k.a. Denghan), who was also involved in arms procurement for the Khomeini regime and who represented Iran's Defense Ministry.[84] In a series of interviews with the author and other journalists in April 1989, Mr. Lavi acknowledged having met on either October 19 or 20, 1980, with Col. Deghan, Cyrus Hashemi, and Manucher Gorbanifar at the Raphael Hotel in Paris (not the Florida hotel, as Brenneke claims).

Mr. Brenneke revealed that pilot Harry Rupp had not only flown William Casey to the Paris meetings of October 19–20, 1980, but that he was a "frequent pilot" of the CIA director.[85] "The Director liked Harry," he said. "Harry [Rupp] had proven over the years that he could definitely keep his mouth shut. Casey was very comfortable with him. . . . I know he'd ask for Harry on occasions, depending on how sensitive what he was doing was." Informant "Y" confirmed to the author that Rupp was "a favorite pilot of Casey's. When Casey became CIA Director, he picked him as his pilot 'out of nowhere,' " he said.[86] Brenneke also claimed that Rupp had told him that he had seen William Casey on the tarmac not only at Le Bourget Airport outside of Paris on October 19, 1980, but also at Washington, D.C., National Airport on the night of October 18, 1980, before the flight to France.[87] Brenneke claimed that he was told by his CIA "control," Robert Kerritt, that he would not need to reserve a room at the Hotel Florida in Paris, where he allegedly stayed on the nights of October 18, 19, and 20, 1980, before leaving on the 21st. If true, this would explain why a subsequent check of the hotel's records did not reveal Mr. Brenneke as having been a guest on those nights.

There is little doubt that Richard Brenneke spent a great deal of time in

Europe from 1980 to 1984, as he claims, negotiating arms agreements. He has produced letters, telexes, travel receipts, and other documents showing that he was in contact with Omnipol, a Czechoslovakian arms trading company, during this period when he travelled to Czechoslovakia.[88] Other sources claim that Brenneke's 1980 flights on behalf of Omnipol were arms deliveries to Iran intended to benefit the 1980 Reagan-Bush campaign. The Czech connection is significant to Mr. Brenneke's "October Surprise" claims for three additional reasons. First, Robert Benes, who was allegedly at the October 20th if not also at the October 19th Paris meeting, is the grand-nephew of the founder of the Czechoslovak Republic. Second, Brenneke's background is also from Czechoslovakia, where a major arms producer still manufactures Brenneke ammunition. Third, Informant "Y" told the author that part of the $40 million used to pay for the arms negotiated at the Paris meetings for the U.S. hostages was deposited in a Czech account in Bank Leu in Zurich, Switzerland. The remainder of the funds, he said, had been deposited in Iran's account in the same bank.

MR. QUALLS GETS NERVOUS

According to pilot Harry Rupp and Richard Brenneke, the two British-made BAC-1-11's flown to Paris from Washington, D.C., National Airport on the night of October 18, 1980 were registered with the FAA as HZM01, Rupp's jet, and N120TA. N120TA was then owned by Tiger Air, a subsidiary of Tiger Leasing, which had previously been a CIA proprietary airline. Rupp's plane, HZM01, which he recalled rather as having had the call letters HZ MFA, had been leased to Tiger Air by its Saudi Arabian owner, Prince Mohammed Fahd Azis.[89]

In an interview with the author, Mr. Brenneke said that records found in Rupp's files showed that a Mr. Kenneth Qualls may have been the pilot of the second BAC-1-11 jet, N120TA, which flew to Paris on the night of October 18, 1980.[90] Documents, in fact, show that in October 1980 Mr. Qualls was the manager of Tiger Air and was the pilot in charge of N120TA. Though the plane's flight logs show that it was in Burbank, California, from October 16–20, 1980, Mr. Qualls told the *Boston Globe* that these records "do not rule out that the plane was involved in an international flight" at that time.[91] Though Rupp's own log books were blank during the same period, he still claims to have made the trip. When asked if he flew N120TA to Paris on October 18, 1980, Mr. Qualls responded that he did not *believe* that he had.[92]

On October 15, 1988, Richard Brenneke telephoned Mr. Qualls in an attempt to get him to testify on behalf of Harry Rupp about the October 1980 flights to Paris for the CIA. Without Qualls' knowledge, Brenneke tape-recorded the conversation. During the telephone call, Qualls effectively admitted that the Paris deal had been made and that he had offered the 1988 Bush presidential campaign to perjure himself to squelch the "October Surprise" story:

> "You know, like I told the press [the *Boston Globe* reporter] . . . You guys don't understand the world. Take people who have been around, and I have been around . . . so what if somebody gave somebody $40 million for fifty-two hostages? They're alive, aren't they? If they're alive, then who cares? I mean, who really cares? . . . I said, who cares if he [Bush] was there and he lied? You know, the fact is that he made a deal, and I said, deals like that are made in the Middle East all the time. . . . The potato farmer in Iowa is going to be pissed at Bush and want an impeachment. But the people that know about the world are gonna say, 'Hey, they did what they had to do . . .' Like, get me [they said], you know, free these guys and gals after I get elected and you got $40 million and you can buy some of this outdated s--- that we gotta get rid of anyway. . . . Let me tell you this, the Bush [campaign] people are aware of what's going on . . . because I've talked to them. They are very much aware of Harry [Rupp]. I sent them that outline that Honegger did. I told 'em what everybody's going through. I said, you know, if you need it, I'll make a statement saying I don't know s--- about nothin'. And that they're barking up the wrong tree."[93]

Kenneth Qualls told Mr. Brenneke that he had gotten word to James H. Baker, then Vice-President Bush's campaign manager, about his apparent perjury offer through "my channel," who turned out to be Harold De-Moss, an attorney then working in the research division of the 1988 Bush presidential campaign. Qualls also acknowledged having flown for President Reagan shortly after his inauguration in 1981. Though the *Boston Globe* did not include the information in its October 23, 1988, story on the "October Surprise," Mr. Qualls had also reportedly told the *Globe* that

Tiger Air, which he then managed, was operating covert flights all over Europe in 1980, including to Paris.[94]

THE STRANGE CASE OF "MR. Y"

On September 6, 1988, the "October Surprise" story took a strange turn. A little over two weeks after the author's press conference in Washington, D.C., she received a telephone call from an anonymous informant who claimed to have been in the Operations Directorate (originally Plans Directorate) of the CIA from the mid-1960's until the mid-1980's. He explained that he had seen "Cover Up," a video documentary produced by the Empowerment Project of Santa Monica, California, for which the author had been interviewed about reports of pre-1980-election meetings between Reagan-Bush campaign and Iranian officials. He had learned of the press conference and the author's reports of Mr. Brenneke's charges, he said, and had additional information to add to the picture. He said just to refer to him as "Mr. Y." (At the time, the author referred in public to Richard Brenneke as "Mr. X," as Mr. Brenneke's court testimony had not yet been made public and his identity revealed.)

"Mr. Y" also claimed to be connected with Israeli and French intelligence and to have read a copy of a report filed by the SDECE, the French equivalent of the CIA, about the October 19–20, 1980, Paris meetings. The report, he said, had been written by one or more agents of French intelligence who, as Mr. Brenneke had revealed, had attended the October 20th meeting, if not the other Paris meetings as well. "Y" claimed that the French intelligence report, which he at first said he had read in Agency files on the seventh floor of CIA headquarters in Langley, Virginia, in December 1980, confirmed that then vice-presidential candidate George Bush; Reagan-Bush campaign manager William Casey; and the CIA's NSC liaison Donald Gregg, who was then technically working for President Carter, had left Washington, D.C., National Airport at approximately 10:00 P.M. the night of October 18, 1980, for Paris, France, with a stopover at Stewart Air Force Base in New York. (He later changed his story, claiming that he had not read the report at CIA headquarters, but had been given a copy to read by a "friendly foreign intelligence ser-

vice.'') "Mr. Y" made no mention of an additional refueling stop in
Gander, Newfoundland, as recalled by pilot Harry Rupp, although he
admitted that his information was based upon memory of a document that
he had read eight years earlier. As he recalled the report, he said, the
parties landed at a "military airport" outside of Paris—he did not at first
specify Le Bourget—about 10:00 A.M. Paris time on the morning of the
19th. Bush, he said, had wanted no Secret Service agents on the trip, to
keep it "sealed," but had compromised with the Service and had allowed
one agent to accompany him to Paris. Intriguingly, a male caller had
phoned KGO radio in San Francisco, to the Ray Taliferro program, in the
spring of 1987, identifying himself as a "former [Secret?] Service officer," and said that as an active agent he had accompanied Bush to Europe
in the "fall of 1980" to a meeting at which Bush "paid an Iranian money
to prevent the hostages from being released until President Carter left
office."[95]

"Mr. Y" claimed, again based upon his memory of the alleged French
intelligence report, that the Iranians at the meeting were Jalal al-Din Farsi,
a major political rival of then Iranian President Abolhassan Bani Sadr and
a representative of Khomeini's number-two man, Ayatollah Mohammed
Beheshti; the speaker of Iran's Parliament, Hashemi Rafsanjani himself
(which is confirmed by William Herrmann); and Iran's arms buyer and
intelligence chief for Europe, Manucher Gorbanifar. "Y" 's recounting
was the first mention of the possible presence of Farsi and Rafsanjani in
Paris, although Richard Brenneke had mentioned that he had a "close
relationship" with Rafsanjani. Although Brenneke had not mentioned
Farsi by name, a reporter for West Germany's news weekly *Der Spiegel*
later told the author that Brenneke told him that he had met Farsi in
Paris.[96] "Y" also claimed that "back channel"—secure communication
line—records at the CIA showed traffic indicating Bush and Casey's
presence in Paris at the time.

Again based on his memory of the report, "Mr. Y" claimed that
Reagan's then campaign foreign policy adviser, Richard Allen, had been
involved in the Paris meetings. When subsequent research revealed that
Mr. Allen had had an interview with a major television station in Washington, D.C., on October 19th and therefore seemed to have an airtight alibi at
least for that date, "Y" stated that the French intelligence report had also
referred to the earlier L' Enfant Plaza Hotel meeting in which Allen had
participated and that he may, after eight years, have gotten the two
meetings confused in his memory. Mr. Herrmann, however, claims that
Iranian official Hamid Nagashian told him that Richard Allen was involved
in Paris meetings in October 1980.

"Y" claimed that the French intelligence report had been initialled by the then head of the SDECE, Alexandre de Marenches, who had discussed its contents with then President-elect Ronald Reagan during a "courtesy visit" with Reagan in California in late November 1980, not long after his election. This meeting between Reagan and the French intelligence chief is reported by *Washington Post* reporter Bob Woodward in his book about the Iran/Contra affair, *Veil*.

"Y" alleged that Rafsanjani had demanded that either Reagan or Bush personally show up at the meeting in Paris so that he could be certain that any deal that might be made would be "for real"—and to have a black-mail card to hold over the new administration to ensure that it carried out its end of an arms-for-hostages agreement once the hostages had been released. It was to be an "eyeball-to-eyeball" meeting, he said, to establish the "bona fides" of the Republican camp.

"FOLLOW THE MONEY"

During the unravelling of the Watergate scandal in the early 1970's, *Washington Post* reporter Bob Woodward's source "Deep Throat" urged him to "Follow the money." The most incredible claim "Y" made had to do with the source of the $40 million. Richard Brenneke had reported that William Casey and George Bush took proof of the wire transfer of the $40 million to the Paris meeting of October 19, 1980. If what he says is true, the Reagan-Bush arms-for-hostages deal with Iran before the 1980 election was literally an extension of Watergate. "Y" claimed that the money was left over from an illegal $60 million "campaign contribution" made by the Shah of Iran to the 1972 presidential campaign fund of President Richard Nixon, the Committee to Re-Elect the President (CREEP). The original $60 million "contribution," he said, had been deposited in a secret bank account in Mexico, and the $1 million used by CREEP for political espionage and sabotage operations against the Democrats in 1972, which formed the basis of the Watergate scandal, had been drawn from this same Mexican account by its "gatekeeper" at the time, Fred Malek. George Bush, "Y" said, knew about the account, since transferred to European banks, and that it still contained the funds because he had been the Republican National Committee chairman during Watergate and was, and still is, a friend of Malek's. During the 1988 presidential election campaign, in fact, Malek was forced to resign another post at the Republican National Committee in a mini-scandal over his involvement in alleged anti-Semitic activities ordered by President Nixon in the early 1970's. Alexander Haig, who reportedly authorized secret U.S. arms shipments to Iran by the Israelis in 1981,[97] would also have been in a position to know about the Mexican account, having been President Nixon's chief of staff.

"Y" claimed that the $40 million from the $60 million Mexican CREEP fund from the Shah of Iran had been wired, in two parts, to separate accounts in Bank Leu in Zurich, Switzerland—one account controlled by Iran and the other by the Czechs—by Merrill Lynch, whose chairman and chief executive officer was Donald Regan, President Reagan's future White House chief of staff. Regan had gotten to know and like William Casey when Casey was head of the Securities and Exchange Commission (SEC), also during the Nixon Administration.[98] The Czechoslovakian connection is confirmed by Richard Brenneke's records, which show that he had had numerous dealings with Czech arms manufacturers in the early 1980's, and by reports that Brenneke's friend Robert Benes, whom he said also attended the Paris meetings, was a double agent for France and the Czechs.

Probably not coincidentally, a subsidiary of Merrill Lynch, Merrill Lynch Futures, reportedly loaned between $400,000 and $500,000 to Dr. Cyrus Hashemi, one of the Iranian arms dealers who had reportedly attended the Paris meetings, shortly after Reagan and Bush gained office, to finance both the transport of arms to Iran and activities against anti-Khomeini dissidents abroad.[99] This amount is comparable to that reportedly loaned to now-imprisoned ex-CIA covert operative Edwin Wilson in 1979: $500,000. With the loan, Wilson and George Bush's longtime CIA associate Theodore Shackley became 49 percent partners in EATSCO, the Egyptian American Transport and Services Corporation, which reportedly received an exclusive contract from the Pentagon to ship U.S. arms to Cairo following the signing of the Camp David Accords between Egypt and Israel in 1979. According to Wilson, silent partners in EATSCO were indicted Iran/Contra co-conspirator, Richard Secord, "off the reservation" CIA operative Thomas Clines, and Erich von Marbod who was then Deputy Director of the Pentagon's Defense Security Assistance Agency which, in an obvious conflict of interest, had recommended approval of the EATSCO contract.[100] The reported president of EATSCO was Hussein K. Salem, an Egyptian. In 1983, EATSCO's partners, including Secord, were indicted for overcharging the U.S. government $8 million—intriguingly the same amount that Secord and his Iranian-American partner Albert Hakim are charged with having illegally skimmed from the Reagan-Bush Administration's secret operation to ship U.S. arms to Iran. In 1982, State Department advisor Michael Ledeen intervened in the case, suggesting to Assistant U.S. Attorney E. Lawrence Barcella that any alleged "billing abuses" in the EATSCO matter may, as in the Iran/Contra scandal, have been used to fund covert operations. The implication of the above reports is that Cyrus Hashemi's $500,000 loan may have gone to start what we will call "IRANSCO" in 1981, just as Edwin Wilson's $500,000 loan went to start EATSCO in 1979, with the same $8 million figure ending up in contention in U.S. courts and involving almost the same cast of characters. When Richard Secord retired from the Pentagon in 1983 in the wake of the mini-scandal, which had developed over his involvement with EATSCO, he became partners with Iranian middleman Albert Hakim, to whom he had been introduced by none other than Wilson, in another military equipment trading company, Stanford Technology Trading Group. The cycle then repeated itself, with Iran instead of Egypt being the recipient of arms. According to Informant "Y," EATSCO was in fact a "shake down cruise" for the far larger IRANSCO operation that followed it. "They used EATSCO to get the 'bugs' out of the system," he said. "The Egyptian operation was used as a model for future operations. The $500,000 in both instances was needed to get things going—as deposits for the shippers."

When asked how his account regarding the transfer of the $40 million to Bank Leu in Zurich, Switzerland, squared with Richard Brenneke's claim that it had been wired to Banque Lambert in Brussels, Belgium, "Y" said that the reports were "not necessarily inconsistent" because the money from the Mexican account had long since been moved to an account or accounts in Europe, perhaps at Banque Lambert. The funds, he contended, may have been wired from Banque Lambert to the two accounts at Bank Leu. Alternatively, he said, after eight years his memory of the French intelligence report may have been incorrect, and the funds may have originated in Bank Leu in Switzerland and been transferred *to* Banque Lambert, as Brenneke claimed. This latter account squares better with one given by the former U.S. chief of the Shah's secret police, Mansur Rafizadeh.

The Shah of Iran's secret $60 million "campaign contribution" to Richard Nixon's Republican CREEP fund in 1971–72 is reported by Mansur Rafizadeh in his 1987 book, *Witness*. Note the reference, once again, to $8 million in "missing funds," the same amount skimmed from the later EATSCO and IRANSCO operations:

"I knew that the Shah liked to give gifts to everyone. The reported amount of the Shah's donation to Nixon's campaign fund was $60,000,000. Of this money, $8,000,000 was stolen by Iranian intermediaries; of the $52,000,000 remaining, some was transferred to Mexico for laundering and [some] brought into the United States in the form of cash [the Watergate 'dirty tricks' fund]. The remainder was deposited in Switzerland in the accounts of Nixon's best friends."[101]

Over a year before Richard Brenneke, Heinrich Rupp, or "Mr. Y" had come onto the scene, Mr. Rafizadeh confirmed George Bush and Donald Gregg's presence at a pre-1980-election Paris meeting and, in a telephone interview, added that "millions and millions of dollars changed hands at the meeting."[102] Clark McGregor, then acting head of President Nixon's 1972 campaign organization also told *Washington Post* reporter Bob Woodward that CREEP had "raised" $60 million,[103] and when he learned of the Watergate break-in at Democratic national campaign headquarters, President Nixon reportedly feared that "They must have found out about Mexico." Intriguingly, the 1980 Reagan-Bush campaign's Iran expert, Michel Smith, told the author that one of the former CIA officers who had worked with him on the Bush side of the 1980 campaign had been stationed in Mexico, where the secret CREEP fund had been located, when Bush was chairman of the Republican National Committee during Watergate.[104]

According to Richard Brenneke, then Reagan-Bush campaign chairman William Casey had said that he would "handle" the financial arrangements for the $40 million worth of arms deliveries to Iran discussed at the Paris meetings. Informant "Y," in fact, claimed that Casey and George Bush carried a copy of Merrill Lynch wire transfers to the Paris meeting of October 19, 1980, to prove that the deal was legitimate.

In a post-election forum with William Casey, President Carter's 1980 campaign pollster Patrick Caddell asserted ironically that Casey and the Republicans would not have been able to counter an "October Surprise" hostage release before the 1980 election, to which Casey replied, "Well, wouldn't that depend on when it happened, and how it happened, and what the price was?"[105] Even more ironic, in January 1987, only four Americans out of ten thought that Irangate was more serious than Watergate.[106] The following year, 1988, George Bush authorized the appointment of a Watergate felon, President Nixon's former appointments secretary Dwight Chapin, to an advisory position on his presidential election campaign.[107] Chapin had been convicted for lying about his connection to Nixon's 1972 "dirty tricks" campaign which, according to "Y," had been financed with $1 million from the Iran account in Mexico. During Watergate, as chairman of the Republican National Committee, George Bush worked to interfere with the Senate Watergate Committee's investigation into the larger covert operations that lay behind the "dirty tricks" fund, going so far as to smear a key committee counsel, Carmine Bellino, on false charges in an attempt to sidetrack the inquiry.[108] Bush then continued the attack as President Ford's CIA director in the wake of Watergate, making one of his primary goals to squelch the flow of information about the CIA's covert operations to the Senate Committee on Intelligence headed by Senator Frank Church.

If "Mr. Y" is correct that the source of funds for the Republicans' sabotage campaign in 1972 was the secret Iran account, Mr. Bush had good reason to want to cover up what informant "Deep Throat" had called the "real Watergate story"—a web of covert operations "involving the entire U.S. intelligence community." According to "Deep Throat," the use of the illegal CREEP funds was "all a Haldeman operation." In July 1988, media reports noted that President Nixon is still blocking the release of more than 40 boxes of Haldeman's 1972 campaign files,[109] in all likelihood many of which have to do with the disposition of the "campaign contribution" from the Shah of Iran. Of the total forty million pages in the Nixon presidential archives, in fact, as of 1988 only five million, or a little over 10 percent, have been made public.[110] Henry Kissinger, Nixon's national security adviser, and Alexander Haig, his Chief of Staff, also maintained possession of their "personal" White House files from the Watergate period, which they have declined to make public. Kissinger's papers have been donated to the Library of Congress, on the condition that they be kept under lock and key until his death, or the year 2001, whichever comes first.[111]

In addition to the alleged $40 million in arms negotiated at the pre-1980-election Paris meetings, Informant "Y" claimed that a promise had also been made that $5 *billion* in U.S. and other Western arms would be made available to Iran once the Republicans gained the White House in January 1981, through "back channels." These "back channels," he said, would include "private" arms dealers, whose deals the new Reagan-Bush Administration would look the other way from, and "friendly third countries." "Iran wanted French-made fighter jets," he explained, "and those cost big money."[112] Intriguingly, the Carter Administration had reportedly conducted secret negotiations with Iranian Prime Minister Mehdi Bazargan and the Iranian armed forces for the delivery of this same quantity of U.S. military equipment, $5 billion, which the Shah had ordered before his fall. Bazargan, however, was shortly removed from power, making the agreement moot. Five billion dollars was also the figure reportedly mentioned by President Reagan's personal emissary Robert McFarlane in his discussions with Iranian officials during his late May 1986 mission to Tehran.

WHO IS "MR. Y"?

Though he repeatedly refused to identify himself to the author, "Mr. Y" did reveal considerable information about himself and his background. He is Jewish, was born in Germany, came to the United States at a young age, and is a U.S. citizen. He claims to have worked in the Plans Directorate of the CIA (which later became the Operations Directorate) beginning in the mid-1960's and to have left the Agency in 1984–85. During his twenty years with the CIA, "Y" claims to have been stationed in a number of European countries including West Germany, in the Middle East, and in Greece. He stated that his "main concern" at the Agency was NATO.

"Mr. Y" claimed to have known John McMahon. McMahon was Deputy Director of Operations (DDO) for the CIA from 1977 to 1981, which would have made him DDO at the time of the October 1980 Paris meetings. Perhaps significantly, in his book *Perilous Statecraft,* Iran/Contra middleman Michael Ledeen notes that the highest ranking Jewish CIA officer had been an executive assistant to a former Deputy Director of Operations/Plans, which was McMahon's position in October 1980.[113] During a telephone interview with the author, "Y" claimed that he had worked closely enough with McMahon that he had referred to him by his nickname, "Mother Hen." Informant "Y" also claims to have known and worked with Tom Polgar, a long time CIA veteran who had been station chief in Saigon and who had served in West Germany, presumably at the time "Y" was also there. Polgar was brought onto the investigative staff of the Congressional Iran/Contra Committee by Senator Warren Rudman, according to "Y" to keep the Israeli and NATO connections to Irangate from surfacing and to steer the inquiry away from links to the 1980 election campaign.

When asked why he was going public with what he knew, "Mr. Y" gave two straightforward and immediate answers. First, he said, there was a faction in the CIA that was angry at the way George Bush had "hung his boys out to dry." "There are a dozen guys in prison who have no reason being there," he said. "They were just following orders—a lot on Contra/ drug raps, and others for bank fraud. When a covert operation gets 'blown,' the Agency lets its agents take the rap along with the guys they've penetrated. It happened to me once, and I didn't appreciate it. Bush doesn't care what happens to his own people. I'm angry and so are a lot of other guys in the Agency," he explained. "Y" 's second reason for going public, he said, was to "protect the State of Israel." "A lot of people would like to 'hang' the Iran/Contra operations on the Israelis," he said. "But the Saudis were even more centrally involved. And anybody with half a brain can see that the 'October Surprise' deal wasn't for Israel's benefit. We did have the 'Exodus' operation [getting Iranian Jews out of Iran in exchange for arms and intelligence], but the big fish had to do with winning the 1980 election."

Intriguingly, "Mr. Y" is fluent enough in Farsi, the Iranian language, to have recited a flowing stanza of Persian poetry to the author. In his book *Perilous Statecraft*, Michael Ledeen notes that George Cave, a former Iran expert at the CIA, had a taste for Persian poetry.[114] Cave accompanied Robert McFarlane, Oliver North, and Israeli counterterrorism adviser Amiram Nir on their secret trip to Tehran on behalf of President Reagan in late May 1986, and remained central to the Iran operations even after the administration's secret arms sales became public. It is therefore possible that "Mr. Y" 's revelations in the "October Surprise" story may be the parable of George Cave.

"Mr. Z"

On April 28, 1988, while *Playboy* magazine was investigating the "October Surprise" story for an article in its October 1988 issue, an anonymous caller telephoned the magazine's headquarters in Chicago, claiming to work with the "shadow" CIA's arms-and-drugs operations. During the course of the conversation, the *Playboy* reporter asked the caller if he had heard any rumors about an Iran deal with the Reagan-Bush campaign in 1980. According to notes of the call, the informant brushed aside the word "rumor" and said matter-of-factly that "all this definitely happened. William Casey and Ollie North were involved, along with Bardon Blizzard, Jr., Terry Matkey, General Dale Duncan, and the ISA'' (Intelligence Support Activity, a top-secret, covert operations division of the U.S. military). "Also involved," he said, "was Richard Armitage and Ross Perot." "Mr. Z" said that the arms-drugs-and-hostages dealings began a year before the 1980 election (which was the same time that an Iran-Israel "Exodus" operation began), and that Sergeant Charlie Beckwith, the ground commander of the Desert One hostage rescue operation, had been involved. Stansfield Turner had fired the best CIA operatives, he said, and they had agreed among themselves to stay in touch and continue to operate. He also mentioned that George Bush's code name in the Iran operation was "White Rose."

THE ROLE OF FRENCH INTELLIGENCE

If any dignitary visits France, the French government knows about it, especially French intelligence. If there was any meeting in Paris involving V.I.P's from the 1980 Reagan-Bush campaign, let alone someone of the stature of vice-presidential candidate and former CIA director George Bush, the SDECE, France's equivalent of the CIA, would have been aware of their every move and involved in providing round-the-clock security. Pilot Heinrich Rupp, in fact, recalls seeing limousines and security men in dark suits at the V.I.P. section of Le Bourget airport outside of Paris on the morning of October 19, 1980, when he also claims to have seen George Bush and William Casey on the tarmac there. Richard Brenneke claims that a veteran of French intelligence, Robert Benes, facilitated Bush and Casey's entry into France, attended at least portions of all three meetings, two on October 19th and one on October 20th, and wrote a detailed report about the sessions for the head of the SDECE, Count Alexandre de Marenches. According to Michael Ledeen, de Marenches "delighted in staging melodramatic scenes,"[115] and a clandestine, midnight-launched rendezvous with Iranian radicals in a Paris hotel certainly qualifies as one. Informant "Y" claimed that Benes' participation in arranging security protection for the meetings had been specifically requested by the Iranians, to whom he was well known. "Y" also claims that the French intelligence report he read was written, at least in part, by Major Robert Benes and signed off on by Count de Marenches, who later went over its contents with Ronald Reagan in California in late November 1980.

Richard Brenneke was so certain that Robert Benes would confirm the details of the pre-1980-election Paris meetings that he agreed to fly to France with a reporter from *Der Spiegel*'s Washington, D.C., bureau, Martin Kilian, in late September 1988 to interview him. Brenneke claims that Benes had told him on the phone that he might even be able to gain access to documentation about the Paris meetings. Shortly before they were scheduled to leave the East Coast, the author received an excited call from Mr. Kilian informing her that he had learned that Interpol, the international police organization, had gotten to Benes first and that Benes had acknowledged that George Bush had been in Paris. The information had reportedly come from *Playboy* magazine's sources in France. When the author called the *Playboy* reporter who had been working on the "October Surprise" story to check the report of the Interpol visit to Benes, he snapped nervously, "I can't tell you anything about that. Just don't even ask me about that! Period."

When Richard Brenneke and the *Der Spiegel* reporter met with Benes a few days later in Paris, he was accompanied by another French intelligence agent, Madame Robert, who Brenneke later acknowledged was probably "the woman" who had participated in the October 20, 1980, meeting at the Hotel Florida. Also present was Nicholas Ignatiev, who, according to Brenneke, had been with the French government.[116] Following his reported meeting with Interpol, Benes backed down, denying that he had ever been at a meeting in Paris before the 1980 election or that he had ever seen George Bush. At first he claimed to have had a major heart operation at the time.[117] According to Brenneke, however, later in the conversation he changed his story and recalled that his heart ailment had been earlier in 1980, and that he must have been "out of town" at the time. He said that he had never met Alexandre de Marenches, never wrote or saw a "French intelligence report," and had never had anything to do with French intelligence.[118] A check of hospital records, however, reportedly showed that Benes was not being treated for a heart condition at the time[119] and a source close to French intelligence told the *Boston Globe* that Benes was "well-known" to them.[120] Informant "Y" laughed when told that Benes claimed not to know de Marenches. "They went to school together," he said.[121] Brenneke later confirmed to the author, based upon subsequent telephone conversations with Benes, that Benes had been visited not only by Interpol, but also by "an old friend of William Casey's," an American, and that their "warnings" had "given him real cause for concern."[122]

While in Paris, Mr. Brenneke and the *Der Spiegel* reporter checked the records at the Hotel Florida, where Brenneke claimed the meeting on October 20, 1980, had taken place. He recalled that it had been in a room on one of the top floors, and that it had begun around 9:30 a.m. Paris time and ended about 2:30 p.m. The hotel's records, however, had not been kept in proper order, and the clerk who assisted the search said repeatedly, "The records are not good." There was no entry for Mr. Brenneke, but this was as he had predicted. Brenneke told the author prior to his September 1988 trip to Paris that he had not required a reservation—that Mr. Kerritt of the CIA had "taken care of the details." The records did show that an Iranian named Soleimany had checked into the hotel on October 18th, the day Mr. Brenneke said that he himself had arrived. The Iranian, however, did not use the room, and according to the records, it was vacant from October 18th through October 20th, the same three nights that Brenneke said he stayed at the hotel. The room that had been reserved by the Iranian, was not, however, on one of the top floors.

Alexandre de Marenches, now retired from the SDECE, agreed to an interview with *Der Spiegel,* but only, his office said, after the election. Although the magazine assumed that the former French intelligence official had meant after the presidential election in the United States, it turned out that de Marenches had meant after the Israeli election of November 1, 1988. The interview was held the next day, November 2nd. De Marenches reportedly denied having any knowledge of the October 1980 Paris meetings and said that he had not given a written report to Ronald Reagan during his late November 1980 visit with the President-elect in California. He was not, however, as absolute in his denial of an oral discussion with Reagan relating to the hostages. The issue of the fifty-two American captives, he had said, according to the *Boston Globe,* had "not especially" been a topic of conversation at the meeting.[123] This latter claim is simply not believable. The hostage crisis remained the number one issue on the minds of Americans and therefore also with the President-elect, until the moment of their eventual release just after Reagan's inauguration.

According to Informant "Y," de Marenches, who later lobbied the U.S. Congress on behalf of the Contras for President Reagan,[123] had good reason not to be forthcoming in his response to questions about pre-election negotiations between the Reagan-Bush campaign and Iran. Like Richard Allen and Robert McFarlane's "failure" to report Houshang Lavi's October 2, 1980, arms-for-hostages offer to President Carter's State Department, de Marenches, according to "Y," specifically chose not to inform President Carter's CIA Director Stansfield Turner about the Paris meetings. After warning Reagan not to trust the CIA,[124] de Marenches left the United States after his "courtesy visit" with Reagan in November 1980 without placing the "courtesy call" to President Carter expected under the rules of protocol. Not surprisingly, therefore, Stansfield Turner has said that he "never saw any documentation" on the alleged Paris meetings. He also said, however, "I'm persuaded that some meetings took place that could have led to a deal."[125] Mr. Turner also told London journalist Patrick Edlin, who worked with the author on the "October Surprise" story, "There's something there. If you can get at it, you'll win a Pulitzer prize."

On the eighth anniversary of the main Paris meeting, October 19, 1988, the right-wing French publication *Minute* published an article entitled "A Bomb Under George Bush" which acknowledged the de Marenches report and defended George Bush's participation in the pre-1980-election negotiations with Iranian officials in Paris. The article included Hashemi Rafsanjani, then the speaker of Iran's Parliament, as one of the participants in the October 19, 1980, meeting, along with Bush, William Casey, and Manucher Gorbanifar. "As is customary," the report said, "the SDECE was closely following the negotiations and knew everything about them." The writer claimed that the negotiations were "incredibly strained." "The Iranians knew what great pressure [President] Carter was under, and they continually hardened their position."[126]

According to a reporter for *Der Spiegel* who asked a local investigator to check for records at Le Bourget Airport outside of Paris, one employee was at first helpful and recalled that an "important party" had arrived at the airport sometime in October 1980. He said that he would check for documentation, and the investigator was to return in a day or two to see what he had found. When the reporter checked back, the employee would no longer talk and claimed to have "no memory" of anything that might have happened in October 1980. According to Informant "Y," who said that he had checked with a source with connections to French intelligence, following *Der Spiegel*'s query French agents and "some people from the U.S. embassy in Paris" arrived and removed airport records covering the period in question. "Y" also claimed to have a source of his own at Le Bourget who said that three planes had landed on October 19, 1980, that lots of limousines had been involved, and that whatever it was, it obviously was "very important."[127]

RICHARD ALLEN'S STORY

Richard Allen's involvement in the alleged October 1980 Paris meetings has been claimed by a number of sources. In the spring of 1987, a caller claiming to be a retired (Secret?) Service agent telephoned the Ray Taliferro radio program on KGO radio in San Francisco. He said that in the fall of 1980 he had accompanied George Bush and Richard Allen to a meeting in Europe—he did not specify Paris—at which they paid money to an Iranian to delay the release of the U.S. hostages until after President Carter had left office.[128] As the station's policy is that callers not identify themselves on the air, the man gave only his place of residence. This report, which may or may not be apocryphal, was made a year and a half before the author was told by Informant "Y" that Mr. Bush, in a compromise with the Secret Service, had allowed only one Secret Service agent to accompany him to the Paris meeting. According to "Y," Bush finally approved the single agent because he realized that his expertise would be needed to "sweep" the meeting room for electronic listening devices. Though having only one agent on a mission with a vice-presidential candidate would have violated standard Secret Service procedures, Secret Service spokesman William Corbett told the author in a telephone interview that only the President and Vice-President are required by law to have security protection at all times. If a vice-presidential candidate insisted on not having protection, or on having only one agent accompany him on a trip, the spokesman said, the Secret Service would have to have bent to his wishes. As the former "Service agent" who called KGO did not specify Paris as the site of the meeting he had allegedly attended with George Bush and Richard Allen, and as Allen appears to have an airtight alibi at least for October 19, 1980, it is possible that there was an additional pre-1980-election meeting, which they both attended on a different date, or that the key Paris meeting itself happened at a different time than Rupp, Brenneke, and Informant "Y" recall. U.S. businessman William Herrmann, in fact, has quoted Iranian Revolutionary Guards official Hamid Nagashian that Richard Allen was in Paris with Robert McFarlane and Dr. Fred Ikle, Allen's campaign aide, in October 1980.

There is reason to believe that Richard Allen knows more about the 1980 Reagan-Bush campaign's "quiet diplomacy" of October 1980 than he has been willing to acknowledge. After insisting repeatedly to a number of reporters that there was "absolutely nothing" to reports of anything having come of his October 2, 1980, meeting with Houshang Lavi, Mr. Allen finally admitted to the *New York Daily News* in late August 1988 that he "could not deny that some 'self-starters' in the [1980] Reagan-Bush campaign 'might have met some Iranian geeks in Paris,' as Honegger alleged, but insisted that no such meeting was authorized."[129] Significantly, Mr. Allen had in the past used language similar to "self-starters"—"free-lancers"—in attempts to distance himself from the Reagan-Bush campaign's discussions of arms-for-hostages as a solution to the "October Surprise" dilemma. In April 1987, Mr. Allen told the *Miami Herald* that "There was no 'authorized' contact, at any time, with any Iranians on such deals. However, he said that he could not vouch for 'free-lancers' who might have invoked Reagan's name in talks with the Iranians."[130] Mr. Allen also told the Knight-Ridder wire service that "[Robert] McFarlane was 'decidedly not part of the 1980 campaign apparatus. Whether Mr. McFarlane was a 'free-lance' . . . there was no connection with us.' "[131] These are rather astonishing denials in light of the fact that one of Mr. Allen's "October Surprise" Group members told a meeting of professors that Mr. McFarlane had attended some of Allen's own meetings, and in light of the fact that one of the meetings which "self-starter" McFarlane attended with Houshang Lavi had also been attended by Mr. Allen himself. As Mr. Allen was candidate Reagan's chief foreign policy and defense adviser at the time, any meeting between Allen and an Iranian (which Mr. Houshang Lavi was and is) would by definition have been an "authorized" one. In other words, by his own definition, Mr. Allen himself was a "free-lancer" and a "self-starter." It is therefore extremely unlikely that he would not have been aware of follow-up meetings to the L' Enfant Plaza rendezvous in which some additional "self-starters"—George Bush and William Casey—met some "Iranian geeks" in Paris. Of course, according to informant "Y" and former CIA contract agent William Herrmann, Mr. Allen himself was one of the many Reagan-Bush "geeks" who met with top Iranian officials in Paris in mid-October 1980.

There is another reason why Richard Allen is likely to have been aware of other "unauthorized" follow-up meetings between a group of "self-starters" from the Reagan-Bush campaign and "Iranian geeks in Paris." According to Informant "Y," "Y" 's source with connections to French intelligence told him that Fred Ikle, one of the key foreign policy advisers on Richard Allen's own "October Surprise" committee, was also involved in pre-1980-election meetings with the Iranians.[132] Likewise, William Herrmann quotes Iranian official Hamid Nagashian as saying that Dr. Ikle was also in Paris in October 1980.

In 1968, Richard Allen reportedly participated in campaign sabotage strikingly similar to the reported arms-for-no-hostages negotiations of October 1980, also involving Paris. At the time, Mr. Allen was the chief foreign policy adviser to another Republican presidential candidate, Richard Nixon. In collusion with Henry Kissinger and Anna Chennault of the U.S. "Taiwan lobby," he reportedly initiated another piece of "quiet diplomacy" to sabotage Democratic candidate Hubert Humphrey's White House bid, which would have received a major and perhaps decisive boost from a planned Paris peace conference to negotiate an end to the Vietnam War.[133] Allen is said to have "activated" Chennault, who in the 1950's and 1960's had been an ardent advocate of the Chiang Kai-Shek dictatorship, to interfere with President Lyndon Johnson's efforts to get South Vietnamese President Nguyen van Thieu to hold the peace conference before the 1968 election. Chennault reportedly called Thieu on October 30, 1968, to make it "perfectly clear" that South Vietnam would receive a better deal from the Republicans than from President Johnson if they held off the conference until after the U.S. vote.[134] On November 2, 1968, two days after Johnson announced that he would participate in the expected Paris peace talks, and only three days before the presidential election, Thieu took the bait and suddenly withdrew from the negotiations. The Republicans, of course, had no intention of holding peace talks after the election, and the war dragged on for a number of years. In 1987, Anna Chennault became the chair of the Republican Heritage Groups Council.

Despite this piece of "quiet diplomacy," which produced the opposite of what had been promised, Richard Nixon told the American public during the 1968 election campaign that he had a "secret plan" to end the Vietnam War. Years later, on October 21, 1980, the day after the last of the three reported meetings in Paris, Ronald Reagan told voters, also in a campaign address, that he too had a "secret plan," this time to end the hostage crisis in Iran. Ironically, on October 27, 1980, President Carter compared Reagan's "secret plan" to end the hostage crisis to Nixon's earlier hint that he had a "secret plan" to end the war in Vietnam in a speech in Waco, Texas. Unfortunately for the nation, Mr. Reagan's "secret plan" apparently resulted in a delay in the release of the hostages, just as Nixon's "secret plan" had resulted in a delay in the end of the southeast Asian war.

DONALD GREGG'S ALIBI

Donald Gregg has an interesting alibi for October 18, 19, and 20, 1980. He told the *Boston Globe* and the Portland *Oregonian* that his private calendar for those days shows that he and his wife spent October 17–19 at a beach house in Bethany Beach, Delaware, which he said had been lent to them by a neighbor. Mr. Gregg, however, did not produce copies of his alleged calendar, and the neighbor, Mr. John Davis, told the *Oregonian* that, though he did sometimes lend the beach house to the Greggs, he had no records or memory based upon which he could confirm the dates.[135] The owner of the beach house also told *Der Spiegel* that he had no recollection of having given the keys to the Greggs, or of their having used the cottage.[136]

Gregg told the *Oregonian* that he had "played tennis and run on the beach" during their stay at the vacation house. A check of the weather that day, however, revealed that it was cold, damp, and rainy. When asked whether anyone had seen him during the stay, rather than mentioning his wife, Mr. Gregg responded, "I have no recollection of that."[137] This is a surprising answer in light of the fact that Gregg's own daughter, Lucy Gregg Buckley, told the paper that she recalled spending time that weekend with her parents. Whether that was just on the 17th, the day before Heinrich Rupp's plane left Washington, D.C., for Paris, or also on the 18th and 19th, was not reported. If Mr. Gregg was in fact at the beach house, and if his daughter saw him that weekend, as she recalls, it is curious that he told the *Boston Globe* there were "no witnesses" to he and his wife having been at the cottage.[138]

On October 20, 1980, when Richard Brenneke claims Mr. Gregg was at a meeting with him taking notes in Paris, France, Mr. Gregg claims to have been at work in Washington, D.C., presumably at the White House National Security Council where he was employed at the time. His only evidence for this, however, is that he claimed to have had three memoranda assigned to him for action that day and to have, he says, "originated" a memorandum on the 20th.[139] Mr. Gregg has not produced any such alleged memorandum, however, nor has he said what "action" he was to have taken on October 20, 1980, whether he took it, or where.

Curious as to what he had meant by "originating" a document—as memoranda can be dictated over the telephone or in some other manner that would not have required him to be in Washington—the author asked for clarification in a telephone interview on January 3, 1989. Mr. Gregg avoided answering the question. He again used the same language, stating that "Computer records show that I 'originated' a document in the Carter NSC that day." When the author asked again whether this meant that he had actually written the document at the National Security Council in Washington, D.C., Mr. Gregg cut off the question curtly, saying, "I stand by my statement in the *Boston Globe*." The *Globe* report stated that he had "generated" a memo. Asked again if "generated" meant that he had actually been in his office in Washington, he simply repeated that he stood by the *Globe* statement. He was unwilling to provide any further information. When the author asked whether he had been in Paris on October 19th or 20th, 1980, Mr. Gregg answered only with a question, "Why do you believe Brenneke?! Mossad [the Israeli intelligence agency] is angry with him." He also said, "Mr. Brenneke is a liar, and you can quote me on that."

One should, of course, examine the veracity of Mr. Donald Gregg's own statements. Mr. Gregg testified under oath on April 29, 1988, for example, that he had no knowledge of any White House-directed efforts to supply the Nicaraguan Contras prior to a meeting of August 8, 1986, with former CIA officer Felix Rodriguez. Oliver North's notebook however, contains an entry that records that Gregg attended a meeting on the Contra supply operation on September 10, 1985, nearly a year before he claims to have first learned of it.[140] Confronted with the evidence of North's note, Mr. Gregg then said that he did not recall having attended the earlier meeting, although his calendar, he admitted, showed no conflicting entry for that date and time.

Mr. Gregg also had no explanation for an agenda typed by his own secretary, which he himself had initialled, for a meeting on May 1, 1986 between Mr. Rodriguez and Vice President Bush, to whom Gregg reported at the NSC. This document, dated three months before he claimed to have learned of the Contra supply operation, stated that Mr. Rodriguez would "provide a briefing on the status of the war in El Salvador and the resupply of the Contras." "I am baffled by how that agenda item appears," Gregg said. "It baffles me to this day."

Donald Gregg must have been even more "baffled" by documents obtained by Washington, D.C., attorneys that showed there had been not just one, but seventeen meetings between himself and Mr. Rodriguez regarding the illegal Contra supply operation.[141] Clearly, the veracity of Mr. Gregg's own statements and memory remains open to serious question.

Given the problems with the above alibi, could Donald Gregg, who was a manager in the Operations Directorate when George Bush was CIA Director in 1976, have acted to interfere with a U.S. presidential election on behalf of the man whose staff he would join only months later in 1981, and whose own national security adviser he would become shortly thereafter? Mr. Gregg, in fact, was an old hand at fixing national elections. In a speech at the University of Texas in 1976 while working for George Bush at the CIA, Mr. Gregg recalled that he had taken part in a covert operation to interfere with an election campaign in Japan.[142] That same year, 1976, the CIA also reportedly intervened to affect the outcome of elections in Jamaica.

WILLIAM CASEY'S ALIBI

Just before his brain seizure, and only hours before he was to testify in Congress on the Iran/Contra operations, William Casey told his long time friend and personal counsel that he had decided to tell everything he knew. Unfortunately, the brain surgery then performed on Mr. Casey rendered him literally speechless, and now he cannot say anything at all: William Casey is dead. Before the advent of his untimely speech difficulties, however, he did reveal to a reporter the "moral criteria" he would use in deciding whether to interfere in a national election. In an interview in his office in the Old Executive Office Building next to the White House after the 1980 election, Mr. Casey said:

> "When you try to intervene in internal affairs or to influence an election, as we [the U.S.] did in Italy in 1948, I think that kind of thing you only do when it is of the highest interest of the U.S."[143]

Did William Casey apply his "moral criteria" to the United States' own presidential election in 1980? Would the World War II covert operative known as "Wild Bill" and "Cyclone" have believed that it was in the "highest interest" of the United States to apply his decades of experience in clandestine craft to illegally influence the American political process at a time when he felt strongly enough to have become the top campaign official for the only viable candidate opposing an administration which he thought, rightly or wrongly, was leading the economy and national security of the nation into ruin?

According to an associate of Texas journalist David Armstrong who checked the 1980 Reagan-Bush files at the Hoover Institution in California in October 1988, William Casey's campaign schedule is blank for October 18th through October 21st, 1980, precisely the dates that pilot Heinrich Rupp claims that Casey was flying to Paris, was in France, was flying to Frankfurt, West Germany, and was returning home to the States.[144] Mr. Casey's more detailed personal appointment book, partial contents of which were obtained by the *Boston Globe* in 1988, also show no entries for Saturday and Sunday, October 18th and 19th, 1980, the day he was reportedly flying to Paris and in Paris with Mr. Bush. Though there are entries in the schedule book for October 20th, when Mr. Casey was allegedly still in Europe, the *Globe* could find no evidence that any of the appointments listed for the 20th had actually been kept. One was for the Washington, D.C., Metropolitan Club, at 8:00 a.m.; one for "Cincinnati" at 10:00 a.m., and a third for "Campaign '80" at 4:00 p.m., presumably a reference to a Reagan-Bush staff meeting at national campaign headquarters in Arlington, Virginia. Mr. Casey's former secretary could not recall whether he had actually made any of the appointments that day, or whether the entries on the calendar were simply notes for planned events. Significantly, Richard Allen's handwritten logbooks for October 18–20, 1980, he says, show that he spoke with Casey on the telephone that same day, October 20th. Mr. Allen has not, however, said where Mr. Casey was when he spoke to him on the phone, and the Los Angeles *Times* reported only that this was "presumably in Washington, D.C." Why Mr. Casey would need to call Mr. Allen, or visa versa, when he could simply have walked into his office at national campaign headquarters in Arlington, Virginia, if in fact he was in town at all, remains a mystery. It is far more likely that Mr. Casey was not in Washington, D.C., when he called Mr. Allen.

On the night of October 23, 1980, William Casey met in New York with Herbert Cohen, a hostage negotiations specialist who was then also a consultant to President Carter's U.S. Hostage Task Force. If Richard Brenneke and Heinrich Rupp's versions of events are true, or close to being true, Mr. Casey met Mr. Cohen shortly after Casey had returned from Europe. As a result of their October 23rd meeting, Mr. Cohen prepared a strategy paper at the request of the Reagan-Bush campaign manager proposing a plan under which the hostages would be brought home on Reagan's inauguration day, January 20, 1981—the day they were in fact released.[145] Cohen's report, dated October 25th, was sent immediately to Casey, who would then have had it in hand before the election.

Though Mr. Cohen claims that Casey appeared "not to know what the h--- was going on with Iran" during their meeting,[146] the mumbler and master deceiver's demeanor were never necessarily a clue to his real intentions. If the man who successfully penetrated the Third Reich in World War II had just negotiated a secret agreement with Iran before the election to hold the hostages until his candidate's inauguration, it would have been in his and the campaign's interest to have a written "plan" on file proposing how the campaign might, *after* the election, obtain their release on inauguration day. This was, in fact, Informant "Y" 's explanation for Mr. Casey's request for the Cohen strategy paper. "It was," as he put it, "a cover-your-ass operation."

WHERE *WAS* GEORGE?

Like the "missing" eighteen minutes of Richard Nixon's Watergate tapes and the unaccounted-for days in William Casey's campaign calendar, George Bush's October 1980 campaign schedule has a 21-hour "gap" covering precisely the period that he was reportedly flying to meetings with Iranian officials in Paris. From approximately 10:00 p.m. on the night of October 18, 1980, to between 7:00 and 8:00 p.m. on the night of October 19th, Mr. Bush's whereabouts are unaccounted for. This twenty-one hours would have been more than sufficient time for him to make a round trip to France with time left over for meetings in the U.S. or in Europe.

Mr. Bush's campaign records show that he was in Philadelphia on October 18th, where he met with newspaper editors at 1:55 p.m. EST and later that night gave a speech, beginning at 8:40 p.m., at Widener University in Delaware County, Pennsylvania. After the speech, he was scheduled to fly to Washington, D.C., and had nothing on his campaign calendar for another 21 hours. At 7:00 p.m. on the 19th, Mr. Bush was scheduled to give an address to the Zionist organization of America in Washington, D.C. He did give the speech. However, as we will see, Secret Service records indicate that he may have arrived over an hour late for the appointment.

Though the national press carried numerous stories before the 1988 presidential election reporting the extremely serious allegations that Mr. Bush may have met secretly with Iranian officials in October 1980 to effectively fix the 1980 election, incredibly, no one of national stature, either in the U.S. media or national politics, asked Mr. Bush himself to respond to the charges. Like the very possibility that the hostages' ordeal might have been prolonged for political gain, it was as if the very thought, let alone the question, was taboo in official Washington.

As the "October Surprise" story began to be carried on nationwide radio in September and October 1988, Washington journalists began calling Mr. Bush's White House office for a response. His official spokesman, Stephen Hart, "strongly denied" the charges, claiming that the then vice-presidential candidate had taken "private 'down' time" at his temporary campaign residence in Washington, D.C., on October 19, 1980, to prepare for his speech that night to the Zionist Organization of America. Mr. Hart, however, provided no documentation or proof that Mr. Bush had in fact been at the campaign residence at 4429 Lowell Street, in Washington, D.C., during the time in question, and at the time of this writing not a single eyewitness has stepped forward to corroborate his claims. The closest such statement was given by Mr. William Corbett, a spokesman for the Secret Service, who told the Portland *Oregonian* that he had "personally supervised" some of Mr. Bush's "security arrangements" on October 19, 1980, but he acknowledged that he had not personally seen the vice-presidential candidate during the time in question.[147]

Of more concern, however, is the fact that the account of Mr. Bush's own spokesperson, Mr. Hart, as to the vice-presidential candidate's whereabouts on the night of October 18th, when he was allegedly flying to Paris, conflicts with the Secret Service's own version of events. Mr. Hart told the Portland *Oregonian* that Mr. Bush flew from Philadelphia, where he had had campaign appearances, on the night of October 18th, to Andrews Air Force Base outside of Washington, D.C., and went from there to his temporary residence in the nation's capitol.[148] Secret Service records obtained by the author, however, assuming they are accurate, show that Mr. Bush instead flew to Washington National Airport that night, October 18th, arriving at approximately 9:25 p.m. EST—the same airport and about the same time at which pilot Harry Rupp says he met Reagan-Bush campaign manager William Casey and, by inference, where Mr. Bush would also have departed for Paris via New York. Clearly, one of the two accounts must be wrong. Mr. Bush would not have flown into both Andrews Air Force Base and Washington National Airport the same night.

Of even greater concern is the fact that, though the Secret Service records show Mr. Bush arriving at Washington National airport at 9:25 p.m. EST on the night of October 18th, the *Oregonian* obtained a conflicting account from the manager of the hotel where the vice-presidential candidate had gone after his speech at Widener University in Pennsylvania that night. The manager of the Howard Johnson motel in Chester, Pennsylvania, told the *Oregonian* that Mr. Bush did not check out until approximately 11:00 P.M. EST, an hour and a half *after* the Secret Service puts a "George Bush" at Washington, D.C., National Airport the same night.[148] Clearly, Mr. Bush could not have been in both places at once. Either the hotel's records or the Secret Service's records are wrong, or the CIA, as Harry Rupp noted in his October 5, 1988, interview with KUSA TV in Denver, may have used a "double," a look-alike for Mr. Bush, in one of the two locations. Intriguingly, the Secret Service document recording Mr. Bush's arrival at Washington Airport the night of October 18th at 9:25 p.m. EST was not filled out until twelve days later, on October 30, 1980.

The initial response of the Secret Service—which until shortly before it was asked to make a statement had been under the direction of George Bush's 1988 campaign manager James Baker when he was secretary of the treasury—to the "October Surprise" charges was to issue a flat denial that then vice-presidential candidate Bush had been out of the country during the "missing" twenty-one hours in October 1980. Unfortunately, most reporters seemed only too willing to take the Service's word for Mr. Bush's whereabouts, without asking for documentation. When the behavior of the Secret Service is analyzed in detail, however, it is evident that its spokesmen acted in a very bizarre manner: different answers were given to different reporters.

After first issuing flat denials that Mr. Bush had been out of the country on October 18th or 19th, 1980, a Secret Service spokesman then stated that the Service "had no evidence that Mr. Bush *had* left the country" during the period in question. Then, in response to a request by *Newsweek*, an officer for the Service said in a letter that, *to its knowledge*, Mr. Bush had not been out of the country at the time. A Washington, D.C., publication received a different response from the Service. It was told that Mr. Bush was "out of the city for twenty-four hours." The Secret Service then told the Portland *Oregonian* that it could only "generally" account for Mr. Bush's whereabouts on the night of October 18th and on the 19th, but refused to identify any agent who might corroborate its statements.[149]

In addition to the major discrepancies between Mr. Bush's own spokesman Stephen Hart's claim (that Mr. Bush flew to Andrews Air Force Base on the night of the 18th) and the Secret Service's record, which shows that he arrived instead at Washington National Airport that night; and between the Service's claim that he arrived in Washington at 9:25 p.m. on the 18th and the hotel manager's claim that he was still in Pennsylvania at 11:00 p.m. the same evening; even the Secret Service's own records are *not consistent with one another* as to Mr. Bush's whereabouts during the period in question. One record obtained from the Service by the author for the night of October 19, 1980, records that Mr. Bush arrived at the Capitol Hilton Hotel for his speech to the Zionist Organization of America at 7:00 p.m. EST. Another Secret Service document provided in the same set, however, shows him arriving at the same event not at 7:00 p.m., but over an hour later, at 8:12 p.m. EST. Again, either one of the two Secret Service documents is wrong, or the Agency was using a look-alike, or "double," as one of the "vice-presidential candidates" who arrived at the Capitol Hilton Hotel that night.

Many reporters ignored the "October Surprise" story before the 1988 presidential election on the grounds that the Secret Service was "infallible." They took at face value its assertions that it knew for certain where Mr. Bush had been from the time that he completed his address at Widener University on the 18th until he arrived at the Capitol Hilton Hotel the night of the 19th. The above analysis, however, reveals that the Secret Service is far from infallible. Its statements, as well as its records, are inconsistent. Critical records were filled out long after the events in question, and no agent has been produced to corroborate any of its multiple versions of events. These problems are, of course, in addition to the fact that the Secret Service's version of a key event, Mr. Bush's arrival in Washington, conflicts fundamentally with that of Mr. Bush's own White House spokesman.

Amongst the Secret Service documents obtained by the author covering Mr. Bush's alleged whereabouts on October 18th and 19th, 1980, only two records provide any information that might throw doubt on reports that he could have been in Paris on the morning of October 19th. These two documents purport to show that Mr. Bush was at the Chevy Chase Country Club in Chevy Chase, Maryland, between 10:29 a.m. and 11:56 a.m. EST on the morning of October 19, 1980, presumably for his customary Sunday tennis game. If these records are accurate—and we have established that there is reason to doubt the reliability of any of the Service's records—Mr. Bush would have had to have taken a faster plane than a Grumman Gulfstream for the trip back to the East Coast from Paris, where he allegedly left Le Bourget Airport between noon and 1:00 p.m. Paris time on the 19th. He could have taken a supersonic Concorde, which can make the trip in a little over three hours, or a military aircraft, however, and still have easily been at the Chevy Chase Country Club by 10:30 a.m. EST on the 19th.

Regardless, there are a number of problems with the Chevy Chase records provided by the Secret Service. One of the two documents, first of all, was filled out by an individual identified as the "lead advance" person. Secret Service spokesman William Corbett informed the author in a telephone interview that "lead advance" referred to one of Mr. Bush's own political campaign personnel. Second, whoever filled out the document did so over a week after Mr. Bush was allegedly at the country club. This record also states that "security" was "N/A" that day, normally meaning "not applicable." The second Secret Service document mentioning the Chevy Chase Country Club is dated on the same day as Mr. Bush's alleged appearance there, October 19th, but is heavily censored.

An investigator working with the author called the Chevy Chase Country Club and spoke with the secretary of its Board of Governors, Mrs. Gochman, on December 12, 1988. He asked whether Mr. Bush may have been at the club on the morning of October 19, 1980. Mrs. Gochman said, "Well, I don't remember that," and added that she did not recall a Secret Service advance party having been there at that time. She said that there were no records at the club to show whether Mr. Bush had been there, one way or the other, and stated that the vice-presidential candidate was not a member of the club in October 1980. Mr. Bush's wife, however—who also had Secret Service protection at the time—used the club "quite often," Mrs. Gochman recalled. Though Mr. Bush's alleged reason for visiting the country club would have been to play tennis, Secret Service records obtained by the author for October 19th show that the weather that day was "rainy," "cool," and "overcast," and Mrs. Gochman stated that there were only outdoor courts at the club. Again, no "tennis partner" or other witness has come forward with a statement about Mr. Bush's whereabouts on October 19, 1980, and the Secret Service will not provide the names of any of the agent(s) it alleges were watching the temporary campaign residence on Lowell Street in Washington, D.C., that day.

As the eighth anniversary of the reported October 19, 1980, Paris meeting approached, word circulated in Washington, D.C., that a former CIA officer, David McMichael, was trying to get former President Carter to hold a press conference at the National Press Club on that date to reveal what he knows about the "October Surprise" story. Shortly before the proposed press conference, as Mr. McMichael was talking with Mr. Carter's former White House press secretary, Mr. Jody Powell, the author received a call from Informant "Y" alerting her to the fact that a source inside Vice-President Bush's office had said that his staff was preparing a "cover story" to answer increasing press inquiries as to why the White

House had not released proof of Mr. Bush's whereabouts during the "missing" twenty-one hours in October 1980. According to the informant, a Secret Service agent had "leaked," off the record, to a Washington, D.C., reporter that the reason no proof had been forthcoming was that Mr. Bush had been with his mistress during the period in question. At the same time, a report about this alleged mistress appeared in the *Los Angeles Weekly*. The story coincided with rumors circulating in Washington, D.C., that the *Washington Post* was about to publish an article that would be "damaging" to the Republican presidential candidate, after which the New York stock market fell thirty-four points in thirty-eight minutes. In the wake of these events, the *Post* issued an unprecedented statement that it had no such plan to publish a "damaging" article about Mr. Bush in its upcoming edition.

Was the man whom President Carter refused to keep on in his cherished post as director of the CIA in 1977 more likely to have committed adultery or treason at the height of the dreaded "October Surprise" window of vulnerability on October 19, 1980? Was George Bush, the man who wanted the White House more than anything else in the world, more likely to have chosen the Lady—or the Tiger?

Mr. Bush, in fact, had a record of being unaccounted for for periods of up to twenty-four hours at a time during his previous presidential campaign. In August 1988, the *Washington Post* reported that a "mystery about George Bush" and the CIA had arisen in interviews regarding the period after he had left the Agency. According to those involved with Mr. Bush's first political action committee, it said, there were a number of occasions in 1978 and 1979, during his first run for the presidency, that Mr. Bush set aside periods of up to twenty-four hours during which he told aides that he could not divulge his whereabouts. Mr. Bush had claimed that during these "missing days" he had attended "meetings with former CIA directors." According to senior Agency officials and even former CIA Director Stansfield Turner, however, there had been no such meetings of former Agency directors during the times that Mr. Bush had been unaccounted for. Mr. Bush's White House spokesman, Stephen Hart, recalled only that the candidate had taken some "personal time off" for tennis visits with friends during his first run for the presidency. On October 19, 1980, as in 1978 and 1979, in other words, Mr. Bush was allegedly playing tennis at a time during which others claim he was on a secret mission.

In addition to the "missing days" during Mr. Bush's 1978–79 presidential bid and the "missing" twenty-one hours on October 18–19, 1980, according to former Green Beret, Lieutenant Colonel James "Bo" Gritz, Vice-President George Bush went on yet another secret mission—before the

1988 presidential election. According to Gritz, who received his information from Delta Force members at Fort Bragg, Mr. Bush held secret negotiations with Iranian officials on board an oceanliner off Antigua during the 1988 presidential election campaign between 10:00 p.m. on the night of August 11 and 2:00 a.m. on the morning of August 12, 1988.

So, where *was* George on October 19, 1980? Was he at the Raphael Hotel in Paris, France? The *Los Angeles Times* checked the books at the Raphael and found a reservation for a "Bush" for September 28, 1980. It had been made together with another reservation for a "Wachs," but neither party had showed up to take the rooms. This is quite remarkable, as the hotel's management had told the West German news weekly *Der Spiegel,* when one of its reporters checked in late September 1988, that it had no records dating back to the September–October 1980 period. When the author mentioned the Bush-Wachs record to a journalist she believes to have intelligence connections, his anxious response was, "I thought the French police got all the records from the Raphael!" Was "Wachs" the sole Secret Service agent whom Mr. Bush reportedly allowed to accompany him to Paris? Had the reservation for Mr. Bush and his Secret Service agent been made too early and then cancelled?

In the final analysis, whether then vice-presidential candidate George Bush personally attended the October 19, 1980, Paris meeting with Iranian officials is not the critical issue. The critical question is whether the Reagan-Bush campaign *per se,* through the mediation of *any* of its agents or officials, secretly negotiated with the Khomeini regime to delay the release of the U.S. hostages until Ronald Reagan's inauguration. Whether Mr. Bush was personally in Paris or not, if the negotiations took place, he would be certain to have known about them and to have either authorized them or not vetoed them. It is the author's belief that Mr. Casey is far more likely to have made the rendezvous in Paris than Mr. Bush.

What is very probable is that Mr. Bush flew to New York from Washington, D.C., on the night of October 18, 1980, to meet secretly with Iran's prime minister Mohammed Ali Rajai before Mr. Rajai left the East Coast for Algiers the same night. Rajai was a member of Iran's critical hostage policy committee and had conveniently refused to meet with President Carter, President Carter's Secretary of State Edmund Muskie, or any other Carter Administration official during his visit to the United Nations over the three-day period prior to his departure from New York the night of October 18th. Mr. Bush could easily have flown to New York to meet with Mr. Rajai that night, and even flown with him on his jet to negotiate a secret agreement, and been back on the East Coast in plenty of time to "play tennis" the next morning. An associate of CIA pilot Heinrich Rupp, in fact, told the *Rocky Mountain News* in Denver that Bush's plane had been in New York the night of the 18th, where it rendezvoused with Rupp and Casey's plane before Rupp and Casey headed for Paris.

At the time of this writing, despite all the reports contained in *October Surprise*, there is some doubt as to whether then vice-presidential candidate George Bush was in Paris on October 19, 1980. His Secret Service records are heavily censored for that day. More importantly, as this book goes to press, the author has received information from sources in Europe that, although the reported date of October 19th may be "off," Mr. Bush and his CIA associates were involved in not just one, but multiple meetings with Iranian officials before the 1980 presidential election. It is the author's hope, therefore, that the information presented in these chapters will spur an official investigation to uncover the real facts of Mr. Bush's involvement in negotiations with Iran over the fate of the fifty-two hostages.

III

THE PLO CONNECTION

**"He said he wanted the PLO to use its influence
to delay the release of the American hostages
from the embassy in Tehran until after the election."**

**Bassam Abu Sharif, Chief Spokesman and Adviser
to PLO Chairman Yassar Arafat**

On December 14, 1988, a geopolitical earthquake shook the Middle East. After hastily arranged secret meetings with leaders of the U.S. Jewish community and Swedish Foreign Minister Sten Andersson, PLO Chairman Yassar Arafat shocked the world by renouncing terrorism and recognizing Israel's right to exist in peace and security. As great a surprise was the sudden willingness of the Reagan-Bush Administration to implicitly recognize the Palestine Liberation Organization by agreeing to hold an official dialogue with a group that had become synonymous with terrorism. The big question, of course, is why? Despite voluminous press coverage proposing various explanations for the sudden switch in policy, there still exists a fundamental mystery as to why the about-face happened—why it happened at all, and why at that particular time, in the final month of the outgoing Reagan-Bush Administration?

The official explanation is that Yassar Arafat finally said the "magic words" that Washington wanted to hear, renouncing terrorism and admitting that, yes, Israel was real after all. A careful look at his "before" and "after" language, however—at the PLO leader's "magic" words versus what he had said only twenty-four hours before—only deepens the mystery. For some reason the following wording in Arafat's speech before a United Nations special session in Geneva on December 13, 1988, was not yet acceptable to President Reagan, Vice-President Bush, or Secretary of State George Shultz:

> "The P.L.O. will seek a comprehensive settlement among the parties concerned in the Arab-Israeli conflict, including the state of Palestine, Israel, and other neighbors, within the framework of the international conference for peace in the Middle East on the basis of [U.N.] Resolutions 242 and 338 and so as to guarantee equality and the balance of interests, especially our people's rights in freedom, national independence and respect for the right to exist in peace and security for all."[1]

PERFECTLY "CLEAR"

Shortly after Arafat's U.N. address, the *San Francisco Chronicle* reported that a Reagan Administration spokesman had said that the speech was unacceptable because the PLO chairman had failed to "clearly" address U.S. conditions for the start of a substantive dialogue with the PLO (their quotations). One day later, after uttering the "magic word" at a hastily arranged press conference, the world suddenly changed for Yassar Arafat:

> "In my speech yesterday, it was *clear* that we mean our people's rights to freedom and national independence, according to [U.N.] Resolution 181, and the right of all parties concerned in the Middle East conflict to exist in peace and security, and, as I have mentioned, including the state of Palestine, Israel, and other neighbors, according to the [U.N.] Resolutions 242 and 338."[2] [authors emphasis added]

Upon hearing the above statement, Secretary of State Shultz gave the following explanation for the sudden turnaround in the administration's position: "I didn't change my mind. They [the PLO] made their statement *clear*." Clearly, Yassar Arafat had said *the* magic word. Was it a code? And if it was a code, what was it a code for?

Resolution 242, adopted by the United Nations in 1967, requires respect for "the sovereignty, territorial integrity and political independence of all states in the Middle East"; and Resolution 338, adopted by the United Nations in 1973, calls for all countries in the region to carry out the earlier Resolution, 242. Resolution 181 was the original United Nations Resolution, which partitioned British mandate Palestine in November 1947 into two jerrymandered regions, one for a Palestinian homeland and the other for a Jewish homeland, and is the legal basis for the existence of the state of Israel today. Though the founders of the state of Israel originally accepted Resolution 181, from the beginning the Palestinians and their Arab allies rejected it and fought unsuccessfully with Israel in 1948–49 in an attempt to gain control of the entire territory. In his statement of December 14, 1988, therefore, Yassar Arafat took the historic step of finally accepting Resolution 181, under which Palestinians would receive title to lands that are now part of the state of Israel.

In accepting Mr. Arafat's language, which included a reference to U.N. Resolution 181, Secretary of State Shultz said that the PLO leader had finally made himself "clear." A careful look at the "unacceptable" language of December 13th versus his "acceptable" language of December 14th, however, reveals little or no real difference between the two wordings. The U.S. State Department, in fact, did not specify how the two versions significantly differed from one another; and an official spokesman for the PLO, Ahmed Abdul-Rahman, stated that it was the United States that had reversed course in those frenetic hours in mid-December 1988, not the PLO.[3] Clearly, something else must have been behind the hastily arranged coming to terms between Washington and the PLO. What could it have been?

To find the most likely answer to that question we must, again, go back to the 1980 presidential election campaign. In the fall of 1980, when the Reagan-Bush camp was at the height of its fear of an "October Surprise"— the successful negotiation of a pre-election release of the American hostages by President Carter—something of major importance happened. Yassar Arafat's senior adviser and top spokesman, Bassam Abu Sharif, claims that he then received a visit in Beirut, Lebanon, from an emissary of the Reagan-Bush campaign. A native of the town of Kafr Aqab near Jerusalem, Sharif had received guerrilla warfare training in Palestinian camps and shares the same name, "Abu Sharif," with the man who was appointed commander of the Ayatollah Khomeini's radical Revolutionary Guards in May of 1980.[4] In an interview with journalist Morgan Strong in May 1988, the PLO spokesman revealed this startling account of his meeting with one of presidential candidate Ronald Reagan's closest friends and advisers before the 1980 election:

Sharif: During the first campaign the Reagan people contacted me.

Strong: During the 1980 campaign, when he was running against Carter?

Sharif: Yes. One of Reagan's closest friends—I will not name him now—and a major financial contributor to the campaign. He was on Reagan's campaign staff.

Strong: You personally spoke with him?

Sharif: Yes. We met in Beirut. He said he wanted the PLO to use its influence to delay the release of the American hostages from the embassy in Tehran until after the [1980] election.

Strong: . . . Can you substantiate that?

Sharif: It's true, there's no question. They asked that I contact the chairman [Arafat] and make the request. We have the proof if it is denied. And they said they would deny it if it ever became public. I hope it does, because I would like to drop the bombshell on them.[5]

Sharif told Morgan Strong that the Reagan emissary with whom he had met was close to presidential candidate Ronald Reagan and continually referred to him as "Ronnie." This might mean that he was one of Reagan's California inner circle. This possibility is given some weight in light of *Washington Post* reporter Bob Woodward's report in *Veil* that Reagan's close-knit group of West Coast friends arranged a later meeting with the head of French counterintelligence, Alexandre de Marenches, in November 1980. According to Informant "Y," de Marenches had received a report of the alleged October 19–20, 1980, Paris meetings attended by representatives of his French intelligence agency, Reagan-Bush campaign manager William Casey, and Iranian officials including, according to "Y," radical Islamic ideologue Jalal al-Din Farsi who had trained with and knew the PLO well. Farsi was a staunch supporter of the Ayatollah Khomeini's Revolutionary Guard. Members of the Guard (which also trained with the PLO) present at the meeting were reportedly Minister Moshen Rafiq Dust and his deputy, Hamid Nagashian.

The more explosive possibility, however, is that the Reagan emissary who asked for the PLO's help in getting Iran to delay the release of the hostages until after the 1980 election was a top official of the Reagan-Bush campaign itself. According to former CIA contract agent William Herrmann in a letter to the author, campaign manager William Casey was that secret "Reagan friend." Herrmann wrote: "It was Casey and [campaign foreign policy aide Dr. Fred] Ikle that flew to Lebanon in August or September 1980 and approached Abu Sharif to make the same deal [to delay the release of the hostages] with the PLO." If this claim can be demonstrated to be true, it would surely qualify as the "bombshell" that Abu Sharif mentioned to journalist Morgan Strong.

If Abu Sharif's story is true, it would, of course, not have been in the PLO's long-term interest to make the name of "Reagan's friend" public. Rather, Sharif and Yassar Arafat would have been likely to use the threat of its release, and the threat of publication of their alleged "proof" that the meeting took place, as a wild card to be exchanged for future U.S. recognition of the PLO. The first historic steps toward that very recognition were taken by the Reagan-Bush Administration in December 1988, only weeks after the first report of the secret pre-1980-election meeting between Sharif and Ronald Reagan's "emissary" appeared in the September 1988 issue of *Playboy*.

The White House, of course, perfunctorily denied Sharif's story.[6] Again, however, if the PLO did have proof that the meeting took place— probably in the form of a secretly made tape-recording—the threat of its exposure would go a long way towards explaining the sudden change of heart by the White House only a few months after Strong's revelations were made public. This is especially true in light of what else Arafat's spokesman told Morgan Strong:

> *Strong:* What promises were made to the PLO by this Reagan representative if the hostages were held beyond the [1980] election?
>
> *Sharif:* We were told that if the hostages were held, the PLO would be given recognition as the legitimate representative of the Palestinian people and the White House door would be open for us.[7]

Implicit recognition, in fact, was precisely what Secretary of State George Shultz, reportedly with the encouragement of then Vice-President Bush, conferred upon the PLO when he authorized U.S. Ambassador to Tunisia, Robert H. Pelletreau, Jr., to begin a "substantive dialogue" with Arafat's representatives in mid-December 1988.[8] Could there be a link between Abu Sharif's threat to release proof of the pre-1980-election meeting and the Reagan-Bush Administration's sudden agreement to hold talks with the PLO? Could there be a link between Abu Sharif himself and Ambassador Pelletreau, the man whom Shultz chose to be the "*sole* designated U.S. representative" [author's emphasis] to the U.S-PLO talks? The answer to both questions is yes, and the key appears to be Sharif.

In September 1970, Robert Pelletreau was taken hostage off the streets of Amman, Jordan, by the radical Marxist faction of the PLO, George Habash's Popular Front for the Liberation of Palestine.[9] Shortly before his capture, Abu Sharif and other members of Habash's organization had hijacked three airliners, forcing them to land in the Jordanian desert.[10] The planes were then blown up and their passengers taken hostage. Pelletreau found himself herded along with the others to a hotel in downtown Amman where the Front announced its demands to the press. George Shultz's future "sole designated representative" to talks with the PLO, however, managed to escape Sharif and the other hijackers by slipping unseen into the crowd of waiting journalists.[11] Sharif later left Habash's hard-line Popular Front to join Yassar Arafat's more "moderate" mainline PLO camp.

It was therefore with one of the terrorists who had taken him hostage eighteen years before that U.S. Ambassador Robert H. Pelletreau, Jr., was authorized to begin a dialogue with the "moderate" PLO on Thursday, December 15, 1988.[12]

In addition to the reported Beirut meeting between Bassam Abu Sharif and the adviser to Ronald Reagan, there may be another link to the PLO in attempts by the Reagan-Bush campaign to delay the release of the 52 hostages before the 1980 election. Informant "Y," who says he received his information from the Israelis and from a French intelligence report filed about the meeting, claims that an Iranian official who worked with the PLO was a participant in the alleged Paris meeting of October 19, 1980, with Reagan-Bush campaign manager William Casey where details of future U.S. arms shipments to Iran were finalized. His name, according to "Y," was Jalal al-Din Farsi. Like Bassam Abu Sharif, Farsi had trained in Palestine Liberation Organization camps and was a promoter of the Ayatollah Khomeini's radical Revolutionary Guards, which an "Abu Sharif" formally commanded in May 1980.[13] The Revolutionary Guards, also called the Pasadran, are the organized armed force of the radical religious clerics in Iran, formed as a counterweight to the Iranian regular army, which Khomeini distrusted. Another early promoter of Khomeini's personal paramilitary force was Hadi Ghaffari, who also had received guerrilla training in PLO militia camps.[14]

Why would representatives of the 1980 Reagan-Bush campaign have felt it necessary to approach the Palestine Liberation Organization in an effort to get the Ayatollah Khomeini to delay the release of the fifty-two hostages then held in the U.S. embassy in Tehran? What was the link between the PLO and those who controlled the American hostages?

THE POISON AND THE CURE

According to a key Shiite Moslem leader interviewed by Middle East correspondent for the *San Francisco Examiner,* John Wallach, the PLO was directly responsible for the taking of the U.S. embassy in Tehran in the first place, with the goal of forcing U.S. recognition of the organization as part of subsequent negotiations for the release of the American hostages.[15] Had it succeeded, Yassar Arafat's "Iran strategy" would have effectively nullified an understanding between then Secretary of State Henry Kissinger and Israel under the 1975 Israeli-Egyptian disengagement accords that the United States would not recognize the PLO until it first acknowledged Israel's right to exist and accepted pertinent United Nations resolutions. "It was their [the PLO's] idea and their project," the senior Shiite leader interviewed by Wallach said. "Everyone in the Iranian Revolution among the activists were working for [PLO leader Yassar Arafat] in the Amal organization."[16]

Though the PLO did not carry out the actual attack on the embassy in Tehran, it was reportedly responsible for training the radical "students" who did. According to Wallach's sources, the PLO and the Syrian-backed Amal faction in Lebanon recruited Iranian Shiites for the U.S. embassy operation and trained them in cooperating PLO and Amal militia camps in southern Lebanon. Amal is the Syrian-backed political and paramilitary group that represents Lebanon's one million Shiite Moslems. Iranian middleman Manucher Gorbanifar's close associate, Iranian Prime Minister Mir Hossein Mousavi, reportedly headed the Islamic Amal faction, an organization of some 350 radical Iranian Revolutionary Guards who trained terrorist recruits in southern Lebanon. (Gorbanifar reportedly later took part in the October 19–20, 1980 meeting in Paris with Reagan-Bush campaign manager William Casey and perhaps also vice presidential candidate George Bush.) An associate of then President of Iran, Abolhassan Bani Sadr, claims that some of the top leaders of the group that took the sixty-six Americans hostage on November 4, 1979, had been graduate students at the University of California at Berkeley who founded the PLO-linked Amal militia camps in southern Lebanon where the radical "students" who stormed the embassy were trained. In all, some twenty thousand Shiite militiamen, including those from Islamic Jihad ("Holy War") and Hezbollah ("Party of 'God' "), received terrorist and guerrilla training at Amal camps close to the PLO's own camps in southern Lebanon where an additional twenty thousand Palestinians received similar instruction. Hezbollah advocates the establishment of a radical Islamic Republic loyal to Iran and the Ayatollah Khomeini in Lebanon, whereas Amal advocates increased power for its own group to the benefit of Syria. Until the capture of U.N. Interim Force Commander U.S. Marine Lieutenant Colonel William Higgins in Tyre on February 17, 1988, Amal and Hezbollah, both Shia organizations, had worked closely together in southern Lebanon. After his kidnapping, however, they had a violent falling out and have been fighting for supremacy in the region ever since.

Yassar Arafat's "Iran strategy" was designed to position him to emerge as a hero for having secured the release of U.S. hostages from their Iranian captors. Evidentally, the PLO leader had no strong preference as to whether they were released to President Carter or to the Reagan-Bush camp, as long as he received the desired promise of future U.S. recognition from either side.

The Ayatollah Khomeini had long supported the Palestine Liberation Organization, and the PLO had numerous supporters within fundamentalist Islamic groups in Iran. Khomeini's first official visitor after he took power on February 1, 1979, in fact, was Yassar Arafat. During this "state" visit, the PLO leader was given the "gift" of Israel's mission headquarters in Tehran, which had flown the PLO flag since the first days of the Iranian Revolution. A year later, in November 1979, shortly after the seizure of the American embassy, Arafat was invited back to Tehran on a "good will" mission to discuss the fate of the U.S. hostages. But the PLO leader, who had hoped that all sixty-six Americans would be released in his name, was to be sorely disappointed. Khomeini, in the meantime, had realized the value of their continued detention as a tool to consolidate his Islamic revolution at home, and he agreed to free only thirteen of the hostages as a result of Arafat's "intercession." On Thanksgiving Day 1979, the first thirteen U.S. citizens held hostage in the U.S. embassy in Tehran thus gained their freedom. "We released the first hostages from the embassy, the first thirteen embassy personnel," Arafat said in an interview in 1988. "They were released according to my personal efforts."[17] The U.S. government, however, never acknowledged the PLO's role in the early hostage release, no doubt because the hand that offered the cure had also administered the poison.

The official story of Arafat's November 1979 "goodwill" mission to Tehran is that Khomeini had obtained the upper hand with the radical students holding the hostages and allowed Arafat to claim credit for the release of the first thirteen Americans. Arafat, however, may have held the real power then and for some time thereafter. According to Informant "Y," the CIA had to pay $15 million to the PLO at a secret meeting in late July or early August 1980 to get Arafat to instruct the students holding the hostages to follow Khomeini's orders, and some of the $1.4 billion involved in Italy's P-2-linked Vatican Bank and Banco Ambrosiano scandal may have been used.[18] Former CIA pilot Richard Brenneke also referred numerous times to a PLO connection to the secret negotiations by the Reagan-Bush campaign before the 1980 election, but would provide no details. In addition, "Y" claimed that the PLO had obtained a report of the alleged October 19–20, 1980, Paris meetings between Reagan-Bush campaign manager William Casey and the Iranians, probably from either PLO-schooled Iranian official Jalal al-Din Farsi or from Hamid Nagashian, a top arms procurement officer for the PLO-linked Revolutionary Guards, both of whom were reportedly there.[19]

Only four months before the November 4, 1979, seizure of the U.S. embassy in Tehran by PLO- and Amal-trained Iranian "students," PLO guerrillas had seized the Egyptian embassy in Ankara, Turkey. Their successful blackmail of the Egyptian government in the wake of that raid set the precedent for the subsequent operation in Iran.[20]

In 1980, therefore, anyone who desired to influence the radical "students" holding fifty-two American citizens hostage in Tehran had to negotiate not only with the Ayatollah Khomeini but with the PLO leadership. Just as the Reagan-Bush campaign reportedly attempted to influence Arafat and Bassam Abu Sharif to delay their release until after the November 4, 1980, election, President Carter tried to influence the PLO leader to expedite their freedom.[21] "There was a special and permanent contact between me and President Carter," Arafat said in a 1988 interview. "I have written documents from President Carter himself."[22]

The fate of U.S. hostages held at the time of this writing by Iran-loyal terrorists in Southern Lebanon is intimately linked to a resolution of the PLO's demand for a Palestinian homeland in the Israeli-occupied West Bank and Gaza Strip, and to demands for the return of the Golan Heights, also captured in the 1967 war, to Syria. When the Ayatollah Khomeini came to power in February 1979, he immediately ended formal diplomatic relations with Israel, called for Israel's withdrawal from all territories captured in the wars of 1948–49, 1967, and 1973, and ordered the passports of the country's eighty thousand Iranian Jews to be stamped with a red seal forbidding their travel to "occupied Palestine."[23] On CBS's *Face the Nation* in February 1987, one of Iran's delegates to the United Nations intoned, ". . . Resolve the Palestinian issue and most all your

problems [with U.S. hostages in southern Lebanon] will be solved."
During Robert McFarlane's trip to Tehran in late May 1986, a senior
Iranian official, Mr. Najafabadi, informed President Reagan's secret emissary that "The people holding the hostages [in Lebanon] have made
demands before they will release the Americans. They asked for Israel to
withdraw from the Golan Heights and South Lebanon."[24] At the time of
this writing, nine U.S. citizens are still held captive by the Khomeini-
loyalist Hezbollah Shiite militia in Southern Lebanon.

When President Reagan, Vice-President Bush, and Secretary of State
George Shultz agreed to begin a "substantive dialogue" with the PLO in
mid-December 1988 and Yassar Arafat agreed to recognize Israel's right to
exist, Iran, Syria, and Libya, the radical states in the Middle East, were
not pleased. All three are committed to the annihilation of the state of
Israel. When Khomeini came to power in Iran in February 1979, he had
called not only for Israel to withdraw from all territories captured in its
wars with Arab nations, but also for the complete elimination of Israel
from the Middle East and for a Palestinian state to be "built on its ruins."
The Iranian leader was therefore outraged by Arafat's recognition of
Israel's right to exist. Libya had been at odds with the PLO even longer
than Iran had been. Since the late 1970's when Khadafy outraged Arafat
by proposing to provide him with an atomic bomb to destroy the Suez
Canal,[25] the two leaders had not been on good terms. For Iran and Libya,
therefore, Yassar Arafat's December 14, 1988, pledge to recognize and
live in peace with Israel was anathema, as was President Reagan's war
against the Sandanistas in Nicaragua where the PLO, Libya, and Iran were
all well represented in Managua.[26]

The Palestinian Liberation Organization is the umbrella group that represents Arab people of Palestinian origin. It includes at least eight Palestinian guerrilla groups, three of which are considered relatively "moderate"
and mainstream: Arafat's own Fatah ("opening" or "conquest" in Ara-
bic) founded in 1959; the Popular Front for the Liberation of Palestine
founded by Marxist Christian Dr. George Habash in 1967; and the Democratic Front for the Liberation of Palestine headed by Nayef Hawatmeh,
which split with Habash's group in 1969. Of the other five guerrilla
organizations under the PLO umbrella, a second faction which split from
Habash's group—called the Popular Front for the Liberation of Palestine-
General Command, led by former Syrian army captain Ahmed Jibril—was
particularly unhappy with Arafat's December 1988 recognition of Israel.
His organization has the backing of Iran's Khomeini, Libya's Khadafy,
and Syria.

Also unhappy with Arafat's recognition of Israel's right to exist were two Palestinian guerrilla leaders now ostracized by the PLO: Abu Nidal, who split from Arafat in 1972 and founded his Fatah Revolutionary Council in 1976, which has since been held responsible for over one hundred terrorist attacks in Europe, Asia, and the Middle East; and Abu Mussa, whose Fatah Uprising split from Arafat in 1983. The day after Arafat recognized Israel's right to exist, Abu Mussa issued a clear threat: "We fully reject the Arafat concession and will prove our stand practically in a way that neither Israel nor the U.S. would expect."

On December 5, 1988, the U.S. embassy in Helsinki, Finland, received a telephone tip that a bomb carried in a suitcase would go off on a Pan American flight originating in Frankfurt, West Germany, bound for the United States before Christmas day, December 25, 1988. This tip came only nine days before President Reagan's sudden decision to hold talks with the PLO on December 14th, and ten days before U.S. Ambassador Robert Pelletreau, as part of his first authorized contact with Arafat's representatives, warned that the United States would hold the PLO leader responsible for terrorist acts carried out by any faction of his organization, which would include that headed by Ahmed Jibril. This tip was also received only a little over two weeks before a bomb did go off, as predicted, on a Pan American flight, 103, originating in Frankfurt, West Germany. After stopping in London, the plane crashed on December 21, 1988, in southern Scotland, killing all 258 passengers and at least 12 people on the ground. According to an Associated Press bulletin on Christmas day 1988, on board the plane was the CIA's Beirut station chief, the successor to William Buckley who died in captivity in Lebanon a year and a half after having been taken hostage by Khomeini-loyal Hezbollah kidnappers on March 16, 1984. The night of the crash, an anonymous male caller claimed responsibility for the sabotage on behalf of the pro-Khomeini Guardians of the Islamic Revolution as revenge for the destruction of Iran's civilian airbus over the Persian Gulf by the U.S. cruiser *Vincennes* on July 3, 1988. Four days after the air bus was shot down, the Khomeini-loyal Hezbollah in Lebanon had put out an order to its foreign agents to prepare for a retaliatory terrorist strike against "U.S. or western interests."[27] And on December 31, 1988, ten days after the crash of Pan American Flight 103, a second anonymous caller telephoned news organizations in London, again claiming "credit" on behalf of the Khomeini-loyal Guardians of the Islamic Revolution, threatening more terrorism against Americans unless the son of the former Shah of Iran, who lives in Virginia not far from CIA headquarters, was deported to the

Khomeini regime.[28] Weeks later, in January 1989, a gunman fired into a crowd of children playing in a schoolyard in Stockton, California. "Hezbollah," the name of the Khomeini-loyalist guerrilla force in southern Lebanon, which holds most of the remaining American hostages, was burned into the butt of his rifle.

Though the Iranian government officially disavowed any connection with the sabotage of Pan American Flight 103, it wasn't long before investigators focused on a former aide to the Ayatollah Khomeini as the leader of the group most likely responsible—Ahmed Jibril. Jibril had reportedly served as Khomeini's personal bodyguard and was the disciple of Adolf Hitler's closest Nazi associate in the Middle East, the Grand Mufti of Jerusalem, Haj Amin el-Huseini.[29] In the wake of the disaster, London's press quickly reported that Jibril's Syria-and Lebanon-based Popular Front for the Liberation of Palestine-General Command—a group under Arafat's umbrella, not yet formally ostracized by the PLO leader but often described as one of his foes—was a key suspect. By the end of December 1988, British investigators zeroed in on Jibril, who had activated a terrorist cell in Frankfurt, West Germany, some eighteen months before a bomb was placed aboard the Pan Am plane in the same city. On February 1, 1989, *CBS News* charged that Jibril's organization was responsible for the sabotage, as did Israeli minister Ariel Sharon on February 6, 1989.[31] On March 26, 1989, the *Sunday Times* of London reported that western intelligence and the PLO itself had also determined that Jibril was the culpable party. According to a PLO source, the Khomeini regime had paid some of the $10 million received by Jibril's organization to blow up the plane in retaliation for the downing of Iran's civilian airbus over the Persian Gulf on July 3, 1989.

Despite these obvious links to Iran, British authorities downplayed numerous claims of responsibility by spokesmen for the Khomeini-loyalist Guardians of the Islamic Revolution, apparently desiring to deflect attention from the Ayatollah, who had personally called for an increase in international terrorism against "U.S. and western interests" immediately after the August 1988 cease-fire in the Iran-Iraq War.[32]

Finally, in January 1989, the CIA and Israeli investigators focused suspicion back on Iran and on sub-groups of the Khomeini-loyalist Hezbollah organization in southern Lebanon whose goal is the establishment of a radical pro-Khomeini Islamic state in that country to the north of Israel. The Hezbollah sub-groups under investigation were the Islamic Jihad ("Holy War"), the Islamic Amal, and the Iranian Revolutionary Guards.[33] Hezbollah and Islamic Jihad control the fate of most of the U.S. hostages still held in southern Lebanon and were behind the 1983–84 bombings of the U.S. embassy and Marine barracks in Beirut in which 290 Americans were killed, precisely the number of dead from the shoot-down of the Iranian airbus over the Persian Gulf on July 3, 1988. Amal, together with the PLO, had trained the radical "students" who held fifty-two Americans hostage in the U.S. embassy in Tehran. And a 1980 commander of Khomeini's own Iranian Revolutionary Guards, "Abu Sharif," named himself after Bassam Abu Sharif, the man who claimed to have received a request from Ronald Reagan's friend and campaign adviser before the 1980 election to delay the release of those same hostages to ensure President Carter's defeat. At the time of this writing, U.S. government authorities believe that the plan to sabotage Pan American Flight 103 originated with Khomeini's Revolutionary Guards and was then carried out by the Popular Front for the Liberation of Palestine-General Command headed by Khomeini's former bodyguard, Ahmed Jibril.

Assuming Bassam Abu Sharif is telling the truth, the existence of a taped record or other documentation of his alleged meeting with Reagan's "friend" before the 1980 election may have been part of a wider PLO scheme connected to the Iran/Contra affair. In November and December 1985, the Palestinian Liberation Organization reportedly approached CIA officers in the Middle East offering to negotiate with Hezbollah for the release of the U.S. hostages held captive in Lebanon.[34] The obvious quid pro quo Yassar Arafat would have expected for this "assistance," as in the case of his strategy for the takeover of the U.S. embassy in Tehran in November 1979, would have been U.S. recognition of the PLO. Intriguingly, Iran/Contra middleman Adnan Khashoggi had also had a plan to reconcile the PLO to Israel and the United States. As part of this scheme, he had reportedly obtained a document signed by then Israeli Prime Minister Shimon Peres in which Peres agreed to recognize the Palestine Liberation Organization.[35] Arafat did not sign the counterpart letter recognizing Israel on behalf of the PLO, however, probably because he insisted on obtaining recognition from the United States first, and, according to Informant "Y," the PLO leader returned Peres's document to Israel under duress. Italy's *La Repubblica* reported that a longtime close associate of Khashoggi's, Adnan Rousan, had been a representative of the PLO; and that Rousan's notebooks contained the classified telephone number of a top adviser to President Reagan.[36]

When Ali Hashemi, a nephew of the second most powerful man in Iran, paid a secret visit to the White House in 1986, he told Iran/Contra defendant Richard Secord and other presidential aides that one of the groups under PLO Chairman Yassar Arafat, George Habash's Popular Front for the Liberation of Palestine, was working to gain influence inside Iran. Iran knew this, he said, because former CIA Beirut station chief William Buckley had revealed it under torture at the hands of Khomeini-loyalist Hezbollah forces in southern Lebanon.

Even Oliver North's Iran/Contra associate Richard Secord had a connection with the PLO. One of the middlemen Secord used to supply arms to the Nicaraguan Contras was Manzer al Kassar, a Syrian arms dealer who also supplied weapons to Palestinian terrorist Abul Abbas, the leader of the hijackers of the *Achille Lauro* cruise ship.[37] Oliver North himself sold rifles bought from Kassar to a CIA-linked arms dealer in Georgia to generate "profits" for the Contras in Nicaragua.[38]

Although Khashoggi's plan to reconcile Israel and the PLO, and the PLO's offer to the CIA to negotiate the release of U.S. hostages with Hezbollah both fell through, their actions reveal that the resolution of the "Palestinian problem" and the fate of Americans still held captive in southern Lebanon are inextricably linked.

IV

IN LIKE A BURGLAR

"You're in like a burglar."

**George Bush to Ronald Reagan,
Election Day, November 4, 1980**

On Election Day, November 4, 1980—before the polls closed and with the hostages still in Tehran—a journalist delivered a personal message from soon-to-be-vice-president-elect Bush to Ronald Reagan at Reagan's voting place in California: "George Bush says you're in like a burglar."[1] While Reagan shrugged off the remark with characteristic aplomb, "the joy in the corridors at CIA headquarters at Langley was palpable." Ironically, in light of the reported pre-election Paris meeting between Reagan-Bush campaign manager William Casey and Iranian officials, "many treated Reagan's victory like Liberation Day in Paris."[2] The celebratory mood was especially great among the six hundred to eight hundred covert operatives whom Carter's CIA director Stansfield Turner had fired or sent to an early retirement in the "Halloween Massacre" of 1977. Some of the "massacred" thought George Bush "walked on water"[3] and had worked for him in the 1980 presidential campaign.

As Bush's premature congratulations were being delivered to Reagan in California, halfway around the world, in Iran, President Bani Sadr's political rivals, the Rafsanjani-Beheshti forces, delivered a letter to the secretary of Iran's Parliament calling for his banishment.[4] Bani Sadr's foes, who had reportedly sent representatives to meet with Reagan-Bush campaign manager William Casey and George Bush in Paris before the election, instantly targeted the one person who had worked with President Carter to obtain an early release of the hostages.

President Bani Sadr had an admittedly selfish motive for wanting the hostages released early to President Carter. In his opinion, their continued captivity tarnished the reputation of the new Islamic Revolution and served only the cause of the radical mullahs who wanted to use the continuing crisis to consolidate their power base at the expense of both himself and the American president. "When I became president in January 1980," he told *New Perspectives Quarterly,* "I felt it was essential to free the American hostages to Carter in order to firmly establish the authority of my government."[5] The radical mullahs wanted that authority destroyed and Bani Sadr removed from office.

Bani Sadr maintains that Beheshti and Rafsanjani were behind the letter to Parliament calling for his banishment because three months earlier, in August 1980, he had refused to sign a written "waiver" agreeing to abide by whatever deal they made with "the Americans" for the release of the hostages.[6] By "Americans," he insists, "they meant that a delay in the release of the hostages could be used to establish a relationship with 'the other side'—the incoming Reagan Administration." As Bani Sadr had already refused to sign the waiver, and as Beheshti's and Rafsanjani's representatives reportedly had come to an understanding with William Casey and George Bush in October 1980 that Iran would receive U.S. arms for its war with Iraq, Bani Sadr had to be banished for their agreement to take force. Unless he was removed from power, as Commander-in-Chief of Iran's armed forces, he would take possession of the arms that would soon begin arriving as a result of his opposition's secret negotiations with the Reagan-Bush camp.

The Ayatollah Beheshti was a powerful religious cleric at the time, second only to Khomeini. According to the Iranian students who took over the U.S. Embassy, he had close ties to the CIA and saw the continuation of the hostage crisis as the best way to consolidate the power of the radical clergy in Iran. Bani Sadr maintains that, in a meeting of the Revolutionary Council, Beheshti and the mullahs sought to exacerbate the hostage crisis as an excuse for removing him from power as President and Commander-in-Chief of Iran's armed forces, and that a tape recording was made of that meeting.[7]

Beheshti and Rafsanjani, who subsequently became the powerful speaker of Iran's Parliament and, in June 1988, also the Commander-in-Chief of Iran's armed forces, clearly saw the same linkage between which U.S. candidate gained credit for a hostage release and which side eventually prevailed in Iran. The fates of Bani Sadr, Carter, and multi-party democracy in Iran were linked—as were those of Reagan, Bush, and the religious theocrats, led by Rafsanjani and Beheshti, with their goal of consolidating political power in a single party, the Islamic Republic Party, led by the radical mullahs.

Back in the United States, President Carter's CIA director, Stansfield Turner, briefed the new President-elect a little more than two weeks after the election.[8] On November 20, 1980, Turner passed to Reagan information about the CIA's most secret and sensitive operations, which probably included a $160 million fund the Agency had set aside for "reconciliation" with Iran.[9] This amount was close to $150 million worth of U.S. arms and spare parts that President Carter, in an official message of October 11, 1980, had told the Iranians that the United States would be willing to deliver upon a resolution of the hostage crisis.[10] Carter's October 11th arms offer, however, was never acknowledged by the Iranians, who instead reportedly met the following week with the man who would become the new director of the CIA, William Casey.

On November 21, 1980, the day after Turner briefed Reagan on the most tightly-held secrets of U.S. covert operations, the new President-elect returned to California. Shortly thereafter, at the instigation of his elite circle of California supporters, Reagan met with Count Alexandre de Marenches, the head of the SDECE—Service of External Documentation and Counterespionage. Though technically a military intelligence agency, SDECE is France's equivalent of the CIA.[11] According to a source who claims to have been told by the Israelis, de Marenches brought with him a copy of an alleged French intelligence report filed with the SDECE on the secret October 1980 Paris meeting between Reagan's campaign manager William Casey, vice-presidential candidate George Bush, French intelligence agents, and Iranian arms procurement officials. In their discussions, the flamboyant Frenchman left Reagan with one other major message: "Don't trust the CIA."[12]

Shortly after the de Marenches meeting with Reagan in California, another critical meeting took place in Washington, D.C., in December, at the request of the Israeli government. The purpose of the meeting was to obtain approval from the future Reagan-Bush Administration for Israel to ship U.S. military equipment to Iran. At the meeting were the then head of Reagan's foreign policy transition team, Richard Allen, soon to become Reagan's first national security adviser, and Morris Amitay, who newly represented the Israeli embassy and had just left his previous post as executive director of the American-Israel Public Action Committee, Israel's top lobby in Washington.[13] It was Allen who had met in early October at the Washington, D.C., L'Enfant Plaza Hotel with Houshang Lavi, a Jewish-Iranian arms dealer who also had long ties to Israel, at which meeting Lavi had offered to arrange the release of the hostages to the Reagan-Bush camp in exchange for U.S. aircraft parts.

Amitay told the *Miami Herald* that he arranged the December 1980 meeting with Richard Allen at the request of General Menachem Meron, Israel's military attaché at its Washington, D.C., embassy and a former head of Israel's Defense Ministry. Amitay said that he asked Allen, who was soon to become Reagan's first national security adviser, "What's the attitude of the [future] Reagan Administration to Israeli shipments of U.S. arms to Iran?" According to Amitay, Allen replied, "Tell your friends I heard what you said."[14] According to Meron, Amitay took Allen's response as authorization with an eye to future plausible deniability and conveyed the same to the general.

In light of Richard Allen's post-election meeting with the Israeli official over U.S. arms shipments to Iran, it may be significant that, according to Bob Woodward's book *Veil,* he later charged that the National Security Agency had intercepted his telephone messages during the transition period and reported them to President Carter. NSA denied the charge.

Richard Allen's meeting with Morris Amitay was not the only December meeting of importance in making arrangements for U.S. arms shipments to Iran during the transition period, and beyond. Sometime during the transition period, Saudi billionaire and middleman Adnan Khashoggi met several times with William Casey in London.[15] Casey, who had already come to know Khashoggi during the Nixon Administration, listened intently to the Saudi's vision of using Israel, with whom he was also on friendly terms, to influence U.S. policy on Iran. By this time, Khashoggi had also already developed a close relationship with Israeli arms dealers Yaacov Nimrodi and Al Schwimmer. Casey, Khashoggi, Nimrodi, and Schwimmer would all figure prominently in the later U.S. arms shipments to Iran that became a focus of the Iran/Contra affair.

Yet another important transition-period meeting involved Alexander Haig, soon to become secretary of state. The *Wall Street Journal* reported that Haig and U.S-Israeli liaison Michael Ledeen met with Italian master criminal Francesco Pazienza on December 9, 1980, about the same time that Richard Allen gave the green light to Amitay in Washington.[16] Significantly, it was Haig who, in February 1981, as secretary of state, subsequently gave the official authorization to Israel to ship U.S. arms to Iran.[17] Ledeen became an adviser in Haig's State Department and later a consultant to President Reagan's third national security adviser, Robert McFarlane, who secretly received Iranian arms dealer Houshang Lavi's arms-for-hostages offer in Washington a month before the election. Ledeen also worked out of Oliver North's office in the Old Executive Office Building next to the White House.

The man with whom Haig and Ledeen reportedly met, Francesco Pazienza, was a top-ranking member of an illegal Italian secret society known as "P-2" which, according to sources who wish to remain unidentified, was involved from the beginning in the Reagan-Bush Administration's secret shipments of U.S. arms to Iran. A scandal involving P-2, whose members included leaders of the Italian administration, military, media, and intelligence community, brought down the Italian government in the first half of 1981, only months after Reagan and Bush gained office. According to these sources, P-2 became involved in billions of dollars worth of arms deliveries from both the U.S. and European NATO countries to Iran in the 1980's. Details of many of these European shipments, and their relationship to P-2 and to "Project Democracy" run by Oliver North from the National Security Council are found in the Chapters VIII and IX.

In an interview with the Israeli newspaper *Ma'ariv*, General Meron, presumably based on Richard Allen's veiled green light to Amitay in Washington in December 1980, said that Israel had shipped U.S. arms to Iran beginning in 1981 with the implicit consent of the Reagan-Bush government.[18] In fact, Israeli deliveries of U.S. arms to Iran began even *before* Richard Allen became national security adviser and Alexander Haig took the post of secretary of state—during the transition period between the November 4, 1980, election and Reagan's inauguration of January 20, 1981.

According to the *London Observer*, Yaacov Nimrodi, an Israeli arms dealer and former military attaché and Mossad station chief in Iran, sold U.S.-made Lance missiles and Copperhead anti-tank shells to the Khomeini regime during the transition period between the 1980 election and Reagan's inauguration.[19] Nimrodi was at the time, and remained throughout the 1985–86 U.S.-Iran arms dealings, Iranian middleman Manucher Gorbanifar's chief Israeli contact.[20] Gorbanifar, a former official in the Shah's secret police, SAVAK, a reported Iranian Jew with links to the Mossad (Israel's intelligence agency), and then head of Iran's arms-buying and intelligence operations in Europe from his comfortable domicile in Paris,[21] had reportedly told CIA agent George Cave in 1980 that he could "buy" freedom for the fifty-two U.S. hostages.[22] He then attended the reported October 19,

1980, meeting in his home city with William Casey, George Bush, French intelligence agents, and representatives of Iran's Ayatollah Beheshti and Hashemi Rafsanjani where $40 million allegedly changed hands.

Besides Gorbanifar and Nimrodi, Cyrus Hashemi, a second reported participant with William Casey in the alleged October 20, 1980, Paris meeting, also began making arrangements to ship U.S. arms to Iran during the transition period between the election and Reagan's inauguration. A multimillionaire banker who claimed to be a cousin of Bani Sadr's rival Hashemi Rafsanjani, Hashemi had also worked closely with Gorbanifar, Khashoggi, and Israeli intelligence, and had been an agent for the CIA since 1975.[23] The FBI made audio and video tapes of conversations in Hashemi's New York trust company offices during the transition period, from November 1980 through January 1981. These tapes reportedly show that he and his brothers, Reza and Djamshid, were then making arrangements to ship U.S. military equipment to the Khomeini regime,[24] including radar equipment, flight direction indicators, night-vision systems, and 60 miles of field communication wire.[25] Hashemi also sold U.S. arms to Iran in 1981 and 1982, the first two years of the Reagan-Bush Administration, claiming that the deliveries were part of an effort to get the original fifty-two hostages released from Iran.[26] In July 1984 he was indicted for these early shipments, but told his attorney, Elliot Richardson of Watergate renown, that they had been secretly sanctioned by the CIA, and he was never prosecuted. CIA Director William Casey had, after all, reportedly met with Hashemi himself at a secret Paris meeting on October 20, 1980, to work out details for the shipments.

In 1981, the first year of the Reagan-Bush Administration, one of Cyrus Hashemi's brothers, Djamshid, also began shipping U.S. arms to Iran. According to the former President of Iran, Abolhassan Bani Sadr, Djamshid made his illegal deals under the false name Mohammad Ali Hashemi-Balanian, representing himself as the president of RRC Company, Inc. of Stamford, Connecticut, and of Yorkhouse Trading Company. According to Bani Sadr, Cyrus Hashemi's brother received letters of credit for his 1981 arms deals with the Khomeini regime through the Lebanese-owned BBC Bank of London and worked with Israeli arms dealers Jamie and Andre Frydel, co-owners of both the British West Indies-registered company JSC International and the Liberian-registered company Kendall Holding, Ltd. Copies of some of the invoices for these early U.S. arms shipments to Iran were obtained by the author from the former President of Iran, Abolhassan Bani Sadr, the earliest dated March 8 and 9, 1981. In 1982, Hashemi-Balanian moved his arms business to London.

Some reports have tried to blame Cyrus Hashemi's transition-period arms arrangements on the Carter Administration. Whereas this is possible, as President Carter's NSC-CIA liaison, Donald Gregg, reportedly attended the October 20, 1980, Paris meeting with Iranian arms procurement officials, a number of facts and reports argue against this conclusion. First, William Casey, soon to become Reagan's CIA director, was also reportedly present with Gregg at the Paris meeting. Second, Gregg was an old friend of George Bush and soon to become the new vice-president's national security adviser. Third, Hashemi's main contact in the Carter Administration was reportedly Stanley Pottinger, also an old friend of George Bush.[27] Fourth, Hashemi's attorney, Elliot Richardson, campaigned for Reagan and Bush and travelled on Reagan's campaign plane. Fifth, documented arms-for-hostages offers to the Carter Administration before the election by Iranian arms dealers Houshang Lavi and Hashemi himself were turned down, whereas Lavi's parallel offer of early October 1980 to Richard Allen of the Reagan-Bush campaign was kept secret from Carter's government. Sixth, Hashemi's major arms deliveries to Iran occurred during the first ten months of the Reagan-Bush Administration, when William Casey's CIA, though knowledgeable, allowed them to proceed without interference. And, seventh, indictments in a $2.5 billion Iran arms sales sting operation, in which the defendants had called Bush to testify as a witness, were dropped shortly before he was inaugurated as President in 1989 because the federal prosecutor said that he knew he "would lose a headline case." Details of Hashemi's 1980 and 1981 arms sales and later collusion with Lavi in this New York sting operation were contained in court affidavits in the case. In summary, it is unlikely that the onus for Cyrus Hashemi's transition-period arms dealings with Iran can be laid at the door of the Carter Administration.

Having already worked with William Casey on the reported arms-for-hostages swap of January 20, 1981, in June 1985 Hashemi made the CIA director a similar offer to free the lesser number of U.S. hostages then held captive in Lebanon. Hashemi was the originator of this second arms-for-hostages proposal—the one that eventually led to the Iran/Contra affair. In exchange for the Americans' freedom, he demanded: 1) the dismissal of his own indictment for the earlier 1981–82 U.S. arms deliveries to Iran, which was granted; 2) the sale of TOW anti-tank missiles to Iran, which was granted in the late 1985 TOW deliveries that became a core focus of the Iran/Contra scandal; and 3) the release of all seventeen pro-Iranian terrorists held in Kuwaiti jails for the bombing of the U.S. embassy in Kuwait in 1983.[28] Of these three conditions for release of the U.S.

hostages held in Lebanon, only the third, of which President Reagan was fully aware, remains unfulfilled at the time of this writing. At a meeting in West Germany in October 1986 shortly after Hashemi's death, and just before the Iran/Contra scandal broke, Oliver North and CIA consultant George Cave told Iranian officials that President Reagan had also agreed to the third and last of the demands. National security adviser John Poindexter also testified to the Congressional Iran/Contra Committees that President Reagan had agreed to do what he could to see that the ''Kuwaiti 17'' were released, which made George Shultz ''sick to his stomach'' (when he heard about it). The continued detention of the ''Kuwaiti 17'' has also been the cause of numerous subsequent Iranian-backed terrorist actions, including the hijacking of a Kuwaiti airliner on April 5, 1988.

Cyrus Hashemi died in London on July 21, 1986, of a ''rare and virulent form of leukemia'' diagnosed only two days before his death. This was only three months before the Reagan-Bush Administration's secret 1985–86 arms-for-hostages deals with Iran became public, and shortly after Hashemi worked with Houshang Lavi on the above-mentioned New York sting operation. Lavi has told the author and other journalists that U.S. agents had Hashemi killed.[29]

In summary, there were at least six meetings, in September, October, November, and December of 1980 involving Reagan-Bush campaign officials and associates at which it is known or can be inferred that arrangements for U.S. arms deliveries to Iran were discussed and concretized: the alleged September 1980 meeting in Zurich between Robert McFarlane and Iranian arms procurement officials; the October 2, 1980, meeting among Iranian arms dealer Houshang Lavi, McFarlane, Reagan-Bush foreign policy adviser Richard Allen, and Allen's aide Laurence Silberman in Washington D.C.; the alleged Paris meetings among William Casey, George Bush, and Bani Sadr's Iranian rivals of late October 1980; the November 1980 meeting between de Marenches and Reagan; the December 1980 meeting between Richard Allen and Israeli agent Morris Amitay; and the reported December 1980 meeting among Alexander Haig, Michael Ledeen, and Francesco Pazienza of P-2. As a result, hundreds of millions of dollars worth of U.S. arms were reportedly delivered to Iran during the transition period between the November 4, 1980, election and Inauguration Day, and throughout 1981.

Though the Carter CIA, in mid-October 1980, set aside $160 million for ''reconciliation'' with Iran—almost exactly the amount of President Carter's never-acknowledged arms offer to Iran of October 11, 1980—it is probable that neither Carter nor President Bani Sadr were privy to the probable use of this money to cover transition-period arms sales. That transition-period arms deliveries to Iran took place and that President Bani Sadr was kept in the dark about them would account for the discrepancy between his and Iranian parliamentary speaker Rafsanjani's assessments of Iran's arms stocks in November 1980. The Foreign Broadcast Information Service reported Rafsanjani as having said that Iran possessed "huge quantities of weapons" at that time.[30] By contrast, President Bani Sadr, the political rival of Rafsanjani and Beheshti, claimed that, as of Iraq's invasion of Iran on September 22, 1980, Iran "had only five to ten days [military] supplies."[31] It was Rafsanjani and Beheshti's representatives, not Bani Sadr's, who had reportedly met with Reagan-Bush campaign manager William Casey in Paris in late October 1980 to work out the first successful arms-for-hostages swap and who would have thus become the likely recipients of those arms. Bani Sadr, in fact, has asserted that "the certitude of an arms supply from the U.S. was a key factor in the decision of the mullah conspiracy to launch the [June 1981] coup which forced me from power."[32]

Iranian democracy and Presidents Bani Sadr and Carter were the triple victims of this reported series of October, November, and December 1980 meetings between their political rivals in both countries. Truly, Ronald Reagan *and* the Ayatollahs were "in like burglars."

V

ONCE UPON A PERFECT TIMING

**"In the eyes of many in the world,
this every-four-year ceremony we accept as normal
is nothing less than a miracle."**

**President Ronald Wilson Reagan
Inaugural Address to the Nation, January 20, 1981**

Two "miracles" happened when Ronald Reagan took the oath of office as President of the United States. The first was made in heaven, the second very much on earth.

As I and other Reagan staffers huddled in the gray chill that twentieth day of January, 1981, awaiting the moment when everything we had worked so long and so hard for was about to come true, an unexpected and heightened sense of anticipation came over me. It had to do with something more than the joyous initiation ritual we were about to experience—it felt as if something else, something "greater," . . . even *miraculous* were about to happen.

I became alert. Far in the distance, on the inaugural platform, for the first time in U.S. history facing west to the White House instead of east, Ronald Reagan stepped to the podium. As he placed his hand upon a well-worn family Bible, a hush fell over the crowd. Was this "it"? Was the "miracle" I sensed about to happen now?

But the oath passed without incident. Then, as Reagan stood before the podium and lowered his head before beginning the inaugural address, the feeling of anticipation heightened. It couldn't be the speech, I thought, for I knew what he was going to say. I had read the draft. But, surely, something momentous was about to happen now.

But the inaugural address, at least from my perspective, seated far back in the crowd, also passed without incident. Still, something told me that "it" had just happened.

After the ceremony, the dignitaries on the platform, including my mentor and boss Dr. Martin Anderson who was about to become Reagan's chief domestic policy adviser, dispersed. They joined Reagan and members of Congress for a post-inaugural event. During the new President's remarks, he was handed a note, which I was later told originated from Richard Allen, Anderson's friend and Reagan's national security adviser who had followed the situation of the hostages. As Reagan read from the note, the crowd burst into applause. The fifty-two American hostages had just been set free in Iran.

Only later would we be told the precise timing of this "miracle." Their plane, which had been held up at Tehran Airport, had received the "go" signal from a guard on the ground holding a radio to his ear with one hand and walkie-talkie in the other. The guard had waited to receive word that Ronald Reagan had just completed his oath of office and was about to begin his inaugural address before giving the signal for the plane to take off.[1] The Iranians, in other words, had waited until the exact moment they could be sure that Ronald Reagan was President to release the hostages to freedom.

The next day, at the White House, when I first heard of this timing, I was stunned. I sat alone at my desk on the second floor of the West Wing, thinking. It had to have been prearranged. The very moment that Reagan had begun his inaugural address, just after completing the oath— when I'd had the feeling that "it" had happened—was the exact instant, halfway around the world, that the plane had been allowed to leave Tehran.

Was that the "event" I had anticipated as Reagan had stepped up to the podium? Incredible as the timing of the release of the hostages was, somehow I knew that this was still not "it." I would have to wait a little longer to find out.

That night was the Inaugural Ball. I was dressed in an emerald green gown—an "original" of which there were at least three identical copies on the dance floor. When Reagan and Nancy arrived at ten o'clock, like starry-eyed lovers at their freshman prom, the room went wild. Throughout the revelry and dancing that followed, my thoughts kept going back to the moment of the oath. Something had to have happened other than the "miracle" of the timing of the hostages' release . . . something *really* miraculous.

The next day, January 21, 1981, I walked through the main gate of the White House on Pennsylvania Avenue for the first time as Special Assistant to the Assistant to the President for Policy Development. I had been in the White House just a few days before, on one of the last days before President Carter left office, as part of a small team sent by Reagan-Bush transition headquarters to receive instruction on operations from the outgoing staff.

As I walked up the stairs to the second floor of the West Wing, where our offices were to be, I was again struck by how incredibly small everything was. Despite the grand images of schoolbook days, the White House is exactly that—a house. And the West Wing, where the Oval Office and main staff offices are located on two floors and a basement, is a small part of that house. Its offices felt more like living rooms in a home than suites.

The first, and main, event that first day was to be a swearing-in ceremony, for major political appointees, in the East Room, one of the few rooms in the White House that definitely was not small. Its size and grandeur had been designed for just such an occasion. My boss and mentor, Martin Anderson, was to be among those sworn in that morning by the Chief Justice—as Assistant to the President for Policy Development, the domestic policy counterpart to the President's White House national security adviser who would be Richard Allen.

That morning, for the first time, I walked past the press quarters, where Jim Brady had his office, through the lanai and the red-carpeted hall of the main mansion, and up the brass-railed stairway to the State level on the second floor. The Marine band was playing across from the great door, which was in the center of the main hall with its brightly painted presidential seal overhead. The East Room, just down the hall, was already filling with new staffers and proud family who had come to watch the ceremony.

I took a seat on one of the folding chairs a few rows back from the front. The new President was not there. His top political advisers were seated on a makeshift platform at the front of the room—among them James Baker, White House Chief of Staff; Ed Meese, Counselor to the President; Richard Allen, the new national security adviser; and the man who had brought me on this amazing journey, Martin Anderson, the new domestic policy adviser. The Chief Justice entered and was introduced by Jim Baker. Then, after a few brief remarks, those seated on the platform were directed to stand and to raise their right hands.

As the direction was given I raised my hand, thinking that this was intended for political appointees in the audience as well. A quick glance to the right and left, however, made it clear that this wasn't the case. Embarrassed, I lowered my hand. But then, in a moment of private commitment, I decided to raise it again and voluntarily take the oath along with the others.

I had just taken an oath to uphold the Constitution of the United States of America to the best of my ability.

The ceremony was surprisingly short: just a brief introduction of the Chief Justice and the administering of the oath. When it was over, to my surprise, Jim Baker announced that those who had taken the oath should form a line under the main door in the entrance hall for a photo opportunity with the President. Amused at the unexpected development, I decided to join the line.

As the President's top political appointees entered the long cue with their family members, I let the newcomers go ahead. As a result, whenever the President looked to the right to see who was next, he always saw me at the end of the line. After twenty minutes of this, he caught my eye with a quizzical look.

As the guests finally dwindled in number, I moved to just behind the purple velvet cord where a Secret Service agent stood with her hand on a large brass ring. When he saw that I was the only person left behind the rope, only a few feet away, the President waved for me to come forward. The Secret Service agent dutifully began to unclasp the rope, but then stopped for a second, thinking. She looked at the President, then at me, and back at Reagan. Again, he motioned for me to come ahead. Again, she hesitated.

"Did you take the oath?" she finally asked, apparently confused.

"I did," I replied firmly.

With graceful but obvious impatience, the President waved his right arm in my direction, nodding. But once again the agent hesitated, torn between her instructions and his clear wish.

"But—did you take the oath—on the platform?" she asked.

"No, ma'am," I said as the President listened intently. "I took the oath on my own, voluntarily, from the audience."

This made the Secret Service agent very uncomfortable. She thought again for a second, looking once more from me to the President, who motioned one last time to get on with the picture.

The agent stiffened. "I'm afraid that we can't allow you—" she began.

I looked at Reagan, he at me. A look of empathy came over his face.

"It doesn't matter," I shrugged. "I don't need to have my picture taken, even though I did take the oath—if it breaks your rules."

I looked at the President one last time and he, too, shrugged, as if to say, "See, I told you. I only do what they tell me."

Though I was disappointed, I was also amused. The Secret Servicewoman had decided that the President of the United States could not overrule her petty bureaucratic instructions. Of all my experiences in Washington over three and one-half years, that first incident, more than any other, embodied the very thing that Ronald Reagan had said for so long that he was coming to Washington to fix. Yet he let it happen. Such a blatant contradiction wouldn't be witnessed again until the world, and I with it, learned that the man who had campaigned on a pledge to stand tough against Iran had sold arms to the Ayatollah Khomeini himself.

I politely thanked the agent and walked a few feet over to one of the large marble pillars in front of the main hall door. So that the President could not see my disappointment, I forced myself to look down and read a copy of the program we had been handed upon entering the East Room.

Though I was looking down, I knew that I was only a few feet away from the cameramen who were packing up their lights, and I was aware that the President had walked to my left a few feet away around the pillar. The Marine band finished a march, and I could hear him thanking the bandmaster for doing such a fine job.

It was then that a human miracle of sorts occurred, in one of those rare moments when the President found a few seconds between pre-scripted cues. As the band struck up again, though I was still looking down, I became aware that a tall figure was approaching me from the front. When he was only a foot away, I looked up. It was the President.

He still had the same look of sympathy in his eyes, and my first thought was that, so close, I wouldn't be able to hide my feelings. Then, suddenly, without saying a word, he raised his hand and nodded. Somehow, I knew what he meant for me to do, and I raised my hand, too. We just stood there, our two hands raised upright, almost touching, while he looked into my eyes and winked. Then he walked on without saying a word.

I stood stunned for a moment, and then, without looking to see where he had gone, walked as fast as I could back to my desk in the West Wing.

What had just happened? Was that "it"? Had I been wrong after all? Did the feeling that a "special event" was coming, which I had experienced just after Reagan took his oath of office the day before, refer to today, not yesterday? As I asked myself this question, still wondering at the meaning of what had just happened, Dr. Anderson returned from the East Room.

"Marty, I've got to tell you what just happened," I intoned.

"Come on in my office," he said jauntily. He motioned for me to take a seat in the Queen Anne chair by his sleek, new, dark mahogany desk.

"So what happened? What did you think of the ceremony?" he asked cheerfully.

"Well—" I began, "I don't know." And I related what had just happened. He thought for a moment, and then, to my surprise, laughed heartily.

"Oh! Well, that's just Reagan!" he said. But I could tell from his expression that there was something else he wanted to tell me, something, perhaps, related to my experience. But he caught himself, as if to say, "Not here."

I returned to my desk, still mulling over the experience, which had deeply touched me. It epitomized Reagan's legendary empathy and character—the simple, spontaneous humanity that was so much a part of his nature. But what did it mean?

Then with a sudden rush I realized—he had led me in the sign of the oath. It was all I could do to keep from crying, it was so wonderful. Yet, as wonderful as it was, I thought, that still wasn't "it."

That first day in the White House was full of meetings and the bustle of housekeeping chores—setting up the offices, changing the locks on safes, checking paper supplies. One evening later in the week, Marty stopped by my desk after it had turned dark. It was common for our White House staff to work long hours, sometimes even late into the night. At first he seemed hesitant, then he spoke.

"Can you come with me to get my car?" he asked.

I was surprised at the request. Dr. Anderson had always been careful to keep his relations with staff confined strictly to business hours. I thought for a moment. His expression told me it was important.

"Of course, Marty. When do you want to go? Now?" I asked.

He nodded. I straightened my desk, grabbed my coat, and followed him down the narrow stairway and into the parking lot on the side street between the White House and the Old Executive Office Building, which towered in the dark.

As we got in the car and Marty started up the engine he explained. "Annelise [Marty's wife, a top political appointee in the Office of Management and Budget] has to work late tonight, and our other car is being repaired. It's ready, and I need someone to drive one of the cars back for me. OK?"

"Sure," I nodded. Then, watching for a cue, I said nothing as we drove on for miles in the night. What was going on? I knew that Marty could have asked Annelise to go get the car with him. I sensed that he must have something on his mind, something he wanted to tell me where no one could hear. A feeling of certainty then came over me. "This is finally going to be 'it'!" I thought. What Marty's about to tell me has something to do with yesterday, when Reagan took the oath of office.

It was everything I could do to keep from asking. We drove on for several more miles in the dark. Finally, when we reached the open freeway, Marty cleared his throat.

"Did you see it?" he asked hesitantly.

I wasn't sure I'd heard him right. "Did I what?"

He spoke louder this time, still looking ahead at the road. "Did you see it?" he repeated.

I didn't know how to answer because I didn't know what he meant.

"Did I see—what?"

"The *oath*," he managed, still looking ahead. "Did you see what happened right after Reagan took the oath of office?"

"No, I didn't—I don't think so. What was it?"

It was then, on the road to Seven Corners, that I learned what "it" had been from the man who had just become the chief domestic policy adviser to the President of the United States. Even though it had happened in front of an audience of thousands, I kept the secret for seven years. I only share it now because he has done so himself. This is what Martin Anderson told me that night, with awe in his voice, in his own words, from his now-published book *Revolution*:

> "Everything was perfect.
>
> "It got even better. President-elect Reagan stood and took the oath of office, administered by the Chief Justice of the United States, Warren Burger. Then came his inaugural address. Reagan walked to the podium, and, as he raised his head to look out at the crowd assembled in front of him and speak, a strange thing happened.
>
> "The dark cloudy sky over his head began to part slightly. Within seconds there was a gaping hole in the gray overcast, and a brilliant, golden shaft of wintery sun burst through the clouds and bathed the inaugural stand and the watching crowd. As Reagan spoke, a slight breeze ruffled his hair and the warm golden light beamed down upon him. Later, a few minutes after he finished speaking, as if on cue from some master lighter backstage, the hole in the clouds shrank, the sky darkened, and Washington grew gray and cold once again.
>
> "It was a fortuitous coincidence of timing and weather, but for those who did not know that, it sure could have looked like a sign from Heaven. At the very least, it was a bright, golden symbol of the passing of the old and the coming of the new, one more proof that even when it came to weather, Reagan was lucky."[2]

This is what Dr. Anderson had said publicly, but that night on the road to Seven Corners, I knew that he knew that it was more than just a lucky coincidence of the weather. Whatever the explanation, he wanted to believe it was more. He wanted to believe that it was a sign from Heaven.

KEYHOLE TO THE KINGDOM

Years later, a retired intelligence officer told me that what happened on the day of President Reagan's inauguration might have been caused by a special kind of satellite. He said that one kind of satellite—he thought it was called a "Keyhole"—uses a beam to burn holes in cloudcover below, so that photographs can be taken regardless of the weather; and that these satellites can "read" the numbers on a car's license plate from 150 miles overhead. I have no way of knowing whether what the agent said is true. If it is, it would explain why the sun shone that noon through what looked like a round hole in the cloudcover. Somehow, though, that explanation didn't satisfy. Like Marty, I wanted to believe that God, not man, was the old "Master Lighter backstage."

The thought of a military satellite taking photographs of the President's speech notes from 150 miles in the sky struck me as incredible, at first. But as I thought about what the retired intelligence official had said, I remembered the other "miracle" that happened just as the "keyhole" had opened up in the heavens. A very human Iranian guard with a very man-made walkie-talkie somehow had received word that Ronald Reagan had just completed his oath of office, and the Iranians had waited until precisely that moment to wave the Algerian plane carrying fifty-two American hostages to freedom.

I had to wonder. Was it really God behind the "miracle" at the inauguration, or was it—the "Party of God"?

The "Party of God," or "Hezbollah," is the name of one of the Ayatollah Khomeini's most radical group of followers—the group responsible, in part, for taking the fifty-two hostages in the first place. Hezbollah was also behind the bombing of the United States embassy and Marine barracks in Beirut in 1983–84 and the taking of a dozen more American hostages in Lebanon during President Reagan's second term in office.

Was it possible that the inaugural timing, which was "too good to be true,'' had to do with some secret arrangement, arrived at between the Iranians and the Reagan-Bush campaign or transition team, not to release the hostages until they were absolutely certain that President Carter could no longer receive credit?

Like a grain of sand in an oyster, that thought simply would not go away. Over the years, piece by piece, other bits of information began building around it. There may not be a worldly explanation for the beam of light at Reagan's inauguration, I realized, but there had to be a down-to-earth explanation for the "coincidence" of the timing of his completing his oath of office and the take-off of the plane.

It wasn't until late 1986 and 1987 that the pieces of the puzzle, which would explain that "coincidence," began appearing in the press, and falling into place.

On November 29, 1986, in a front-page article, the *Washington Post* reported that Richard Allen, who had been Reagan's chief foreign policy adviser in the 1980 campaign, and Robert McFarlane, who later became his third national security adviser, had met secretly in Washington, D.C., in early October 1980 with a self-proclaimed Khomeini emissary who offered to arrange a release of the fifty-two hostages to the Reagan-Bush campaign, and not to Carter, in exchange for arms. Shortly thereafter, the *Miami Herald* reported that Iran's parliamentary speaker, Hashemi Rafsanjani, had been in charge of the timing of the release of the hostages on Iran's end, and that Richard Allen had been the person on Reagan's end who had informed him of their release.

When I read those two articles, I vowed to find every bit of information publicly available to answer the gnawing question: Had Richard Allen said "yes" to the Khomeini emissary's arms-for-hostages offer, despite his public denials? And—was the "lucky" weather more than merely luck?

Ironically, one of the first leads came from Richard Allen himself, the man who became Reagan's first White House national security adviser. On the *MacNeil/Lehrer Newshour* on November 7, 1986, just after the Iran/Contra scandal broke, Allen recalled President Reagan's first full day in the White House—the same day as my "oath" experience after the swearing-in ceremony in the East Room. Allen explained to the nationwide television audience that on that day, January 21, 1981, there was still one other American hostage who had not yet come home, and what President Reagan said when he told him about her plight:

> "When the Iranian hostages—our hostages in Iran—were released on Inauguration Day, one was left behind. It was a journalist. As it turned

out, that journalist, a woman, Mrs. Dwyer of New York, was the wife
of a former classmate of mine in school. I went to the President the next
day [January 21, 1981], and said: 'There's one still not out.'

"And the President said, 'Get the word out that the deal is off unless
she's on the plane.' ''

I was stunned, first, that the moderator hadn't picked up on what was
being said and had not asked the obvious question: "What deal?" Second,
I suddenly realized that the same man, Richard Allen, who had met, in the
last two weeks before the 1980 election, with an Iranian claiming to
represent the Khomeini regime offering an arms-for-hostages deal, "happened" to be the friend of the husband of the one hostage Iran had held
behind. He also "happened" to be the person who had informed President
Reagan of the all-too-perfectly-timed release of the plane carrying the
other fifty-two hostages to freedom.

If there had been a deal—if Allen or someone else in the Reagan-Bush
campaign had said "yes" to Khomeini, maybe not at that first Washington, D.C., meeting, but at a later one with "the right Iranians"—it would
make sense of everything. President Carter claimed that the Algiers Accord, the formal agreement between Iran and the United States that ended
the hostage crisis which was signed in late January 1981 just before he left
office, contained no promise of U.S. arms. But at the time of the accord,
Iraq had just begun its war with Iran, and the Ayatollah's army was in
desperate need of U.S.-made arms and spare parts for its military equipment, which was almost 100-percent U.S. made: U.S.-made weapons
needed U.S.-made spare parts. One would not expect the wily Iranians,
known to be some of the shrewdest bargainers on earth and desperate for
arms, to settle for billions of dollars less of their money than President
Carter had frozen when the hostages were taken (which they did) without
extracting a secret promise for at least that dollar difference in weapons.
One would also expect these canny negotiators to hold something back as
"collateral" against President Reagan's coming through with his end of
the bargain after the inauguration and after the hostages were released.
Otherwise, the Iranians would have no guarantee that the new President
would keep his word. And here was Richard Allen, Reagan's first national
security adviser, admitting on national television that the President had
referred to "a deal" on his first full day in office.

Something important was going on that first day in the White House—
January 21, 1981—the day that Richard Allen later said Reagan told him
to tell the Iranians "the deal was off" unless Mrs. Dwyer was released in

Iran. I knew that Allen, the new national security adviser, was scheduled to meet with the National Security Council and other top advisers that day to discuss two major agenda items: Libya and Iran . . . and that Manucher Gorbanifar, the man later at the center of the Iran/Contra scandal and Iran's number-one arms buyer in Europe, was also on the agenda.[3]

Why the need to focus on Iran so soon if, as the public had been led to believe, there was nothing more to be discussed on the hostage question? As far as the public knew, the fifty-two hostages were safely home, and Iran had received its unfrozen assets, as agreed to by President Carter under the Algiers Accord, signed shortly before he left office.

In *Caveat*, President Reagan's first secretary of state, Alexander Haig, writes that on that same day, January 21, 1981, some of President Reagan's top advisers argued that *"Carter's* agreement" [author's emphasis added] with Iran on the hostage release should not be kept, and that he, Haig, was "horrified" at the suggestion and argued strongly against it. In his book, he also said that William Casey, Reagan's new CIA director, and Richard Allen, the new national security adviser, were the two other top officials who found the idea of not keeping "President Carter's" agreement with Iran "unthinkable."[4]

What "Carter agreement" could they have been referring to? By January 21, 1981, as far as the media and the public knew, Iran had already received that part of its unfrozen assets it had agreed to accept under the Algiers Accord and had agreed to put the rest in escrow accounts to await future court decisions, which could be expected to take a long time. So what "Carter agreement" could Casey, Haig, and Allen have been referring to?

The first possibility for a "Carter agreement" is President Carter's public announcement only a few days before the election that the United States would be willing to allow Iran to receive some $250 million in U.S. arms and spare parts that it had already paid for under the Shah upon the safe release of the hostages. But this was not a formal offer and would certainly not have bound the incoming administration.[5]

A second possibility for a "Carter agreement" could have been an early "scenario," as it was called, signed in January 1980 by President Carter and then President of Iran Abolhassan Bani Sadr. This "scenario" outlined a proposed process for releasing the fifty-two hostages. One of its conditions involved a U.S. agreement to unblock $400 million in U.S. arms and spare parts belonging to Iran—of which the $240 million referred to above were part—which President Carter had frozen in the pipeline when the hostages were first taken. However, that proposal fell through as a result of disagreements among President Carter's advisers, and no spare parts were delivered to Iran while President Bani Sadr was still head of state.[6] As he remained in office until late June 1981, well into the Reagan-Bush Administration, it is highly improbable, if not impossible, that this early "scenario" could have been what Haig, Casey, and Allen referred to as "Carter's agreement."

As a third possibility, it is conceivable that there was a secret part to the Algiers Accord signed by President Carter. Was it possible that he, and not the Reagan-Bush campaign, had made a secret promise of arms and spare parts to the Khomeini regime—an agreement that was not part of the publicly acknowledged accords? If this were true, such a secret agreement to return, grant, or sell U.S. arms to Iran under the next administration, whoever won the election, would have to have been negotiated, at least in part, by one of President Carter's own officials. The Foreign Broadcast Information Service reported in mid-October 1980, a few weeks before the election, that President Carter's CIA *had* set aside $160 million for "reconciliation" with Iran within the context of the arms it needed for its war with Iraq.[7] Could the "Carter agreement" Haig referred to have had something to do with this $160 million fund? If so, one thing was certain. A Carter official closely connected with the CIA would have to have been involved in the negotiations.

One man in President Carter's White House fit that bill—someone who would shortly become Vice-President Bush's national security adviser. He not only had intimate knowledge of the Middle East,[8] but was the CIA's liaison to President Carter's National Security Council. His name was Donald Gregg.

But what if President Carter didn't win the election? Such a top CIA official, whether Donald Gregg or someone else, couldn't have been certain before the election that President Carter would win. Therefore, if Carter did make a secret arms agreement with Iran, how would he have been able to guarantee the Iranians that Reagan and Bush, should *they* win, would abide by a "Carter agreement"? The answer would be for someone high up, very high up, in a potential future Reagan-Bush Administration to also attend the negotiations and to convince the Iranians that he, too, would live up to such an agreement. The Iranians would likely demand that such a top official from the Reagan-Bush campaign be able to speak on behalf of a future Reagan Central Intelligence Agency. Again, there was one man who fit the bill: William Casey. Casey was *the* top Reagan-Bush campaign official, the campaign manager, and there was little question, for those in the know, that he was in line to become Reagan's CIA director.[9]

Given these facts, it should not be surprising that a number of sources claim that precisely these two men—William Casey, representing the Reagan-Bush campaign, and Donald Gregg, representing the CIA and nominally the Carter Administration, attended a secret meeting in Paris, France, on October 19 and/or 20, 1980, only two weeks before the election, with Iranian arms procurement officials to finalize just such a secret arms-for-hostages agreement. For details of these claims and an assessment of their credibility, see Chapter II.

If this information is correct—if a meeting between Casey, Gregg, and the Iranians did occur—whether in Paris on October 19/20 or anywhere else before the election—why would President Carter have agreed to a secret arrangement that would result in the release of the hostages in such a way that he would receive none of the credit? Surely, if he was knowledgeable of such a meeting at all, he would only have agreed to release arms to the Iranians on the understanding that the hostages would be delivered to him. In other words, why would President Carter, after all his efforts to reach an early resolution of the hostage crisis, have agreed before the election to a release of the hostages to Reagan and Bush, almost certainly ensuring his own defeat?

The answer, of course, unless he is a saint, is that he did not. President Carter, in fact, has made it clear that he did not expect the hostages to be released when they were: immediately after he left office. In an interview on the nationwide Michael Jackson radio show on September 2, 1988, he implied that he expected the hostages to be released to *him*, before Reagan took the oath of office: "I thought it was strange, two things. One, that all of the hostages were in an airplane in the airport in Tehran about 10 o'clock the morning of my going out of office, on Reagan's inauguration, and the Ayatollah deliberately held them there until a few minutes after 12 o'clock. And they actually took off and cleared while the inauguration ceremony was still in progress. That seemed very strange to me. And second, now it lately has been revealed that for a good portion of the last eight years we [the U.S., i.e. Reagan-Bush Administration] have either directly or indirectly been delivering weapons to the Ayatollah. That's another strange—maybe—coincidence."

Clearly, if President Carter did authorize Donald Gregg, or anyone else, to meet secretly with the Iranians before the election, it was *not* to agree to a hostage release to Reagan and Bush. And, if he was himself knowledgeable of a "Carter agreement" on arms for Iran, as Alexander Haig intimates in *Caveat*, it would surely have been on the understanding that the hostages would be released not to them, but to him.

If President Carter's National Security Council-CIA liaison, Donald Gregg, did negotiate a secret "Carter agreement" for arms with Iran, it is also clear that President Carter was not aware that a Reagan-Bush campaign official or officials were involved.

In an interview on the nationwide Larry King radio program, on June 15, 1988, President Carter revealed that he had been aware of efforts purely on the part of the Reagan-Bush campaign before the election to hold up release of the hostages so that he would not win the election: "There were reports made to me before the [1980] election that this was going on. That the hostages would not be released [to me] and that weapon sales would be restored to Iran, either directly or through the Israelis." Richard Brenneke, who claims to have been at the October 20, 1980, meeting in Paris with William Casey, Donald Gregg, and Iranian officials, confirmed that he had been told that President Carter was not aware of Gregg's presence at the negotiations.

The "Carter agreement" referred to by Alexander Haig could not have been a secret part of the Algiers Accord, which formally settled the hostage crisis. Captain Gary Sick, who was President Carter's Iran expert on the National Security Council throughout the hostage crisis, emphatically denies that there was any secret codicil to the Algiers Accord.[10] In any case, the Algiers Accord makes no mention of arms. Sick, in fact, points out that President Carter's only actual offer of arms and spare parts to the Iranians—a presidential message of October 11, 1980, offering $150 million in U.S. weapons upon safe release of the hostages—*was received but never acknowledged by the Iranians*. Sick considers this official silence to be one of the great mysteries of the entire hostage crisis. And though President Carter's $150 million offer is close to the amount of the secret CIA "reconciliation" fund for Iran, $160 million, he clearly could not, and would not, have made an agreement based upon an offer that the Iranians never even acknowledged having received. Besides, Carter's CIA was reported to have discussed the $160 million CIA "reconciliation" fund within the context of a hostage release before, not after, the election.[11] On October 11, 1980, the Foreign Broadcast Information Service noted that the Kuwaiti paper *Al-Qabas* reported that the head of Khomeini's secret police (SAVAMA), General Hoseyn Fardust, had recently met with CIA officials in Washington, D.C., to discuss a plan to release the hostages *before* the November 4, 1980, election; and that Fardust's U.S. visit was with Khomeini's knowledge and in the clear context of Iran's need for U.S. arms and spare parts.[12] When the hostages were not released before the election, any understanding reached between the Carter CIA and Fardust would have become moot.

Another possibility for what Haig, Casey, and Allen referred to as "Carter's agreement" could have been a response to Iran's request to Israel for U.S. arms and spare parts made only a little over a month before the election. The Khomeini regime did, in fact, approach then Israeli Prime Minister Menachem Begin immediately after the beginning of the Iran-Iraq war, which started September 22, 1980, with a request for some $200 million worth of U.S. military equipment.[13] Iran, 95 percent of whose arms were U.S.-made, had only five to ten days of spare parts in its arsenal when the war broke out and had nowhere to turn *but* to Israel *because* of Carter's arms embargo. Shortly after Khomeini's request, on September 29, 1980, Deputy Israeli Defense Minister Tzipori announced that Israel would be prepared to help Iran with arms.[14] Israel responded to Khomeini's request in October 1980 by immediately shipping 250 spare tires for Iran's U.S.-made F-4 Phantom jets, worth $300,000, without obtaining prior authorization from the United States, as required by law.[15] In mid-October, Begin sent President Carter a cable informing him, after the fact, that a planeload of U.S. military equipment had already been sent to Iran, and requesting permission for additional shipments. The letter read, "Two weeks ago we were approached by Iran, for [U.S.-made] military equipment and spare parts in particular. As friends of the U.S., we believe that the common interest of the free world lies in the support of the present regime in Iran. We agreed to the request and one plane has already left for its destination. We ask your approval for another delivery."[16] An unnamed State Department official recalled Begin's approach to *The New York Times*, "We [the U.S.] felt it would not be a good idea to add the Israelis to an already complex mix and told them to please hold off while we were going about our business to free the hostages . . . I think they did go ahead with one shipment. They asked us almost after the fact, when they were down the line and were right in the middle of the thing." President Carter did not use such diplomatic language when he received Begin's message. He was furious with the Israeli prime minister for interfering with his attempts to negotiate a hostage settlement with Iran, and he immediately ordered Secretary of State Muskie to ask Begin to stop until the hostages were freed.[17] Though Prime Minister Begin officially agreed to do so, U.S. intelligence sources told *Time* that Israel continued to sell tank parts and ammunition to Iran. In his memoirs, President Carter's national security adviser, Zbigniew Brzezinski, recalled the event: "We learned, much to our dismay, that the Israelis had been secretly supplying American spare parts to the Iranians without much concern for the negative impact this was having on our leverage with the Iranians on the hostage issue.''

It is possible, because the hostages *were* freed at Ronald Reagan's inauguration, that the ''understanding'' Israel had, that it could then restart the halted U.S. arms deliveries to Iran, may have been construed by Alexander Haig, Richard Allen, and William Casey as ''Carter's agreement.'' It was not, however, a formal agreement, nor, by the time the hostages were finally released to President Reagan and not to President Carter, was it ''Carter's agreement'' at all.

The most convincing evidence that President Carter made no formal arms-for-hostages agreement with Iran is that he turned down a number of such agreements actually offered to him. During the month of October 1980, the Carter Administration considered an arms-for-hostages offer by Houshang Lavi, the same Iranian arms dealer who approached the Reagan-Bush and John Anderson campaigns with a similar offer, *but turned it down*. The reason the Carter Administration turned it down was because Lavi, they eventually ascertained through a friendly embassy in Tehran, did not represent then President of Iran Abolhassan Bani Sadr, with whom Carter wanted to officially deal. However, by the end of October 1980 Mr. Bani Sadr did not hold the power over the fate of the hostages. That rested with his rivals, Hashemi Rafsanjani and Ayatollah Beheshti—the very men who reportedly sent representatives to meet with William Casey, George Bush, and Donald Gregg in Paris two weeks before the 1980 election. So, clearly, if President Carter insisted on dealing with President Bani Sadr in the Lavi matter, as he did, and as his NSC Iran expert and documents firmly support, he would never have authorized Donald Gregg, or anyone else, to reach a secret agreement with Bani Sadr's rivals. If Donald Gregg did attend the pre-election Paris meeting with William Casey and Bani Sadr's political enemies, it was therefore almost certainly without the knowledge of the President.

Houshang Lavi's arms-for-hostages offer was not the only one turned down by the Carter Administration before the 1980 election. The Carter Administration turned down yet another arms-for-hostages offer in October 1980 by a second arms dealer, Cyrus Hashemi.[18] Hashemi, like Lavi also reportedly met with Casey and Gregg in Paris and shipped U.S. arms to Iran during both the transition period *and* the first ten months of the new Reagan-Bush Administration while Casey looked the other way. Finally, President Carter has stated many times, including on national television, that he neither sent nor contemplated sending arms to Iran.

There appears to be only one solution that makes sense of these facts and reports, assuming that they are correct: that President Carter's NSC-CIA liaison, Donald Gregg, did negotiate a secret arms-for-hostages agreement with the Iranians and William Casey of the Reagan-Bush campaign, as has been reported, but did so, contrary to President Carter's wishes, with Bani Sadr's rivals, not with Bani Sadr, and on the understanding that the hostages would be released to Reagan and Bush, not to President Carter. Then, once Reagan and Bush were inaugurated, Casey would oversee the implementation of "Carter's agreement" from the CIA, and Gregg would shortly join the staff of Vice President Bush. Because their agreement may have been based on the never-acknowledged October 11, 1980, Carter offer of $150 million in arms and/or the $160 million CIA "reconciliation fund," it could have been loosely referred to by Haig on January 21, 1981, as "Carter's agreement." This would explain why those very officials who would have been knowledgeable about the "turning" of President Carter's never-acknowledged arms-for-hostages offer against him— Casey, Haig, and Allen—were the very Reagan-Bush officials who insisted on Reagan's first full day in office that not keeping "Carter's agreement" with Iran would be "unthinkable."

On the same day, January 21, 1981, that Richard Allen insisted that not keeping "Carter's agreement" with Iran would be "unthinkable," Reagan ordered Allen to tell Iran "the deal" was off unless the spouse of Allen's friend, then still held hostage, was freed in Tehran. I believe that history will show that the "Carter agreement," which Casey, Allen, and Haig referred to that same day, *was* "the deal." It was probably based on a combination of President Carter's never-acknowledged and thus forgotten arms offer to Iran and Israel's self-serving "understanding" that it could resume U.S. arms shipments to the Khomeini regime once the hostages were freed. But it had long since become twisted from anything President Carter had had in mind, if he had knowledge of "his" agreement at all.

Whatever the agreement behind President Reagan's threat to call off "the deal" with Iran on his first full day in office, both the Congressional Iran/Contra Committees and Iran/Contra special prosecutor Lawrence Walsh probably know what it is and have covered it up. Both requested White House records, including tape recordings of White House telephone conversations, dating back to Reagan's first day in office[19]—that is, to the very day that the President ordered Richard Allen to call Iran to tell them "the deal" was off unless Allen's friend's wife was released from prison in Tehran. White House spokesman Larry Speaks said that the administration would make any such taped records available to the investigators and acknowledged that some presidentially initiated telephone calls to heads of state had been recorded using a "patching system" to the White House basement situation room.[20] White House counsel Arthur Culvahouse, Jr., told the *Washington Post* that the Administration was complying with these requests from the Congressional Iran/Contra Committees and the special prosecutor for all relevant audio recordings dating back to President Reagan's first day in office.[21] This was the last that the public heard of requests for evidence linking the President's arms-for-hostages deals to events in 1980 or 1981. Despite their requests, both the Iran/Contra Committees and special prosecutor Walsh then focused only on events dating back to 1984: The Committee limited itself to revelations from 1984 forward, and the special prosecutor was restricted by formal mandate to bring criminal charges based only on actions and events dating back to 1984. That mandate had been drafted by the man who would know, more than any other, the true origins of the President's arms-for-hostages negotiations with the Khomeini regime: Attorney General Edwin Meese, Richard Allen's boss in the 1980 Reagan-Bush campaign.

To this day, I believe that the ray of light, which shone down on Ronald Reagan as he began his inaugural address that cold, wintry day in January 1981, was a genuine act of God. But the release of the hostages only moments before, as he completed his oath of office, was almost certainly an act, not of God, but of the "Party of God" and of his own.

VI

THE SMOKING GUNS

"During the course of our secret discussions,
I authorized the transfer of small amounts of defensive weapons
and spare parts for defensive systems to Iran. . .
These modest deliveries, taken together,
could easily fit into a single cargo plane."

**President Ronald Reagan,
November 13, 1986**

Many covert operations, by their very nature, are lies. Even the "revelations" of the Iran/Contra affair were part of a covert operation on a vast scale.

The "Big Lie" of the Iran/Contra scandal was the general impression left with the public that Israeli shipments of U.S. arms to Iran did not begin until 1985, and then only reluctantly in an attempt to get Americans who were first taken hostage in 1984 out of Lebanon. The Senate Intelligence Committee, the Tower Commission, and the Iran/Contra special prosecutor's investigation therefore focused only on events from 1984 forward. This arbitrary time limit on where they looked for an explanation of the origins of U.S. arms deliveries to Iran, whether self-imposed or by outside mandate, was justified on the grounds that the alleged "Contra diversions" didn't take place until Reagan's second term. The real purpose of these 1984-forward limitations, in fact, was to divert attention away from reports that massive quantities of U.S. arms and spare parts had been being shipped to Iran from the United States and Europe, as well as from Israel, beginning almost immediately after Mr. Reagan and Mr. Bush gained the White House, in 1981. Had the Iran/Contra Committees or the special prosecutor been allowed to consider these earlier shipments, they would not have been able to avoid asking the smoking question: Why were

U.S. arms being shipped to Iran in 1981 and 1982 when there were *no* U.S. hostages either in Tehran *or* in Lebanon?

From the moment of President Carter's defeat on November 4, 1980, the Iran desk at the CIA considered President-elect Reagan and Vice-President-elect Bush to be the new chief executives of the United States.[1] According to Mansur Rafizadeh, the former U.S. chief of the Shah of Iran's secret police (SAVAK), after the election, the CIA immediately persuaded Sadegh Ghotbzadeh, Khomeini's foreign minister at the time, to obtain a promise from Khomeini to further delay the release of the fifty-two hostages until Ronald Reagan's inauguration.[2] Rafizadeh explains, not without humor, that Khomeini had agreed *before* the election to release the hostages to Reagan and Bush and not to Carter, but had incorrectly assumed that President Carter would either be killed or imprisoned the moment he was defeated at the polls, as probably would have been the case in Iran. Thus the need for Ghotbzadeh's active intervention to get Khomeini to agree to further delay the release of the American hostages until Reagan's inauguration.[3] President Carter's Iran expert at the National Security Council throughout the hostage crisis, Captain Gary Sick, confirms that the Iranians were genuinely surprised to learn that Ronald Reagan would not take office on November 5, 1980, the day after the presidential election. There was, of course, a price for the additional delay—arms and intelligence, which the Khomeini regime desperately needed to fight its wars against both Iraq and its political opposition at home and abroad.

As we have already seen, U.S. arms began flowing to Iran not in late 1985, but immediately after the 1980 presidential election, during the transition period between November 4, 1980, and the inauguration on January 20, 1981. Chapter IV sets forth what is known of U.S. arms and spare parts deliveries to Iran by Israel, Israeli-linked arms dealers, and U.S.–based arms suppliers during this three-month period before President Reagan's inauguration. The present and following chapters take up where Chapter IV leaves off, addressing what is known of U.S. arms deliveries to Iran once Ronald Reagan, George Bush, and William Casey took office in January 1981.

The second "Big Lie" of revelations in the Iran/Contra scandal was the general impression left with the public that the United States had, against its better judgement, shipped a scant $30 million worth of U.S. arms to the Khomeini regime—only enough to "fit into a single cargo plane." That is not even close to the actual dollar amount, which was not millions, but billions.

When the Shah was forced to flee his country in 1978, almost 100 percent of Iran's military equipment was American-made. The planes and arms Khomeini inherited, therefore, had to have American-made spare parts to keep them in working order. When Iraq invaded Iran in late September 1980, a little over a month before the 1980 U.S. presidential election, Iran had "only five to ten days [worth of military] supplies" according to the Commander-in-Chief of the country's armed forces at the time, Abolhassan Bani Sadr.[4] By the time Reagan had won the election, Iran was therefore in desperate need of U.S.-made spare parts to fight its burgeoning war with Iraq, which had just started on September 22, 1980.

There is no question that Iran received billions of dollars worth of U.S. military equipment long before the relatively minor deliveries of U.S. TOW and HAWK missiles, which became one of the main focuses of the Iran/Contra scandal. Mr. Bani Sadr, who was President of the Islamic Republic of Iran from January 1980 until June 1981, answered the question of whether there were any "smoking guns" best when he said: "Iran fought the war with Iraq for *eight* years with American arms. What else do you need?"[5] Precisely how many billions of dollars worth of American-made arms Iran received over the seven-and-one-half years of the Iran-Iraq War, which virtually coincided with the eight years of the Reagan-Bush Administration, varies somewhat depending on the source. All reliable sources agree, however, that the volume was not only magnitudes greater, but began years earlier than the Reagan-Bush Administration led the American public and the Congress to believe.

The New York Times reported that Iran purchased over $9 billion in U.S. and Western European arms between 1981 and 1988, and that European NATO countries accounted for only about 20 percent of that total.[6] This leaves over $7 billion in military equipment which had to have come from the U.S., either directly or through Israel and other "third countries." *The New York Times* also estimated that Iran received some $313 million in military equipment from nine nations, including the United States, prior to 1983—that is, three years before the so-called "first" U.S. arms shipment to Iran of late 1985 acknowledged by the Reagan-Bush White House. President Reagan's CIA director William Casey himself told *Time* magazine that Iran annually purchased between $3 and $4 billion in arms.[7] A quick accounting based on the first *New York Times* report cited above reveals that one-third to one-fourth of $3–$4 billion in arms, or about $1 billion a year, went to Iran from the U.S. and/or its client state, Israel. *Business Week* reported that Iran had received $30 billion in arms since the beginning of the Iran-Iraq War, of which Israeli deliveries accounted for some 20 percent of the total, or at least $6 billion.[8] This $6–$7 billion figure for Israel's arms traffic with the Khomeini regime tallies with that of the other reports, and as we shall see, many of these Israeli deliveries were of U.S.-made, not Israeli-made, arms and spare parts.

A quick look at the trade figures for Iran and the United States from 1979 to 1986 shows that in one year only, 1981, the first year of the Reagan-Bush Administration, Iran received a large boost in exports from the United States.[16] In that year alone the U.S. shipped Iran $300 million in U.S.-made products. These figures do not reflect what percentage of that $300 million is represented by arms.

Trade Deficit with Iran
1979–1986
$4.97 billion dollars

(numbers below are in millions of dollars)

	1979	1980	1981	1982	1983	1984	1985	1986
Imports	$2784	339	64	585	1130	700	725	569
Exports	$1021	23	300	122	190	162	74	34
Deficit	–$1763	– 316		– 463	–940	–538	–651	–535
Surplus			+236					

Total Deficit $4,970 million = $4.97 *billion*

The Secretary-General of the World Association of Jews from Islamic Countries (WAJIC) has stated that early on the Reagan-Bush Administration promised Iran $5 billion in military equipment and financing for its war with Iraq.[9] This same $5 billion figure comes up again in reports of Robert McFarlane's late May 1986 mission with Oliver North to Tehran— the now-famous trip with the cake. The Greek Newspaper *Dimikratikos Logos* reported that a tape-recording of Mr. McFarlane's negotiations with Iran during that trip reveals that he reminded Iranian officials that they had already received $1.3 billion in U.S. arms from a total commitment of $5 billion.[10] The Israeli on that mission, a man who would therefore know about the $5 billion promise and who had personally briefed Vice-President Bush during Bush's trip to Israel on July 29, 1986,[11] Amiram Nir, died under questionable circumstances in a plane crash in Mexico on November 30, 1988, not long after telling Bob Woodward of the *Washington Post* that he intended to go public in the future with what he knew about the mission.[12] Nir told Woodward that "less than half" of the truth about Mr. McFarlane's May 1986 trip to Tehran and U.S.-Israeli arms transactions with the Khomeini regime was yet publicly known.[13] According to *Time* magazine, $5 billion happens also to be the value of U.S. military equipment that the Shah of Iran had ordered before his fall from power. Finally, a $5–$6 billion figure is also the amount of still-frozen assets that Iran, as of October 1988, claims that it is owed by the United States.[14]

Having established that U.S. arms shipments to Iran over the eight years of the Reagan-Bush Administrations were worth not millions but *billions* of dollars, we will now turn to what is known of U.S. government involvement in arms deliveries to Iran beginning in 1981. In this chapter, we will first review reports of 1981 arms deals involving participants at the alleged pre-election meetings between Iranian officials and Reagan-Bush campaign representatives in October 1980. We will then look at reports of early Israeli deliveries of U.S. military equipment to Iran. Chapters VII and VIII then detail what is known about U.S. government involvement in massive diversions of American and other Western arms to Iran throughout the period of the 1980's, again long before the so-called "first" U.S. arms deliveries to the Khomeini regime of late 1985.

U.S. ARMS DELIVERIES TO IRAN IN 1981-82 WHICH MAY HAVE RESULTED FROM PRE-1980-ELECTION MEETINGS BETWEEN REAGAN-BUSH CAMPAIGN REPRESENTATIVES AND IRANIAN OFFICIALS

Cyrus Hashemi

According to Oregon businessman and sometimes arms dealer Richard Brenneke, who became a key source for some of the most startling revelations in the Iran/Contra affair, Cyrus Hashemi attended an October 20, 1980, meeting in Paris, France, with Brenneke, Reagan-Bush campaign manager William Casey, Carter CIA-NSC liaison Donald Gregg, Iran's chief European arms buyer Manucher Gorbanifar, Iranian officials representing President Bani Sadr's rivals Hashemi Rafsanjani and the Ayatollah Beheshti,[17] and for part of the time, Iranian arms dealer Houshang

Lavi. According to Brenneke, the purpose of the pre-election meeting was to finalize arrangements for U.S. arms shipments to the Khomeini regime based on the clear understanding that Iran would not release the hostages until Ronald Reagan was inaugurated as President. Though there is as yet no concrete proof that this meeting took place as Brenneke alleges, one of the reported participants, Cyrus Hashemi, did begin arrangements to ship U.S. arms to Iran immediately after Reagan's election victory. The FBI reportedly taped his telephone conversations from November 1980 through January 1981, which show that he and his brothers Reza and Djamshid were arranging U.S. arms deliveries to Iran during that transition period between the election and Reagan's inauguration.[18] Hashemi then went on to ship U.S. arms to Iran throughout the first ten months of the new Reagan-Bush Administration, later claiming, shortly before his untimely death in 1986 just before the Iran/Contra scandal broke, that his early deliveries were necessary to get the original fifty-two hostages released on Reagan's inauguration day.[19] After Reagan and Bush gained office, William Casey's CIA was aware of Hashemi's 1981 shipments and did nothing to stop them.

Richard Brenneke

Richard Brenneke, who says that he was at the same October 20, 1980, meeting in Paris attended by Cyrus Hashemi, Gorbanifar, Casey, Gregg, Lavi, and Iranian officials likewise claims to have flown U.S. arms to Iran in 1981.[20] He claims that William Casey and the CIA, among others, worked with a London company called Jericho International in 1981 and 1982 to arrange for U.S. arms deliveries to Iran, and that a CIA operative directed much of this early U.S. weapons traffic out of the U.S. embassy in London.[21]

The author obtained a partial record of Mr. Brenneke's flights covering this early period, which he had provided to a former U.S. Customs agent. These records, if accurate, show a trip from Bandar Abbas, Iran, to Ankara on October 10-11, 1981; and a trip from Lyon, France, to Tehran in March of 1982. (Cyrus Hashemi also claimed to have arranged U.S. arms deliveries to Iran in 1982.[22]) Mr. Brenneke's partial flight logs also show that he made numerous round trips between Nice, France, and Iran in 1980, before the 1980 election. Mr. Brenneke told a reporter for a major news weekly in 1988 that he also flew arms to Iran from a Czechoslovakian arms company named Omnipol before the 1980 election, to benefit the Reagan-Bush campaign. Former U.S. Customs special agents Gary

Howard and Ron Tucker have uncovered information that international arms dealer Ian Smalley, known as "Dr. Doom," was shipping tank engines to Iran through Nice, France, during the same period that Brenneke's 1980 flight logs show Nice-Iran deliveries. (See "Dr. Doom Gets Off," below.)

In an interview with Oklahoma City radio journalist Jerry Bohnen of October 6, 1988, Mr. Brenneke stated that for a period of approximately a year and a half beginning in March 1981, he flew 707's and DC-8's with cargoes of U.S. arms to Iran. He claims that he was brought into the operation by French arms dealer Bernard Veillot and piloted some dozen flights in the early 1980's, mostly from France. His flights to Tehran and Bandar Abbas, Iran, Brenneke told Bohnen, included stop-offs in Nice, Ankara, or Cyprus. He said he was aware that his cargo was arms, which included shoulder-fired missiles, rifles, ammunition, aircraft tires, and military spare parts. The arms were usually pre-loaded in France, though Mr. Brenneke said that he sometimes stopped in Nice, Turkey, or Germany to pick up weapons. His co-pilots, whom he knew only on a first-name basis, were selected by the CIA. He says that he sometimes flew with Harry Rupp, the pilot who claims to have flown Reagan-Bush campaign manager William Casey to Paris in October 1980, and with Frenchman Bernard Veillot.

Brenneke's interview with Bohnen leaves no doubt that he understood that his 1981 arms deliveries to Iran were in exchange for the release of the fifty-two U.S. hostages on January 20, 1981, the day of Ronald Reagan's inauguration as President:

> *Bohnen:* "Were you ever told during the course of these flights you were making . . . how high up in the [Reagan-Bush] Administration they were aware of this?"

> *Brenneke:* ". . . Bill Casey, who was a cabinet member by that time, certainly was aware of it. He'd been sitting in Paris [allegedly on October 20, 1980] talking about it."

Brenneke declined to comment when asked whether any of his arms flights originated at U.S. military bases in Europe, whether he was assisted by the U.S. military in any way, or if any of his deliveries were undertaken on behalf of a country other than the United States, specifically Israel.

In an earlier interview with the author, Mr. Brenneke added that he was not the only pilot flying U.S. arms to Iran as a result of negotiations at the alleged pre-election meetings between Reagan-Bush campaign officials, Reagan-Bush sympathizers in the CIA, and Iranian representatives. He stated that some of the planes making arms deliveries flew Paris-Istanbul-Tehran as well as Paris-Tehran or Nice-Tehran routes.

Mr. Brenneke claims that one of the arms companies reflected in early invoices covering U.S. arms deliveries to Iran, made available to the author by the former President of Iran, Abolhassan Bani Sadr—Kendall Holding, Ltd.—is related to one of the companies with which he himself did business: Kendall International Arms Company of Kentucky. Intriguingly, a knowledgeable source told a major news weekly that Richard Brenneke and Houshang Lavi "talked constantly" with one another in the mid-1980's, which means that they may have known and worked with one another earlier.[23] Lavi is the alleged Khomeini emissary who offered an arms-for-hostages deal to Reagan-Bush campaign foreign policy adviser Richard Allen, Allen's aide Laurence Silberman, and then aide to Senator John Tower, Robert McFarlane, in Washington, D.C., a month before the 1980 presidential election, and, according to one report, attended at least part of the October 20, 1980 Paris meeting with William Casey, Mr. Brenneke, and Iranian officials.

Manucher Gorbanifar

According to Richard Brenneke and Mr. Bani Sadr, who is now in exile near Paris,[24] Iran/Contra middleman Manucher Gorbanifar was one of the participants at the alleged Paris meetings of October 19–20, 1980, with Reagan-Bush campaign manager William Casey. (Houshang Lavi also claims to have met with Gorbanifar and Cyrus Hashemi in Paris at the Raphael Hotel on either October 19 or 20, 1980.) A former officer in the Shah's secret police, SAVAK, and then the head of Iran's arms-buying and intelligence operations in Europe [25] who worked directly with the office of Iran's Prime Minister Mir Hossein Mousavi, Gorbanifar wasted no time in arranging for U.S. arms deliveries to Iran once Reagan had won the election. On November 30, 1980, less than three weeks after the vote, Gorbanifar, whom CIA Director of Operations Claire George, Oliver North, and Iranian sources all claimed was an agent for Israel,[26] reportedly worked with Israeli arms dealer Yaacov Nimrodi to arrange for the delivery of U.S. Lance missiles (which can be made nuclear-capable) and Copperhead anti-tank missiles to the Khomeini regime.[27] Nimrodi was Gorbanifar's chief Israeli contact.[28] After being contacted by the CIA in London, [29] Gorbanifar went on to facilitate further U.S. arms deliveries to

Iran in 1981.[30] Gorbanifar later became a central figure in the Reagan-Bush Administration's secret U.S. arms shipments to Iran in late 1985 and 1986.

Houshang Lavi

Jewish-Iranian arms dealer, Houshang Lavi, claims that he was the "Iranian emissary" who proposed an arms-for-hostages deal to then Reagan-Bush foreign policy adviser Richard Allen, Allen's assistant Laurence Silberman, and then aide to Senator John Tower Robert McFarlane at the L'Enfant Plaza hotel in Washington, D.C., on October 2, 1980.[31] Until Hashemi's death in July 1986, Lavi had also been an associate of Iranian arms dealer Cyrus Hashemi who had reportedly attended the alleged October 20, 1980, meeting in Paris with William Casey. Lavi himself now admits to having met with Hashemi and Gorbanifar in Paris on October 19 or 20, 1980 at the Raphael Hotel (which Brenneke claims included his meeting with Casey of October 20). Mitchell Rogovin, Lavi's personal attorney at the time of the earlier L'Enfant Plaza meeting, was a neighbor of Richard Allen's campaign associate Laurence Silberman.[32] Rogovin was also, Lavi says, "very close to [George] Bush."[33] Lavi claims to have placed numerous calls to James Baker, Bush's top campaign aide, a number of times prior to the 1980 election, including one just before his meeting with Allen, Silberman, and McFarlane on October 2, 1980, in Washington, D.C. Lavi's note of the L'Enfant Plaza meeting refers to this call to Mr. Baker.

In the early 1980's, after getting a go-ahead from Israeli Prime Minister Menachem Begin, Houshang Lavi claims to have worked with a Belgian-based arms company, Asco, one of whose directors had been a colonel in Israel's intelligence service, Mossad, to supply Iran with U.S. -made HAWK anti-aircraft missile parts, tank parts, night vision equipment, rifles, and other arms.[34] He claims that the total dollar value of arms, "all of them made in the U.S.," shipped by Asco and others associated with Asco to Iran in the 1980's "amounts to billions."[35] According to Richard Brenneke, some of the $40 million dollars made available for arms discussed at the October 20, 1980 Paris meeting had been deposited in Banque Lambert in Brussels, Belgium.

In April 1981, the same month that top Iranian official and Khomeini's former hostage negotiator Sadegh Tabatabai signed a $200 million arms deal with Israel,[36] Western Dynamics, Inc., a company owned by Houshang Lavi's brothers, closed a $11.2 million deal with Iran for F-14 fighter jet fuses.[37] In October 1981, the same company signed a second contract with the Iranian air force for over \$4 million worth of F-14 parts—some of the same equipment Houshang Lavi had proposed exchanging for the fifty-two hostages at his meeting with Reagan-Bush campaign officials and Mr. McFarlane a month before the 1980 election. In these deals, the Lavi brothers' agent was Ahmad Tabatabai, who, according to Houshang Lavi, is a relative of Sadegh Tabatabai, Khomeini's chosen hostage negotiator in 1980.[39] When then President of Iran Abolhassan Bani Sadr discovered that Sadegh Tabatabai had made arrangements to purchase U.S. military equipment from Israel in April 1981, he called a meeting of his Defense Council to protest the deals, to no avail.[39] Three months later, after Mr. Bani Sadr was forced to flee Iran, the arms from Tabatabai's agreements began arriving in Tehran.

In 1981, a Customs Service agent at the U.S. embassy in London alerted the State Department to the Lavi brothers' arrangements to ship U.S. military equipment to Iran. Once the State Department received the information, Customs was ordered to drop all investigations into the Lavis' business dealings.[40]

The Lavis may have been associated with Iran/Contra defendant Albert Hakim, also reportedly an Iranian Jew. According to court records, the Lavis may have served as foreign agents for Hakim's Olin Corporation in the 1970's. According to a former employee of Hakim's who corresponded with the author in 1988, Albert Hakim worked in the 1970's with Israel's intelligence service, Mossad, specializing in "fixing" HAWK missile part deals between the U.S. and Iran.[41] The former President of Iran, Abolhassan Bani Sadr, has reported that Hashemi Rafsanjani, the powerful speaker of Iran's Parliament, who reportedly sent a representative to the October 19–20, 1980, Paris meetings with Reagan-Bush campaign officials, used "a Geneva company with ties to Iran" to arrange for U.S. arms deliveries to Tehran in the early 1980's. Hakim's company maintained a corporate office in Geneva.

ISRAEL

Israel has a long-standing tradition of using sales and barters of military equipment to maintain relations with nations who do not wish to establish diplomatic ties with the Jewish state. Although the Ayatollah Khomeini vowed from the beginning of the Iranian Revolution in February 1979 to "eliminate" Israel, Israel nevertheless considered Iraq to be its greater enemy. Israeli leaders therefore saw benefit in doing whatever was necessary to keep Iran fighting with, and preoccupying, its historic adversary Iraq. It was for this reason, as well as Iran's strategic position, its great economic potential, its history of economic cooperation with Israel under the Shah, and its centuries of enmity with Israel's other enemies in the Arab world, that the Jewish state made the decision to maintain secret relations with its non-Arab near-neighbor, Iran. The *Jerusalem Post* quoted U.S. officials as stating that "The link between the military establishments and intelligence organizations of both countries [Israel and Iran] has survived the fall of the Shah, with slight interruption caused by the chaos of the Iranian revolution. It is a case of both nations holding their noses and acting in their own self-interest."[42]

Chapter V reviewed reports that Israel has acknowledged having sent at least one unauthorized shipment of military equipment to the Khomeini regime in the month before the 1980 election, and that President Carter ordered all deliveries stopped until the hostages were freed. When the hostages were finally released the day of Reagan's inauguration, Israel had reason to want the shipments resumed. As a result of the Shah's fall and the ensuing Iranian revolution, she had lost an estimated $225 million in annual military sales to the Persian state and was anxious to recoup her losses. Once the hostages were freed, both the Israeli Parliament and the Israeli defense ministry were eager to resume business-as-usual, though underground, relations with Iran. On September 28, 1980, Israeli Knesset member Yehuda Ben-Me'ir argued that Israel was a "natural source" for military aid to Iran as the Israelis could supply the Khomeini regime with sorely-needed U.S.-made spare parts and equipment. The next day, September 29, 1980, CBS news reported Israeli Deputy Defense Minister Mordechai Tzipori's statement that the Jewish state was prepared to help Iran (with her recent military request), "if it changed its policy towards Israel."[43] That "policy," in all probability, had to do with Iranian oil.

At the time of the siege of the U.S. embassy in Tehran, it has been reported that the Khomeini regime had agreed to a major oil-for-arms deal with Israel. In exchange for U.S. and Israeli arms desperately needed to wage the new war with Iraq—especially anti-aircraft HAWK missiles and anti-tank TOW missiles to counter Iraq's superiority in planes and tanks— Khomeini would provide Israel with a continuous flow of Iranian oil at rock-bottom prices. Regardless of the reason or the method of payment, there is no longer any question that Israel supplied U.S. arms and spare parts, as well as its own, to Iran in 1981. Vice-President Bush, CIA Director William Casey, and the U.S. State Department have all now acknowledged these early arms shipments to the Khomeini regime.

Vice President Bush told the Tower Commission, which investigated Iran/Contra allegations, that U.S. interests were "in the grip of the Israelis," who, he said, had used the now-famous 1985–86 U.S. arms deliveries to Iran to "cover" previous arms deliveries to the Khomeini regime "going back to the early 1980's."[44] This is no doubt true. An early invoice from an Israeli-owned company, made available to the author by the former President of Iran, Abolhassan Bani Sadr, includes an order for U.S.-made Sidewinder missiles. On October 3, 1985, immediately after the release in Lebanon of Reverend Benjamin Weir, Iranian middleman Manucher Gorbanifar, who has been claimed by many to be an Israeli agent, demanded these same Sidewinder missiles before Iran would consider prevailing upon its friends in Lebanon to release any more U.S. hostages.[45] Israel could only have "covered" earlier missile deliveries to Iran, as Vice President Bush alleged, however, if it had kept at least some of the U.S. arms that the Reagan-Bush Administration approved for delivery in 1985 and 1986. If this in fact is what happened, it would explain why planes flying U.S. arms to Iran in 1986 stopped off first in Tel Aviv, and why the Iranians rejected a shipment of HAWK missiles as "outdated" in late 1985. Those spurned HAWKS were not only older models; some reportedly bore the Israeli star of David. Obviously, there had been a switch. They were not the HAWKS from U.S. stores expected by the Iranians.

CIA Director William Casey himself confirmed U.S. arms dealings with Iran in 1981, President Reagan's first year in office. He told Bob Woodward of the *Washington Post,* "In '81, Israel was telling us to work with the Israelis," and he revealed to an associate, Ray Furmark, that "The U.S. supplied and permitted the supply of arms to Iran" long before 1985.[46] Casey's deputy CIA director Bobby Inman has also confirmed that the Agency was aware of the U.S. arms shipments to Iran in 1981.[47] And Duane "Dewey" Clarridge, another top deputy of CIA director Casey, told the Congressional Iran/Contra Committees that the "opening to Iran" through the Israelis began early, "probably going back to '81, certainly '82, in the form of General Haig," who was then President Reagan's secretary of state.[48] And a U.S. military source told the *Wall Street Journal* that "This thing [i.e., U.S. arms sales to Iran under a conscious policy of "plausible deniability"] goes back to 1981. Shultz was involved, [James] Baker knew, Weinberger knew, and Haig knew."

Senior Israeli officials, including then Israeli ambassador to the U.S. Moshe Arens, insist that the Reagan-Bush Administration knew about and had approved their 1981 U.S. arms shipments to Iran "at almost the highest levels." U.S. Ambassador to Israel Samuel Lewis, who had reportedly been informed of the deliveries by Israel's defense ministry, gave "no clear-cut veto" they maintained, and then Israeli defense minister Ariel Sharon said that the Reagan-Bush Administration was informed in advance and in detail of Israel's early U.S. arms shipments to Iran and did not object. "We gave them the lists," he said. "They [the U.S. government] knew exactly."[49] Israeli officials maintain that U.S. government approval was given with the "implicit" understanding that Israel would be compensated for its early weapons deliveries—that is, that it would either be reimbursed for U.S. arms shipments to Iran or that its stores of American-made arms would be replenished by the Reagan-Bush Administration.[50] A U.S. intelligence source has since confirmed to the *Wall Street Journal* that "It was implicit that any time the Israelis sent anything . . . that they would be compensated. If they sent their own stuff, it was understood that we [the U.S. government] would replace it."

These claims are consistent with information provided by William Northrop, a former Israeli intelligence agent who has flight logs, pro forma invoices, manifest lists, and bank telexes documenting a series of U.S. arms deliveries to Iran by Israel beginning in the spring of 1981, which he claims were made with the full knowledge of U.S. Ambassador to Israel Samuel Lewis. These shipments included $7 million in U.S. C-130 aircraft spare parts delivered in the spring of 1981; $200 million in spare parts for U.S. tanks, F-4 Phantom jets, radar, rifles, and ammunition delivered in the summer of 1981; $40-plus million in rifles, mortars, and ammunition delivered in the spring of 1982; one thousand U.S. TOW anti-tank missiles delivered in November of 1982; and $16.5 million in two hundred AIM-9L Sidewinder missiles and ten missile launcher sets delivered in January 1983. Northrop claims that these arms deliveries—all of which occurred years before the so-called "first" shipments of U.S. arms to Iran in

1985—were secretly sanctioned by the U.S. government and were later replenished from U.S. stores.

HOW OFFICIAL WAS THE AUTHORIZATION?

Israel has raised these "implicit understandings" and "lack of clear cut vetoes" to defend its early U.S. arms deliveries to Iran. An important question, however, is whether the Israeli government ever received explicit authorization for any of the shipments. The *Wall Street Journal* reported on December 12, 1986, that shortly after President Reagan took office in 1981, the Administration made the decision to "tacitly" condone Israeli arms sales to Iran. That decision, however, may have been more than just "tacit."

Before his death in late November 1988, Amiram Nir, the former counterterrorism adviser to Israeli prime ministers Peres and Shamir, told Bob Woodward of the *Washington Post* that the U.S.-Israeli arms transactions with Iran were authorized under a secret agreement, called an "accord," between the Reagan-Bush Administration and then Prime Minister Peres, which had not been shared with Congress as required by law.[51] Although most joint U.S.-Israeli covert operations allegedly covered by this secret accord took place in 1986, the agreement itself may have been signed much earlier—even as early as 1981. If not—if there was no official authorization from the U.S. government, Israel's shipments of U.S. arms to Iran during Reagan's first term would have been in violation of the Arms Export Control Act, which requires advance presidential approval before any such arms transfers can be made. The act also requires timely notification of Congress by the President of any shipments by another government without U.S. approval. A Congressional attorney familiar with the Arms Export Control Act told the *Miami Herald,* however, "I don't know of any presidential approval for Israeli arms shipments to Iran in 1981, or of any notification to Congress that Israel shipped the weapons without authorization."[52] Unless there was some kind of official authorization for Israel's 1981 arms deliveries to Iran, another U.S. law requires the suspension of all military aid to a country found in violation. Surely the Israelis would not have risked $3 billion dollars a year in U.S. economic and military aide without covering itself legally in some way. Could the still-secret "accord" referred to by Nir have been that "way"?

The former President of Iran, Abolhassan Bani Sadr, claims to have seen some $53 million in contracts between his country and Israel for U.S. arms and spare parts in May of 1981, none of which were received until after he was forced to flee the country in late July 1981 following a coup d'etat against him. He has since made public some early-1981 invoices covering U.S. arms and spare parts deliveries to Iran by Israeli-owned companies. The earliest of these invoices is dated March 8, 1981. To have been legal, the arms deals represented by these documents had to have been covered by either a signed presidential finding—similar to the one President Reagan signed on January 17, 1986, to legitimize the now-famous Iran/Contra arms shipments of 1986—or by a still-secret "accord" like the one referred to by the late Mr. Nir.

The day after the earliest of these invoices provided by Mr. Bani Sadr, on March 9, 1981, CIA director William Casey presented President Reagan with a covert action proposal to support pro-U.S. forces with relation to Iran.[53] Did President Reagan sign an as-yet-unacknowledged secret finding or accord with Israel for covert operations relating to Iran as early as March 1981? That same month, March 1981, the secret Intelligence Support Activity (ISA) special operations force, an elite group of military covert operations and intelligence specialists commanded by Colonel Jerry King, went operational.[54] Gary Howard, a former covert operations specialist and current Texas border patrol officer told the author in 1988 that the ISA, as well as the Defense Intelligence Agency (DIA) and the elite military Delta Force, had been involved in the supply of U.S. arms to Iran throughout the 1980's. ISA relied for planning and support on the Army's Special Operations Division, which *also* became operational in March 1981.[55] This Special Operations Division had been organized under the direction of Iran/Contra defendant Richard Secord after the failed Desert One hostage rescue attempt in Iran of late April 1980.

On the same day that William Casey asked Reagan for a covert operations authorization on Iran, he also proposed covert operations relating to Nicaragua.[56] The use of "profits" from secret U.S. arms sales to Iran for covert operations is believed to have begun only in 1986. However, it may have begun as early as 1981. In 1983, a member of one of the just-mentioned secret military units claims to have seen a secret CIA plan for financing the Contras using profits from arms sales to "foreign countries."[57] Iran is such a foreign country. From the beginning of the Iran-Iraq war in late September 1980, Iran was desperate for U.S. arms and spare parts and was willing to pay marked-up prices to obtain them. As the date of the secret CIA plan for arms profit diversions seen by the special operations officer was not specified, it may be that it, too, was formulated shortly after President Reagan and Vice-President Bush gained office, in early 1981.

In other words, the entire Iran/Contra scheme, not only the Israeli-mediated U.S. arms sales to Iran, may date back to 1981 and may have been covered by the still-secret U.S.-Israeli accord referred to by Mr. Nir, or one like it. After all, the President of Nicaragua, Daniel Ortega, has stressed that the United States and Israel created a joint military force to counter his revolution not in 1983 or 1984, but at the very beginning of the Reagan-Bush Administration, in 1981.[58] By 1981, in fact, Israel was already the largest arms exporter to Central America, including to the Nicaraguan resistance. NBC Television reported that, by April 1984, Israel had armed one quarter of the Contra army.[59] Israel provided the Contras with liberal amounts of military equipment in return, in part, for ousted Nicaraguan leader Anastasio Samoza's father having been among the first to support Israel's 1948 war of independence and for having been among the first to supply her with arms for her 1967 war against the Arabs. The senior Samoza's Nicaragua had also been among the first nations to recognize the new Jewish state in 1948 and had supplied passports for Israeli agents in 1949.

On July 8, 1981, President Reagan signed National Security Decision Directive (NSDD) #5, entitled "Conventional Arms Transfer Policy," under which his administration made overseas sales of U.S. arms a high priority.[60] This was only a few weeks before the President of Iran, Abolhassan Bani Sadr, was forced to flee his country and the first Israeli-mediated U.S. arms shipments began arriving in Tehran. National Security Decision Directive #5 required "effective United States Government control and direction over arms transfers." As the Arms Export Control Act requires U.S. government control over all "third-country" transfers of American-made arms—including any transfers of U.S. arms to Iran by Israel—it is clear that Israel's 1981 shipments must have been with the knowledge and official blessing of President Reagan himself, who had signed the national security decision directive.

The first official authorization of U.S. arms shipments to Iran, however, may have happened even earlier than March of 1981. When the fifty-two American hostages were released on the day of President Reagan's inauguration, one U.S. citizen who had been taken hostage on May 5, 1980, Mrs. Cynthia Dwyer of New York, was still held captive in Iran.

She happened to be the wife of an old friend of Richard Allen, the President's new national security adviser and his top White House foreign policy official. The next day, January 21, 1981, after being told about Mrs. Dwyer's plight, President Reagan ordered Allen to "tell the Iranians the deal is off" unless she was also freed.[61] Shortly thereafter, Secretary of State Alexander Haig announced that "U.S. policy" toward Iran would depend on the outcome of her "case." In other words, some already-agreed-to U.S. arms shipments to Iran would be delayed pending her release.

At a meeting with then Israeli defense minister, Ariel Sharon, in late January 1981, Secretary of State Alexander Haig reportedly authorized Israel to resume its deliveries of U.S.-made F-4 and F-5 fighter plane parts to Iran.[62] Haig reportedly was urged to approve Sharon's request by his then counselor and liaison to Israel Robert McFarlane, by National Security Adviser Richard Allen,[63] and by the then director general of Israel's foreign ministry and a former Mossad chief for Western Hemisphere operations, David Kimche, who had sought out McFarlane's support.[64] Though Haig and McFarlane now deny having given the authorization, written minutes of the meeting reportedly show otherwise.[65] "When we saw [in the minutes of the private meeting] what Haig had done," according to one senior U.S. official interviewed by *Newsweek,* "we almost panicked." On January 28th, shortly after giving his reported green light to Israel to ship U.S. arms to Iran, Haig announced at his first press conference as secretary of state that the *United States* would not be providing arms or spare parts to Iran.[68] In fact, right from the beginning, the State Department looked the other way from continuing deliveries of U.S. arms to the Khomeini regime. "It is true that we have not done all we can to stop Israel's re-export of U.S.-made [military] equipment to Iran," a high-level State Department official told *Time* magazine in 1983. "[But] we don't give a d--- as long as the Iran-Iraq carnage doesn't affect our allies [i.e. Israel] in the region or alter the balance of power."

Though the Israelis claim that its U.S. weapon shipments to Iran in 1981 amounted to only some $10 to $15 million, they were in fact preparing to resume delivery of $200 million worth of arms, which had been requested by Khomeini before the 1980 election and forcefully stopped by President Carter when he learned of a shipment in October of 1980.[67] Khomeini's former hostage negotiator and a top arms procurement official, Sadegh Tabatabai, signed the contract for this $200 million deal on April 7, 1981.[68]

Two men who reportedly urged Secretary Haig to go ahead with these early 1981 U.S. arms shipments to Iran, Richard Allen and Robert McFarlane, had met in early October 1980, before the election, with Iranian emissary Houshang Lavi, who offered a release of the U.S. hostages in exchange for U.S. military equipment. According to former CIA contract agent William Herrmann, McFarlane and Allen also met with Iranian officials in Paris after the Washington D.C. Lavi meeting. As soon as Reagan gained the White House, these same two men, Allen and McFarlane reportedly recommended establishing a secret arms relationship with Iran, and Houshang Lavi's brothers began making arrangements for U.S. arms deliveries to the Khomeini regime.[69] As noted earlier, when Customs alerted Haig's State Department to the Lavis' Iran arms dealings in 1981, Department officials ordered that all Customs investigations be dropped.[70]

Mrs. Dwyer was finally released by Iran on February 9, 1981. Eleven days later, on February 20, Secretary Haig, who had vowed that "U.S. policy" toward Iran would depend on an end to her detention, again reportedly approved an Israeli proposal for U.S. arms sales to Iran in a meeting with then Israeli foreign minister Yitshak Shamir.[71] According to testimony before the Congressional Iran/Contra Committees, McFarlane's close associate Howard Teicher, who was chief of political-military affairs at the National Security Council, and U.S.-Israeli liaison Michael Ledeen both counseled approving the sales.[72] According to Abolhassan Bani Sadr, Ledeen may also have accompanied McFarlane on his now-famous secret trip to Tehran of late May 1986, at which McFarlane was reportedly taped reminding the Iranians of a $5 billion commitment of U.S. arms by the U.S.[73] Ledeen, however, denies the charge.[74] Ironically, the same day that the first report of this $5 billion commitment appeared in Greece, on November 29, 1986, halfway around the world the *Washington Post* published the first report of Richard Allen, Robert McFarlane, and Laurence Silberman's secret meeting with an "Iranian emissary" offering to release the fifty-two hostages to the Reagan-Bush camp to defeat President Carter.[75]

Once formal, though secret, U.S. authorization had been given, huge quantities of U.S. arms and military equipment began flowing to Iran. On July 25, 1983, *Time* reported that large quantities of U.S. arms had been sold to Iran by Israel "in clear violation of the law" in cooperation with an Athens-based Iranian arms dealer, Faroukh Azzizi. Based on a report by the Tel Aviv Jaffe Institute for Strategic Studies, a West German newspaper estimated that Israel sold at least $500 million in military equipment to Iran between 1981 and 1983.[76] The *International Herald Tribune, The New York Times,* and numerous other publications reported that Iran had received $100 to $200 million in arms, spare parts, and ammunition, almost all of it U.S.-made, through Western Europe between 1981 and early 1982, half supplied by Israel and the other half by "free-lance" arms dealers, many with close connections to Israeli intelligence.[77] Bani Sadr, the former President of Iran, has confirmed that "Israelis were present at all the arms sales."[78] As the former U.S. chief of SAVAK (the Iranian secret police under the Shah), Mansur Rafizadeh, put it: "Almost as soon as President Reagan came into office, shipments of [U.S.] arms started from Tel Aviv. This is 1981 we are talking about, not 1985."[79]

In the spring of 1981, Iranian agents contacted a number of arms dealers in Europe asking them to arrange for transportation of 360 tons of M-48 tank spare parts and ammunition from Israel to Iran. Swiss arms merchant Andreas Jenni and a Miami-based Scottish international arms dealer Stuart Allan McCafferty teamed up to provide a plane for the mission. According to Jenni, a twelve-shipment contract was signed by a British middleman operating out of a Tel Aviv cover firm (probably "Dr. Doom") on behalf of the Israelis, and also by Sadegh Tabatabai, Khomeini's former hostage negotiator and a relative of the Ayatollah's by marriage. Jenni and McCafferty's crew reportedly completed two runs before the "smoking guns" finally hit the fan.

On July 18, 1981, on its third run to Iran from Israel, their C1-44 turbo-prop crashed, making headlines in Europe, the United States, and the Middle East.[80] The plane, using the call sign "Tango November" and answering to the radio signal "Yankee Romeo," had been hired from a small Buenos Aires, Argentina, air company called Transporte Aereo Rioplatense by McCafferty on behalf of the Israelis to carry part of the 360-ton, $27.9 million deal for tank parts from Tel Aviv to Tehran. On the return trip through Larnaca, Cyprus, it flew seriously off course and either went down or was shot down in Soviet Armenia, just over the Turkey-USSR border, after being intercepted by two Soviet MIG-25 jets.[81] Depending on the report, the pilot was either McCafferty or, one of three Argentinians also on the mission, Captain Hector Cordero, who liked to "fly planes for fun." All of the crew members died.

Until the crash of "Tango November" and press reports that followed in its wake, the Reagan-Bush Administration and Israel had been able to maintain the public fiction that U.S. arms were not being delivered to the Khomeini regime. Even after the fiasco, as Jody Powell, President Carter's former press secretary, put it, "The response from the U.S. and Jerusalem was, 'We didn't do it, and we ain't gonna do it anymore.' " But Alexander Haig's State Department finally admitted that Israel had sold "at least

$27 million in [U.S.] military equipment to Iran.''[82] This, of course, was admitting to almost the precise amount of the $27.9 million Jenni-McCafferty-Tabatabai deliveries exposed by the crash.

Despite the State Department's reluctant acknowledgement, to the best of the author's knowledge neither the U.S.-Israel-Iran arms deal revealed by the July 18, 1981, crash nor any of the other hundreds of millions of dollars worth of U.S. arms shipments to Iran by the Israelis in 1981 or 1982 were ever reported to Congress as required by the Arms Export Control Act. That law prohibits all such arms transfers unless the President has given his explicit consent and has affirmed that 1) the U.S. itself would transfer the arms to Iran; 2) the transferee nation, Iran, has agreed *in writing* not to ship the arms elsewhere without the President's approval; and 3) the President has notified Congress of the sales. There have been no press reports that any of these requirements were met by the Administration or by Iran covering the 1981 U.S. arms deliveries to the Khomeini regime.[83]

On July 21, 1981, only three days after "Tango November" went down, the Reagan-Bush Administration's Senior Interdepartmental Group, referred to as SIG, met to rethink its policy on arms sales to Iran by allied nations. The decision reached was that "U.S. efforts to discourage third country transfers of non-U.S. origin arms would have only a marginal effect on the conduct of the [Iran-Iraq] war."[84] Some present even expressed concern that "a rigid U.S. policy against all arms transfers to Iran would not serve overall U.S. interests."[85] In other words, arms shipments to Iran by Israel and other countries would not only be allowed to continue, they would be quietly encouraged. "It was an experimental program," one National Security Council staffer recalled. "We anxiously awaited the result." CIA Director William Casey himself told the *Washington Post* that: "The initiative seemed credible to us, based on the future post-Khomeini era." This was the same rationale used for the U.S. arms shipments to Iran in 1985 and 1986, the so-called "first" deliveries, which became a focus of the Iran/Contra affair.

Less than a week after the White House SIG meeting—on July 24–27, 1981—and shortly after President Reagan signed National Security Decision Directive #5 requiring strict U.S. government control over all transfers of American-made arms, Israeli arms dealer Yaacov Nimrodi reportedly signed a $135 million contract with Iran for fifty U.S. surface-to-surface Lance missiles, fifty mobile missile launchers, and sixty-eight HAWK anti-aircraft missiles—the same kind Israel shipped to Iran in late 1985—with Colonel K. Denghan of the Iranian Defense Ministry.[86]

Intelligence/Parapolitics has even reported that the U.S. military, under the direction of the Reagan-Bush Administration, sent secret teams to Iran in the early 1980's to train the Iranians in the installation and use of the HAWK missiles.[87] Even earlier, during the transition period, Nimrodi had reportedly made a deal to sell Lance missiles and Copperhead anti-tank shells to Iran.[88] Then, in September 1981, he and Israel's defense minister Ariel Sharon reportedly made yet another deal to supply Iran with Howitzer shells and ammunition captured by Israel in its war with Syria.[89]

Despite these reports, author Samuel Segev claims that Mr. Nimrodi did not sell military goods to Iran until March 1985.[90] He claims that another unnamed Israeli arms dealer, not Nimrodi, negotiated the July 1981 contract with Iran with the assistance of a French firm and a representative of Iran's military Chief of Staff, Ahmed Khudari. Segev reports that the deal was for $200 million, not $135 million, for 250 Phantom jet tires, communications equipment, artillery, mortars, and ammunition purchased by Iran on the condition that Israel deny the deal if it ever became public.[91] According to Segev, after the first shipment under the contract was delivered, Khudari reportedly defrauded Iran's Defense Ministry of some $56 million and fled to France. Iran sued for the money, but according to the former Iranian President, Bani Sadr, Iran dropped the suit on a technicality after he informed French officials of the possible relationship between the deal and negotiations by the Reagan-Bush camp. Despite Khudari's reported fraud, the shipments continued, the third of which was reportedly the one that crashed in Soviet Armenia on July 18, 1981. Whether Yaacov Nimrodi was personally involved in these early U.S. arms deals or not, there is no question that he and his government supported them. In February 1982, Nimrodi appeared on the British BBC television program *Panorama* stressing the importance of Israel's continued arms supply relationship with Iran.[92]

Israeli shipments of U.S. arms to Iran continued throughout 1981 and in 1982. In May 1982, top Israeli officials acknowledged that Israel had been selling substantial amounts of arms and spare parts to Iran and informed Secretary of State Alexander Haig and Secretary of Defense Caspar Weinberger that the Jewish state had signed yet another arms agreement with Iran the same month.[93] Israel's minister of defense, Ariel Sharon, however, publicly acknowledged only the $27 million in arms sales [94]— roughly the amount of the $27.9 million July 1981 shipment exposed by the plane downed over the Soviet Union, and the same amount admitted to by the U.S. State Department.[95] Following these revelations, on May 21, 1982, columnists Evans and Novak reported that secretary of state

Alexander Haig appeared ready to reward, not punish, Israel for its surreptitious arms deliveries to Iran.[96]

In July 1982 the attitude of the Reagan-Bush Administration towards arms deliveries to Iran began to change when George Shultz replaced Alexander Haig at the Department of State and "Operation Staunch," Shultz's program to stem the flow of Western arms to the Khomeini regime, began to take shape. The government now said that it had received "definitive evidence" that Iran had been behind terrorist and hostage-taking operations—as if the holding of fifty-two American hostages against their will for 444 days had not been proof enough. This "new information" was said to cause a rethinking of the secret U.S. and U.S.-Israeli policies towards Iran. But the new concern wasn't yet enough to move the administration to stop Israel's sale of more TOW anti-tank missiles to Iran in November of 1982,[97] the same kind of weapons President Reagan and his national security adviser Robert McFarlane later authorized to be shipped to Iran in late 1985. According to *Time,* in November 1982, Iranian arms dealer Faroukh Azzizi purchased additional U.S.–made TOW missiles from the Israelis for delivery to Tehran through Amsterdam.[98]

The same month that the Reagan-Bush Administration claimed it received the first definitive proof of Iran's links to international terrorism and hostage taking, the tables were turned, as the first *Iranian* officials were taken captive in Lebanon. On July 4, 1982, three top Iranian officials were taken hostage by Christian Phalangist militiamen in the northern portion of the country—Iran's chargé d'affaires Hussein Moussavi, Revolutionary Guard Commander Colonel Ahmed Motevaselian, and Iranian press bureau chief Kazem Akhavan.[99] Iran has since stated that freedom for Briton Terry Waite and for the American and other Western hostages held by Khomeini-loyalist Hezbollah forces in southern Lebanon depends on the release of these three Iranian officials.

In early 1982, a number of claims appeared in the international press that Israel's arms sales to Iran, including some of the U.S. equipment, was intended to support a planned coup attempt against the Ayatollah Khomeini. On February 1, 1982, BBC Television in London aired a story on its *Panorama* program that Israel's arms shipments to Iran were intended to topple the existing regime. The program was based, in part, on an interview with then director of Israel's foreign ministry, David Kimche. Kimche, however, vigorously denied the BBC report, insisting that he had said nothing about arms supplies to Iran during his interview with the network.[100] Israel, in fact, did not receive its first request for assistance from an opposition group organizing to reinstate the Shah's son until seven months later, in September 1982.[101] The confusion arose because arms dealer Yaacov Nimrodi called openly on the same BBC program for an overthrow of the Khomeini regime. Seven months after the show aired, in September 1982, it would be Nimrodi who would ask Israeli Defense Minister Ariel Sharon for assistance in bringing down the Khomeini regime. Nimrodi and another influential Israeli arms dealer, Al Schwimmer, had worked out the scheme with Saudi middleman Adnan Khashoggi in mid- to late 1982. They had reportedly put together a $2 billion plan to reinstate the former Shah's son, Reza Pahlavi, with the assistance of King Fahd of Saudi Arabia and CIA Director William Casey.[102] These same four men—Nimrodi, Schwimmer, Khashoggi, and Casey—would later be at the center of the Iran/Contra scandal in 1985 and 1986.

But the planned Iranian counter-revolution of 1982 never got off the ground. To succeed, it required the support of Israel, but Defense Minister Ariel Sharon, whom Nimrodi and generals loyal to the crown prince had contacted for support, resigned in February 1983 before the plan could be put into effect, in the wake of the 1982 scandal over the slaughter of civilians in Sabra and Chatila refugee camps. Israel's new foreign minister, Yitshak Shamir, and Sharon's successor, Defense Minister Moshe Arens, were not interested in helping the crown prince, who had declared himself Shah, to regain the Peacock Throne. Unlike the release of the American hostages at the moment of Ronald Reagan's inauguration, the timing didn't seem to have been made in heaven.

VII

A NEAT IDEA

"You can get killed for just knowing about this stuff."

A Reagan-Bush National Security Council official, 1988

It had become clear that billions, not just millions, of dollars worth of U.S. arms had gone to Iran beginning in 1981. The question was, where did they come from? The entire Iran/Contra scandal and the international furor it caused had resulted from revelations that only a relatively small quantity of U.S. arms had been shipped to Iran. Where could the Reagan-Bush Administration have found billions of dollars of American weapons and spare parts to assist Khomeini in his war with Iraq without Congress finding out?

Still without an answer, I decided to hold a press conference in Washington, D.C., in late August 1988 to focus media attention on the fact that U.S. arms worth hundreds of times the amount revealed in the Iran/Contra hearings had been going to Iran since 1981. I had an interview with C-SPAN television on August 23rd, and arrived three days early to meet with a few journalists who had also been investigating the "October Surprise" story. I had gone to Washington with no expectation that the trip would uncover anything radically new. I was soon to receive a few surprises of my own.

THE FIRST CLUE

The corner table in the bar of the Hay Adams Hotel, opposite the White
House, was the perfect setting for a meeting, late the afternoon of August
21st. I was waiting for Mickey Smith, an old friend from the 1980
Reagan-Bush campaign who had been its Iran expert and one of the four
senior watch officers in the Operations Center. The Operations Center had
been the communications command center of the 1980 Reagan-Bush campaign, where calls went in and out, to and from the Reagan and Bush
planes. Mickey had also served in the Department of Commerce as head of
its Iran desk for years and had been stationed at the U.S. embassy in
Tehran not long before its take-over by radical Iranian students, which
had started the hostage crisis.

I had already conducted numerous interviews with Mickey in which he
recalled having been phoned in early October 1980 by a colleague in
President Carter's State Department who had asked him whether the
Reagan-Bush campaign had received an approach from an Iranian arms
dealer named Houshang Lavi. At the time, President Carter's State Department was considering an arms-for-hostage offer by Lavi similar to the one
he had made to Richard Allen of the Reagan-Bush campaign in Washington the same month. Mickey recalled that the campaign had indeed had
some interaction with Lavi. He remembered the name having been mentioned. He thought he had been asked about Lavi by Stephan Halper, one
of Bush's key foreign policy functionaries, who had a number of former
CIA people working under him in the campaign. Halper constantly busied
himself on hush-hush projects, including "October Surprise" preparations.
Mickey wasn't sure whether the former Carter official who had called him
during the 1980 campaign was a colleague then working on the Reagan-
Bush National Security Council or whether he had been another longtime
acquaintance then with the Department of State. Mickey said he was going
to try to bring his NSC friend to the Hay Adams for a drink, and he was as
eager as I was to find out if he was the one who had made the October
1980 inquiry about Lavi.

As fate would have it, Mickey had the "wrong" man. He knew nothing
about Houshang Lavi, and Mickey decided that it had to have been his
other friend at State who had called him in October 1980. His NSC friend
was interested, though, in why I was in Washington, and after some
background I raised the big question. If one believed reports in the

European press, I explained, it seemed clear that billions of dollars in U.S. arms had been flowing to Iran since the early 1980s. Did he have any idea where they could be getting them from?

"There's only one place they could have come from without being detected," Mickey's friend said matter-of-factly. "The Reforger stores."

"The what?" I asked.

"The Reforger stores," he repeated. "They're the 'black' [secret] stores of weapons and spare parts our forces in Europe would use in case of a surprise Warsaw Pact invasion."

I knew we were onto something. "Do you know about this directly, or is this—"

"A draw-down of Reforger stores would be consistent with what we already know," he said, "but my portfolio at the NSC doesn't allow me to officially follow it up."

"I see," I said.

Mickey's friend then suddenly got nervous. "Don't use my name in connection with any of this!" he said in a loud whisper, red-faced. "You can get killed for just knowing about this stuff!"

"Great!" I managed, scribbling "Reforger" on a napkin in my lap. Reforger . . . I'd heard the name before. Perhaps in the White House, where I had been Policy Analyst in the Office of Policy Development in 1981 and 1982, the first two years of the Reagan-Bush Administration. But I couldn't yet place just where. Within twenty-four hours, I would receive a reminder.

Late the next morning I had a prearranged appointment with *Newsweek* reporter Bob Parry at the International Center for Development Policy, downtown. Parry had just completed a major article on the National Security Council's use of CIA psychological warfare experts to "disinformation-manage" the Congress and the media, and therefore the American public, about Iran/Contra events. But the topic we were there to discuss wasn't the Reagan-Bush Administration's use of disinformation specialists. Parry was one of only a few journalists who had taken the time to look seriously into the "October Surprise" story, and I hoped that he would have some new information.

Again, however, there was nothing. Parry had been focusing on the other story and did not have anything new on "October Surprise." It had just occurred to me that perhaps something else of interest on the story was to be found at the Center when a man stopped in the door of the conference room to say hello to Parry.

"Hi, Bob," he said, as if they were old friends. They exchanged a few words and then the man walked on. I could hear him climbing a flight of stairs.

"Who was that?" I asked.

"That's Richard Brenneke," Parry offered.

"Brenneke? Wasn't he the source on Donald Gregg's connection to the Iran/Contra story?"

"That's him," he nodded.

"And also the first source on Saudi money for the operation?" I asked, recalling some articles I had read, some of them Parry's own in *Newsweek*.

"That's right. In fact, I'm going to go up and talk with him," the *Newsweek* reporter said. Parry followed the shy man with the thinning hair up the stairs.

For reasons that would soon become clear, my internal radar was on high alert. This man was important. I, too, would have a talk with him. I hoped that he might know something about the Reforger stores. After a few minutes I navigated the narrow stairs to the third floor and waited outside Mr. Brenneke's office. As Bob left, I stood to introduce myself.

"Sure, come on in," Brenneke said, gesturing for me to take the second chair in his small office while he lit up a cigarette. I took a deep breath and decided to lay it all on the table.

"I'm in town for a press conference on the 25th where I'm going to present evidence that there was a series of meetings before the 1980 election, in October, between top officials of the Reagan-Bush campaign and Iranians. I believe a deal was cut at these meetings to delay the release of our fifty-two hostages in exchange for a promise of arms once Reagan and Bush gained the White House. The former President of Iran and the former U.S. chief of SAVAK have already both written about it. A caller to a radio station in California claimed to have been the secret service officer at one of the meetings, in Europe. Bani Sadr, the former President of Iran, says that the meeting happened in late October in Paris. I thought maybe you might know something that could help us get to the bottom of this."

The next fifteen seconds were the longest in my forty-one years. The slight man opposite me seemed suddenly to flatten against the back of his chair, like an astronaut unexpectedly caught in a gravity simulator. I waited, watching him intently.

"Yes. I . . . do," he finally said. When I heard the response, it was everything I could do to keep from leaping from my chair.

"You know about the *Paris* meeting?" I asked, astonished.

"Yes. About the Paris meeting," Brenneke said.

My pulse must have jumped fifty points. I expected him to say more, but he didn't.

"Are you afraid that someone can hear us?"

He laughed. "This isn't the best place to talk about this, no," he said. After that, things went easier.

"Look. This stuff's already been in the papers." I tried to encourage him. "My briefcase is full of articles about pieces of the puzzle. I'm just trying to find out who was there. You know, the details."

There was still no answer. Brenneke was watching me intently. Then he broke the silence.

"I'll tell you what I know about the meeting if you promise to keep me completely out of it."

"Alright," I said. "I promise. Look. What if I give you a list of names and you just put a mark by anybody you know was there?" I thought this might make it easier for my newfound source.

"O.K.," he finally said, lighting up another cigarette. They were the short filterless kind. Horrible. I dug into my briefcase for a piece of paper and quickly wrote out the following list of names:

> BUSH
> GREGG
> CAVE
> GORBANIFAR
> HASHEMI
> HAKIM?

As I put the question mark by Hakim, Brenneke spoke.

"Not Hakim," he said. "Gregg, Gorbanifar, Hashemi were there. And William Casey," he added definitively.

"Casey!" I exclaimed, almost falling back into my chair. This was the first information from any source that Ronald Reagan's campaign manager himself had been at the Paris meeting.

"You mean *William* Casey?" I asked again to make sure. "Reagan's campaign manager?"

Brenneke nodded. "That's right. Casey was there with Gregg."

"Jesus!" I thought. Rafizadeh, the former U.S. chief of SAVAK, had been the first to say that Gregg had been at a meeting in Europe with the Iranians before the 1980 election. But—Casey! If true, that would put this thing in a whole new light.

"OK, let me get this straight," I said. "You say Casey, Reagan's campaign manager, was there with Gregg, and Gorbanifar, and Cyrus Hashemi?''

Brenneke nodded. He looked certain.

"And you are talking about *Paris?* The Paris meeting of October 1980?''

"Right. Paris. It was in mid- to late October." Then he hesitated for a moment. "Actually, there was more than one meeting. Two, I think. The one I'm talking about would be the second one."

"The second one?" I asked, stunned. I had only heard about one meeting.

"Yes. I learned that there had been a meeting the day before the one I was first told about—but I don't have anything directly on that first meeting," he tried to explain. I was still confused.

"We're talking *before* the election?"

"Oh, definitely, yes. Before the election."

"And what about the date—or dates? You said there were two meetings . . . may have been two meetings?"

Without hesitation, Brenneke answered. "As I recall, the second meeting was the Monday or Tuesday of the last full week in October 1980. That last week wasn't a full week. I remember that. Do you have a calendar?''

"What would I be doing with a 1980 calendar?" I asked, and we both laughed. The ice had been broken.

Then came *the* question, "How do you know this?"

There was another long silence.

"Want a cigarette?" he asked, avoiding the question for the moment. I hadn't smoked in years, but decided to try anything to keep him talking. "Sure." After he lit it, I tried again.

This time I tried relaxing. "So how do you know? Were you there, or did somebody tell you about it?"

"Cyrus told me—"

"Cyrus Hashemi?"

"Yes. Cyrus Hashemi—and also one of the Iranians who knew about the meeting, from the day before."

"Do you mean there was a third Iranian at the meeting?" I queried.

"Maybe." He didn't want to say anything more about the other Iranian. I thought back to his previous answer.

"Just a minute. You said Monday or Tuesday. You mean *you* were in Paris?''

"Yeah. I was there. On other business. I met the next day—that was the

Monday or Tuesday—with a couple of the people who knew about the meeting from the day before.''

I took a deep breath. ''So the meeting with Casey wasn't *your* meeting?'' He shook his head ''no.'' ''Then the meeting with Casey and Gregg happened, what? The day before your meeting with the Iranians?''

''Right. I was told that Casey was there in Paris with Gregg and the Iranians, the day before I happened to get together with Cyrus Hashemi and one of the other Iranians.''

The interview was getting more and more interesting. I didn't feel that Brenneke was leveling with me about the degree of his own involvement in the meetings. But that could wait.

''Can you tell me who the Iranians were? Bani Sadr says that representatives of Hashemi Rafsanjani and the Ayatollah Beheshti attended the Paris meeting.''

''That's right.''

''So, can you tell me who they were—the Iranians?'' I tried again.

''I really don't think I ought to go into that. They—they're friends of mine, still in Iran—still in positions in the government in Iran. I don't think it would help anybody to know right now who they were.''

Again, a seemingly impenetrable armor had been raised around the identity of the two Iranians at the Paris meeting. Bani Sadr wouldn't name them. Houshang Lavi wouldn't name them. Now Brenneke wouldn't name them. I decided to try again later.

''OK. Look, why don't we both try to find a 1980 calendar, and then let's have dinner tomorrow night,'' I suggested.

Mr. Brenneke was agreeable. We made an appointment to meet at 6:00 the next evening in the lobby of his hotel next to the Capitol. I left some articles with him and called a cab to take me to the house where I was staying, in Georgetown. I had a lot to think about that night.

AN AMAZING COINCIDENCE

I didn't know whether to believe Richard Brenneke or not. On the one hand, he had been the source for a number of major breaks in the Iran/Contra story that had proved to be true—big breaks, like the Saudi connection and Donald Gregg's being a link between the Contra operation in Central America and Vice President Bush. Clearly, he had access to accurate and important information, but something told me that he was not leveling about *how* he knew what he knew about the Paris meeting.

The following evening when I met Mr. Brenneke in the lobby of the Capitol Hill Hotel, we were both nervous. I was afraid that he might have decided not to say anything more. We exchanged small talk and then walked outside and down the sidewalk to one of his favorite restaurants around the block from the hotel. The waiter seated us at a small table close to the front of the room, next to some other diners. As I was wondering how best to break the ice, the sleeve of my dress caught on a napkin under one of the waterglasses, spilling a torrent of ice-cold water out over the tablecloth and onto the floor. We both laughed.

I suggested that we move to a corner table, where we could talk more privately. He agreed, and after that everything went more smoothly.

That night I learned that Richard Brenneke had worked with Mossad, the Israeli secret service, and that he claimed to have been one of the pilots running some of the arms, which had resulted from the agreement made at the Paris meeting, to Iran. He told me the details of the flights: where he flew out of, usually France. In the middle of the conversation, I remembered what Mickey's friend from the NSC had said two nights before. I might as well ask him, I thought. I had nothing to lose.

"Were any of those arms from the—Reforger stores?" I asked. From Brenneke's instant change in expression, you would have thought a bomb was about to go off under the table.

"You know about the *Reforger* stores?" he exclaimed, stunned.

I nodded.

"Is there anything to indicate that these arms you were shipping, that any of them were from the Reforger stores?" I pressed.

Brenneke said that he didn't want to talk about it. At least not then. He said he knew, but that I should talk with someone else, soon, at his office. I said I needed to spend the next day preparing for my press conference on the 25th, and I asked if we could meet the day after the conference. He found that agreeable and said that he'd try to make the press conference.

When I arrived at the National Press Club the morning of August 25, 1988, the room we had rented for the press conference had been expanded on both sides to accommodate more journalists and camera crew. The event was sponsored by the Association for Responsible Dissent (ARDIS), an organization of former CIA officers and agents and other former government employees who joined together to critique U.S. foreign policy;

and by the Women's Peace Initiative. John Stockwell, a former CIA officer and Executive Director of ARDIS, was to be the anchor, and Professor Margaret Brenman-Gibson would introduce me. There, as promised, sitting in the center of the front row was Richard Brenneke.

My prepared remarks incorporated the information Brenneke had revealed. Respecting his wish to remain anonymous, in that section of my remarks I referred to him as "Mr. X." The irony of his being in the room did not escape me.

The event went well. Stockwell stressed that the purpose of the press conference was to get the media to begin asking the right questions, rather than to impart any definitive new information. The appropriate emphasis was, so far, missing from the "October Surprise" story—that was what we were trying to get across. The event lasted for two hours.

That afternoon I had an interview with *Der Spiegel* Television at the West German weekly's offices in downtown Washington. Martin Kilian, *Der Spiegel*'s senior correspondent for Washington, D.C., was keenly interested in the "October Surprise" story and had already done considerable background work on it himself. He wanted to know more about "Mr. X," and I said that I would try to get him to do an interview with *Der Spiegel* off the record. Meanwhile, Kilian wrote an overview article on the "October Surprise" story, which was published in the magazine's September 5, 1988 issue.

"IT'S ALL A HAIG OPERATION"

West Germany was very much in the air. The next morning, the day of my third meeting with Richard Brenneke, the *Washington Post* broke a headline story about a former U.S. Army sergeant who had just been arrested in Bonn as part of a major espionage ring, which had sold NATO war plans and other top-secret information to the Soviets through Hungary. The man who had been arrested, Clyde Lee Conrad, had reportedly had access to NATO's defense plans from 1980 until his retirement in 1985 through his job at a military documents center in West Germany. On an inside page, the article described the stolen NATO documents as "lists of supply facilities for American forces in Europe." Could these be the Reforger stores? I asked myself. It was with this question in mind that I arrived at Brenneke's office at the Institute for Policy Studies that afternoon.

When he closed the door to his office, I pointed out the *Washington Post* article.

"I read that," he said. "I don't know if there's a connection."

Brenneke then explained that, while making a series of arms deliveries to Iran in the 1980's, something didn't feel right about the whole thing. He contacted a friend who, at the time, was a liaison to NATO in the Marine reserves. The Marine colonel had suggested taking down some of the numbers off the cargo boxes so that he could have them checked against supply lists. After checking the numbers, Brenneke said, his friend told him, "You can't be running this stuff. They're not supposed to exist!" "But I am running them," Brenneke had insisted, at which point his friend told him that his cargo was from secret NATO stores—military weapons and spare parts supplies at various locations throughout Europe paid for under the Pentagon's "black budget." They weren't to be touched for any purpose except for the defense of Europe. They weren't supposed to be moved anywhere else, for any reason.

My heart skipped a beat. Was Brenneke telling the truth? In two interviews in as many days, and now also perhaps in the newspaper, the NATO stores had come up. Brenneke could not have known about Mickey's friend, I thought. They could not have compared notes.

Brenneke dialed the number of the now-retired NATO liaison he had mentioned—the man who had "checked the numbers" for him. His name was Richard Muller. A former colonel in the Marine reserves, he also happened to be Brenneke's attorney.

"He wants to talk with you," Richard said, and handed me the receiver.

That morning I learned quite a bit about the NATO stores that I hadn't known before. Muller explained that the first large-scale draw-down of secret NATO military supplies had occurred in 1973, when massive quantities of arms and spare parts were moved out of Europe to Israel to help the Israelis win their war against Egypt. That left the NATO stores in urgent need of replenishment. In the five years following its first draw-down, Alexander Haig, who was Supreme Allied Commander of NATO in Europe from 1974 to 1979, undertook a huge program to restock the facilities.

"Then Stansfield Turner and George Bush would have known about this, too?" I asked.

"Of course," Muller said. "Turner was commander of the allied forces in southern Europe from '75 to '77."

And, I thought, became President Carter's CIA director in time for the 1977 "Halloween Massacre" when hundreds of covert operatives were fired or demoted at the Agency.

"And Bush was then head of the CIA," he added.

"So it wasn't a Turner operation? It was Haig's?" I asked.

"It was Haig who built them up," Muller summarized, "and it was Haig who was in a position in 1981 to draw them down. It was all a Haig operation."

"You mean as Secretary of State? In the Reagan Administration?" I asked, aghast.

"That's the implication," he said.

I was stunned. The timing was incredible. Just the night before, on *Nightline,* Alexander Haig had been asked about the Army sergeant who had passed secret lists from NATO's supply facilities to the Warsaw Pact. He had responded that perhaps the spy had passed information about "support bases and facilities which cannot be changed or moved." A former KGB agent also on the program, Stanislav Levchenko, had warned slyly that "doctoring of information" about American weapons and supplies in Europe might be dangerous to our [U.S.] national security.[1]

"Israel, our ally, wanted the Iran-Iraq War to go on," Muller continued. "That took arms, lots of arms. They had to come from someplace."

"But the Iran-Iraq War caused half a million deaths!" I protested. I couldn't believe what I was hearing.

"Well," he said, almost smugly, "Israel had to do something to occupy its number one enemy, Iraq. It kept 'em busy for over seven years. I don't know, I think it was a pretty neat idea."

A "neat idea"! My thoughts raced. Did these guys all think alike? That was what Oliver North had said about taking "profits" from the Iran arms sales to fund the Contras. But he had also said that that "neat idea" was a covert operation, and covert operations are often counterintelligence operations—lies. North had also talked about "replenishments." Could there be a connection? Some sources, after all, had reported that Iran's payments for the arms had gone to Israel.

Muller continued, "So you know about the island?" he asked.

I didn't, but I thought I'd pretend I hadn't heard him. Maybe he would give more information.

"Excuse me?" I said.

"The island—where the stores are? You know about the island?"

I tried a guess. In unpublished chapters from Mansur Rafizadeh's book *Witness,* I had read about the island of Masira off Oman, near the Persian

Gulf, which the U.S. had leased for a secret military base and supply facilities, which were used in the Desert One hostage rescue operation.

"You mean off Oman?" I asked. Muller was silent. I later read that, as a result of the increased U.S. presence in the Persian Gulf towards the end of the Iran-Iraq War, U.S. facilities "in Oman" had been beefed up to a degree "greater than expected."

The man on the phone believed that it was a "neat idea," if I understood him correctly, to loot secret NATO stores of billions of dollars worth of arms for Iran so that Israel could perpetuate a deadly war and also profit from it. He was now asking me for the name of Mickey's friend at the National Security Council who had told me about the Reforger stores. I wouldn't tell him.

CURIOUSER AND CURIOUSER

On August 30th, after having put Richard Brenneke together with Martin Kilian of *Der Spiegel,* I returned to California. I continued to receive calls from journalists as a spin off from the press conference, and with the presidential election approaching, interest was building in the "October Surprise" story.

The trip to Washington had resulted in a wealth of unexpected new information, particularly the possibility that military supplies from our NATO stores in Europe may have been secretly drawn down to supply Iran with arms, with part of the "profits" being used to support William Casey's now-famous "off-the-shelf, stand-alone, self-financing" covert operations with Israel. If true, there was still one major question about the use of NATO stores to fuel the Iran-Iraq War. However disgusting, the perceived benefit to Israel was clear. But why would top officials of the U.S. government have approved of an operation that would leave Europe less able to defend itself against a conventional attack from the Warsaw Pact? The rationale for the stores, as I understood it, was to give NATO additional time, in case of such a conventional attack, before a decision to use nuclear weapons would have to be made. Surely, I thought, no one in a position of authority would willfully jeopardize the security of all of Europe for Israel. Or would they? There had to be another piece to the puzzle, or some explanation I had not yet thought of.

The apparent answer came, as always, in an unexpected way. In early September 1988 I received a call from a former journalist with Cable News Network who said that someone wanted to talk to me who seemed to have important information about the "October Surprise" story. The following day I received my first call from Informant "Y," who wishes to remain anonymous.

"Y" claimed to have worked for the CIA for twenty years and to have retired around 1984. He didn't want to talk about the circumstances of his leaving the Agency, and I didn't press. He provided a considerable wealth of detail about the October 1980 Paris meeting which, if true, would move the story a major step forward. The details of what he had to say can be found in Chapter II. What is important here is the light he threw on the rationale for the reported draw-down of the NATO stores.

"Y" explained, without hesitation, that the intention of the draw-down had been to *reduce* the amount of time after a conventional Warsaw Pact invasion of Western Europe that NATO commanders would have to go nuclear. He said that the Soviets had been "let know" of the situation as proof that the West had the *will* to use nuclear weapons. This, he explained, was necessary to counter their more than two-to-one superiority in conventional forces. The implicit threat of the use of what nuclear weapons the West did have, he insisted, was what had brought the Soviets to the Intermediate Nuclear Forces (INF) bargaining table, not, as he said, "Reagan's blue eyes."

I restated what he had just told me, "So they killed two birds with one stone, as it were—scared the Soviets to the bargaining table and kept Israel's enemy Iraq busy for eight years fighting the Iran-Iraq War? Is that what you're telling me?"

"That's about the size of it," he said.

"And how do you know about all this?" I asked the obvious question.

"My specialization was NATO. I was stationed in Germany for a number of years. Other places, too. Greece, for instance."

If "Y" had really been in the CIA all those years, I thought, he should be able to provide more specifics. "What about details?" I asked. "Where are the stores drawn down, for instance? And how did the arms get to Iran?"

"It wasn't just Iran," he responded. "They also used the supplies for other 'Contra' operations—Angola, Afghanistan, Nicaragua, as well as Iran. And a lot of other places you don't know about."

"And what about the stores? Name some."

"Because of the draw-down, there are problems at Kitzigen, Bavaria, and at Bad Tolz and Germanhausen. The information on the emptying of NATO Rapid Deployment Force supplies are in BND files."

"How do I know you aren't giving me disinformation" I asked him. "This information is obviously all classified, so there's no way for me to check it."

"You don't," he came right back. "But think about it. It makes sense. The Russians are taking the position that they came to the INF table because they love peace. That's b--- s---. The truth is, we drew down the conventional weapons back-up in Europe and let them know about it—under the table, of course—so they'd know we meant business when we told them NATO would go directly nuclear if they attacked us on the ground."

"And how did we let them know?" I asked.

"In 1986, we swapped one of their top spies, a guy named Koecher, for Shcharansky—the Jewish dissident. We have intelligence that one of the 'presents' Koecher took back to his KGB bosses in Prague was the scoop on the draw-down of NATO stores. Shortly after that, Gorbachev decided to get serious about the INF negotiations."

I thought for a moment. "How do we know Koecher wasn't still really working for us., and that the draw-down story is just a piece of disinformation—like we got Hitler to buy before we invaded Normandy? How do I know you aren't part of that same disinformation strategy, right now?"

"Y" laughed. "You don't. But if there's anything else you've heard of that makes sense of everything that's happened these last eight years, let me know."

I thought for a moment. "Alright. But what about our allies? Do they know? I can't believe that West Germany would agree to a draw-down, regardless of the logic. They're the ones who would have to pay if this strategy turned out to be wrong."

"Only a few know about it, at the *very* top. Almost all of the politicians were given false lists, 'doctored' totals."

"Does Genscher know?" I asked.

"Yeah. He's been a CIA asset for years. He got the straight stuff from Tom Polgar. He's also 'in tight' with Tabatabai."

"Tabatabai? You mean *Sadegh* Tabatabai? The man who was Khomeini's main hostage negotiator in the hostage crisis?"

"That's right. Genscher was at the table with Tabatabai and Carter's man, Warren Christopher, in Bonn, the only time they met on the hostages.''

I knew he was right about that.

"What about what a former Marine liaison to NATO told me? He said it was all a Haig operation. He said that Haig built up the stores in the mid- to late-70's, and then drew them down for all these Reagan-Bush covert operations, including Iran, in the 1980's.''

"That's absolutely right. But you have to understand, Haig wasn't the guy at the top. He's Kissinger's man. It was really a Kissinger operation.''

"Alright,'' I said. "What about how they got there? How did the arms get to Iran?''

"Beginning in 1981, the RDF [Rapid Deployment Force] shipments went through Turkey to Iran. They used the trucking company of a leading German politician.''

"Genscher?'' I asked.

"You'd think so, but no. I won't give you the names over the phone. But—check out the name of the finance minister then, and an official with a name like a famous composer.''

"Y" was ticking me off. "What else?''

"Some of the RDF stores were bought from European dealers. It's not all U.S.-made stuff.''

"What about the amount? Robert McFarlane was reported to have reminded the Iranians during his May 1986 trip to Tehran about a five billion dollar commitment. And that they had already received 1.3 billion dollars towards that total.''

"Y" laughed. "By late May 1986, the looted RDF stores were worth three times that much. At *least* fifteen billion dollars. But the McFarlane report could still be true. Those arms went other places besides Iran— Afghanistan, Angola, Central America—''

I remembered my conversation with Richard Muller. "I simply can't believe that anyone would decide to do this,'' I said. "I mean, those arms resulted, by some counts, in a million deaths and injuries! How can you justify this?''

For the first time in our long conversation, "Y" seemed to get impatient with me. "Look,'' he said firmly, almost in a grandfatherly way. "Some- times you have to do these things. The world isn't an easy place. It worked, didn't it? The world has an INF treaty, the Russians are pulling out of Afghanistan and Angola. Israel didn't have to worry about Iraq for almost eight years, and—''

"—and Casey got his off-the-shelf, self-financing, stand-alone, covert operations, right?" I anticipated "Y."

"Yeah, that's right," he said, with satisfaction. "All in all, I think it was a pretty neat idea."

VIII

PROJECT DEMOCRACY

**"The embargo on weapons exports to Iran is a comedy . . .
By using roundabout means, an increasing number
of companies in the U.S. military-industrial complex
are involved in shipping weapons, munitions, and equipment
to Iran and are earning fabulous profits in the process."**

An Iranian officer, Al DUSTUR, London

In Chapter VI, we saw how Vice President Bush, CIA Director William Casey, and the U.S. State Department have each acknowledged American arms shipments to Iran beginning in the early 1980's. President Reagan himself told NBC's Chris Wallace in November 1986 that he had been aware of "major" U.S. arms shipments to Iran by "private" dealers. By his choice of the word "private," the President wanted viewers to believe that, although he had been aware of these shipments, there had been no U.S. Government approval or involvement. In this chapter we will show how misleading that statement was.

After Eugene Hasenfus's plane was shot down over Nicaragua on October 5, 1986, President Reagan used the same language when he told reporters, "We've been aware that there are 'private' groups and 'private' citizens that have been trying to help the Contras . . . but we did not know the particulars of what they're doing." It wasn't long before Congress and the American public learned that it had been the President's own idea to ask those "private" citizens and "private" groups to fund the Nicaraguan resistance.

From the day that President Carter imposed his formal embargo on U.S. arms deliveries to Iran shortly after the hostage crisis began in November 1979, all U.S. arms sales to Iran have been illegal. Since that day, the

State Department has issued no export licenses to private dealers for the shipment of military equipment to Iran. Any American weapons sent to Iran during the eight years of the Reagan-Bush Administration, therefore, were either illegal or had to have had the secret blessing of the United States government.

In this chapter we will review reports that huge quantities of U.S. and other-nationality Western arms shipped to the Khomeini regime in the early- and mid-1980's had, in fact, not only the secret blessing of the Reagan-Bush White House, but the active assistance in some cases of the U.S. military. A common thread throughout many of these reports of arms deliveries to Iran from both the United States and Western Europe is the oversight provided by the Marine liaison to President Reagan's National Security Council, Oliver North, under the umbrella of a program called "Project Democracy." Under its aegis, North was given what amounted to a global charge account, through Iran/Contra middleman Richard Secord and Albert Hakim, with which he could set up covert operations anywhere in the world with no Congressional oversight and no public accountability. The idea behind Project Democracy was to "privatize" U.S. foreign policy worldwide. But what was that policy, as it pertained to Iran?

ENTER MACDUFF

The first hint that something was terribly wrong, appropriately enough, came from a man whose surname sounds like Macduff, a central character in Shakespeare's famous play *Macbeth*. In that drama, Macduff is the good thane who discovers the horrible crimes of the Scottish king, Macbeth, and vows to do something about them. Committed and deeply loyal to his country, he returns with an army of soldiers disguised as the trees of Burnham Wood to defeat the king and set the kingdom right.

I first learned of Mr. McDuffie from Mansur Rafizadeh, the former U.S. chief of SAVAK, the Shah of Iran's secret police. In late August and early September of 1987, I had visited Mr. Rafizadeh's office to review documents and information that he had put together on the Desert One hostage rescue attempt. Shortly after I had returned to California, his assistant forwarded materials, which they had received from Mr. Glenn McDuffie, a former 35-year employee of Westinghouse Corporation who, as part of his job, had worked with the U.S. Army Missile Command (MICOM).

Mr. McDuffie was suing Westinghouse Corporation. He claimed that he had been wrongfully fired in March 1982, after thirty-five years of outstanding service and numerous promotions, for having protested to the company's management that his supervisors may have diverted critical HAWK missile parts to Iran beginning in the early 1980's. The parts that he said had been sent to the Khomeini regime were upgrades for critical digital signal processor boards for the missiles' new Pulse Acquisition Radar (PAR) system.[1] These upgrades represented a significant improvement in the anti-aircraft HAWK missile's low-altitude radar capability.[2] What was more disturbing, however, was that McDuffie claimed that the PAR boards that had been sent to Iran were supposed to go instead to NATO for the defense of Europe, and that the CIA, FBI, and White House had all been aware of the diversions and did nothing to stop them. The author had already received some information that secret NATO weapons stores were being diverted to Iran from Western Europe, but this was the first hint that similar diversions were taking place out of the United States itself.

In court papers and correspondence, Mr. McDuffie held that these particular HAWK parts were critical to the defense of NATO and that without enough of them, NATO's own anti-aircraft missiles would not work. His documents showed that in mid-March of 1981, in fact, MICOM's commander, Major General Moore, had made a special trip to Europe to try to discover first-hand the reason for a "quiet crisis," which had developed there over the HAWK situation.[3] A memo provided by Mr. McDuffie dated March 12, 1981, states that "MG Moore, MICOM commander, has returned from Europe with burning questions relating to the on-line availability of HAWK missile systems in Europe." March 1981, I recalled, was the same month that CIA Director William Casey had asked President Reagan to authorize secret covert operations with respect to Iran,[4] and only three months before Israeli arms dealer Yaacov Nimrodi reportedly signed a contract to deliver HAWK missiles to the Khomeini regime.[5] The following year, 1982, the "Khomeini emissary" who had approached Richard Allen of the Reagan-Bush campaign in early October 1980 with an arms-for-hostages proposal, Houshang Lavi, said that he had received Israeli Prime Minister Menachem Begin's go-ahead to ship HAWK missile parts to Iran. Intriguingly, the $250 million in U.S. military equipment that President Carter had frozen upon the taking of the fifty-two American hostages included "$20.8 million [worth of] improved HAWK air defense units."[6] Although that embargoed equipment has never been delivered, the presence of improved HAWKS on the list showed Iran's need for the weapons.

Like the reported draw-down and diversion to Iran of secret NATO stores in Europe, Mr. McDuffie said that the HAWK radar parts he claimed Westinghouse had sent to Iran had been upgraded and diverted to the Khomeini regime under a "black" (secret) Pentagon program. The U.S. military, he said, was centrally involved in the operation. According to McDuffie, key individuals from the U.S. Army's Missile Command at Redstone Arsenal, Alabama, Westinghouse Corporation, and a number of other defense companies had covered up a massive "private" pipeline of HAWK missile parts and other U.S. arms shipments to Iran beginning in 1981.

Significantly, the Congressional Iran/Contra Committees later reported that the secret shipment of HAWK anti-aircraft missile parts to Iran authorized by President Reagan had substantially, and in some cases completely, depleted the U.S. Army's own supplies of several critical items and had damaged the U.S. Army's war readiness. As part of the U.S. negotiations to trade arms for hostages, it said, the Iranians had demanded a list of HAWK missile parts and the CIA had approved that list to Army depots. With the CIA as middleman, the Army had provided the Iranians with thirteen shipping pallets of HAWK parts after National Security Council officials, including Oliver North, ordered the usual readiness review for U.S. arms transfers bypassed "in the interests of secrecy." Fully one-third of almost 150 HAWK parts demanded by Iran, the report said, existed in Army stocks in only such small amounts that the CIA- and NSC-approved transfer to Iran could have had a devastating impact on the readiness of U.S. forces. For fifteen of the requested HAWK-related items, Army stocks would have been completely depleted if the Pentagon had provided the full requested amounts. "Supplying eleven of the items would have depleted more than half the available stocks." Army officers were able to adjust some of the requests, but, the Congressional report emphasized, all of the requested parts were shipped on the order of the CIA and the White House with a resulting impact on readiness that "remained critical for ten to twelve of the parts." The report continued that "The parts were ordered to be shipped even though U.S. HAWK missile batteries would be deficient if they were needed. . . . The availability of one part was particularly acute. The Iranians had requested a quantity of this one particular part used in the HAWK radar [to guide the missiles to their targets]. If the part fails, the system does not work; if there are no replacements, the system remains useless. The Army had only a limited supply of this part. Shipping the parts would put the readiness impact in the 'high risk' category,'' the report concluded.[7]

When I read these reports I was aghast. This was exactly what Glenn McDuffie said had happened with the Westinghouse HAWK parts. Now the Congressional Iran/Contra Committees were saying that this had been going on with the approval of the President of the United States.

Though the Congressional Iran/Contra Committee's report leads the reader to believe that the problem with U.S. and NATO readiness caused by the diversion of HAWK missile parts to Iran began only in the late 1980's, McDuffie's documentation makes it clear that a policy of sacrificing U.S. and NATO security to the interests of Iran and Israel may have began as much as five years earlier—almost as soon as President Reagan and Vice President Bush gained office. The Congressional Iran/Contra Committee's report and 99 percent of press reports also claimed that the decision to ship HAWKs and HAWK parts to Iran was taken in the context of the Reagan-Bush Administration's secret efforts to obtain the release of U.S. citizens who were not taken hostage in Lebanon until 1984. HAWKs and HAWK parts, however, had been flowing to Iran since 1981, when there were no U.S. hostages in Lebanon—or in Iran. It is therefore far more likely that the entire secret U.S. policy of supplying the Khomeini regime with U.S. arms was arrived at within the context of the Reagan-Bush campaign and/or Reagan-Bush transition team's attempt to win freedom for a very different group of hostages—the original fifty-two who were released on Reagan's inauguration.

A depletion of HAWK radar spare parts in West Germany, which would be the key battleground in any conventional (non-nuclear) military confrontation with the Warsaw Pact, would result in the greatest damage to NATO security. This would be especially true if terrorists attacked existing HAWK radar facilities, in which case a shortage of spares would suddenly become a matter of life and death for millions of people. In August 1985, Red Army terrorists, in fact, carried out four such attacks against U.S. military facilities in West Germany.[8] The following month, in September, three bomb blasts destroyed HAWK radar equipment at the U.S. Army's anti-aircraft missile site near the West German town of Nohfelden.[9] Only a few weeks later, in November 1985, the National Security Council, as part of Oliver North's ''Project Democracy,'' authorized the shipment of even more HAWK missiles by Israel to Iran. These are the shipments that became a major focus of the Iran/Contra investigations.

According to Mr. McDuffie, Don Howard, who was an attorney for

MICOM from 1979 to 1984, told him that HAWK missile radar systems were being shipped to Iran through Taiwan and South Korea in 1981. Significantly, a publication by the former President of Iran, Abolhassan Bani Sadr, has also reported that these same two countries, Taiwan and South Korea, began shipping U.S. military spare parts to Iran the same year. An employee of Iran/Contra defendant Albert Hakim's Tehran office of Stanford Technology Corporation during the 1970's has told the author that Hakim specialized in "fixing" HAWK missile part deals between the United States and Iran while secretly reporting to Mossad, the Israeli intelligence service. *Time* magazine reported that in the 12-month period prior to July 1983, (South) Korean Airlines (KAL) and two government-controlled South Korean companies made *sixty* separate purchases of HAWK missiles and spare parts for shipment to Iran. The above-mentioned Stanford Technology Corporation employee told the author that papers documenting Iran/Contra middleman Albert Hakim's involvement in organizing these early HAWK shipments with KAL were amongst documents conveniently "stolen" from Hakim's California office safe just as the Iran/Contra affair broke in the press in 1986. Mr. Hakim's involvement in the HAWK deliveries to Iran under the Reagan-Bush Administration may, in fact, have begun as early as 1981. According to former CIA contract agent William Herrmann, Albert Hakim attended at least one of the secret Paris meetings in mid-October 1980 between Reagan-Bush campaign representatives and Iranian arms procurement officials to work out arrangements for the shipment of U.S. arms to the Khomeini regime following Reagan's inauguration.

According to Mr. McDuffie, the critical HAWK missile radar parts manufactured by Westinghouse Corporation were smuggled into Iran under the auspices of Intergraph Corporation of Huntsville, Alabama. He says that the trucks that transported them to Mexico, from where they were shipped to Iran, returned with partial "payment" in the form of drugs.[10] During a break in his trial against Westinghouse for wrongful dismissal, McDuffie claims that one of his former supervisors tried to run him down in a car whose license plate was traced to an Iranian employee of Intergraph Corporation, who then escaped to Iran.

On the weekend of November 9, 1984, an Intergraph employee, Charles White, of Huntsville, Alabama, was murdered as he was preparing to make similar knowledge of the Iran arms diversions and drug connection public. The night of White's murder, someone also attempted to break into McDuffie's house. According to McDuffie, the CIA was behind White's murder, and its involvement was covered up by the Justice Department, which called off a local FBI investigation into the case.[11] In April 1987, the *Wall Street Journal* confirmed that the FBI had withheld information about U.S. arms shipments to Iran long before disclosure of the so-called "first" HAWK deliveries in 1985.[12]

Not long after White's murder, an attempt was made on the life of an employee of one of Intergraph Corporation's contractees, Anthony Parker, whom Mr. McDuffie says was also knowledgeable about the diversion of U.S. military equipment to Iran. A private detective hired by McDuffie to look into the possible relationship between the threats to his own life, the attempt on Parker, and the White murder told him that to continue the investigation would "antagonize the FBI and the local (Huntsville, Alabama) police department."[13]

The harrassment and intimidation experienced by McDuffie and Parker was not reserved for civilians. In 1985, Petty Officer Robert Jackson reported that his life was threatened when he tried to alert the Navy to the theft of F-14 fighter jet parts from the U.S.S. *Kitty Hawk* and the Miramar Naval Supply Depot and their attempted diversion to Iran. A subsequent Congressional investigation headed by Congressman Jim Bates revealed that Khomeini agents had gained access to a wide inventory of U.S. naval weapon stores. At last report, Iran/Contra special prosecutor Lawrence Walsh was considering whether to take on a pending court case in which two Navy men had charged ten defendants with plotting to divert U.S. military parts from Navy ships to Iran with the assistance of a London-based arms dealer.[14] The author's expectation is that this case, like the major conspiracy and theft counts against Oliver North, will be dropped because the diversions were in fact part of secret National Security Council and CIA policy.

In light of these murders, attempted murders, and coverups, it should be recalled that Oliver North, who oversaw President Reagan and Vice-President Bush's "Project Democracy," had reportedly threatened anyone who leaked information about the secret arms diversions to Iran with assassination.[15]

According to McDuffie, Iran Electronics Industries (IEI) had the facilities to manufacture HAWK missiles, given that it could obtain critical U.S.-made parts and subsystems from U.S. military stores. IEI had been established and operated for the Shah by McDuffie's company, Westinghouse Corporation. According to a former U.S. employee of IEI, some fifteen to twenty former Iranian employees of that company became Khomeini agents and later worked with the CIA inside major U.S. defense contractors. If so, they are part of one hundred secret Khomeini agents that reporter Jack Anderson estimated had infiltrated the U.S. defense establishment as of 1987.[16]

Mr. McDuffie informed all major U.S. governmental authorities of the diversions of HAWK missiles and other U.S. military equipment to Iran beginning in 1981, with no response. He notified President Reagan on June 24, 1985; the U.S. Attorney General on November 9, 1986, and on April 21, 1987; U.S. Judge MacKinnon, who appointed Iran/Contra special prosecutor Lawrence Walsh; and key members of the Senate Intelligence and Congressional Iran/Contra Committees, including Senator David Boren, Representative Lee Hamilton, and Senator Daniel Inouye. After writing to the Federal Bureau of Investigation on October 5, 1984, he met personally with its agents who refused to take written notes of his evidence of early U.S. arms diversions to Iran.

If what Mr. McDuffie reports is even partially true, it is evident that Iranian agents may have been bribing high-level officials of the U.S. government, the U.S. military, and U.S. defense contractors to facilitate and keep quiet about these early arms and spare parts diversions to Iran. McDuffie brought his charges to court in June 1988. On June 14, 1988, FBI agents conducted a massive surprise search of U.S. military and defense industry offices in an attempt to document accusations of fraud and bribery.[17] A top U.S. official was later reported to have said, in connection with this FBI procurement fraud investigation, that it was "time to stop the Iranian arms bazaar" in the United States.

Mr. McDuffie's information may also make sense of one of the central mysteries of the Iran/Contra affair: why, in November 1985, Iran refused to accept eighteen HAWK missiles it received from Israel, and why President Reagan's emissary Robert McFarlane delivered advanced HAWK missile parts during his now-famous late May 1986 trip to Tehran. If Iran had already received upgrades for its HAWK systems beginning in 1981, as McDuffie claims, Khomeini's agents would have been expecting the advanced equipment and would have recognized that they were being delivered outmoded merchandise in 1985. It is possible that the "particular part used in the HAWK radar" subsequently sent to satisfy their demands was the upgraded HAWK radar subsystem McDuffie says had been delivered to the Iranians in the early 1980's. During the Iran/Contra hearings, Oliver North confirmed that Iran had rejected Israel's HAWK missile delivery of November 1985 because they had expected to receive "SUPER HAWKS," or I-HAWKS, capable of destroying high-flying Iraqi bombers, instead.[18]

THE BLUE PIPELINE

From McDuffie's material it was clear that the U.S. military, as well as the National Security Council, the CIA, and the FBI had been involved in making arrangements for, and covering up, U.S. arms deliveries to Iran long before 1985. What the author did not know was whether this activity was sporadic—whether it happened on a case-by-case basis—or whether it had been centrally organized.

In 1988, while researching this question, the author received a call from a man who claimed to have been a former G-2 (General Intelligence) officer for the U.S. in Europe and, more recently, an investigator for the U.S. Department of Labor. Since retiring from that job, he had been researching the same question and had information to share about the U.S. military's participation in so-called "private" U.S. arms shipments to Iran, which President Reagan had acknowledged knowing about to *NBC News*.

The man's name was Dick Murray. He claimed that a steady stream of U.S. military equipment had flowed, always at night, to Iran from the mainland United States in the 1980's through what was called the "Blue Pipeline." It had been given this code name because the sea containers bound for Iran had been painted blue. He said that his research, which he claimed had been given to WLS-TV in Chicago, revealed that beginning at least as early as 1982, a company called Capital Engineering & Manufacturing of Chicago had trucked air-cooling units, night vision kits, and assault bridge launchers for U.S. tanks in blue sea containers to Intermaritime Forwarding Company in New York where they were loaded onto waiting ships. The ships then carried the military equipment to ports in Spain, Italy, and Greece, from where it was transported to Iran by members of the Danish Seamans Union. Murray claimed that Intermaritime was a CIA proprietary—a CIA front company. Based on interviews with the Danish Seamans Union and individuals familiar with the operations of Intermaritime, Murray estimated that at least fifty to sixty boatloads of American military equipment had left New York harbor for Portugal, Spain, Italy, Germany, Greece, and other European ports en route to Iran throughout the 1980's.

Capital Engineering, Murray claimed, was one of at least a dozen companies that were part of the "Blue Pipeline." This report checked with *Time* magazine, which reported in 1983 that hundreds of millions of dollars worth of U.S.-made arms and military equipment had flowed annually to Iran in the first years of the Reagan-Bush Administration from at least a dozen American companies, facilitated by international arms dealers operating out of the United States. Mr. Murray said that the "holding point" for "Blue Pipeline" arms bound for Iran was a naval base located on a peninsula near the Statue of Liberty, which was part of the U.S. military's Sealift Command. The Sealift Command, he said, used a fleet of "private" ships, which operate for civilian companies as well as for the U.S. Navy. Under the auspices of the Command, "private" vessels receive U.S. military protection. Murray claimed that Capital Engineering & Manufacturing's union in Chicago had asked Senator Paul Simon, the FBI, and the U.S. Customs Service to investigate labor practices at the company. During the resulting investigation, he says, Department of Defense officials refused to take written notes about evidence for "Blue Pipeline" arms deliveries to Iran. According to *Time,* two other companies among the dozen or so U.S. firms that supplied Iran with military equipment in violation of U.S. licensing laws prior to 1983 were Fort Worth based Bell Helicopter and Textron, Inc.

Because they were central to both the Iran/Contra scandal and Glenn McDuffie's information, I asked Mr. Murray about HAWK missile shipments.

"Is there any evidence that these 'private' ships carried HAWK missiles or HAWK missile parts to Iran?" I asked.

"Absolutely. The Danes shipped HAWK missiles from Italy to Iran, armed and loaded by the U.S. Army. You can't get HAWKS out of U.S. arsenals, whether here in the U.S. or out of European stores, without official authorization. They also shipped M-60 tanks, artillery, and ammunition. The Danish Seamans Union has been monitoring the flow of U.S. arms to Iran for years. The American Seamans Union is also ready and willing to give its testimony that this has been going on," he explained.

Murray's information checked with reports by the New York publication *Newsday,* which interviewed British merchant marine captain Thomas Screech. Screech had worked with the Danish Seamans Union to run a shipload of two thousand U.S. serial bomb fuses from Portugal to Bandar Abbas, Iran, in July-August of 1982.[19] Cargo containers on board his ship showed that the fuses originated at one of the U.S. Government's own ammunition plants operated on contract by "private" firms. Significantly, Screech's mission in 1982 was on behalf of a company owned by Houshang Lavi's brothers, Western Dynamics International of Long Island, New York. Western Dynamic's Iran representative was reported to have been

Sadegh Tabatabai, Khomeini's designated negotiator in the hostage crisis. Houshang Lavi had been the man who offered Reagan-Bush campaign officials Richard Allen and Laurence Silberman, in the presence of Robert McFarlane, an arms-for-hostages deal in Washington one month before the 1980 election, and reportedly also attended at least one meeting with Reagan-Bush campaign manager William Casey in Paris two weeks later, on October 19 or 20, 1980. When Captain Screech reported his U.S. arms deliveries to Iran to the U.S. embassy in London, the U.S. State Department told embassy personnel to drop their inquiry into the matter. Screech also reported his experience to the Congressional Iran/Contra Committees and to Iran/Contra special prosecutor Lawrence Walsh.

"DR. DOOM" GETS OFF

Reports of the Blue Pipeline, and Glenn McDuffie's revelations, were just the tip of the iceberg of high-level government involvement in U.S. arms deliveries to Iran long before the late-1985 shipments that became a focus of the Iran/Contra scandal.

In early 1981, the U.S. Customs Service contracted with Texans Gary Howard and Ronald Tucker to work with Green Beret veteran Richard Meadows. Howard, now a U.S. border patrol officer, had been in Texas law enforcement; Tucker was a narcotics investigator for the State of Texas; and Meadows had been a key operative in President Carter's Desert One hostage rescue mission in April 1980. Howard, Tucker, and Meadows's mission, called "Houston I," was, they were told, to stop an arms smuggling operation. In March of 1981, under "Houston I," Customs seized 360 handguns, 100 M203 40M grenade launchers, and 1,146 Colt M16 machine guns from a Boeing 707 at Houston International Airport.

Shortly after the successful completion of "Houston I," the U.S. Customs Service re-contracted with Howard and Tucker for another, larger mission called "Houston III." "Houston III" 's goal was to catch one of the world's biggest and reportedly most ruthless arms dealers, Briton Ian Smalley, in the act of making what they were told would be illegal U.S. arms shipments to Iran. Smalley had named himself "Dr. Doom."

According to Howard and Tucker, in 1981 Smalley worked with Mr. M. Sarkis Sogahlian, a Miami-based arms dealer with close links to

Vice-President Bush's office. Their evidence shows that a number of Bush's top national security aides, including Colonel Sam Watson, General Stubbelheim, and Daniel Murphy used Sogahlian's planes for various purposes.[20]

When Howard and Tucker began "Houston III," "Dr. Doom" was reported to be in the process of making arrangements to sell over 8,000 U.S. TOW anti-tank missiles, eight C-130 transport planes, 100 M48A-5 tanks, and loads of ammunition to Iran. The agents invested over a million dollars of their own money setting up front companies for the "sting" operation and performing the numerous sub-operations required by Customs. Then Customs headquarters unexpectedly shut down the operation.

In the early summer of 1982, Tucker and Meadows claim that they were told by Defense Intelligence Agency (DIA) agent Wayne Long, who was DIA's liaison to the anti-terrorist Delta Force, that "Dr. Doom" was to be left alone because of pressure that had been brought to bear by Secretary Alexander Haig's State Department. It was Haig, according to the *Washington Post*, who had authorized the first U.S. arms deliveries to Iran as early as February 1981.[21] Long himself had reportedly been involved in U.S. arms deliveries to Iran.[22]

In the spring of 1982, according to Howard and Tucker, Iran was defrauded of some $56 million by "Dr. Doom" in cooperation with an Iranian fugitive named Ahmed Khudari (also sometimes spelled "Heydari" or "Heidari"), at which time Smalley changed plans and prepared to ship arms to Iraq. "Doom," however, apparently continued to do business with the Iranians.

Months before the so-called "first" U.S. arms shipments to Iran in August-September 1985, Howard and Tucker received invoices and letters dated February and March 1985 documenting a shipment of 5,000 U.S. TOW anti-tank missiles to Iran. The letter covering the deal was signed by Iran/Contra middleman Manucher Gorbanifar, Iran's top arms buyer in Europe. When they brought these incriminating documents, relating to what they thought were unauthorized arms deals with the Khomeini regime, to the attention of the U.S. Customs Service, agent Rod Hale, they say, was nervously ordered by Washington to under no circumstances accept copies of documents on the TOW missile agreements with Iran.

"Doom" had also reportedly been involved in earlier arms deals with Iran. Howard and Tucker's investigation reveals that in 1980 he shipped sixty tank engines from England to Nice, France, from where they were flown to Iran through Israel.[23] U.S. businessman and arms dealer Richard Brenneke, who claims to have met in Paris with Reagan-Bush campaign manager William Casey and Iranian officials before the 1980 election, has flight records showing that he piloted flights from Nice to Iran during this same period.

Howard and Tucker claim that a number of high-ranking U.S. military and government officials were fully aware of these early U.S. arms deliveries to Iran, including then deputy director of the CIA General Sam Wilson, President Reagan's NSC aide Oliver North, Customs Commissioner William van Raab, London Customs attaché Calvin White, former CIA operative Richard Brenneke, CIA case officer Bob Kerritt who worked with Brenneke, former Israeli intelligence agent William Northrop, Colonel Wayne Long of the DIA, State Department official Ralph Johnson, CIA agent Bob Ellis, Thomas Allen Twetten, Donald Hoirup, Customs agent William Rudman, and Customs agent Harvey Wayson.[24]

After the Iran/Contra revelations of 1988 and 1987, Howard and Tucker realized that their mission to stop "Dr. Doom" had to have been sabotaged by Alexander Haig's State Department, the FBI, the U.S. Customs Service and the Pentagon. Top-level officials had put an end to their "sting" operation against Smalley because they were afraid that a genuine investigation would reveal the secret stream of U.S. arms, which had been flowing to Iran with the blessings of the Reagan-Bush White House and the CIA since early 1981.

Ian Smalley was arrested in 1982, but all charges against him except one were dropped, and he returned to Texas. In June 1987, Gary Howard and Ron Tucker sued the U.S. Government in Washington, D.C., for over $100 million in lost commissions and expenses from the aborted "Houston III" mission.[25] Their trial, which is pending at the time of this writing, was put on hold when the judge in the case received documents on the operation from the CIA. When their suit comes to trial, Howard and Tucker plan to call former NSC aide Oliver North as a key witness.

FROM EUROPE WITH LOVE

At the Williamsburg Summit where leaders of the seven Western powers met in 1983, President Reagan called for restoring Western economic ties to Iran. The implementation of that decision led to an increase in Iranian oil exports to the West and therefore to increased revenues, which the Khomeini regime used to purchase arms and ammunition for its war with Iraq. It was this boost in income and new weapons purchases that allowed Iran to achieve military equilibrium in the Iran-Iraq War by the mid-1980's.

THE FRENCH CONNECTION

Hashemi Rafsanjani, the powerful speaker of Iran's Parliament, set off a firestorm when he charged that French Prime Minister Jacques Chirac had asked Iran to delay the release of French hostages then held by pro-Iranian kidnappers in Lebanon until after the March 16, 1986, election, which Chirac went on to win.[26] According to the *Independent* of London, Chirac promised Iran French-made arms in exchange for the delayed release of the French hostages.[27] In September 1986, shortly after the election, Iranian-backed Hezbollah militants released one French hostage, after which France paid off the first one-third on a loan owed to Iran from the time of the Shah.[28] After a second French hostage was released the following month, in October, France reportedly promised Iran yet more arms, citing "the evolution of French policy in the Middle East."[29] In all, Iranian-backed militants released four French citizens during the period following Chirac's reported arms-for-hostage-delay deal.

Where would the Prime Minister of France have gotten the idea that the Khomeini regime might agree to such an outrageous hostage-delay-for-arms deal? According to an informant who claims to have read a French intelligence report on the alleged 1980 Paris meeting among Reagan-Bush campaign manager William Casey, middleman Manucher Gorbanifar, and Iranian officials to work out a similar hostage-delay-for-arms agreement before the 1980 U.S. election, French intelligence officials participated in this October 1980 Paris meeting and filed an official report on the negotiations with their government. This document, which was allegedly filed with the French intelligence service SDECE, was reportedly discussed with then President-elect Ronald Reagan during Reagan's meeting with SDECE chief Alexandre de Marenches in late November 1980 in California. Chirac could easily have gained access to, or knowledge of, such an SDECE report.

Chirac's March 1986 deal with Iran was not the only arms-for-hostages agreement that he reportedly made with Khomeini. In the summer of 1987, after French police tried to question an Iranian interpreter suspected of involvement in a wave of terrorist attacks in Paris the summer before, Wahid Gordji, Iranian militants surrounded the French embassy in Tehran causing Chirac to break off diplomatic relations with the Khomeini regime. But in November 1987, in yet another secret deal, France reportedly paid Hezbollah a large ransom, agreed to Gordji's release, and paid off the second of three installments on its billion dollar loan from the Shah.[30] When the remaining French hostages were released on November 27, 1987, with the reported assistance of Iran/Contra middleman Manucher Gorbanifar, France bowed to Iran's wishes one more time by expelling dozens of anti-Khomeini dissidents who had been granted political asylum in France,[31] paid off the final third of its loan, promised the Khomeini regime even more arms, and pledged not to ship weapons to Iran's enemy, Iraq.[32]

Chirac's numerous reported arms-for-hostage-delay and arms-for-hostages deals with Khomeini fit a pattern. In June 1986, "to improve relations with Iran," he expelled Khomeini's number-one opponent in exile, Mojahedin leader Massoud Rajavi, in exchange for two French hostages, who were released days later.[33]

In addition to the apparent link between the reported 1980 Reagan-Bush and 1986 Chirac arms-for-hostage-delay deals with Iran, there have also been numerous reports that both the White House and the U.S. military assisted France in shipping arms to Iran. Oliver North's "Project Democracy," which was run out of the National Security Council's offices in the White House, reportedly worked with the French SNPE Corporation and Swedish-born arms dealer and Israeli liaison Karl-Erik Schmitz to arrange weapons deliveries to the Khomeini regime.[34] In August 1981, former Iranian President Abolhassan Bani Sadr, who had then just taken up exile in France, revealed that his government had recently purchased U.S. arms from Israel over his objections with the active assistance of the French government and a French trading company called SETI.[35] In February 1982, BBC Television in London reported that a Frenchman, Jean Luc Deverent, had been involved in SETI's 1981 arms deals with Iran, which included engines for British-made Scorpion tanks, radios, and U.S. F-4 Phantom jet tires. BBC said that a "French government agent" had put SETI in touch with the Israeli embassy in Paris, which helped the company make arrangements with Israel to ship the equipment to Iran.[36] This "French government agent" may well have been Major Robert Benes, an agent of the SDECE, the French equivalent of the CIA, who had expertise in the Middle East. It was Benes, according to former CIA operative

Richard Brenneke, who represented the French intelligence agency at the alleged October 20, 1980, meeting in Paris with Reagan-Bush campaign manager William Casey shortly before the 1980 election to work out an arms deal with Iran in exchange for the delayed release of the fifty-two U.S. hostages. After the French government put SETI in touch with the Israeli embassy in Paris in 1981, the Israeli embassy then reportedly contacted Ahmed Khudari (also "Heydari" or "Heidari"), an Iranian arms dealer well connected to Tehran's military command, who oversaw arrangements for the arms deliveries from Iran's end. SETI is probably also the "French firm" to which author Samuel Segev has referred in connection with Israel's arrangements with Ahmed Khudari to sell U.S. arms to Iran in 1981 (see Chapter VI).[37] "Dr. Doom," British international arms dealer Ian Smalley, was also reportedly working with Khudari at that time, apparently on the same tank engine deals.[38]

According to journalists who have investigated the companies involved, SETI may be related to the SATI Company of Zug, Switzerland. Like SETI, SATI was also reported to be involved in black market arms deals with the Iranian regime in 1981 and 1982.[39] According to a book about the early arms shipments to Iran published in Germany, SATI also dealt with notorious terrorist and P-2 member Stefano della Chiaie who used the company to camouflage P-2's underground weapons deals with the Khomeini regime. Della Chiaie was charged with blowing up the Bologne train station in Italy in 1980, an act of terrorism in which eighty-five people were killed and two hundred more injured. For more information on P-2's dealings with Iran, see Chapter IX.

Top U.S. military officers in addition to Lt. Col. Oliver North, Colonel Robert McFarlane, Admiral John Poindexter, and retired Major General Richard Secord were reportedly involved with early, secretly sanctioned U.S. arms sales to Iran. In the early 1980's, an office of European Defense Associates (EDA) was set up in Paris to supply Iran with up to $1 billion in advanced U.S. military equipment, including M-48 battle tanks, twenty-five or more attack helicopters, thirty-nine F-4 fighter jets, F-4 surveillance equipment, submarines, and Harpoon and Sidewinder missiles from U.S. Army stockpiles in Europe.[40] Beginning in 1983, EDA's manager was Colonel Ralph Broman, chief of the Pentagon's own Office of Defense Cooperation in the U.S. embassy in Paris. There, as part of his official position, Broman was entrusted with monitoring international shipments of the same U.S. arms EDA was making arrangements to sell to the Khomeini regime. Also connected with EDA was Col. William Mott IV, an officer at the U.S. embassy in London and the founder of a "private"

British company, Spearhead Atlantic, which dealt with European Defense Associates.

A co-owner of EDA was U.S. Army Colonel Paul Cutter (aka Paul Sjeklocha).[41] Cutter has been linked both to the Mossad, Israel's intelligence service,[42] and to the CIA.[43] In 1982, Cutter reportedly met with then Israeli Defense Minister Ariel Sharon, the chief of staff of Israel's defense forces Rafi Eitan, General Amos Gilboa, and the head of Israel's military intelligence service, after which he began arrangements to ship 1,140 U.S. TOW anti-tank missiles to Iran. In his dealings with the Khomeini regime, Cutter reportedly had the assistance of Lieutenant Colonel Wayne Gillespie of the U.S. Army's Material Command. Cutter then worked with Iranian arms smuggler Fabrin Sanai and with Amir Hosseni (aka Hossein M. Azar), an officer in Khomeini's secret police SAVAMA, to ship U.S. arms to Iran.[44] In July 1985, Cutter and Gillespie were indicted for their activities, but only Cutter was prosecuted. In December 1985, he was convicted of attempting to smuggle U.S. arms to Iran and sentenced to five years in prison. In November 1986, he filed a $1 million lawsuit against the U.S. Government for false prosecution, claiming that the FBI had used the Mafia to entrap him in his later deals with the Khomeini regime. Cutter was released from prison in Safford, Arizona, on February 19, 1987, still insisting that his arms dealings with Iran had been authorized by the Pentagon and the White House.

When the Reagan-Bush Administration's own secret arms dealings with Iran were exposed in 1986 and 1987, Paul Cutter told *The New York Times*, ''We all worked under the umbrella of [U.S.] Defense Department approval.''[45] In a radio interview from prison in 1987, he estimated that U.S. arms deliveries to Iran had amounted to $1.3 billion—$1.3 billion is the precise amount of U.S. military equipment that President Reagan's own emissary, Robert McFarlane, reportedly reminded Iranian officials they had already received during his now-famous late May 1986 trip to Tehran.[46] According to other reports, it was Cutter's associate, EDA manager Colonel Ralph Broman, who called Colin Powell, later to become President Reagan's White House national security adviser, at the Pentagon in late 1985 to request the release of U.S. TOW anti-tank missiles to the CIA for secret delivery to Iran. It was this delivery that became a central focus of the Iran/Contra investigations.

In June 1985, the U.S. Army investigated charges that Colonel Ralph Broman and the Paris office of EDA had violated conflict of interest laws, which prohibit U.S. military officers from using information gained in the course of their employment for private gain. The investigation also focused on allegations that EDA's activities may have undermined U.S. efforts to keep American arms out of the hands of Iran-loyal terrorists. The Army's report on EDA was referred to the CIA, the DIA, and the National Security Agency, but no prosecutions resulted. That is, neither the U.S. military nor top U.S. intelligence agencies did anything to stop active and retired U.S. Army officers from making arrangements to sell weapons from U.S. Army stockpiles in Europe to the Khomeini regime.

Marine Lieutenant Colonel Oliver North's reported dealings with the French SNPE Corporation and EDA's activities in Paris may be explained by the close association between French businessman John Delaroque, who was involved in a number of large weapons deals with Iran linked to Israeli intelligence, and U.S. Marine Corps Commandant, General P.X. Kelley. Delaroque is reported to have been a boyhood friend of Commandant Kelley, who was Oliver North's boss before he joined President Reagan's NSC staff at the White House.[47] Another close associate of John Delaroque is former French Navy pilot and arms dealer Bernard Veillot. Veillot and CIA-linked Claude Lang set up a Panama-based company, Daloe Finance, to handle the financial end of their arms deals with Iran in the 1980's. Both men reportedly met in France with Iran/Contra defendant Richard Secord's associate, Ret. Air Force General Swede Svendsen, to discuss the project. Another associate of Veillot's and Delaroque's is U.S. arms dealer Richard Brenneke, who claims to have attended an October 20, 1980, meeting in Paris (when EDA had an office) with Reagan-Bush campaign manager William Casey, French agents, and Iranian officials to finalize an arms-for-hostage-delay deal before the 1980 election. According to Brenneke, another close associate of Commandant Kelley, Lieutenant Colonel George Alvarez of Marine Corps counterintelligence, was also involved in the Reagan-Bush Administration's secret arms sales to Iran.

Considerable pressure was brought to bear on French officials not to stop France's arms deliveries to the Khomeini regime. On January 15, 1985, the France-based terrorist group Direct Action reportedly joined forces with Germany's Red Army Faction. Ten days later, on January 25th, French General Rene Audran, whom some sources reported had tried to block France's secret arms deliveries to Iran, was gunned down by a Direct Action hit team. Ten days later, leading West German arms manufacturer Ernst Zimmerman was killed outside his home in Munich by assassins of the German-based Red Army Faction, which had just joined forces with France's Direct Action.[48]

France has its own "Irangate" scandal, which broke into the mainstream press in Paris in November 1987, although sporadic accounts had surfaced as early as two years before.[49] An official June 6, 1986, report by the comptroller general of the French armed forces, Jean-François Barba, based on the investigative work of French Magistrate Michel Legrand, revealed secret shipments by the French company Luchaire of between $117 million and $133 million in heavy artillery shells and other arms to Iran between 1983, the year that Colonel Ralph Broman joined EDA, through 1985. Reports from Paris claimed that French President François Mitterrand, French Defense Minister Charles Hernu, and the French Ministry of Finance had all known of these deals as early as 1983. The French government awarded Daniel Dewavrin, Luchaire's president, its highest civilian honor, the Medal of the Legion of Honor, despite his involvement in questionable arms deliveries to Iran.[50] During an investigation into the scandal, Defense Minister Hernu's adviser, Jean-François Dubos, reportedly told the head of France's foreign intelligence service DGSE, "Let them catch me if they can."[51] The chief investigator in the French "Irangate" scandal, Comptroller General Barba, was reportedly told by Luchaire's president Daniel Dewavrin that financial arrangements for his company's arms deals with Iran had been handled by Italy's Banca Nazionale del Lavoro (BNL). BNL, whose board members included Henry Kissinger, had been closely linked to Oliver North's "Project Democracy," to Italy's "Irangate," and to the outlawed weapons-trafficking Italian "Masonic lodge," P-2.[52] (See Chapter IX)

Informant "Y" insisted that the movement of U.S. and other Western arms from Europe to Iran during the 1980's had been "a Kissinger operation." Richard Brenneke's attorney, the former liaison to NATO for the Marine reserves, had said that it was "a Haig operation." Alexander Haig, President Reagan's secretary of state in 1981 and 1982, had been an associate of Kissinger's for years. Haig's State Department adviser on France, Italy, and Israel at the time, Michael Ledeen, had reportedly counseled Haig to approve arms deliveries to Iran beginning in 1981.[53] Ledeen would therefore have been the obvious choice to communicate Washington's secret policy of authorizing early arms shipments to the Khomeini regime to French officials, who then followed the lead of the United States.

Italy's "Irangate" and its links to "Project Democracy" are reviewed below in "The Italian Connection."

Gene Wheaton, an ex-Marine with twenty-five years of experience in criminal investigations for the U.S. military, has documentation on U.S. arms deliveries to Iran dating back to 1982. Wheaton's deposition in a Miami, Florida, case closely linked to the Iran/Contra affair confirms his knowledge of a secret U.S.-Iran arms relationship dating back to 1981.

Wheaton claims that the "French Connection" to the U.S. "Irangate" includes then Senator Dan Quayle, President George Bush's choice for vice-president in 1988. According to Wheaton, a major source of Quayle's political power in Indiana, his home state, is a longtime associate of former CIA director William Casey, Beurt SerVaas. SerVaas, Wheaton says, was on the Executive Board of the Veterans of the O.S.S. (the predecessor organization to the CIA), which "runs the CIA from behind the scenes." SerVaas's daughter, Joan, according to Wheaton, is married to an "off-the-books" French intelligence asset and Indiana resident, Bernard Marie. In 1982, Wheaton claims to have introduced Marie to Defense Intelligence Agency (DIA) officials who then played a key role in the Reagan-Bush Administration's secret deliveries of U.S. arms to Iran in the 1980's.[54] DIA was one of the military intelligence agencies that was uninterested in prosecuting Colonel Ralph Broman for his arms dealings with the Khomeini regime out of Paris in the early to mid 1980's.

Oliver North's courier in the Iran/Contra operation, Robert Owen, was introduced to another Indianan, John Hull, and to Contra commander Luis Rivas in Senator Dan Quayle's office on July 21, 1983, when Owen was Quayle's legislative aide. Senator Quayle reportedly stayed for the beginning of the meeting.[55] That summer, Quayle authorized Owen to travel to Hull's ranch in Costa Rica at Hull's expense. The ranch was being used by the CIA as a military supply site for the Nicaraguan Contra rebels, a relationship that continued throughout the period during which "profits" from the administration's secret arms sales to Iran were illegally diverted to the Contras. In November 1983, Robert Owen left the staff of Senator Dan Quayle and went to work for Oliver North's "Project Democracy," which oversaw secret U.S. arms shipments to both the Contras and to Iran.

Considering Senator Quayle's reported link to French intelligence through Beurt SerVaas and Bernard Marie, and his link to Oliver North's "Project Democracy" through their mutual aide Robert Owen, it is more than likely that Mr. Quayle had also been made aware of secret U.S. arms shipments to Iran in the first years of the Reagan-Bush Administration. If so, it is probable that he was also privy to the genesis of those early arms deliveries to the Khomeini regime in alleged pre-1980-election meetings among future CIA director William Casey, Iranian representatives, and French intelligence agents. According to Gene Wheaton, "SerVaas brought Quayle into the Casey network early in the game."[56] A formerly classified "Memorandum for the Record" by then Assistant Secretary of State Harold Saunders, dated October 15, 1980, reveals that a "Bob Owen" had been made privy to the details of a pre-1980-election arms-for-hostages offer made by Iranian arms dealer Houshang Lavi to President Carter's State Department and CIA.[57] Lavi, whose attorney, Mitchell Rogovin, was, according to Lavi, "close to George Bush," had made a *simultaneous* arms-for-hostages offer to Robert McFarlane, then of Senator John Tower's Senate Armed Services Committee staff, and to Richard Allen and Laurence Silberman of the Reagan-Bush campaign at a secret meeting in Washington, D.C., on October 2, 1980. Informant "Y" also alleged that Robert Owen may have worked for Carter's then CIA liaison to the National Security Council, Donald Gregg, at the time that Gregg reportedly attended the late October 1980 Paris meeting with Casey and the Iranians, which would be consistent with the Saunders memo's reference to "Bob Owen." In a telephone interview with the author, however, Gregg denied that Owen had worked for him at the time. Owen's employment record does show that he had returned to the United States in the fall of 1980, having recently served in the United Nations refugee program in Thailand.

Gene Wheaton's research also revealed that another associate of William Casey's, with a French background, Glenn Souham, was part of the secret U.S.-Iran arms delivery network. According to Wheaton, Souham worked with Saudi middleman Adnan Khashoggi and Iranian arms dealer Cyrus Hashemi and was murdered on September 24, 1986, while his father, a former high-level civilian official in NATO, was on a visit to the White House. Hashemi, who died under questionable circumstances the same year, had reportedly participated in the late October 1980 meeting in Paris with William Casey to work out the details of an arms-for-hostage-delay deal with the Khomeini regime. For more details on this reported Paris meeting, see Chapter II.

Oregon businessman and former CIA pilot Richard Brenneke has also stressed the central role of France in the secret U.S. arms relationship with Iran in the 1980's. "Follow the French connection," he said in an interview of August 28, 1989. "It's the key to the whole thing." At one time, Brenneke was slated to become a defense witness in a federal case in New York against seventeen defendants, including his French arms dealer associates, Bernard Veillot and John Delaroque, who had been indicted in April 1986 as part of an alleged Customs "sting" operation, for attempting to ship $2.5 billion in U.S. arms to Iran. The two Frenchmen, Veillot and Delaroque, were never apprehended by U.S. authorities and their indictments were soon dropped. Intriguingly, arms dealers Cyrus Hashemi and Houshang Lavi—both reported to have been involved in pre-1980-election meetings with Reagan-Bush campaign officials—worked with the U.S. Customs Department to set up this "sting."

Both Richard Brenneke and Houshang Lavi have flatly stated that the defendants in this Manhattan "sting" case are innocent. Brenneke claims that they had been assured that their planned arms sales to Iran had received explicit authorization from Vice President Bush, as part of the secret White House policy of allowing U.S. arms shipments to the Khomeini regime. Defense attorneys had even subpoenaed Vice President Bush as a witness in the case. At the first high-level White House council called to decide what to tell Congress and the American public about the newly exposed U.S. arms sales to Iran, one participant in the Situation Room meeting acknowledged that the defendants' $2.5 billion arms deals were "Probably 'private,' but with [U.S.] government knowledge." Tapes of telephone conversations with defendants in the case confirm that they understood they had received White House authorization for their arms deals at the very time that President Reagan signed a "draft" finding on January 6, 1986, authorizing secret U.S. arms sales to Iran. The President signed the final version of this funding eleven days later, on January 17, 1986. Shortly before George Bush's inauguration as President, the prosecuting attorney in the case dropped all indictments against the defendants, stating that the Department of Justice knew that it would be "losing a headline case."

One of the most interesting pieces of information provided by Richard Brenneke was his claim that former Secretary of the Navy and President Reagan's Ambassador to the European Economic Community, J. William Middendorf II, who had also headed Reagan's CIA transition team after the 1980 election, had been one of Brenneke's contacts in Brussels, Belgium, in relation to U.S. arms shipments to Iran. According to *The Octopus Eagle,* a book about the above-mentioned "sting" operation from the point of view of one of the defendants in the case, Hans Bihn, a Reagan-Bush official involved in that secret program to ship U.S. arms to Iran was this same man, William Middendorf.[58] Brenneke claimed that the operation overseen by Middendorf started out "legitimate" and only later was turned by Customs into a "sting." If true, the central involvement of Reagan's top appointee to the European Economic Community would go a long way towards explaining reports of secret collaboration between Oliver North's "Project Democracy" and governments throughout Europe in shipping arms to Iran in the 1980's. In 1980, William Middendorf had been a top adviser to the Reagan-Bush campaign.

THE ITALIAN CONNECTION

We have already reviewed reports of Michael Ledeen's early involvement in the Reagan-Bush Administration's secret Iran arms policy. Ledeen was an adviser on French, Italian, and Israeli affairs to President Reagan's first secretary of state, Alexander Haig, who (Haig) reportedly oversaw a secret draw-down of NATO military supply stores for delivery to Iran. Ledeen was later at the center of the genesis of the 1985–86 U.S. arms sales to Iran, which became a major focus in the Iran/Contra scandal. It should therefore come as no surprise that the U.S. government, the Italian government, Italian arms companies, and U.S. military bases in Italy were reportedly involved in major arms deliveries to Iran beginning long before these later "Irangate" sales. The Israeli publication *Davar* reported on November 24, 1986, that Mr. Ledeen worked with Iranian arms dealer Cyrus Hashemi and Israeli Foreign Ministry official David Kimche on arms deals between Italy and Iran. Mr. Ledeen himself has reported that top Italian officials were aware of the secret White House policy on arms shipments to the Khomeini regime. In *Perilous Statecraft*, he notes that Italy's military intelligence service, SISMI, was aware of the U.S. Iran/Contra initiative.[59]

The former President of Iran, Abolhassan Bani Sadr, has reported that U.S.-mediated arms shipments to Iran beginning in the early 1980's involved "a vast international network—a real multi-national." Subsequently, European press reports in the latter 1980's revealed a massive covert operation to move Western arms from the U.S. and Italy to Iran with the cooperation of the CIA, the Defense Intelligence Agency (DIA), and the National Security Council. According to Carlo Palermo, the chief investigative judge in Italy's "Irangate" scandal, this huge arms operation was code-named "Demavand" after a mountain near Tehran and resulted in between $1 and $2 billion worth of military equipment being secretly diverted to the Khomeini regime.[60] The reader will recall that the Greek publication *Dimikratikos Logos* reported that, on his secret May 1986 trip to Tehran, President Reagan's emissary Robert McFarlane was tape-recorded reminding Iranian officials that they had received $1.3 billion in arms out of a total $5 billion commitment[61]—within the range of the $1 to $2 billion "Demavand" deliveries. McFarlane reportedly accompanied another 23 tons of arms and spare parts to Iran in a second trip in September 1986.[62] Intriguingly, according to *Interlock* by Mark Hulbert, editor of a Washington, D.C.-based financial newsletter and an Oxford graduate, $1.3 billion happens also to be the amount of four questionable loans made by Chase Manhattan Bank to the Shah of Iran. The loans had been deposited in the Shah's private Pahlavi Foundation accounts. William Casey's law firm, Rogers and Wells, reportedly represented the U.S. branch of the Pahlavi Foundation.[63] Under the Algiers Accord, which officially settled the hostage crisis in January of 1981, Iran paid off all loans it had received from U.S. banks, including Chase Manhattan, leaving this $1.3 billion Pahlavi Foundation fund "free and clear."

These dollar amounts tally with reports in the Italian press that, by October 1986, at least sixty "Demavand Operation" shiploads of arms and spare parts had left the Italian port of Talamone for Iran. Former French Naval Air pilot Bernard Veillot (the same man cited earlier as part of the "French connection" to the Iran/Contra affair); his associate, CIA-linked Claude Lang; and American arms dealer Michael Austin had reportedly begun arrangements for this operation as early as 1980.[64] One of the board members of Austin's company, Austin Aerospace and Universal Aerospace of Manhattan, was General John Singlaub. *Time* magazine reported in July 1983 that the Italian Agusta Company and Fort Worth based Bell Helicopter supplied Iran with Chinook helicopters in violation of U.S. licensing regulations.

Italian judge Carlo Palermo compiled a six thousand-page report on the background of the "Demavand" deals, which reportedly demonstrated that CIA headquarters, the U.S. embassy in Rome, and U.S. military bases in Italy, including the naval base of Maddelena near Sardina, had all been involved in this massive operation to ship U.S. arms to Iran. His report revealed that both Italy's Foreign Minister Andreotti, an advocate of "friendlier relations with Iran," and the U.S. ambassador to Italy Maxwell Rabb had known about the deals and had looked the other way while they were being carried out.[65] *The New York Times* has also reported that Ambassador Rabb was suspected of high-level complicity in Italy's "Irangate" scandal.[66]

At last report, Italian prosecutors Augusto Lama and Giovanni Panebianco had arrested thirty-four of forty-five defendants charged with taking part in an illegal drug ring associated with the U.S.-Italy-Iran "Demavand" arms operation. This ring reportedly involved prominent members of the Trapani-based Sicilian Mafia, Italian industrialist Count Ferdinando Borletti, and Borletti's son Giovanni. Significantly, court affidavits show that Houshang Lavi's brothers' New York companies, Western Dynamics and Omega Industries, also worked with the Borletti Company of Milan,

Italy.[67] Houshang Lavi claims to have met with top Reagan-Bush campaign officials and Robert McFarlane, then-aide to senator John Tower, before the 1980 election, offering an arms-for-hostages deal with the Khomeini regime.

At the time of the "Demavand" arrests, Borletti's company near Milan, Valsella Corporation, which is 50-percent owned by a Fiat subsidiary, had contracted to ship 25 million sea mines to Iran. Documents in the possession of Italian authorities reportedly show that this Valsella operation was only part of a far larger arms-to-Iran trade undertaken in partnership with the Boviga Company of Barcelona, Spain.[68] In *Secret Warriors, U.S. News and World Report* reporter Stephen Emerson confirms the Barcelona connection. He quotes a former covert operative who claims to have seen a CIA document dated May 1984 showing that the CIA had evidence as early as 1983 that a company headed by Iran/Contra defendant and Iranian arms dealer Albert Hakim "may be associated with Iranian terrorist-supported activities being run out of official Iranian installations in Vienna and Barcelona."[69] Former CIA contract agent William Herrmann has quoted Iranian offical Hamid Nagashian that Hakim met in Paris in October 1980 with George Bush, William Casey, Robert McFarlane, and Dr. Fred Ikle to finalize an arms-for-hostages agreement with the Iranian Revolutionary Guards. The Israeli publication *Davar* reported in November 1986 that Israeli Foreign Ministry official David Kimche worked with the consultant to Secretary of State Alexander Haig and NSC Adviser Robert McFarlane, Michael Ledeen, to arrange arms deliveries to Iran through both Italy and Spain.

Apparently beginning about 1984, the Khomeini regime ran low on cash to buy arms and turned to heroin as a medium of exchange to finance its military needs. The source of this heroin was reportedly both Iran and the Syrian-controlled Bekaa Valley of Lebanon.[70] The drugs, used as partial payment for arms, were shipped by truck to the Italian towns of Verona and Trento. With the reported assistance of the former chief of Italian military intelligence (SISMI) and P-2 member, General Santorito, and other top Italian officials, the narcotics were then exchanged for weapons which were smuggled to numerous destinations, including Iran.[71] Significantly, Manucher Gorbanifar, Iran's chief arms buyer in Europe, has been reported to be a drug dealer as well as an arms dealer who "bartered" protection for the shadier side of his operations in exchange for intelligence information and assistance in the secret Iran/Contra deals.[72] Both the Senate Intelligence Committee and consultant to Robert McFarlane Michael Ledeen have reported that, according to Israeli sources, Gorbanifar was connected with Iranians involved in drug running as well as arms smuggling and terrorism.[73]

According to Italian prosecutor Lama, Syria, Iran's only Arab ally in its war against Iraq and the controller of drug centers in the Lebanese Bekaa Valley, also played a key role in facilitating arms shipments from Italy to Iran. On September 17, 1987, Lama announced that the owner of Spain's Boviga company, which had worked with Borletti's Italian firm in the above-mentioned "Demavand" operation, worked with Syrian intelligence. The head of Syria's intelligence network in Spain was Firaas al Assad, a nephew of Syrian President Hafez al Assad. Firaas reportedly oversaw the opium traffic out of Lebanon's Syrian-controlled Bekaa Valley, proceeds from which were used as partial payment for arms deliveries to Iran.[74]

Judge Carlo Palermo claims to have shown that some of the profits from these massive drugs-for-arms deals were used by an outlawed Italian terrorist-linked organization called "P-2" to influence political events in Italy. P-2 is an abbreviation for Propaganda Due, nominally a Masonic lodge founded in the late 1960's by powerful Italian businessman and underworld figure Licio Gelli.[77] Over a period of some twenty-five years, Gelli's "lodge" worked to systematically corrupt top political, military, intelligence, press, and business leaders to control a secret government-within-a-government in Italy. P-2 was finally exposed in a scandal that shook the country to its core in 1981. Chapter IX addresses P-2's links to the Iran arms sales.

Given the importance of Italy and P-2 to the Reagan-Bush Administration's secret Iran arms sales, it is not surprising that the CIA's Rome station chief in the early 1980's, Duane "Dewey" Clarridge, became a favorite of CIA Director William Casey. Casey later made Clarridge co-chairman, with Oliver North, of the National Security Council's critical "Operations Sub-Group," a newly integrated intelligence directorate for counterterrorism policy,[78] where they worked together on the Iran/Contra program.[79] It was Clarridge who supervised the drafting of the CIA's now-infamous assassination manual for use by the Contras when he was head of the CIA's Latin American Directorate in the mid-1980's[80] and who oversaw the mining of Nicaragua's harbors, which led to Congressional restrictions on military funding to the Nicaraguan resistance.[81]

The Italian publication *La Repubblica* reported in 1987 that a longtime associate of Saudi middleman Adnan Khashoggi, Jordanian Adnan Rousan, worked closely with a personal adviser to President Reagan, NATO official Peter Aley, on arms arrangements with Iran.[82] Rousan, who was also reportedly a former representative of the PLO, had founded Nabila Trading, Ltd. in 1972, an Italian company named after Khashoggi's daughter Nabila, reportedly as a front for international arms smuggling operations. At the time of his arrest in June 1986, Rousan's notebooks reportedly contained Aley's classified phone number, a number released only at the personal request of President Reagan.[83] Italian authorities retrieved a list of armaments, which Aley was making available to Rousan for purchase by Iran, including U.S.-made missiles and fighter aircraft. In February 1987, Rousan was released from prison and escaped Italy, probably returning to Jordan.

In late 1985 and early 1986, when it became apparent that the "Demavand Operation" was in danger of being exposed by Italian investigators, the U.S. government hastily organized a "sting" operation to net some of its key operators. At a trial in Manhattan, General John Singlaub's associate, Michael Austin, one of the U.S. arms dealers involved, pleaded guilty to arranging contraband shipments to Iran. Austin was given the ridiculously light sentence of only twenty weekends in jail and was warned not to talk about the operation. Shortly thereafter, on April 22, 1986, seventeen defendants were indicted in the New York "sting" operation discussed earlier, including a key operative in the "French Connection," French arms dealer Bernard Veillot. The defendants were charged with attempting to sell over $2 billion in U.S. TOW anti-tank missiles, Cobra helicopters, howitzer shells, and tanks to Iran. When the truth about the larger operation threatened to become public, "government agents" reportedly killed "sting" informant Cyrus Hashemi.[84] Some reports claim that Hashemi was killed by U.S. agents, others by Israeli agents. Arms dealers Houshang Lavi and Richard Brenneke insist that Israel was not the country at fault.

THE WEST GERMAN AND SWISS CONNECTIONS

When the Reagan-Bush Administration's secret arms relationship with Iran became public in late 1986, former NATO Ambassador David Abshire was made special counsel to President Reagan to "manage" revelations from the White House.[85] In light of what is known about the reported secret draw-down of NATO stores to supply the military needs of the Khomeini regime, it is not surprising that someone with intimate knowledge of NATO's affairs would be appointed to such a hastily-created position to focus attention away from Europe and onto the so-called "Contra diversion." Because the draw-down of NATO stores has the greatest impact on West Germany, the "German Connection" to the Iran/Contra affair takes on special importance.

West German law forbids the sale of military equipment that could be used in active war zones, as in the Persian Gulf and Iran and Iraq during the Iran-Iraq War. Nevertheless, West German Foreign Minister Hans Dietrich Genscher is reported to have supported his country's secret arms shipments to Iran. Italian investigators reportedly revealed his involvement in plans to deliver twenty thousand U.S. TOW anti-tank missiles to the Khomeini regime.[86] Genscher had long been a protector of Sadegh Tabatabai, who was Khomeini's designated hostage negotiator in 1980 and a top Iranian arms procurement official.[87] In September 1980, Tabatabai had asked the German foreign minister to sit in on Iran's formal negotiations in Bonn with the United States Government on the hostage crisis.[88] Evidentally, Genscher and Tabatabai reached a "special understanding" about how West Germany might help Iran meet its arms needs in the Iran-Iraq War.

On November 20, 1984, a year before the so-called "first" U.S. arms shipments to Iran of 1985, Oliver North and Richard Secord reportedly met with Iran's ambassador to Bonn, Javad Salari, and British business-man Ben Banerjee in Hamburg, West Germany. North's "Project Democracy" is then said to have worked with the West German Dynamit Nobel and Silberkraft companies and Swedish-born Israeli liaison, Karl-Erik Schmitz, to arrange for massive arms deliveries to Iran.[89] In October 1987, *Paris Match* reported that a Hamburg shipyard had been the point of origin for illegal shipments to Iran of speedboats used by Khomeini's hit teams in the Persian Gulf.[90] On October 19, 1987, Italian customs authorities seized a shipload of NATO arms bound from Hamburg to Iran. On October 5, 1987, Charlotte Petzold de Gramsch, an agent for the Argentinian Match-box Company, which manufactures German tanks, was reportedly arrested in West Germany for the company's sales of tanks and jet fighters to Iran.[91] West Germany reportedly supplied the Khomeini regime with submarines under a pre-revolution agreement,[92] and Cyrus Hashemi's brother, Mohammad Hashemi, told *ABC News* that he had been assured $48 million in commissions for a $1 billion sale of twelve transport aircraft to Iran by the West German aerospace company, Messerschmitt-Bolkon-Blohm.

As reports of the "German connection" to Irangate were making headlines in Europe, a West German politician who had reportedly protested his country's secret arms arrangements with Iran was murdered. Having met with Iran/Contra middleman Adnan Khashoggi the previous Friday, on October 11, 1987, the governor of the German state of Schleswig-Holstein, Uwe Barschel, died under questionable circumstances in the midst of a bitter fight within the West German government over that country's relationship with Iran.

The Swiss connection to the Iran/Contra affair may be even more important than the German connection. According to sources available to the former President of Iran, Abolhassan Bani Sadr, Robert McFarlane, then an aide to Senator John Tower, met in Zurich, Switzerland, in September 1980, just over a month before the 1980 U.S. presidential election, with a top arms procurement official for the Iranian Revolutionary Guards, Hamid Nagashian, and with another Iranian, purportedly a "Mr. Hakimi." The author believes that "Mr. Hakimi" was in fact future Iran/Contra middleman Albert Hakim. Former CIA contract agent William Herrmann claims that Nagashian himself told him in January 1981, just as the fifty-two U.S. hostages were being released from 444 days of captivity in Iran, that one of the Iranians who had been present at subsequent meetings with Nagashian, Reagan-Bush campaign officials, and others in Paris, in mid-October 1980, had been Albert Hakim.

The author has received information from a major news weekly that the above-mentioned September 1980 meeting in Zurich reportedly attended by Robert McFarlane, Hamid Nagashian, and "Mr. Hakimi" was only one of at least three meetings held in the Swiss city before the 1980 election, involving top Reagan-Bush officials and CIA associates of then vice-presidential candidate George Bush. At the time of this writing, the author has agreed to keep confidential details of reports of these additional meetings in Switzerland. Hopefully, they can revealed in future editions of *October Surprise*.

According to *Fanning the Flames* by author Kenneth Timmerman, the SATI Company of Zug, Switzerland, was involved in black market arms deals with Iran in 1981 and 1982. SATI reportedly dealt with top members of the outlawed Italian secret society P-2, which used the company as a front for its underground weapons deals with the Khomeini regime. SATI may be related to the French company SETI, which was reportedly involved in arms shipments to Iran in 1981, the first year of the Reagan-Bush Administration. Swiss arms dealer, Andreas Jenni, organized the twelve-flight series of U.S. military equipment deliveries to Iran beginning in February-March, 1981, the third of which crashed inside the Soviet Union on July 18, 1981.

One of the international arms dealers with whom White House aide Oliver North reportedly worked, Karl-Erik Schmitz, allegedly had an ongoing relationship with a company called IN-COTRA in Freibourg, Switzerland. IN-COTRA also had reported ties to Mossad, Israel's intelligence service, which was intimately involved in arms deals with Iran throughout the 1980's.

Time magazine reported in July 1983 that Switzerland was a favorite transshipment point for American-made arms bound for Iran from the United States in the early 1980's. Swiss bank accounts were also liberally used to facilitate the Reagan-Bush Administration's secret arms deals with Iran. Informant ''Y'' claimed that some $40 million was transferred to bank accounts in Switzerland in October 1980 to back up the 1980 Reagan-Bush campaign's secret arms-for-hostages agreement with the Khomeini regime.

THE AUSTRIAN CONNECTION

The Vienna *Courier* exposed illegal arms deals with Iran by Voest-Alpina Company, Austria's state military industry. Two major figures knowledgeable about the arrangements, the company's former chairman Herbert Apfalter and Herbert Amry, Austria's former ambassador to Greece who had exposed the deals in May 1984, both died of apparent heart attacks on the eve of their testimony to investigative bodies charged with looking into the matter.[93] A classified CIA document cited by *U.S. News and World Report* reporter Stephen Emerson claims that a company headed by Iran/Contra defendant and Oliver North's associate Albert Hakim ''may be linked with Iranian terrorist-supported activities being run out of official Iranian installations in Vienna and Barcelona.''[94] In 1983, the Iranian-born Hakim, who reportedly attended at least one of the October, 1980 Paris meetings with William Casey and Iranian officals, was made a U.S. citizen on the personal order of Casey, who as CIA director, was allowed by law to bestow citizenship on up to one hundred foreign nationals each year ''for national security and intelligence reasons.''[95]

Austria was also used as a trans-shipment point for contraband arms shipments to Iran from the United States. *Time* magazine reported in July 1983 that Austria became a favorite stopover point for U.S.-made arms bound for the Khomeini regime, because its customs inspection was lax to nonexistent.

THE BRITISH CONNECTION

We have already mentioned the arms deals with Iran of London-based international arms dealer Ian Smalley, the self-proclaimed "Dr. Doom." In addition to "Doom," Israel and Oliver North's "Project Democracy" figure prominently in the British connection.

Iran/Contra defendants Oliver North and Richard Secord reportedly met with British businessman Ben Banerjee and Iran's ambassador to Bonn on November 20, 1984, in Hamburg, West Germany.[96] Beginning the same year, Banerjee, of Britain's B&RW Industries, reportedly made arrangements to ship $300 million in U.S. arms, including 1,250 TOW anti-tank missiles, to Iran. Because large quantities of TOWs were available through Israel, Israeli arms dealer Yaacov Nimrodi reportedly arranged a secret meeting at the Zürich airport on March 14, 1986, between then Israeli Prime Minister Shimon Peres and Iranian officials. Peres was then en route to the funeral of the assassinated Swedish Prime Minister, Olof Palme. Later in the Iran/Contra affair, documents found at the residence of a reported German "bag man" for Oliver North's network linked the courier to British arms dealer Banerjee and to Nimrodi.[97] Banerjee's testimony was sought by special prosecutor Lawrence Walsh in connection with the investigation of possible crimes committed by North in the Iran/Contra scandal.

In addition to his association with Banerjee, Oliver North's "Project Democracy" reportedly worked with Britain's ICI Corporation and Swedish-born Israeli liaison Karl-Erik Schmitz to facilitate other arms deals with Iran. London's Arbuthnot Latham Bank reportedly handled Schmitz's financial arrangements.[98]

THE SWEDISH CONNECTION

In November 1987, *60 Minutes* reported that the February 28, 1986 assassination of Swedish Prime Minister Olof Palme and the January 15, 1987 suicide of Swedish materiel inspector Rear Admiral Carl Algernon may have been directly linked to their involvement in sales of anti-aircraft missiles to Iran.[99] Before his sudden death, Palme had reportedly decided to delay delivery on two hundred RBS-70 missiles, which had already been purchased by Iran, until after the upcoming 1986 elections, which greatly displeased the Iranians. The missiles were manufactured by the giant Bofors weapons company of Sweden. In December 1984, the deputy minister of Iran's radical Revolutionary Guards, Hamid Nagashian, showed former CIA contract agent William Herrmann a contract between Iran and the prime minister's government for ten batteries of the above-mentioned Bofors RBS-70 missiles made in Sweden, including spare parts. The contract, Herrmann recalls, called for the Bofors missiles to be delivered to Iran through South Korea. Herrmann also says that top officials of the Reagan-Bush Administration, including CIA Director William Casey's "cowboys," had encouraged Prime Minister Palme to accept the RBS-70 deal with the radical Iranian Revolutionary Guards in November or December of 1984. According to the Danish magazine *Press*, Rear Admiral Carl Algernon, who committed suicide less than a year after Palme's assassination, had been deeply involved with the missile deal between Iran and Bofors, which was reportedly using false end-user certificates to deliver contraband arms to Iran. Algernon had also reportedly met with an agent of the parent firm of the company that manufactured the missiles just before his death, and only a few days before he was scheduled to testify in the matter.

Swedish Justice Minister Anna-Greta Leijon authorized a private investigation in the spring of 1988 into charges by the former President of Iran, Abolhassan Bani Sadr, that in reaction to the delayed delivery of the Bofors missiles, Kurdish extremists had murdered Palme with Khomeini's blessings.[100] Ironically, Palme had earlier expressed "admiration for the new Iranian democracy" and was an advocate of "improved relations" with the Khomeini regime.[101] In February and March of 1980, he had also served on behalf of then secretary-general of the United Nations, Kurt Waldheim, as a mediator in the U.S.-Iran hostage crisis, without result. According to Informant "Y," Palme had also engineered another major arms deal in which Sweden's Volvo company would supply motors for speedboats used by the Iranian Revolutionary Guards to harrass tankers and escort ships in the Persian Gulf during the Iran-Iraq War.

There have been a number of intriguing leads as to who might be responsible for the assassination of Olof Palme. At the time of this writing, however, no proof has been presented for any of them. Informant "Y" claims that Italian P-2 leader Licio Gelli sent a telegram to an associate shortly before the Palme murder assuring him that "the Swedish tree will be felled" and to "tell our good friend [George] Bush."[102] Danish *Press* correspondent Agmete Vistar also reports that shortly after Palme's death, an attorney for P-2 member Stephano della Chiaie visited della Chiaie in Venezuela and was told by him that he knew who had killed Palme.[103] In the meantime, with no firm evidence to go on, the official investigation into Palme's assassination has been marred by infighting and accusations of incompetence and cover-up. On December 14, 1988, Swedish police arrested its first suspect in the murder, a man with a long history of violent crime, named Karl Gustav Krister Pettersson.[104] His links to Iran or P-2, if any, have not been disclosed.

The former President of Iran, Abolhassan Bani Sadr, has charged that a huge "international arms cartel" worked with the United States in the 1980's to arrange shipments of arms to the Khomeini regime. If any organization fits this description, it is the network of arms dealer Karl-Erik Schmitz, headquartered in Malmo, Sweden. Schmitz and Oliver North reportedly worked with an interlocking cartel of European arms companies in Sweden, Finland, Norway, Austria, Italy, Holland, West Germany, Belgium, France, and Great Britain throughout the 1980's.[105]

Karl-Erik Schmitz also reportedly worked with William Casey's CIA. In July and August of 1985, Schmitz arranged for a CIA proprietary company, St. Lucia Airways, to deliver $1 million worth of Dutch, Israeli, and Belgian explosives to Iran.[106] It was St. Lucia Airways that also delivered the now-famous eighteen U.S. HAWK missiles to the Khomeini regime in November 1985. Between September 1985 and October 1987, Swedish customs officials uncovered details of yet another Schmitz arms deal with Iran for enough explosives to fill one hundred ninety-two railroad cars and four ships.[107] The deal was reportedly arranged in the early 1980's through the arms dealer's companies, Scandinavian Commodities AB and Serfina SA.[108]

According to press reports, Karl-Erik Schmitz's firms worked with other Swedish companies, including Dynamit Nobel, Bofors, and Boliden, on major arms deals with Iran facilitated by Oliver North's "Project Democracy'' network.[109] On August 27, 1987, Schmitz wrote to NDIO, Iran's arms procurement office: "In reference to our previous telex, we would like to inform you that we are now violating *all* existing laws and regulations to make it possible to deliver the goods to your organization."[110]

One of the Swedish businessman's arms arrangements with Iran can be thought of as the "Iran/COTRA" affair. Schmitz is reported to have had an ongoing relationship with IN-COTRA, a company run by Iranian Makhmoud Kaikhosrovi out of Freibourg, Switzerland,[111] which had close ties to Mossad, Israel's intelligence service.[112]

THE BELGIAN CONNECTION

Iranian-American arms dealer Houshang Lavi reports that he dealt with a Belgian company, ASCO, which began shipping huge quantities of arms to Iran—"all of them made in the U.S.," he said—beginning as early as 1982. Mr. Lavi says that the company's board of directors includes a former Mossad (Israeli intelligence) colonel and that his own business dealings with the firm began after he had received a "green light" from Israeli Prime Minister Menachem Begin in a meeting with Begin in late 1982.

Influential Swedish arms dealer Sven Klang told *ABC News'* chief European correspondent, Pierre Salinger, in an interview that the Reagan-Bush Administration had ordered F-4 fighter jet engines to be taken from NATO warehouses in Belgium and delivered to the Khomeini regime in 1981, shortly after Mr. Reagan and Mr. Bush gained the White House. The timing of the delivery of this U.S. military equipment from U.S. NATO stores is significant in light of the fact that Mr. Houshang Lavi not only reportedly attended the Paris meeting of October 20, 1980, with Reagan-Bush campaign manager William Casey and Iranian arms procurement officials to work out logistics for the delivery of U.S. arms to Iran after Reagan's inauguration, but also worked soon after with the Israelis and a leading Belgium firm to ship U.S. arms to the Khomeini regime itself. Intriguingly, according to American arms dealer and former CIA contract agent Richard Brenneke, who was reportedly at the same Paris meeting with Lavi, William Casey, and other Reagan-Bush and Iranian officials on October 20, 1980, some of the $40 million discussed at the meeting, which was to be used for the purchase of arms, had been deposited in Iran's bank account at Banque Lambert in Brussels, Belgium.

THE BRAZILIAN CONNECTION

Brazil reportedly shipped arms to the Khomeini regime in exchange for Iranian heroin. In January 1983, Iranian official Sadegh Tabatabai's alleged middleman in the deals, General Motors executive George Perry, was killed in what was reported to be a professional murder.[113]

THE PORTUGUESE CONNECTION

In February 1985, five Portuguese arms dealers were indicted in Los Angeles for purchasing $600,000 in HAWK missile parts destined for Iran. Arrangements for the deal had begun in January 1984.[114] In July 1982, British merchant marine captain Thomas Screech picked up his boatload of U.S. military equipment bound for Iran in Portugal. (See also "The Danish Connection," below.)

THE DANISH CONNECTION

In his first televised speech from the Oval Office on November 13, 1986, following revelations in the Iran/Contra affair, President Reagan said, "I know you've been reading a lot of stories in the past several days attributed to Danish sailors . . ." The President's apparent purpose was to lead viewers to doubt reports by members of the Danish Seamans Union that they had been involved in large shipments of U.S. arms to Iran.

The Danish Seamans Union was reportedly involved in shipping at least

3,600 tons of arms to Iran on behalf of Israel.[115] Containers for the massive U.S. arms operation to Iran known as the "Blue Pipeline" were loaded onto Danish ships in ports in Valencia, Spain; Livorno, Italy; and Athens, Greece, for shipment to Iran throughout the 1980's.[116]

THE GREEK CONNECTION

Throughout the Iran-Iraq War, Greece sold arms to Iran and also bartered weapons for crude oil. Payment reportedly was delivered to a high-level official in the Greek Ministry of Defense.[117]

THE SOUTH AFRICAN CONNECTION

According to existing documentation, South Africa sold at least $300 million in arms to Iran, including sophisticated missiles, each year of the Iran-Iraq War.[118] According to the *San Francisco Examiner,* the South African government, which has close ties to Israel, exchanged $1 billion in long-range missiles for deliveries of Iranian oil.[119]

THE TAIWANESE AND SOUTH KOREAN CONNECTIONS

The final report of the Congressional Iran/Contra Committees notes that Taiwan and South Korea were involved in U.S. arms and spare parts shipments to Iran in the late 1980's.[120] The former President of Iran, Abolhassan Bani Sadr, however, reports that U.S. arms were being delivered to his country through Taiwan and South Korea beginning in 1981, including tires and parts for U.S.-made F-4 and F-5 fighter jets.[121] Former Westinghouse employee Glenn McDuffie has information that confirms

Mr. Bani Sadr's claims. He reports that an attorney for MICOM, the U.S. Army's missile command, told him that U.S.-made radar parts for the HAWK missile were being shipped to Iran by Taiwan and South Korea beginning in 1981 or 1982. According to *Time* magazine, South Korea was a major supplier of U.S.-made and U.S.-licensed weapons to the Khomeini regime in the early 1980's. It reports that in the twelve months prior to July 1983 Korean Air Lines (KAL) and two government-controlled companies made sixty purchases of HAWK missiles and spare parts which U.S. Customs officials believe were intended for delivery to Iran.[122] A defector from Iran's Air Force confirmed that South Korea provided parts and spares for Iran's F-4 fighter jets. *Time* also reported that large quantities of U.S.-made arms sold to South Korea were resold to the Khomeini regime in the early 1980's in clear violation of American re-export laws. According to former CIA contract agent William Herrmann, the Swedish company Bofors and the Swedish government used false end-user certificates to ship large quantities of RBS-70 missiles to Iran through South Korea in the mid 1980's. In 1984, the French weekly *L' Express* reported that "Washington has constantly maintained underground relations with the Tehran imam (i.e., Khomeini) pertaining to weapons deliveries through South Korea, Western Europe, and the Israeli allies of the United States."

Iran/Contra middleman Albert Hakim, who reportedly attended at least one of the mid-October 1980 Paris meetings between Reagan-Bush campaign representatives and Iranian arms procurement officials to work out an arms-for-hostage-delay agreement before the 1980 election, worked closely with South Korea in his various business enterprises.[123]

THE CHINESE CONNECTION

The Iran-Iraq War was a bonanza for the People's Republic of China,[124] which at the time of this writing is reported to be the fifth largest weapons supplier to Middle East nations. Chinese arms are able to compete effectively because they are durable and are offered at far lower prices than those made by Western companies. By 1987, according to Pentagon and U.S. intelligence officials, China was Iran's leading supplier of arms, including Silkworm anti-ship missiles worth as much as $1 billion,[125] although the Chinese government insists that any Silkworms that found their way to the Khomeini regime did so through the efforts of "third parties."[126] One such "third party" was most likely Israel, which is reportedly helping the Chinese to build an improved version of the Silkworm missile.[127] Of the total $5.2 billion in Chinese arms sales between 1984 and 1987, an estimated 80 percent, including Silkworms, went to both Iran and Iraq to fuel the Iran-Iraq War.[128] The most successful of China's weapons corporations, which is suspected of having been involved in the Silkworm deal with Iran, is Poly Technologies, Inc., a subsidiary of CITIC, China's largest investment concern. Poly's president, Hu Ping, is the son-in-law of China's leader, Deng Xiaoping.

During the 1980's, China sold intermediate-range ballistic missiles to Saudi Arabia so that the Saudis, ironically, could defend themselves against Iran.[129] China also sold jet fighters, missiles, patrol boats, and submarines to Egypt, in the hope of reducing Soviet leverage in the Middle East.

At the other end of the Iran/Contra scandal, the Chinese have even been reported to have worked out a short-lived arrangement with White House NSC aide Oliver North to ship arms to the Nicaraguan Contras.[130]

THE SOVIET CONNECTION

Before the beginning of the Iran-Iraq War, Iraq's main arms supplier was the Soviet Union. With Iraq's invasion of Iran on September 22, 1980, however, the Soviet Union officially suspended all arms shipments to the Iraqis.[131] Deliveries resumed once Iran successfully repulsed Iraq's forces, in the mid-1980's.

Though the Soviet Union has been a key ally of Iraq, like China, Moscow supplied missiles to both sides in the Iran-Iraq War.[132] Soviet-made Scud-B surface-to-surface missiles rained onto both Tehran and Baghdad in the devastating "War of the Cities" in the spring of 1988. Iraq had upgraded its Scud-B's with strap-on boosters, enabling them to reach both Tehran and the Iranian holy city of Qom. Soviet-made AKA-47 assault rifles also found their way into Iran's arm stockpiles. Soviet ally Syria also supplied liberal quantities of weapons to the Khomeini regime throughout the Iran-Iraq War in exchange for a combination of money and oil.[133]

It was the Soviet Union that revealed the first "smoking guns" in the Reagan-Bush Administration's secret arrangement with Israel to ship U.S. arms to Iran, only months after Reagan and Bush gained the White House. Soviet jets shot down, or forced down, the "Tango November" cargo plane over Soviet Armenia on its return flight from delivering U.S. military equipment to Iran on July 18, 1981.

THE PHILLIPINE CONNECTION

The *Virginia-Pilot* and *Ledger-Star* of Norfolk, Virginia, reported in 1988 that the Asian and Pacific Subcommittee of the U.S. House of Representatives Foreign Affairs Committee was investigating charges that former Phillipine President Ferdinand Marcos funnelled millions of dollars in illegal campaign contributions to the presidential campaigns of Ronald Reagan and George Bush in 1980 and 1984.[134] If these allegations prove to be true, it is possible that this money was part of the millions reportedly wired to Iran's Swiss and Belgian bank accounts before the October 19–20, 1980, Paris meetings between Reagan-Bush campaign and Iranian officials. Associated Press has reported charges by a Marcos political opponent that President Marcos, President-elect Ronald Reagan, and Vice President-elect George Bush met secretly in December 1980, shortly after the reported Paris meetings.[135] In any case, President Marcos's friends were personally involved in facilitating illegal shipments of U.S. arms to Iran in the early 1980's. According to sources interviewed by *Time* magazine, false end-user certificates showing the Phillipines as the destination for millions of dollars in U.S. military equipment bound for Iran were signed, for a 5 percent "laundering fee," by a crony of the Phillipine President.[136] Other reports identified this personal friend of Marcos's as General Ver, who allegedly authorized the direct transfer of U.S. arms to Iran from Clark Air Force Base in the Phillipines, using U.S. C-130 cargo planes.[137]

On October 21, 1988, President Marcos and his wife, Imelda Marcos, were indicted by a federal grand jury in New York on charges of fraud, bribery, obstruction of justice, and embezzling over $100 million from the

Phillipine treasury for the purchase of Manhattan real estate. Also indicted in the case was Iran/Contra middleman Adnan Khashoggi, who had reportedly acted as a front to help the Marcoses divert Phillipine assets and conceal their ownership of U.S. properties.[138] This collusion between the Phillipine President and Mr. Khashoggi, who was at the center of the Reagan-Bush Administration's arms-for-hostages negotiations with Iran, suggests that Marcos, as well as his military confidant General Ver, may have been a key player in the secret U.S. relationship with the Khomeini regime dating back to the early 1980's. Shortly before the August 1988 truce in the Iran-Iraq War, President Marcos offered to pay $5 billion for a visa to return to the Phillipines, on the condition that he would be exempt from criminal prosecution.[139] Intriguingly, $5 billion is the exact amount of money the Khomeini regime claimed at that time it was still owed by the United States Government.[140] According to a reported tape-recording of President Reagan's personal emissary Robert McFarlane during his meetings with Iranian officials in Tehran in late May 1986, $5 billion was also the total amount of arms that the Reagan-Bush Administration had secretly promised to the Khomeini regime.[141] According to *Time* magazine, $5 billion was also the amount of U.S. arms ordered by the Shah of Iran before his fall and Khomeini's rise to power.[142]

President George Bush, like former President Ronald Reagan, has his own ties to former Phillipine President Ferdinand Marcos. Texas oilman Robert Mosbacher, a former business partner of Bush's and the finance chairman of his 1988 presidential campaign, had reportedly been involved in a scandal-ridden off-shore oil deal with then President Marcos.[143] Mr. Mosbacher became President Bush's secretary of commerce.

THE BEAT GOES ON

President Reagan announced in November 1986 that U.S. arms shipments to Iran would be stopped in the wake of revelations of the administration's secret arms-for-hostages dealings with the Khomeini regime. Following Secretary of State George Shultz's courageous rebellion against the administration's secret Iran arms policy on November 16, 1986, the White House issued a statement promising no further deals with Iran and put Shultz in charge of future negotiations with the Khomeini regime.[144] Only three days later, on November 19, 1986, however, President Reagan said in a White House press briefing that his arms deals had not been a mistake and stubbornly asserted that "We're going to continue on this path."[145] Despite public outcry, CIA Director William Casey persuaded President Reagan to overrule Secretary of State Shultz's objections and authorized Iran/Contra middleman Albert Hakim, CIA consultant George Cave, and State official Charles Dunbar to meet with Iranian official Ali Samaii in Frankfurt, West Germany, on December 12, 1986, to negotiate even further arms deals with the Khomeini regime. On the second day of the meetings, Iran demanded 1,500 more TOW anti-tank missiles, HAWK missile parts, and a promise that the U.S. would pressure Kuwait to release seventeen Da'wa Shiite prisoners who had bombed the United States and French embassies in that Middle Eastern country.[146] The administration did ask the Kuwaiti government to release the seventeen Da'wa prisoners, and President Reagan's national security adviser, John Poindexter, told the Congressional Iran/Contra Committees that this action was taken with the approval of President Reagan.

As a result of these and other meetings with Iranian officials, U.S. arms shipments to Iran continued long after public revelations of the administration's Iran/Contra dealings, only further underground. As late as June 28, 1988, the *Los Angeles Times* reported that Iran was still receiving arms from the United States.[147] Only a few days before the destruction of Iran's airbus over the Persian gulf on July 3, 1988, the main political group opposing the Khomeini regime announced that they would soon hold a press conference in Washington, D.C., to release proof of the continuing U.S. arms deliveries to Iran. The international furor over the downing of Iran's airliner drowned out their message, and this critical piece of news was all but forgotten. Fifteen days later, on July 18, 1988, Khomeini surprised the world by accepting a cease-fire with his hated enemy, Iraq, a defeat he described as worse than "swallowing a poison pill."

ALL THE RIGHT MOVES

It is no coincidence that the men who would have been knowledgeable about Reagan-Bush campaign manager William Casey's secret arms-for-hostage-delay negotiations with Iranian officials before the 1980 election moved into precisely the "right" positions to authorize and oversee secret U.S. arms shipments to the Khomeini regime beginning in 1981.

William Casey became CIA director. Casey had reportedly met in Paris before the 1980 election with Iranian officials to finalize arrangements for U.S. arms deliveries to Iran once Reagan and Bush gained office.

Richard Allen became President Reagan's first national security adviser. Allen had met with a "Khomeini emissary" in early October 1980 who had offered an arms-for-hostages deal to the Reagan-Bush campaign, and reportedly also attended at least one October 1980 meeting in Paris with Iranian officials.

Alexander Haig became President Reagan's first secretary of state. Haig had reportedly met in early December 1980 with Michael Ledeen and P-2 member Francesco Pazienza. P-2 soon became intimately involved in secret Western arms shipments to Iran.

Robert McFarlane, later to become Reagan's third national security adviser, became counselor to Haig at the Department of State, from which post he reportedly counseled Haig to approve Israel's requests to ship U.S. arms to Iran in 1981.

General John Vessey, Jr., who had been a major critic of President Carter and who had overseen ISA/Delta Force special operations for the Desert One hostage rescue attempt of April 1980, was promoted to the top military post in the Reagan-Bush Pentagon, Chairman of the Joint Chiefs of Staff.

Michael Ledeen became senior adviser on French, Italian, and Israeli affairs to Secretary of State Haig, from which post he reportedly encouraged Haig to approve Israel's request to ship U.S. arms to Iran in 1981. France, Italy, and Israel soon figured prominently in "Irangates" throughout Europe.

J. William Middendorf II, who had been a top adviser to the 1980 Reagan-Bush campaign and a head of the Reagan-Bush transition team, became Ambassador to the European Economic Community (EEC). From this post, he was in a position to facilitate arms deals between European NATO countries and Iran, as reported by Richard Brenneke.

Richard Perle became Assistant Secretary of Defense for International Security Affairs. Together with his deputy, Stephen Bryen, he was responsible for European and NATO high-technology transfers to third countries, including Iran. Both Perle and Bryen reportedly worked hand-in-glove with Israel, which was involved in U.S. and European arms transfers to Iran in the early 1980's. Perle's immediate boss was Undersecretary of Defense Fred Ikle, who had been a member of foreign policy adviser Richard Allen's "October Surprise" Group in the 1980 Reagan-Bush campaign and who reportedly attended an October, 1980 meeting in Paris with William Casey and top Iranian officials. Perle and Bryen were also closely associated with Michael Ledeen.

Richard Secord, who had been a planner for President Carter's Desert One hostage rescue operation, became Deputy Assistant Secretary of Defense for the Near East and South Asia, the chief Middle East arms sales adviser to Secretary of Defense Caspar Weinberger. From this post he was positioned to authorize secret U.S. arms deliveries to Iran from the Pentagon as early as 1981.

Oliver North, who had also been involved in President Carter's Desert One hostage rescue attempt and had worked with Secord in the past, was quickly tapped by National Security Adviser Richard Allen as the Marine liaison to the White House National Security Council, in 1981.

Laurence Silberman, who worked with Richard Allen in the 1980 Reagan-Bush campaign and met with a "Khomeini emissary" reportedly offering an arms-for-hostages deal in Washington, D.C., one month before the 1980 presidential election, was appointed a federal judge by President Reagan. From this judgeship, Mr. Silberman ruled that the actions of the special prosecutor investigating charges in the Iran/Contra scandal were unconstitutional. The Supreme Court overruled his decision.

IX

THE NAME OF THE ROSE

"Wearing the white flower of a blameless life . . .
in that fierce light which beats upon a throne . . ."

Alfred Lord Tennyson, *Idylls of the King*

The previous chapters contain numerous references to an outlawed Italian organization, with international links, called "P-2" and its reported involvement in secret arms deliveries to Iran beginning in the early 1980's. What precisely is P-2? Who are its central players, and what was their relationship to top officials in the 1980 Reagan-Bush campaign and the Reagan-Bush Administration?

"Raggruppamento Gelli—Propaganda Due," or P-2 for short, is the name of a secret, illegal Masonic lodge founded in Italy in 1966 by a rich Italian textile merchant named Licio Gelli. Gelli, who was the first Italian ever to be granted joint Italian-Argentine citizenship, was an ardent member of Mussolini's Fascist party and went on to become Oberleutnant in and "liaison officer" to Hitler's Waffen SS in World War II.[1] After overseeing the triumphant return of President Juan Peron to Argentina,[2] Gelli returned to Italy and joined the Italian secret service in 1956.[3] In 1972, he became Argentina's economic adviser in Italy, arranging for the purchase of large quantities of arms by his adopted homeland.[4]

With the founding of P-2 in the late 1960's, Gelli began consolidating power by extracting official secrets from influential Italians as the price of entry to his secret society. These secrets were the ammunition he needed to blackmail additional leaders in Italy's government, military, police, intelli-

229

gence community, media, business, Mafia, and the Vatican to join his organization.[5] In the late 1960's and early 1970's, with the active support and encouragement of CIA headquarters in Rome,[6] P-2 began plotting the overthrow of the Italian government from the inside and its replacement by a right-wing fascist dictatorship. Around this same time, P-2 began using violence to achieve its ends. On December 12, 1962, bombs since traced to Gelli's secret organization first went off in Rome and Milan. Italian authorities identified the group responsible for these "active measures," intended to frighten voters into "voluntarily" calling for a right-wing take-over, as an elite P-2 cell called the "Rose of Twenty."[7]

One of Gelli's closest associates and a P-2 member was Mafia- and Vatican-linked Michele Sindona,[8] the U.S. manager of the Vatican Bank and also one of Italy's most powerful private bankers. Sindona was involved in the bankruptcy and collapse of Banco Ambrosiano, one of Italy's largest private banks, in 1982, after it had received a fraudulent $1.4 billion loan guarantee from the Vatican Bank. He was arrested in New York in 1980 and sentenced to twenty-five years in prison for the 1974 collapse of yet another bank, the Franklin National. Sindona had purchased the Franklin National in 1971.

Michele Sindona introduced P-2 grandmaster Licio Gelli to Philip Guarino, an adviser to the Republican National Committee on senior citizen affairs and a director of its speaker's bureau, working on behalf of Ronald Reagan and George Bush in the 1980 presidential election campaign. Guarino, who was also one of the planners for Reagan's 1980 inaugural celebrations, arranged a seat for Gelli next to the new President at one of his inaugural galas and introduced Gelli to "members of the entourage."[9] Guarino's involvement with P-2 had begun much earlier, in the mid-1970's, when Sindona financed Americans for a Democratic Italy, an organization co-chaired by Guarino and Paul Rao, Jr., an attorney for the head of the Gambino Mafia family.[10] Sindona and Gambino family members were indicted in 1982 on charges of orchestrating a $600-million-dollar-a-year heroin ring in Sicily and the United States.[11]

Gelli didn't like it when Sindona was put in prison in New York in 1980. *The New York Times* reported that Philip Guarino appealed to his grandmaster for help in springing P-2 "brother" Sindona, and Gelli quickly organized an escape disguised as a kidnapping.

In March 1981, two months after Reagan's inauguration and the month of the assassination attempt on his life, the Italian police issued a warrant for Gelli's arrest on charges of political, military, and industrial espionage and photographed an explosive list of 953 P-2 members in a raid on his private villa. Revelations that the men on Gelli's list had been under his clandestine control soon brought down the administration of Christian Democratic Prime Minister Aldo Forlani in the spring and summer of 1981. On the list were reportedly former prime ministers, including Giulio Andreotti; the chief of cabinet of the prime minister at the time, Mario Semprini; Justice Minister Adolfo Sarti; forty-three members of the Italian Parliament; the chiefs of Italy's three secret intelligence services; fifty-four top civil servants; one hundred eighty-three top military officers, including the commander of Italy's armed forces Admiral Giovanni Torisi, thirty generals, air force brass, and eight other admirals; nineteen judges; numerous lawyers, magistrates, police chiefs, bankers, newspaper owners, editors, journalists, and political party leaders; and fifty-eight university professors.[12] In the wake of the scandal Giovanni Spadolini became Italy's new prime minister, piecing together a coalition government consisting of representatives of the country's five non-communist political parties.

According to papers recovered from Gelli's villa and 150,000 pages of trial documents from the ensuing investigation, P-2 had controlled a "black" secret government whose goal was to destroy the existing constitutional order and substitute a hidden dictatorship in its place.[13] According to the indictment against twenty participants in the conspiracy who went to trial in March 1987, Gelli orchestrated a "secret structure composed of military personnel and civilians" who worked with members of neo-fascist terrorist groups to destabilize the elected government of Italy. His "lodge," the indictment said, "had the incredible capacity to control the state's institutions to the point of virtually becoming a state-within-a-state."[14] One of the prosecutors in the case estimated that any event of importance in Italy over a period of nearly two decades had been anonymously and surreptitiously orchestrated by Gelli, the spider at the center of a vast secret web.

It was a top member of this illustrious "lodge," P-2, and the former number-two man in Italy's military intelligence agency SISMI, Francesco Pazienza, with whom Alexander Haig, soon to be secretary of state, and Michael Ledeen, soon to be Haig's special adviser on Italian affairs at State, reportedly met in early December 1980, one month after Ronald Reagan's election victory.[15] Informant "Y," who claims to have received his information in an interview with Pazienza, alleges that Haig and Ledeen had both been made "honorary" (non-Italian) members of P-2, Ledeen in 1980 and Haig some time before.[16] When the Italian police raided Gelli's home in March 1981, it was Michael Ledeen who, at the instigation of Haig and Henry Kissinger, reportedly offered to buy the list of 953 P-2 members in an apparent attempt to keep it from becoming public.[17] Henry Kissinger had also reportedly sent Ledeen to Italy to try to squash an investigation into his and Alexander Haig's involvement in the founding of P-2.[18] Gelli had also reportedly offered a secret manuscript to Ledeen,[19] and Ledeen reportedly sold a CIA study on terrorism to SISMI through P-2 member Pazienza. Pazienza told an Italian parliamentary commission in 1982 that he had been close to Alexander Haig when Haig was the Supreme Allied Commander of NATO from 1974 to 1979. At the time of his reported December 1980 meeting with Pazienza and Haig, Ledeen was soon to become Secretary Haig's adviser on Italian affairs at the Department of State. When President Reagan's national security adviser John Poindexter warned Oliver North that Attorney General Meese was preparing an investigation into the administration's secret arms relationship with Iran, within minutes of the call North was in a taxi heading to the home of Michael Ledeen,[20] who had been at the center of the genesis of the "new relationship with Iran" in 1985. Much like Licio Gelli's "black" government in Italy, the network behind the Reagan-Bush Administration's secret Iran arms deliveries involved right-wing extremists, "rogue" military and intelligence agents, and organized crime, as well, reportedly, as the outlawed P-2 itself.

Whether or not Alexander Haig and Michael Ledeen were members of P-2 at the time of their meeting with Francesco Pazienza in December 1980, it is the case that shortly after Haig became secretary of state and hired Ledeen to be his adviser on Italian affairs, the Reagan-Bush Administration made the decision not to put pressure on Italy's new government to remove key military and intelligence officials on Gelli's list from their posts, including the country's Defense Chief of Staff, Chief of Counterintelligence, and Chief of National Security.[21]

On the morning of August 2, 1980, a massive bomb since linked to Gelli and to master terrorist and P-2 member Stephano della Chiaie, exploded in the waiting room of the central train station in Bologna, Italy, killing eighty-one people and injuring two hundred others. General Santorito, the chief of Italy's military intelligence agency, SISMI, who was also reportedly a member of P-2, testified in the wake of the bombing that it had been planned by the British-Swiss-American Montecarlo Comite, P-2's "sister" organization based in Monaco. When P-2 had come under increasing scrutiny in 1979, grandmaster Licio Gelli had reportedly made his base of operations the Montecarlo Comite. On April 11, 1980, the bombing of the Bologna train station was reportedly decided upon in Montecarlo's Hotel de Paris, and it was planned by Gelli and P-2 terrorist Stephano della Chiaie shortly thereafter in Buenos Aires, Argentina.[22] Not surprisingly, reported members of the Montecarlo Comite are Gelli, Henry Kissinger, Alexander Haig, and Michael Ledeen.[23]

The European publication *Europa* reported that an Italian parliamentary commission revealed "an entirely American thread" inside the Reagan-Bush Administration involved with the use of funds from SISMI, Italy's military intelligence agency, deposited by Italian General Santorito in secret Swiss bank accounts. The funds reportedly were made available to SISMI's number-two man, Francesco Pazienza, who allegedly paid some of them to Ledeen as "consultant's fees."[24] Ledeen told the *Wall Street Journal* that he had worked with SISMI.[25] General Santorito, in fact, testified that a secret inner core of SISMI, known as "Super SISMI" or "Super S," had been involved in criminal activities including gunrunning, drugs, and the financing of terrorism. Super SISMI was, in effect, a cell of P-2. Santorito himself was reportedly involved in facilitating a massive drugs-for-arms operation in which Iranian heroin was delivered to secret processing centers in Verona, Italy, in exchange for weapons smuggled back to the Khomeini regime.[26]

In 1982, Licio Gelli was arrested in Switzerland on charges of political, military, and industrial espionage, conspiracy, criminal association, fraud, extortion, fraudulent bankruptcy, and forgery. Within a year of his arrest, he had escaped from prison and reportedly fled to South America, probably back to Argentina.[27] Gelli's deputy, Francesco Pazienza, was arrested in New York and extradited to Italy in the summer of 1987, where he faced charges of bank fraud in connection with the collapse of Vatican-linked Banco Ambrosino, and charges of espionage, extortion, possession of drugs, Mafia association, and involvement in Super SISMI's criminal activities.

THE ARGENTINE CONNECTION

Given Gelli's long and unique relationship with the Argentine government as the first Italian ever to be granted joint Argentine-Italian citizenship, that Latin American country's links to the Iran/Contra affair and to secret shipments of U.S. arms to Iran in the early 1980's take on special significance.

According to sources close to the Italian government's investigation of

P-2, Argentina had long been a preferred haven for drug-money laundering operations by the Sicilian Mafia, which has overlapping membership with Gelli's secret organization. P-2 was also reportedly associated with the "Absalom" Masonic lodge in Hamburg, West Germany, which was one of the planning centers for the Iranian revolution.[28] Ayatollah Mohammed Beheshti, who would become the Ayatollah Khomeini's number-two man once he took power in February 1979, was involved with the Hamburg lodge and P-2. Beheshti reportedly sent a personal representative to the secret October 19, 1980, Paris meeting with Reagan-Bush campaign manager William Casey at which arrangements were made for the future Reagan-Bush Administration to ship U.S. arms to Iran in exchange for a delayed release of the fifty-two American hostages. An Argentinian air transport company, Transporte Aereo Rioplatense, then supplied the aircraft used by arms dealers Andreas Jenni and Stuart Allan McCafferty, who worked in collaboration with the Israelis and Iranian arms procurement official Sadegh Tabatabai, a Khomeini confidant, to deliver the first shipments of U.S. arms to Iran in 1981 under the new Reagan-Bush Administration.[29] According to Michael Ledeen, even before the inauguration of President Reagan in 1981, the CIA funded Argentina to provide the first logistical support to the Nicaraguan Contras, which continued until the fall of its military junta in 1983 in the aftermath of the Falklands War.[30] The bombing of the Bologna train station in Italy, in August 1980, likewise, was planned in Argentina, Gelli's second homeland. The P-2 grandmaster reportedly met in Buenos Aires in the spring of 1980 to work out the details of the terrorist attack with saboteur and P-2 member Stephano delle Chiaie.

Even earlier, Argentina had been involved in negotiations to free the fifty-two American hostages held in the U.S. embassy in Tehran. Argentinian Hector Villalon was one of two key mediators who attempted to work out a solution to the hostage crisis with Khomeini's agents and President Carter's chief of staff, Hamilton Jordan, in 1980.[31] After President Reagan's inauguration, in the fall of 1981, Villalon approached the new secretary of state, Alexander Haig, who had already given the Israelis reported authorization to begin secret U.S. arms shipments to Iran.[32] Villalon alerted Haig to an alleged planned coup attempt against Khomeini by former foreign minister Sadegh Ghotbzadeh.[33] Khomeini was alerted to the plot, however, and ordered Ghotbzadeh tortured and assassinated. Abolhassan Bani Sadr, the former President of Iran, claims that it was Michael Ledeen who alerted Khomeini to the planned coup attempt,[34] although Ledeen denies it.[35]

THE VATICAN CONNECTION

We have seen that Alexander Haig and Michael Ledeen, key players in authorizing secret U.S. arms shipments to Iran in 1981, were both reportedly members of P-2. Given this context, it may be significant that P-2 grandmaster Licio Gelli, P-2 member Michele Sindona, Alexander Haig, 1980 Reagan-Bush campaign manager William Casey, and former CIA Beirut station chief William Buckley all were also reportedly members of the Vatican's military order, the Knights of Malta,[36] whose initiates must take an oath of allegiance to the Pope. Through Michele Sindona and others, the Vatican had long ties to P-2. Significantly, Cyrus Hashemi, one of the Iranian arms dealers who reportedly met with William Casey at the secret October 20, 1980, Paris meeting, was also reportedly linked to the Knights of Malta.[37] Hashemi began making his arrangements for U.S. arms deliveries to the Khomeini regime immediately after Reagan's election victory in November 1980, and he told journalists that his 1981–82 arms shipments had been necessary to obtain the release of the original fifty-two hostages.[38]

Given that Knights of Malta member William Casey, Knights of Malta associate Cyrus Hashemi, a representative of P-2-linked Ayatollah Beheshti of Iran, and a representative of alleged P-2 member Alexander Haig reportedly met together on or around October 19 and 20, 1980, at a "hotel named Raphael," it may be more than coincidental that the residence of Italy's Prime Minister Bettino Craxi, himself reportedly a right-hand man of Gelli's,[39] is on the top floor of the Hotel Raphael in Rome.[40] Although former Iranian President Abolhassan Bani Sadr has reported that he believes Reagan-Bush campaign and Iranian representatives met at the Raphael Hotel in Paris, France, it is possible that Mr. Bani Sadr incorrectly assumed that the "Hotel Raphael" referred to by his sources in Iran was the one in Paris, where he was newly exiled. Given Prime Minister Craxi's close association with Michael Ledeen[41] and Ledeen's close association with both William Casey and Secretary of State Alexander Haig who appointed him liaison to Craxi at the Department of State,[42] it is possible that the "Raphael" suite where the secret pre-election meeting reportedly took place was in fact at the Raphael Hotel in *Rome*. When the White House needed to contact Craxi in October 1985 in an attempt to intercept the jetliner carrying the hijackers of the *Achille Lauro* cruise ship, Oliver

North asked Ledeen to call the Italian prime minister at his residence at the Raphael Hotel in Rome.[43] According to Ledeen, Italy's military intelligence service SISMI, many of whose top officers had belonged to Gelli's organization P-2, knew about William Casey's secret initiative to Iran.[44] The CIA's Rome station chief in 1981, Duane "Dewey" Clarridge, became a favorite of the new CIA director, and the Agency's Rome headquarters reportedly facilitated secret arms shipments to Iran from Italian ports beginning in the early 1980's.[45]

According to the Greek newspaper *Dimikratikos Logos,* Alexander Haig's associate Robert McFarlane was tape-recorded reminding Iranian officials during his late May 1986 trip to Iran—the one with the now-infamous cake—that by then Iran had already received $1.3 billion in U.S. arms.[45] Given Haig and Casey's reported membership in the Vatican's military order, the Knights of Malta, and the Vatican's links to Gelli's P-2 through Michele Sindona and others, it may be more than a coincidence that the amount of money reportedly involved in the Banco Ambrosiano-Vatican Bank scandal was almost precisely the same figure—$1.4 billion. According to informant "Y," some of this $1.4 billion was laundered through bank accounts in Panama, where Panamanian General Manuel Noriega has access to records demonstrating the connection.[47] If true, this may explain Noriega's boast that he had information which, if revealed, could substantially affect Vice President Bush's chances in the 1988 presidential election.

POET-IC JUSTICE

P-2 has been reported to have deep links to the Mafia, in particular to the New York-based Gambino crime family.[48] P-2's membership list included Mafia figures,[49] and Licio Gelli himself reportedly acknowledged in a taped conversation with Rizoli Publishers in Italy that P-2 member Francesco Pazienza was connected with the Mafia and the CIA.[50] As already mentioned, Gelli's associate and reported "honorary" P-2 member Philip Guarino founded Americans for a Democratic Italy in the mid-1970's with an attorney for the leader of the Gambino organization. The Gambino Mafia family also has a long reported history of distributing Iranian heroin in the eastern United States.[51]

A number of press reports, taken together, suggest that there may have been a P-2 and Gambino Mafia connection to the release of the fifty-two American hostages from the U.S. embassy in Tehran. Associated Press, Gannett news service, and the *Courier Post* of Cherry Hill, New Jersey, reported that a freighter named *The Poet* was hijacked in the Delaware River off Philadelphia on October 24, 1980, less than two weeks before the 1980 presidential election, by south New Jersey crime boss Carlo Gambino. The ship, which had thirty-four men on board, was reportedly rerouted to Iran, where its cargo of corn was swapped for heroin. *The Poet's* early departure would have given it more than enough time to reach Iran on or before the date that the hostages were released, on Reagan's inauguration. Reuters news service reported that, when the fifty-two American captives were released, Iran took some thirty-two *new* U.S. hostages, identified as "New Jersey heroin smugglers." As the Gambino clan, reported to have hijacked *The Poet*, has a reported history of importing and distributing Iranian heroin in the eastern United States, the obvious question presents itself: Were these estimated thirty-two "New Jersey heroin smugglers" taken hostage by Iran on or around January 20, 1981, the same as the estimated thirty-four men reported to have been on board *The Poet*, hijacked by the New Jersey Gambino clan? Lest the reader think that such an arrangement is beyond the realm of possibility, it should be noted that the CIA reportedly orchestrated a drugs-for-prisoners (i.e., "hostages") exchange with Cuba after the collapse of its disastrous April 1961 Bay of Pigs operation.[52] The reader should also recall the Mafia's close reported ties to P-2[53] and P-2's reportedly close relationship with the CIA.[54] It is also well known that the CIA has worked directly with the Mafia on a number of key covert operations.[55] A Robert Gambino, who had been George Bush's bodyguard during his pre-convention campaign against Ronald Reagan in 1980 and a former head of internal security at the CIA, was appointed one of four senior watch officers in charge of the 1980 Reagan-Bush campaign's communications headquarters, called the Operations Center.

If the inference is correct that Khomeini's agents seized thirty-two or more men linked to the Gambino Mafia organization and to P-2 in Iran on or shortly before Reagan's inauguration, it would account for reports of P-2's involvement in the subsequent secret arms deliveries to Iran outlined in the previous chapter. The shipments may have been a *quid pro quo* for Khomeini's agreeing to their eventual, and probably phased, release. Informant "Y" claims that a number of the transport companies involved in clandestine deliveries of U.S. and European weapons to Iran in the early to mid-1980's were fronts controlled by or influenced by P-2.[56] In fact, he maintains that "almost every 'black' [secret] arms deal since the early 1970's had in some way involved P-2."[57] In *Fanning the Flames*, author Ken Timmerman reports that a company used to front for "black" arms shipments to Iran in 1981 and 1982, the SATI Corporation of Zug, Switzerland, has been linked to Gelli's organization through gangster and P-2 member Stephano della Chiaie, the man implicated with Licio Gelli in the bombing of the Bologna train station in Italy. According to Timmerman, della Chiaie reportedly met with top Iranian arms procurement official and Khomeini insider Sadegh Tabatabai at the Hotel President in Geneva.[58] Contributor to the Danish magazine *Press*, Agmeto Vistar, reports that P-2 grandmaster Licio Gelli had been closely associated with CIA operations officer Theodore Shackley when Shackley was stationed in Rome, and that Shackley was also linked to P-2 through future national security adviser Robert McFarlane's consultant, Michael Ledeen. Ledeen acknowledged to the *Wall Street Journal* that he was an associate of Shackley's.[59] Shackley was George Bush's assistant Deputy Director of Plans (covert operations) when Bush was director of the CIA in 1976. One of Iran/Contra middle-man Albert Hakim's former employees had also reportedly been Theodore Shackley.[60]

If the Khomeini regime did take Gambino family and/or P-2 associates hostage in early 1981, it might also account for reports of a prominent "Italian connection" to the early 1981 arms shipments to Iran. The "Italian connection" in the 1980's would then parallel the "French connection" of the 1960's. During the 60's, the major supplier of heroin to the United States was Turkey, where peasants laboriously gathered raw opium from poppy fields in the Anatolian Plateau. This raw opium was then smuggled into France where it was processed into street-grade heroin in laboratories in Marseilles—hence references to the "French connection."[61]

Italy was the original headquarters for P-2. In the previous chapter we reviewed reports that P-2 was involved in "Operation Demavand," under which large quantities of Western arms were shipped from Italy to Iran with the blessings of the CIA and the assistance of the U.S. military. According to Italian magistrate Carlo Palermo, who directed the team that uncovered the "Demavand" deals, a portion of the arms were paid for with opium originating in the "Golden Crescent" region of Iran, Pakistan, and Afghanistan. As in the "French connection," it was also shipped into Europe through Turkey. In the case of the "Italian connection," Iranian raw opium was reportedly smuggled into Verona and Trento, Italy, where it was processed into marketable heroin. (U.S. NATO General James Dozier was reportedly rescued near a heroin refinery in Verona.) A former chief of Italian military intelligence, General Santorito, then reportedly oversaw shipment of the arms purchased with drugs to numerous terrorist-linked countries, including Iran.[62]

Significantly, Manucher Gorbanifar, CIA Director William Casey's chosen middleman in President Reagan's secret arms deals with Iran, was reportedly a drug smuggler as well as Iran's chief arms buyer in Europe.[63] He reportedly offered to trade his services in the Iran weapons operation, as well as intelligence information, for "protection" for his narcotics-smuggling operations.[64] It was Gorbanifar who, among others, allegedly met with soon-to-be CIA director William Casey in Paris on October 19–20, 1980, to conclude a secret arms-for-hostages agreement with Iran. The question naturally arises whether there may have been an arms-for-*drugs*-for-hostages dimension to this reported pre-election agreement. Reagan-Bush campaign official Max Hugel, a "Casey lackey"[65] with his own reported links to organized crime,[66] was appointed by the new CIA director to be his first Deputy Director for Overseas Operations[67] over protests from intelligence veterans that Hugel had no experience to qualify him for the job. Casey defended his selection of Hugel, however, saying that he had "lots of international experience" and "a key job to do."[68] (Hugel left the Agency in late 1981 in the wake of allegations of improper financial dealings.) Hugel's reputed links to organized crime and the Mafia's links to P-2 raise the additional question as to whether the "key job" that CIA Director Casey put Hugel in charge of in 1981 might have been working with P-2 on its early shipments of Western arms to Iran in fulfillment of Casey's reported pre-election arms-for-hostages agreement with Khomeini's agents.

Besides Hugel, another "Casey favorite" had been the Agency's station chief in Rome. His name is Duane "Dewey" Clarridge. As station chief in the home territory of P-2, which the Agency had backed since its inception,[69] Clarridge would have been the perfect man to oversee the "Italian connection." Clarridge also was later selected by Casey to fill the key Agency post of Chief of European Operations,[70] where he would have been well positioned to work with Manucher Gorbanifar, Iran's chief arms buyer in Europe. Clarridge, in fact, oversaw the secret November 1985 shipment of U.S. HAWK missiles to Iran for the Agency.[71] Another top Iranian official, stationed in Rome, was Khomeini's Ambassador to the Vatican, the Ayatollah Khosrow-Shahi. Shahi had been second in command of the radical "students'' who seized the U.S. embassy in Tehran in late 1979 and had been Khomeini's personal bodyguard.[72]

As the Contra side of the Iran/Contra operations came into play, CIA Director Casey moved "Dewey" Clarridge to the post of chief for the Agency's Western Hemisphere operations[73] and later to the National Security Council's new anti-terrorism planning group, the Operations Sub-Group, where he was Oliver North's co-chairman and CIA mentor.[74] Clarridge later testified to Congress that the U.S.-Iran arms operation dated back "probably to '81," at the instigation of then secretary of state Alexander Haig,[75] reportedly a P-2 member.

THE NAME OF THE ROSE

According to Informant "Y," who claims his source to be Licio Gelli's top associate Francesco Pazienza, George Bush himself was made an "honorary" member of P-2 in 1976, the year that he became director of the Central Intelligence Agency. Though the author has no confirmation for this claim, it is a fact that Gelli's "lodge," especially P-2's sister Montecarlo Comite, has branches in many countries besides Italy[76] and that the grandmaster's key targets for membership have been top civilian and military intelligence officials. The Montecarlo Comite, in fact, has been structured into thirty-three divisions, each of whose chiefs corresponds to a key institution, like the CIA, in the country targeted for take over.[77] According to "Y," shortly before the assassination of Swedish Prime Minister Olof Palme, Licio Gelli sent a message to former Republican National Committee adviser and alleged "honorary" P-2 member Philip Guarino assuring him that "the Swedish tree will be felled" and to "tell our good friend Bush."[78]

There are additional reports that suggest a possible link between George Bush and Licio Gelli's secret organization. An informant who called *Playboy*'s offices in early 1988 while the magazine was putting together a story on the "October Surprise"[79] confirmed that there had been a pre-election meeting and agreement between the Reagan-Bush campaign and Iran, and that George Bush's code name for the secret Iran operation was "White Rose."[80] The reader will recall that in 1973, when police uncovered the P-2 control cell responsible for terrorism in Italy, they learned that its code name was "The Rose of Twenty." Grandmaster Gelli apparently had a fondness for the flower. Whether a white rose has any particular significance for him is unknown.

Another reference to a flower code in connection with the Iran initiative is contained in *Witness,* authored by CIA informant and former U.S. SAVAK chief Mansur Rafizadeh. A number of times in the book, he states that the CIA Iran expert with whom he worked most closely always wore a flower in his lapel. Rafizadeh knew and worked with George Bush and also with Bush's future national security adviser and CIA Middle East expert Donald Gregg.[81] Rafizadeh, in fact, was the author's first source that Bush and Gregg had met in Europe with top Iranian officials in October 1980 to negotiate a secret arms-for-hostages agreement with the Khomeini regime.[82] As former chief of SAVAK in the United States, Rafizadeh himself may have worked with P-2. According to informant "Y," P-2 leader Licio Gelli had been behind removing the Shah of Iran from power, an operation in which Rafizadeh actively participated.[83] Gelli, however, wanted SAVAK officers who had joined P-2, and who were therefore under his control, to stay on as part of SAVAMA, Khomeini's new secret police.[84] Cyrus Hashemi, one of the Iranian arms dealers who reportedly met with William Casey and George Bush in Europe before the 1980 election, was reportedly the New York chief for SAVAMA[85] and was also associated with the Vatican's military order, the Knights of Malta, to which Casey belonged.

Two further references to the "White Rose" should be noted, although they have no known relationship to the Reagan-Bush Administration's secret Iran initiative. "White Rose" was the name of a radical right-wing pro-Batista group of anti-Castro Cubans based in Miami in the early 1960's, at the time of the CIA's Bay of Pigs operation.[86] A source who worked in the Agency in the early 1960's told *The Nation* that George Bush "was [then] involved in the Caribbean . . . There was very definite worry that some Cuban [-American] groups were going to move against Castro and attempt to blame it on the CIA."[87] One such Cuban-American group was the "White Rose." A white rose is also the symbol of the British royal House of York, which fought the War of the Roses against the House of Lancaster, whose symbol was the red rose, in England. President George Bush is related to English royalty.

If Licio Gelli did make George Bush an "honorary" member of P-2 or its sister lodge, the Montecarlo Comite, only he and his small inner circle of cell "chiefs" would know. It has been reported that only Gelli knows the names of all the members of his international secret society, including who is on a top-secret "List of 300" non-Italian members.[88] One thing is certain. If George Bush did become a member of P-2 and/or the Montecarlo Comite, as the price of initiation he would have been obliged to place a compromising document about himself under the grandmaster's control.[89]

What compromising secret document might Licio Gelli have in his possession relating to the 41st President of the United States? Whereas there are many possibilities, given that Mr. Bush was director of the CIA in the wake of the Watergate scandal, one possibility stands out above the rest. That would be a memo or memos written by or to Bush in 1963—the year of President John F. Kennedy's assassination—when Bush was already reportedly a CIA agent or "asset."[90] *The Nation* has obtained one such document from this period, a memo from then FBI director J. Edgar Hoover recounting a 1963 briefing given to then "CIA representative George Bush" following President Kennedy's murder. Vice President Bush's White House office denied that he had ever been a "CIA agent" or "asset" ("only" the CIA director) and claimed that the "George Bush" in the memo obtained by *The Nation* therefore referred to "another" George Bush. However, the publication then contacted this "other" George Bush who insisted that it could not have been he who was referred to in the memo. *The Nation* also reported that another former CIA employee had confirmed the accuracy of its original claim. One of George Bush's first actions as director of the CIA in 1976 was to squelch an investigation by the Senate Committee on Intelligence into the CIA's involvement in the Kennedy assassination.

On the 25th anniversary of his brother's death, Senator Edward Kennedy paid his respects by placing "a single white rose" at the foot of President Kennedy's memorial in Runnymede, England.[91] This act, of course, may be purely coincidental. Then again, it may not. Either way, George Bush came up smelling like a rose.

BEWARE THE 30TH OF MARCH

In an earlier chapter we reviewed reports that the agenda at President Reagan's first White House National Security Council meeting, on January 21, 1981, included Iran. It also included a discussion of reports from Manucher Gorbanifar of assassination threats against the President. We have also reviewed reports that President Reagan ordered his national security adviser, Richard Allen, on the same day as that National Security Council meeting, to tell Iran that "the deal's off" unless American citizen Cynthia Dwyer was freed in Iran. We have seen that this "deal" reportedly involved a secret promise of U.S. arms, and that authorization for the Israelis to ship weapons to the Khomeini regime was not given until *after* Mrs. Dwyer was released in February, a month after Reagan's inauguration. As in the case of the assassination of Swedish Prime Minister Olof Palme,[92] this threat of a delay in a promised shipment of U.S. arms to Iran—i.e., President Reagan's threat to call the "deal" off—may have triggered the attempt on his life.

President Reagan was wounded in an assassination attempt on March 30, 1981. In *The Investigative Reporter,* columnist Jack Anderson revealed that assassin John Hinckley had been associated with a U.S.-based faction of the Khomeini-loyal Islamic Guerrilla Army.[93] Anderson's informant, a former Islamic Guerrilla Army member named Tony Rollini, had reportedly told the Secret Service two months before the shooting—only about ten days after Reagan's inauguration—that Hinckley was planning to kill the President and had been arrested in Nashville, Tennessee, for illegally possessing firearms. Rollini also said that the Islamic Guerrilla Army referred to Hinckley as "Hicks." According to senior White House correspondent Sarah McClendon, the Secret Service agents who accompanied President Reagan as he approached his waiting limousine outside the Washington Hilton Hotel on the morning of March 30, 1981, were not in their usual tight formation around the commander-in-chief.[94]

During the time that President Reagan was under anesthesia for treatment of the wounds he had received in the assassination attempt, a decision was made by his top advisers not to invoke the 25th Amendment of the Constitution, which could have made Vice President George Bush Acting President. This is curious in light of the fact that the opposite decision was reached four years later when Reagan was in far better condition during his surgery for and recuperation from colon cancer. On July 13, 1985, George Bush *did* become Acting President of the United States, under far less compelling circumstances.

The morning of the assassination attempt against President Reagan, March 30, 1981, Vice President Bush was on a scheduled trip to Texas. As his plane was about to land at Austin Airport, he was told that the President had just been shot. The Vice President was in Austin long enough to take Governor Bill Clements, who had purchased President John F. Kennedy's West Virginia estate where Reagan had stayed during the

1980 election campaign, on board. The Hyatt Regency Hotel, formerly the Old Hotel Texas, where Bush had just given a speech, was the hotel where President John F. Kennedy had stayed the night before his assassination.[95] The night of the attempt on President Reagan's life, Vice-President Bush's son Neil had a scheduled dinner appointment with Scott Hinckley, the brother of assassin John W. Hinckley, Jr.

X

THE SOUND OF SILENCE

**"There are more instances of abridgement
of the freedoms of the people
by the gradual and silent encroachments of those in power
than by violent and sudden usurpations."**

**James Madison
The Father of the United States Constitution**

One would think that when the issue might be treason and one of those implicated was a candidate for the presidency of the United States that the media would fulfill its most important function of educating the American electorate. Unfortunately, in the 1988 presidential election campaign, there were no Woodwards and Bernsteins.

As I toured the country, speaking on scores of radio programs in 1987 and 1988, I learned something astounding. "If what you say is true, and there is all this evidence," audiences would ask, "why hasn't it been in the media?" I would then begin to list mainstream newspapers—*The New York Times,* the *Miami Herald,* the *San Francisco Examiner*—that had covered major parts of the "October Surprise" story, many of them in front-page headline articles, only to be interrupted with the same protest, "Yes, but—it hasn't been in the *media.*" Through repeated encounters such as this, I learned that newspapers in the United States, even the best and most prestigious ones, are no longer considered by the general public to be part of "the media." That appellation, sometimes unconsciously, but also consciously, is reserved for television and, in particular, for network television.

Given this distinction in the public mind between television and other media, there both was, and was not, censorship of the "October Surprise"

245

story during the 1988 presidential election campaign. Radio coverage was good, often outstanding, and very thorough. Newspaper coverage was good to fair, and magazine coverage, with the notable exceptions of the West German news weekly *Der Spiegel* and *Playboy*, was poor. But "media"—network television—coverage, also with a few notable exceptions, bordered on the nonexistent.

ABC

The first hint that "the media" had made a decision to squelch serious discussion of any links between the secret 1985–86 U.S. arms sales to Iran and events in 1980 and 1981 came in December 1986, a month and a half after the Iran/Contra scandal broke in the press. On ABC's *Nightline*, on December 18, 1986, as anchor Ted Koppel was interviewing a number of journalists and principals in the Iran/Contra story, Pierre Salinger, ABC's European correspondent, tried to focus attention on 1980: "Iran was willing to exchange hostages for the original $300 million of impounded U.S. weapons and spare parts," he began, but was cut off by a curt Koppel, who quickly steered the conversation back to 1985–86.[1] Koppel's decision not to explore the 1980 origins of the Iran/Contra scandal on the air was ironic, as he had literally made his name as the anchor for ABC's late-night report, "The Iran Crisis: America Held Hostage," which later became *Nightline*.

ABC received a critical piece of information on the "October Surprise" story from Mr. Salinger, which it has so far chosen not to share with the American public. On September 7, 1987, Salinger interviewed an influential Swedish arms dealer, Sven Klang, in Copenhagen, Denmark. In a confidential memorandum to ABC chairman Roone Arledge the following day, September 8, Salinger alerted the network that:

> "Klang says he is sure the United States delivered F-4 [fighter jet] engines to the Iranians in 1981—I REPEAT—1981, which were taken from NATO warehouses in Belgium. If that can be proved, it would give much higher credibility to the charge that Ronald Reagan's aides negotiated a deal with the Iranians in October of 1980 to prevent the release of the U.S. hostages in Iran during the Carter regime, promising them military equipment if they held off."

Klang was an associate of longtime CIA contract agent William Herrmann, who claims to have been told by Iranian Revolutionary Guards Deputy Minister Hamid Nagashian in January 1981 that George Bush, William Casey, Richard Allen, Allen's campaign associate Dr. Fred Ikle, and Robert McFarlane met in Paris in October 1980 with Iranian officials Mohammed Beheshti, Hashemi Rafsanjani, Revolutionary Guards Minister Moshen Rafiq Dust, Iran/Contra middleman Albert Hakim, and Nagashian, Dust's deputy.

On November 3, 1988, a little under a week before the November 8th U.S. presidential election, a *Nightline* producer told *Philadelphia Daily News* columnist Jack McKinney that her ABC staff had found the evidence for the "October Surprise" allegations "very impressive," but had chosen not to air a program on it before the vote. The author had sent numerous summaries of what was known about the story to *Nightline,* as had Mr. McKinney. In early October 1988, after an ABC affiliate television station in Denver, KABC-TV, videotaped an interview with Heinrich Rupp, the CIA pilot who claims to have flown William Casey to Paris on October 18–19, 1980, Capitol Cities Communications, which owns ABC, ordered the tape "held until further notice." Apparently, no "notice" was ever received.

Almost two years later, after millions of Americans had already learned of the "October Surprise" story from radio, I was interviewed on the subject by ABC Television at their headquarters in New York City, on September 30, 1988. As I arrived at the studio, an assistant to Gabe Pressman, the reporter who did the interview, said that ABC had just received a "tip" that Israel was about to come forward with new information on the story. I later learned that ABC had also interviewed the former President of Iran, Abolhassan Bani Sadr on the subject, at his residence outside of Paris. Neither tape was ever used.

Unlike television, ABC radio provided the best, most extensive, and most detailed coverage of the "October Surprise" story, both in 1987 and during election year 1988. The popular KGO radio station in San Francisco devoted dozens of hours to exploring every avenue and detail of evidence in the story. As a result, those who received its signal, which reaches thirty-two states, voted in a telephone poll before the 1988 presidential election to demand formal action in Washington, D.C. This was on the Ray Talliferro program, which airs from 1:00 to 5:00 A.M. weekday mornings. Eighty percent of the first six hundred callers wanted their elected representatives to pay attention and take meaningful action.

On the morning of November 3, 1988, five days before the election,

Don Elliot of ABC Radio in Peoria, on whose program I appeared beginning at 6:00 A.M., told me that he had arranged for the staff of ABC anchor
Peter Jennings, then in Illinois, to listen to the program. His hope was
that, when ABC saw how well the story "played in Peoria," they would
decide to cover it from network headquarters in New York. Audience
reaction, as usual, was overwhelming, but there was still only silence from
this pillar of "the media."

TIME MAGAZINE

I first became aware of the clearest example of censorship in the "October
Surprise" story in the summer of 1987. I had circulated copies of a
summary of my research findings on the story to radio listeners who had
requested them. One such copy evidently found its way into the hands of
an Iranian emigré journalist living in Europe who happened to be visiting
the Monterey Peninsula. He called out of the blue one afternoon and
invited me for lunch to discuss my latest findings. At the restaurant, he
explained that he was on his way to Saudi Arabia where he had been
invited by King Faud to spend six weeks covering the Haj, the annual
Muslim pilgrimage to Islam's holy cities, Mecca and Medina. That happened to be the year that Iranian rioters clashed with Saudi police, during
which hundreds of Khomeini loyalists were killed.

From what the Iranian journalist had to say, I could tell that he was very
well connected, and the conversation became more interesting. He asked
for a copy of my latest research summary, which I had brought along to
the luncheon. During our meeting, I watched as he jotted notes in a
distinctive hand on the back of the summary. At the end of our conversation, the Iranian mentioned that he knew Manucher Gorbanifar, the now-
infamous middleman used by the Israelis and the White House to facilitate
secret arms sales to Iran in 1985 and 1986. Just as I was wondering who it
was I was having lunch with, my guest said that he had to leave for
another appointment.

A few weeks later, I received a second call out of the blue, this time at a
local press. I had just started working there, and only a few of my very
closest friends had the number of the business. The caller, who had a
smooth, deep voice, introduced himself as Mansur Rafizadeh. I was

startled. The man on the other end of the line was the former U.S. chief of SAVAK, the Shah of Iran's dreaded secret police. I was very much aware of who he was because I had recently read his very fine book, *Witness*, which contains the first revelation in print that elements in the CIA loyal to the Republicans in 1980 delayed the release of the U.S. hostages in Iran until Reagan's inauguration.[2] I had, in fact, been hoping to get in touch with him, but had no way of knowing how to reach him. I was delighted that he had found me. It was slightly disturbing, however, that the former American head of the Shah of Iran's secret police knew where I worked, when most of my friends still didn't. When I asked, he said only that "someone high up in media circles in New York" had given him a copy of my latest research summary. Whoever that was had also given him my telephone number.

"I want you to know that I stayed up late last night reading through your summary, and it is absolutely correct," he said. "Except one small detail. Cyrus Hashemi was not a cousin of Mr. Hashemi Rafsanjani." (Rafsanjani is the speaker of Iran's Parliament). He insisted on this a number of times, despite the fact that Hashemi's relationship to Rafsanjani had appeared a number of times in print. We went over my summary of reports on the "October Surprise" story in detail, and he then recommended that I contact a reporter in New York who had done a lot of work on the story, at *Time* magazine.

"*Time* censored the story," he then said. "They won't allow it to be published. Maybe he will tell you more about it."

I thanked Mr. Rafizadeh, who invited me to come to New Jersey to review his research files and unpublished chapters from his book *Witness*, and called the reporter at *Time*'s headquarters in New York. According to Mr. Rafizadeh, he had authored many of the magazine's cover stories on the Iran/Contra affair.

"It's true," he confirmed. "We had the story of the hostage delay in April 1986. I had material from Rafizadeh and a number of other sources as well. It was approved in headquarters, but Washington 'killed' it just before it was to go to press."

I was stunned. I asked the reporter who his other sources were, but he said he had promised them that he wouldn't reveal their names. I learned later, through a journalist at another major news weekly who shared an insider's track, that *Time* had received confirmation for the story from four to five active and former CIA sources, off the record.

"I'm so grateful someone is finally going to follow up this story!" the

Time writer exclaimed. ''Let me know if there's *anything* I can do to help. If you can get it out—oh!—I'd—I'll send you roses!''

Surprised at his sudden display of emotion, I thanked the reporter for coming to the phone and hung up. Here was a journalist at the top of one of the largest news magazines in the country imploring me, a private citizen, to help *him* get the story to the American public.

NBC

Throughout 1987, Mr. Mansur Rafizadeh appeared on numerous programs aired by NBC affiliate stations in major cities nationwide. These interviews invariably focused on the most explosive revelation in his book *Witness*, in the chapter called ''When the Hostages Didn't Come Home,'' about the delay in the release of the fifty-two U.S. embassy hostages engineered by Bush-loyal forces in the CIA. Despite this widespread TV coverage by its own affiliates, however, not a word of the story was picked up by NBC network headquarters in New York for broadcast on the nightly news. Nightly network news, of course, is what my audiences had meant by ''the media.'' ''I'm so mad,'' Mr. Rafizadeh told me in a telephone conversation. ''They ignore it. Even *this*. They just ignore it!''

On September 30, 1988, a little over a month before the 1988 presidential election, I was invited to do a two-hour radio program on ABC's ''Lynn Samuels Show'' in New York City. In the middle of the program, a colleague from Fairness and Accuracy in Reporting (FAIR) came into the studio to say that NBC Television wanted to do an interview at the end of the show. After the program, we were escorted down the street to NBC headquarters, where I was interviewed on video by Tom Brokaw's assistant, Brian Ross. A day earlier, former CIA pilot Richard Brenneke's sworn testimony on the October 19–20, 1980, Paris meetings between Reagan-Bush campaign officials and Iranian representatives had been released by a judge in Denver, and suddenly the networks were showing interest in the story. After our taped interview, I stood next to Brokaw's production assistant as he confirmed, in a call to CIA pilot Harry Rupp's attorney, Michael Scott of Denver, that Rupp indeed claimed to have flown then Reagan-Bush campaign manager William Casey to those Paris meetings in October of 1980. Despite this interview, telephone confirmations, and hours xeroxing documents for use by NBC Nightly News, not one word on the ''October Surprise'' story, except for Mr. Rafizadeh's talk show appearances in 1987, was heard by the network's viewers.

In late August 1988, I took Mr. Rafizadeh up on his invitation to go through his notes and the unpublished chapters from *Witness* on the Desert One hostage rescue mission in his New Jersey offices. There, on the coffee table when I arrived, was the copy of the research summary I had given to the Iranian journalist with whom I had lunched in Monterey months before. On the back of the document was the number where Mr. Rafizadeh had first telephoned me. One mystery, at least, had been solved. The former chief of the Shah's secret police in the United States was well acquainted with the European journalist who was well acquainted with Manucher Gorbanifar and King Faud of Saudi Arabia. Over a year would pass before I would have enough information to realize why an associate of King Faud's might take interest in my research. CIA pilot Heinrich Rupp claimed to have flown 1980 Reagan-Bush campaign manager William Casey to Paris on October 18–19, 1980, in a plane owned by one of King Faud's sons.

In an interview on August 29, 1987, while I was visiting Mr. Rafizadeh's office, he confirmed once again, as he had in earlier telephone conversations, that Donald Gregg, then President Carter's national security council aide and later Vice President George Bush's national security adviser, had been present at a meeting in Europe with vice-presidential candidate Bush and Iranian representatives before the 1980 presidential election. (For reasons that are not clear, Mr. Rafizadeh has since refused to confirm this to other journalists). A few days later, I drove into New York City at the end of my trip, to meet with the *Time* reporter I had spoken to earlier. I wanted to get his reaction to what Mr. Rafizadeh had said about Donald Gregg.

''If Rafizadeh says Gregg was there, he was there,'' the *Time* man said flatly. ''If anyone knows about Gregg, it's Rafizadeh.''

Interestingly, in *Witness*, Mr. Rafizadeh refers repeatedly to a CIA officer with whom he worked closely for many years. Although he would not identify him by name, it is known that twenty-five-year CIA veteran Donald Gregg is a Middle East expert with long ties to George Bush.[3] A photo of Bush and Rafizadeh appears in the book.

CBS

On October 12, 1988, I received an urgent telephone message from Sarah McClendon, the senior White House correspondent. A Washington institution in her own right, Ms. McClendon has covered nine consecutive presidencies from the White House press room. The indomitable Sarah wanted me to know that she had just received news that CBS had recently held a top-level meeting at its New York headquarters at which it had been decided, despite the information from alleged eyewitnesses, not to run the "October Surprise" story before the 1988 presidential election. She was outraged and had called the network to try to get a statement from its chairman, Mr. Tisch, who did not return her calls.

According to Pierre Salinger, ABC News' European correspondent, Swedish arms dealer Sven Klang has been interviewed by CBS's *60 Minutes*. As Klang was ABC's source for information that the Reagan-Bush Administration secretly delivered F-4 fighter jet engines to Iran in 1981, taken from NATO stores in Belgium, it is probable that the arms dealer also shared this important piece of the "October Surprise" story with CBS. To date, however, there has been no report from CBS News of allegations of an early draw-down of U.S. NATO stores in Europe to supply Iran's military needs.

Shortly before the election, I was invited to do an interview on the "October Surprise" story by San Francisco's CBS affiliate station, KPIX Television. The interview aired that night, and I received hundreds of calls from grateful viewers over the following weeks.

CNN TELEVISION

Several days before the 1988 presidential election, following a briefing on the "October Surprise" by the Washington, D.C. based Christic Institute, CNN owner Ted Turner said that his network would run the story before the election. When the broadcast did not happen, he reportedly claimed that his news executives had "overruled him." I had had lunch with Mr. Turner some time before this, at which time he had put a thick summary of published reports on the "October Surprise" story in his breast pocket.

NEWSWEEK MAGAZINE

In July 1987, shortly after my conversation with the *Time* reporter whose story on the hostage delay had been censored in 1986, I received a call from *Newsweek*'s West Coast headquarters in San Francisco. The West Coast bureau chief, Jerry Lubenow, I was told, had received my package of background information and articles on the "October Surprise" story from a former television journalist and was excited about doing an article about it in one of the magazine's forthcoming issues. One of Lubenow's correspondents, Pam Abramson, arrived with a camera crew and spent hours going over every detail of the story while the magazine's photographer shot rolls of film. When no story appeared after a few issues, I called Ms. Abramson, who told me that the *Newsweek* report, like *Time*'s, had apparently been "killed." In this case, it had happened in the magazine's headquarters in New York, despite the active efforts of the West Coast bureau chief to get it into print. A writer who had taken interest in the story in New York had been sent on vacation, she said, and Lubenow was later transferred to London. A few weeks later, after the magazine's bureaucratic machinery had gone into action, two sentences on the story appeared in the "Periscope" section along with a comment from an unidentified staffer from one of the "official" investigations in Washington (which had no time, money, or mandate to investigate it seriously) that it was a "*tentative* 'blind alley.' " This was all that the American people learned of the "October Surprise" from *Newsweek*.

To the author's knowledge, only one *Newsweek* reporter, Robert Parry, paid serious attention to the story before the 1988 presidential election. The author met with Mr. Parry in late August 1988 in Washington, D.C. Not long afterwards, he flew to Denver to cover Richard Brenneke's appearance at the sentencing hearing of CIA pilot Harry Rupp in September. *Newsweek* had run major revelations by Brenneke in the Iran/Contra story, written by Parry, including Brenneke's claim that Donald Gregg had been a key link between Vice President Bush's office and the Contras, and that the Saudi royal family had made a substantial financial contribution to the Nicaraguan resistance. Yet not one word of Brenneke's or Rupp's testimonies on the critical pre-1980-election Paris meetings between then Reagan-Bush campaign manager William Casey, then vice-presidential candidate George Bush, and Iranian officials ever reached print in *Newsweek*.

THE *WASHINGTON POST*

A few months before the 1988 election, I drove to the University of California at Berkeley where *Washington Post* reporter Bob Woodward was presenting a keynote address at the Berkeley Convocation. After the speech, I met with him briefly backstage and gave him a package of updated information on the "October Surprise" story. Previous mailings to his office had produced no response, and I wanted to be certain that he personally received the material. After Mr. Woodward took the package and thanked me, I returned to the Monterey Peninsula. Surely, I thought, Bob Woodward of Watergate fame, of all journalists, would want to get to the bottom of allegations which, if true, would make the crimes of Watergate look like child's play; especially as he had ended his speech that afternoon by urging the audience to remain vigilant so that the country would never again have to suffer a trauma like Watergate. Yet nothing more by Mr. Woodward on the "October Surprise" story appeared in the *Washington Post*. A colleague later called to say that he had telephoned Mr. Woodward to ask whether his office had followed up on the material I had left with him. Woodward reportedly said, "We'll be getting in touch with her" but never did.

The *Washington Post* evidentally had a different agenda. In early October 1988, about a month before the presidential election, I received a call from London *Sunday Times* correspondent, Mark Hosenball, who said that he had been hired by the *Post* to do a story on the "October Surprise." At his request, I quickly overnighted a package of updated material, including dozens of articles, a transcript of Richard Brenneke's testimony from Heinrich Rupp's Denver sentencing hearing, and a summary of my research findings. Mr. Hosenball called back in a couple of days to say that he had received the information and reviewed it, and that his article would be appearing in the "Outlook" section of the newspaper's Sunday edition. On October 9, 1988, a poorly researched, superficial, and blatantly biased piece, "If It's October, Then It's Time for an Iranian Conspiracy Theory" written by Hosenball was published in the *Post*. It distorted many of the key facts and claims in the package I had sent to him. Mr. Hosenball not only attempted to dismiss the story as "rumor," but referred to the serious former President of Iran, Mr. Bani Sadr, as "Charlie Chaplinesque," and called former President Carter's public statements that he had been aware before the 1980 election of attempts by the Reagan-Bush camp to delay the release of the hostages "murmurings." The *Washington Post* had effectively stooped to referring to former presidents of both the United States and Iran as "rumor mongers." Mr. Hosenball had taken the word of an aide to then Vice President Bush that the Secret Service had records allegedly contradicting the charge that Bush had attended a pre-1980-election meeting in Paris. Hosenball wrongly claimed that the "ex-CIA" man referred to in my documentation was Richard Brenneke, when it was instead Informant "Y"; stated incorrectly that Mr. Brenneke had claimed that he had attended the Paris meeting with Bush, when Mr. Brenneke had always stressed that he had *not* been at a meeting with Bush, and my documentation made no such claim; and stated incorrectly that I had claimed that French intelligence agent Robert Benes had also met with Bush, when I had never made such a claim and nothing in my documentation stated anything of the kind, then proceeded to knock this "straw man" down by quoting Benes as saying that he had never met with Bush! Finally, Mr. Hosenball made the additional false statement that I had claimed that Iranian arms dealer Houshang Lavi had offered to hold up the release of the hostages when he had met with Robert McFarlane and Richard Allen in early October 1980 in Washington, D.C. Reports of attempts to delay their release were only in reference to subsequent meetings, not the early Washington meeting, and Mr. Hosenball knew that very well from the materials I had sent him.

When I finished reading the *Post* piece, I had to ask myself who Mark Hosenball was really working for. Luckily, there were other reporters who were as outraged at his misleading and inaccurate reporting as I was. In its October 19–25, 1988, issue, *In These Times* ran an excellent critique of Hosenball's article, along with a political cartoon, which summed up the attitude of Washington's number-one newspaper best. In it, a reporter in a Dick Tracy hat phones his findings on the "October Surprise" story in to his editor, saying, "That's right, Chief. I talked to the CIA, and they said there's *nothing* to it."

THE LARRY KING SHOW

Some of the most curious and convoluted attempts to prevent the "October Surprise" story from reaching the airwaves came from the "Larry King Show." In early December 1986, shortly after the Iran/Contra scandal broke, King's producers arranged for me to call in to his television program the evening that President Carter's former White House chief of staff, Hamilton Jordan, was the guest. I was immediately put on the air. After I summarized allegations that the 1980 Reagan-Bush campaign secretly negotiated a delay in the release of the fifty-two U.S. hostages for political gain, Mr. Jordan was asked by an astonished King for a response. "I know of nothing to contradict what has just been said," Jordan replied, at which King demanded to know who his caller was. I reminded him of his show's explicit policy, as I had just been reminded by his producers, that callers were not to reveal their identities on the air. He nevertheless insisted, and immediately after putting down the receiver at the end of our on-the-air interaction, I received a threatening phone call. Luckily, it was the only such call I received in two years of public speaking on the "October Surprise" story.

After I had already appeared on scores of radio programs nationwide throughout 1987 and 1988, callers began demanding on the air that Mr. King invite me as a guest. In the months before the 1988 election I had received literally dozens of telephone calls from angry listeners and viewers (King has a radio as well as a television program) relaying that the talk show host had promised the previous evening to have me as a guest on the show to get to the bottom of the facts and charges in the "October Surprise" story. On each such occasion, the following morning I would call King's studio and talk with one of his producers to accept the reported invitation, only to be told, in one way or another, that the viewers who had called must have misheard or been mistaken. Finally, angry viewers and listeners began sending audio tapes of King's assurances on the air that his production staff was trying to get me to appear as a guest, so I was able to confirm his statements for myself. Either King or his producers, or both, were trying to have their cake and eat it too—lead viewers and listeners to believe that the popular host was trying to get me to accept his invitation to come on the air, but that there was some problem with *my* being able to accept. At one point, Mr. King even said on the air that his producers were "negotiating with Ms. Honegger" to appear on the program, which was

patently false. I was also told by listeners that King had claimed on the air
that I had turned down appearances on other major television programs,
which was also completely false. I had accepted every invitation to appear
on both television and radio programs to discuss the "October Surprise"
story. The morning after hearing of these further false claims, I again
called King's producer to demand that he retract his misstatements on the
air; he never did. After even further assurances by Mr. King on the air that
the show was trying to have me on as a guest, a colleague personally
delivered my acceptance to the talk show host in Los Angeles on the night
of September 28, 1988, so he could not claim that verbal acceptances to
his production staff had not reached him. Still, there was no call or
invitation from either Mr. King or his producers to be on the program.

LOS ANGELES TIMES

In late September 1988, I received a call from Doyle McManus, Washington, D.C. correspondent for the *Los Angeles Times* and co-author of a
book on the Iran/Contra affair, *Landslide*. We scheduled a full afternoon
appointment for October 9, 1988, in Carmel, California. Over lunch, he
explained that he had himself been researching the "October Surprise"
story for a number of years. After hours of discussion and going over the
story from every angle, he signed a copy of *Landslide* with the inscription:
"For Barbara Honegger. An indomitable investigator in the greatest American tradition." Unfortunately, that personal opinion did not get reflected
in his article, which soon reached the light of day in the *Los Angeles
Times*.

Mr. McManus proceeded to publish an article as obviously biased as
that which had appeared in the *Washington Post*. It was on page one of
the paper's October 25th edition under the loaded headline, "Leads, Leaps of
Faith in Hostage Tale." Although the piece contained some solid information on the story, it was written in a condescending tone, which cued
readers to disregard its contents. The one piece of news in the article—that
thirteen of the fifty-two hostages held in the U.S. embassy in Tehran for
444 days had filed a legal action based on the "October Surprise"
allegations—was buried at the very end of the article, on an inside page.

When I called Mr. McManus at his office in Washington, D.C. after the

election, the first thing he said was, "After what I wrote, I thought you'd
never talk to me again!" I told him that I was willing to put it behind us in
the interest of continued collaboration on the story. The *Los Angeles
Times*, like all too many in the mainstream media, had unfortunately
succumbed to the elitist attitude prevalent in today's newsrooms, which
results in claims from "official" sources being judged by standards far
more lax than those from "nonofficial" sources, when they should at least
be held to the same standard.

THE ATLANTA-JOURNAL CONSTITUTION

Among the journalists selected to question presidential candidates George
Bush and Michael Dukakis in their September 25, 1988 debate was
Atlanta-Journal Constitution political correspondent John Mashek. I was
able to speak with Mr. Mashek shortly before the debate, and arranged for
a package of documentation and articles on the "October Surprise" story
to be delivered to the address he had given me, at a hotel in the city where
the debate was to be held. Although Mr. Mashek read the documentation,
he did not question Vice President Bush during the debate on "October
Surprise" allegations. Afterwards, he published a letter to the editor in
which he acknowledged having had a bias that had caused him to dismiss
the information: "Whatever the merits of the ["October Surprise"] story,
it had a sensationalistic ring to it and was dismissed without much prob-
ing." This was despite the fact that articles on the subject from the
nation's mainstream newspapers, including *The New York Times* and the
Miami Herald, including one from a Pulitzer-prize-winning reporter, had
been included in the package he had reviewed. They couldn't all have been
"sensationalistic." Unlike other reporters with major U.S. newspapers
who had tried to pass off superficial treatments of the story as if they were
based on real investigations, however, Mr. Mashek was at least honest
enough to admit that he had passed judgment without taking the time to
examine the story on its merits.

THROUGH THE "LOOKING GLASS"—DER SPIEGEL

On August 25, 1988, I held a press conference at the National Press Club in Washington, D.C., under the auspices of the Association for Responsible Dissent. The purpose of the conference was to share the latest information on the "October Surprise" story with the national and international press. In attendance, based on the registration list from the event, were CBS News, CBS Radio, ABC News, Gannett Television, the Federal News Service, *Der Spiegel* of West Germany, Associated Press, UPI, the *Village Voice*, IPS, Pacifica News Service, the *Boston Globe*, the Voice of America, the *Guardian* (of Britain), Cable News Network (CNN) Television, McClendon News Service, Scripps-Howard wire service, Hong Kong Commercial Radio, the *Christian Science Monitor*, the *Fort Lauderdale News/Sentinel*, the *Veteran's Daily Life, People* magazine, and the *Los Angeles Weekly*, among others.

Of all the reporters present at the press conference, which lasted over two hours, by far the most serious and genuinely interested was from Europe's prestigious news weekly, *Der Spiegel*. *Der Spiegel* is the equivalent of *Time* magazine in West Germany. That afternoon, following the press conference, I had an appointment to do a videotaped interview with *Der Spiegel* at the magazine's Washington offices. The interview went well, and the reporter had already received permission from his headquarters in West Germany to devote as much time, attention, energy, and money to the story as he felt was needed to get the job done right. On September 5, 1988, *Der Spiegel* published an excellent overview article on the "October Surprise" story for German-speaking readers. Like the article in *Playboy*'s October 1988 issue, it too mentioned reports of the Paris meeting before the 1980 election between top officials of the Reagan-Bush campaign and Iranian representatives. *Der Spiegel* has since invested literally tens of thousands of dollars and hundreds of man hours following the "October Surprise" trail across Europe. At the time of this writing, the magazine has enough information to fill a book and, hopefully, will be revealing what it knows.

THE GOOD NEWS

Despite censorship and biased reporting by the television networks, major news weeklies, and a few major U.S. newspapers, there was some excellent coverage of the "October Surprise" story by a number of papers. The *Boston Globe*, the Portland *Oregonian*, the *Miami Herald*, the *Rocky Mountain News* of Denver, the *Oakland Tribune*, the *Philadelphia Daily News*, the New York *Post*, *In These Times*, the *San Francisco Examiner*, *Playboy* magazine, *Der Spiegel*, and the French publication *Minute* all ran good to excellent articles, many of them front-page banner-headline stories, on the subject. C-SPAN television, the cable network that covers Washington, D.C., aired an hour-long interview program with the author in late August 1988, which resulted in hundreds of grateful letters from viewers.

But it was radio that did the "October Surprise" story real justice during the 1988 presidential election campaign. The author appeared on literally dozens of radio talk shows nationwide, some more than once, and for as long as two to three hours at a time. Included in these informative programs were the nationwide "Michael Jackson Show," the nationwide "Tom Snyder Show," and dozens of talk shows on 50,000-watt stations, whose signals reach listeners in up to thirty states.

The best radio programs on the subject were produced by "The Other Americas Radio" in Santa Barbara, California, and by KFI (ABC) radio in Los Angeles. The "Other Americas" tape, called "The October Surprise," was aired on National Public Radio (NPR) stations nationwide beginning in June 1988, to an overwhelming response. This audio tape led *20-20* co-anchor Hugh Downs to devote an entire radio program to the subject in August 1988. The three-hour KFI program aired on September 17, 1988.

THE HOSTAGE FACTOR

An important element behind media self-censorship on the "October Surprise" story during the 1988 presidential election campaign is the hostage factor. Among nine U.S. hostages held in Lebanon at the time of the campaign (and still held captive at the time of this writing) was the chief

Beirut correspondent for Associated Press, Terry Anderson. Anderson had been kidnapped by Khomeini-loyalist Shiite guerillas on March 16, 1985, and was the longest-held of all U.S. hostages in southern Lebanon. Out of deep concern for his safety, fellow journalists, consciously or unconsciously, may have felt pressure not to publish information that might be expected to displease his overly zealous kidnappers. A group of American reporters had even formed a support organization, the Journalists' Committee to Free Terry Anderson, out of empathy for his plight.

Anderson's Shiite captors were extremely shrewd. By selecting a reporter from Associated Press, they would be able to exert maximum leverage over U.S. media coverage of news relating to Iran. The effect of this leverage could be very real, because, until a story appears on the Associated Press "A" wire, it is rarely picked up by television or becomes a "national" issue. The Watergate story, for instance, had received regional coverage in the *Washington Post* before the 1972 presidential election, but did not become a national issue until after Richard Nixon had won the election, when it was picked up by the AP "A" wire. Watergate-related stories then instantly appeared, not only in the *Post*, but in newspapers and magazines across the country. As long as a top reporter from Associated Press lives at the point of a gun, it is unlikely that any credible report on negotiations by the Ayatollah Khomeini's agents to delay the release of other American hostages in 1980, or any other report likely to anger Terry Anderson's captors, will be carried on his service's "national" wire. In a classic case of Catch-22, it was precisely the absence of such a "national emphasis" in the news that led audiences around the country to protest, "But, if this story is true, why hasn't it been in the 'media'? Why hasn't it been in my local newspaper?" "Media," to the American public, means "mass awareness" as much as it means "network television."

LORD OF THE LIES

Above and beyond the elitist attitude that pervades modern newsrooms and results in reports biased, often unconsciously, towards giving the benefit of the doubt to "official" over "nonofficial" sources, another more insidious factor lay behind censorship and ridicule of any information that the White House deemed not to be in its interest. This applied not just to the "October Surprise" story but to any information or news analysis unfavorable to either presidential candidate George Bush or vice-presidential candidate Dan Quayle. Unfortunately, when the Vice President of the United States becomes a candidate for President, what is merely a personal political interest is too easily equated with the "national interest," and censorship is all too often rationalized in the interest of "national security." This "hidden" factor, which influenced which stories would reach the American electorate and which were likely to be given "credence" by editors, was headquartered at 1600 Pennsylvania Avenue. There, a White House office had been established which treated the American public, its elected representatives in Congress, and the U.S. media as if they were literally enemies in time of war.

In the Fall 1988 issue of the prestigious journal *Foreign Policy, Newsweek* reporter Robert Parry and Peter Kornbluh of the independent National Security Archive revealed that psychological warfare experts from the U.S. military—specialists trained in deceiving and confusing an enemy population in time of war or preparation for war—had been brought on to the staff of the National Security Council in an operation headed by a senior CIA disinformation expert recommended by Vice President Bush's national security adviser, Donald Gregg.[4] In 1982, Gregg—who, if reports about his involvement in the pre-1980-election Paris meetings are correct had much to divert media attention from—recommended Walter Raymond, Jr., a CIA psychological warfare veteran, to head what was euphemistically called the "Office of Public Diplomacy." The mission of this office was to ensure that Congress, the press, and the American public did not get too close to the truth about the administration's covert Iran and Contra operations.

In January 1983, President Reagan formalized this psychological warfare offensive against the American public in National Security Decision Directive (NSDD) #77. A few months later, in July 1983, the National Security Council also took over a second "Public Diplomacy" office in the U.S. State Department, headed by an Otto Reich. Reich had acknowledged in a memo that his State Department operations "responded to NSC [White House] direction." Under Reich at the State Department were U.S. Army psychological warfare specialists, including his executive assistant Lieutenant Colonel Daniel Jacobowitz and five experts from the Army's 4th Psychological Operations Group at Fort Bragg, North Carolina, a key training center for military covert operations. This State Department office, under White House direction, orchestrated the publication of articles in the nation's newspapers that purported to be written by independent scholars. According to one report by the Government Accounting Office (GAO), the investigative arm of Congress, the "Public Diplomacy" program amounted to a "legally prohibited covert propaganda campaign designed to influence the [U.S.] media and the public."

In these efforts, Donald Gregg and Walt Raymond, Jr. were certain to have the enthusiastic support of Vice President George Bush, who himself had a history of influencing with the U.S. press. In the wake of the Watergate's scandal, Mr. Bush, as President Gerald Ford's CIA director, met personally with editors of the nation's major newspapers and news magazines, "gently" pressuring them not to print information embarrassing to the Republican administration—in the alleged interest, of course, of "national security."[5]

By the mid 1980's, according to *Los Angeles Times* reporter Doyle McManus, most of these so-called "public relations" operations directed from both the White House and the Department of State were devoted "not to selling the Administration's programs, but to deceiving the public about the nature of those programs."[6] A senior NSC official acknowledged that the "public diplomacy" apparatus was modeled after CIA covert operations aimed at *enemy* populations overseas: "They were trying to manipulate public opinion . . . using the tools of Walt Raymond's trade craft, which he learned from his career in the CIA covert operations shop," he said.[7] NSC Adviser John Poindexter himself told Oliver North, in a message dated September 13, 1986, "What he [CIA Director William Casey] has in mind [as a person to head up the psychological offense operation] is a political operative who can twist arms and also run a high-powered public relations campaign."

According to *Foreign Policy*, NSC and State Department "public diplomacy" head Walt Raymond, Jr. and his staff pressured journalists and editors into both reporting, and not reporting, information about the administration's Iran operations to suit its own goals. Clearly, chief among these goals was the election of Vice President George Bush in 1988. With the psychological warfare operation already in place, it could easily be activated to advance a purely domestic political agenda.

The existence of the psychological warfare and propaganda offices was so secret and so sensitive that a chapter on their history and operations was censored by Reagan-Bush loyalists from the final report of the Congressional Iran/Contra Committee. This suppressed chapter concluded that "[The propaganda office] did what a covert CIA operation in a foreign country might do—attempted to manipulate the media, the Congress, and public opinion to support Reagan Administration policies. The problem with all this is—they tried to do it in America, to their own people, to their own Congress, and to their own free press.'' A copy of this same censored report from the Iran/Contra investigation formed the basis for Parry and Kornbluh's article, which appeared in *Foreign Policy*.

When it is recalled that the National Security Council's ''Public Diplomacy'' office and its State Department counterpart had access to the massive computerized PACS system created by Richard Beal, the picture of what was going on inside the White House during the 1988 presidential election campaign becomes even more disturbing. For PACS had been designed to ''maintain Reagan's [and Vice President Bush's] popularity, no matter how dangerous, unpalatable, narrow, or delicate his goals.''[8] Given this avowed objective, it is little wonder that the prestige-conscious Washington press corps, after the NSC's psychological warfare specialists had finished their ''friendly discussions,'' either did not cover, or ridiculed, a story as serious as the ''October Surprise.'' It is also little wonder that, after months of hearings and hundreds of thousands of dollars of taxpayers' money, Co-Chairman of the Congressional Iran/Contra Committees Senator Daniel Inouye complained that Congress *still* did not have any idea of the origins of the administration's secret U.S. arms sales to Iran. Such are the wages of a nation that allows the military to enforce silence at the expense of democracy.

Ironically, as the American people were observing the 200th anniversary of their Constitution, President Reagan, Vice President Bush, and CIA Director William Casey chose to unleash psychological warfare operatives against the press, whose rights under the First Amendment were then being celebrated.

THE 1988 BUSH CAMPAIGN

When the ''October Surprise'' story began to get coverage on radio talk shows reaching a nationwide audience, about two months before the 1988 presidential election, even the prestige-conscious Washington press corps began to pay attention. The author appeared on the Michael Jackson and Tom Snyder radio programs in September and October of 1988, and principals in the story, including Richard Brenneke, pilot Harry Rupp, and an attorney for fifteen of the original fifty-two U.S. embassy hostages started going public. When that happened, "respectable" reporters asked the White House for comments. Spokesmen for Vice President George Bush denied all allegations, as expected; but, astonishingly, neither the White House nor campaign press corps pressed the Vice President himself for a response. The question was considered "taboo," apparently because it might be perceived as "political"—that is, the answer might actually affect someone's vote. Also, as a spin-off to the elitist attitude pervading major media, neither Vice President Bush nor his office was asked for proof that he was not in Paris on October 19, 1980, as claimed by Brenneke, Rupp, Informant "Y," and others. The burden of proof was placed instead on those who were trying to break through the effects of a multi-million-dollar psychological warfare campaign by both the White House and the Bush campaign. If a murder had taken place on October 19, 1980, and someone accused one of the major presidential candidates of committing it, the first demand of a detective on the case would be, "What's your alibi? Prove that you were somewhere else on that date and time." But the White House press corps demanded no such proof from the second highest-ranking official in the U.S. government who had been charged with committing an action bordering on high treason.

LAWLESS ATTITUDE

When the former President of Iran, Abolhassan Bani Sadr, claimed on October 4, 1988, that there had been another recent secret U.S. arms delivery to Iran and that a former CIA officer named Richard Lawless had just secretly negotiated with Iranian officials on behalf of Vice President George Bush, journalists failed to report the obvious connection to the "October Surprise" story. Lawless, who had worked in the Agency's operations directorate and had served in the U.S. embassy in South Korea when Bush's national security adviser Donald Gregg was CIA station chief there, denied the allegation. Yet, despite the denials, it was established that Lawless had been in the Middle East at the time Mr. Bani Sadr claimed. White House spokesman Marlin Fitzwater acknowledged that "There is a fellow named Lawless. He is over there [in the Middle East]. What he's up to, nobody knows."

When Associated Press correspondent Terry Anderson, the longest-held

U.S. hostage in southern Lebanon, released a videotaped message on October 30, 1988, three days after his fourth birthday in captivity and a little over a week before the presidential election, claiming that the Reagan-Bush Administration had repeatedly interfered with his release, the Washington press corps again failed to report the obvious connection to the "October Surprise" allegations that Mr. Bush had also acted to delay the release of another group of hostages, eight years earlier. In his taped message, Anderson said:

> "I've been very close to being released several times over the past two years, but each time it seems that the U.S. government uses its influence to stop any agreement from being made . . . I am not asking [President] Reagan to deal with terrorists, although Mr. Bush did so in the Iran/Contra affair and the TWA hijacking."[10]

President Reagan attempted to downplay Anderson's statement, claiming that he had been speaking "from a script." But Anderson's sister, Peggy Say, after reviewing the videotape, denied that characterization of her brother's motives. On November 4, 1988, Islamic Jihad, the pro-Khomeini group holding Anderson hostage, also denied President Reagan's charge: "The videotape, irrespective of its contents, has been issued directly by Terry Anderson without any pressure," they said. Though their claim, of course, is suspect, equally so was that of a President who had used a "script" for nearly eight years without anyone making a similar charge that he was not in control of his communications.

When *Nightline* reported on November 3, 1988, five days before the presidential election, that a volunteer of the 1988 Reagan-Bush campaign's advisory committee on the Middle East, Paul Jureidini, had met secretly in Damascus on August 16th with a high-ranking member of Syrian intelligence with intimate links to the Khomeini regime,[11] again the Washington press corps reported no connection to the "October Surprise" story receiving attention elsewhere in the media.

Journalist Robin Wright visited Iran in August 1988 to interview Hashemi Rafsanjani, the speaker of Iran's parliament, and other top Iranian officials and reported that they were united in their desire to see Democratic candidate Michael Dukakis lose the 1988 presidential election to George Bush.[12] Rafsanjani, apparently, had even taken steps to ensure that Vice President Bush would have the edge in the contest. Although the Reagan-Bush Administration, including President Reagan himself, had repeatedly stated that there would be no U.S. negotiations with Iran until all American hostages had been freed in Lebanon,[13] former Iranian President Abolhassan Bani Sadr reported that Mr. Bush's emissaries had been holding discussions with Rafsanjani since February. Former Green Beret, Lieutenant Colonel James "Bo" Gritz, revealed in a public address that on August 11–12, 1988, Vice President Bush himself had met secretly with top Iranian officials on board a British cruise ship off Antigua. Although American Express records reportedly existed documenting Mr. Gritz's charges, no mention of the meeting appeared anywhere in the U.S. media. According to the former President of Iran, Mr. Bani Sadr, this reported secret shipboard meeting between Vice President Bush and representatives of Iran's parliamentary speaker, Hashemi Rafsanjani, who was also the head of Iran's armed forces, occurred shortly after a personal message had been sent by the Vice President to Rafsanjani in August.[14] According to Bani Sadr's intelligence inside the Iranian government:

> "Mr. Bush sent a message to Mr. Rafsanjani saying that 'If current trends in the presidential elections continue, Dukakis will become President. Then the Democrats will reveal all the facts and documents in the matter of the [1979–81 U.S. embassy] hostage-taking and Irangate affairs because of their domestic needs and their public opinion needs. With these documents and facts revealed, your regime will lose the bare minimum of respect it needs to survive and the American Republican party will suffer a blow, too, which, if it coincides with a completely Democratic-run administration, will be deprived of the presidency for some time to come. So it is in both sides' interests to cooperate. You can help us win in the presidential elections by providing us with a major agreement [i.e., a cease-fire in the Iran-Iraq war].' "[15]

As a follow up to the reported August 11–12, 1988, shipboard meeting between Vice President Bush and Iranian officials, an Israeli weekly, *The Nation*, reported that further secret negotiations between U.S. and Iranian representatives and "other intermediaries" had taken place near Geneva, Switzerland, between September 26 and October 2, 1988, a little over one month before the presidential election. *The Nation* reported that an agreement had been reached on Iran's demand for economic aid, weapons, and the phased return of between $5 to $6 billion of its financial assets in exchange for the future release of eight of the nine U.S. hostages held by Iran-loyalist guerillas in southern Lebanon.[16] In denying the report, President Reagan lamely stated, "We are not negotiating directly with Iran." *The Nation* had reported that the talks were being conducted by "intermediaries" in any case.

When Florida publisher William Loiry released his "Report of the Vice President's Involvement in the Iran/Contra Scandal" at a press conference at the National Press Club in Washington, D.C. on October 20, 1988, including twenty pages of new information and details on the "October Surprise" story, the Washington press corps acted as if it hadn't happened. What *Newsweek* had reported the week before the 1988 election was, unfortunately for the American public, all too true—that the "guidance" from the Reagan-Bush Administration before the election had been to "keep everything off the headlines."[17] Vice President Bush and Donald Gregg's psychological warfare specialists were clearly successful in preventing any word of Bush's secret rendezvous and $5 billion-plus arms-for-hostages deal from reaching public awareness before the election. All that the voting public was allowed to know was that a conveniently-timed cease-fire had been suddenly agreed to by the Ayatollah Khomeini, to take effect eight days after Mr. Bush's reported shipboard meeting with Khomeini's number two man, on August 20, 1988.

BREAKING THROUGH TO "THE MEDIA"

Before the election, angry citizens' groups tried to break through the wall of silence from the television networks on the "October Surprise" story by holding "mock hostage" protests in major East and West Coast cities. A spontaneously formed group, which called itself the October Surprise Committee, held rallies in Westlake and Pasadena, California, on September 29, 1988, during which demonstrators bound themselves and wore blindfolds to represent the original fifty-two hostages held in the U.S. embassy in Tehran. They again demonstrated outside UCLA's Pauly Pavilion, where President Reagan gave an address on October 16, 1988. A group called the October Surprise Truth Committee held another rally in Los Angeles on October 13th, and large groups of citizens demonstrated as mock hostages outside Republican campaign headquarters in Eureka, California, and Boston, Massachusetts. Footage from these rallies was carried by UPI and by local ABC and CBS affiliate television stations, without, however, telling viewers the reason for the demonstrations.

The author received feedback from the 1988 Bush-Quayle campaign through a television journalist in Boston. During a videotaped interview there on September 29, 1988, with a WCVB-TV reporter, the author was told that the station had called Bush campaign headquarters for a comment on the "October Surprise" allegations. "Tell her [Ms. Honegger] that she's operating 'heavy equipment' " was the message.[18]

UP TO THE 'MINUTE' REPORTING

On October 19, 1988, the eighth anniversary of the alleged Paris meeting among Reagan-Bush campaign manager William Casey, George Bush, and Iranian and French representatives, the right-wing French publication *Minute* published an article defending then vice-presidential candidate George Bush's role in the pre-1980-election Paris negotiations.[19] The same day, a rumor swept the nation's capitol that the *Washington Post* was about to release a story that would be damaging to the Vice President's candidacy,[20] followed by an immediate fall in the New York stock exchange. Shortly before this rumor surfaced, the author received a telephone call from a journalist colleague in Washington saying that aides in the Vice President's office were working on a "cover story" to be used in case the French *Minute* report was picked up by the *Washington Post* and other major American newspapers. The *Post*, however, denied that it had any plans to publish a derogatory story about the presidential candidate, and no U.S. wire service or newspaper picked up *Minute*'s report.

"MY TRIP TO IRAN"

After the 1988 presidential election, President-elect George Bush held a White House press conference to introduce his appointee for Director of the Office of Management and Budget, Richard Darman. The Vice President first answered questions from reporters and then turned the microphone over to Mr. Darman. Before he did, however, Sarah McClendon, the senior White House correspondent, asked a question that Mr. Bush said he would leave for his designee to answer. After leaving the podium, according to McClendon, the Vice President started to leave the room, but stopped and was overheard to say [paraphrase]: "If Sarah is going to ask about my trip to Iran, I want to hear it." McClendon claims that this remark was replayed on a television broadcast later that evening, but *The New York Times*, which published a transcript of the "entire" question-and-answer session, left out this critical comment by Mr. Bush—presumably because he was no longer at the microphone and it was considered off the record.[21] After the press conference, Ms. McClendon asked the White House press office what the Vice President had meant by his remark, but did not receive an answer.

This reported reference by Vice President Bush to his "trip to Iran" is as significant as it is astonishing, as there has never been any mention of such a trip in the U.S. press. Again, only the sound of silence. The Vice President has acknowledged having met in Jerusalem on July 29, 1986, with Oliver North's Israeli counterpart, Amiram Nir, but never to having held negotiations in or having travelled to Iran *per se*.

Between the 1988 election and mid-December voting date for the Electoral College, the author mailed an information package on "October Surprise" allegations and evidence to each of the hundreds of Republican electors. Although each had pledged to vote for their party's candidate for President, they had done so without knowing about the "October Surprise" allegations and were not required by the U.S. Constitution to honor their pledges. Each Republican elector still cast his electoral ballot for Mr. Bush, even after being alerted to the fact that a scandal of far greater magnitude than Watergate could cast a shadow over his tenure in office.

THE DUKAKIS CAMPAIGN

In October 1988, at the height of the presidential election campaign, there were hopeful signs that Democratic candidate, Michael Dukakis, would raise the "October Surprise" story to the level of national prominence it deserved. On October 20th, in a campaign speech in New Haven, Connecticut, the Democratic candidate drew a parallel for the first time between Vice-President George Bush's actions in the Iran/Contra affair and the Watergate scandal of the early 1970's. "Truth was the first casualty in the Nixon White House," he said, "and it has been the first casualty in the Bush campaign. Above all, truth should matter a lot in a presidential campaign, because, as we learned in Watergate, it matters a lot in the Oval Office.''[22] The parallel being drawn, of course, was to President Richard Nixon, who won the 1972 election and *then* dragged the country through the trauma of the Watergate scandal.

On November 3, 1988, presidential candidate Michael Dukakis was asked for a comment on the "October Surprise" story by someone in the audience at one of his campaign appearances. By that time, the story had been covered by his local Boston newspaper, the *Globe*.[23] He responded, quite accurately, that "There's no information to prove it [yet], but no information to disprove it."

Except for this lone remark and a few campaign charges leveled at Vice President Bush that he "knuckled under to the Ayatollah" in approving the secret sale of U.S. arms to Iran,[24] however, there was surprisingly little emphasis on the Iran/Contra scandal by the Democratic presidential candidate. Following speeches across the country before the election, especially in the Boston area, the author was constantly asked why the Democrats were not taking advantage of the one issue that could win them the election—the Vice President's reported secret deals with Khomeini in both 1985–86 and in 1980. Although only Mr. Dukakis knows the answer, part of it, almost certainly, was that one of the nine U.S. citizens held hostage by Khomeini loyalists at the time of the 1988 campaign was a native of Dukakis's home city, Boston—journalism professor Alann Steen.[25] According to press reports, Steen had been beaten by his Lebanese Shiite captors,[26] allegedly when he tried to escape. Also during the campaign, a Lebanese woman, Aline Ibrahim Rizkallah, was arrested in Milan, Italy, carrying what she claimed to be a letter written by Steen. According to the head of Milan's anti-terrorism police, Achille Serra, ". . . an American organization is interested in getting this material. You have the experience to understand which one." As Steen is a native of Boston, that "American organization" could very well have been the Dukakis presidential campaign.

According to the former president of Iran, Abolhassan Bani Sadr, the Dukakis as well as Bush presidential campaigns sent emissaries to Iran prior to the 1988 election to discuss the situation of the U.S. hostages in Lebanon.[27] Although the Dukakis campaign denied the allegation, if it were true, it would go a long way towards explaining the candidate's reticence to make an issue of reports of his opponent's secret hostage negotiations in 1988 and 1980. To do so might well have backfired in the national media.

Some of the most astounding feedback received by the author during the

1988 election campaign came in the telephone call from a colleague in late October. He said that he had called a major East Coast newspaper in an attempt to discover why it had not followed the lead of the *Boston Globe*, the *Washington Post*, the *Los Angeles Times*, the *Miami Herald*, the *San Francisco Examiner* and other mainstream newspapers, and run a story on the "October Surprise." To his amazement, he was told that it was the paper's "policy" not to publish a "derogatory" story about one presidential candidate unless it had something "equally derogatory" to print about the other candidate—in this case, Mr. Dukakis. My associate protested that such a "policy" unfairly punished decent citizens who chose to run for public office.

"What if the second candidate has a clean record? Would you still not print a so-called 'derogatory' story about the first candidate?" he asked.

"Look," the reporter said defensively. "That's the policy. Otherwise we'd appear to be too 'political.' "

In 1988, it seemed, the mainstream press would go to any length to avoid educating the American electorate.

Another particularly glaring example of this self-imposed double standard by the American press was the dearth of attention paid to a "derogatory" story about vice-presidential candidate Dan Quayle. A man in prison on drug charges in Reno, Nevada, told a few people beforehand that he planned to hold a press conference before the election. He said he was going to reveal that he had been an acquaintance of vice-presidential candidate Dan Quayle and that he had personally sold marijuana to Quayle, who had once advocated its legalization,[28] some fifteen to twenty times over a period of a year and a half. One-half hour before his press conference was to begin, the man was placed in solitary confinement against his will and with no showing having been made, contrary to prison policy, that he threatened physical danger to himself or to others. According to *Legal Times*, this unprecedented violation of the prisoner's rights and prison policy had been requested by Vice President Bush's campaign manager, James Baker, and by Republican campaign officials Stuart Spencer and Lee Atwater—all three then private citizens, not government officials—through the director of the Justice Department's Bureau of Prisons, Michael Quinlan.[29] Not only was the prisoner's press conference cancelled and the man placed in solitary confinement against his will, contrary to prison policy, he was also not allowed to talk to the press or even to his own attorney. He was finally released from solitary confinement on November 14, 1988, six days after Vice President Bush won the 1988 presidential election.

Like the "October Surprise" story, this critical piece of news was well reported on radio, but was avoided by the mainstream media—probably, once again, because to cover it might have appeared "political." God help the journalist, it seems, who reports a story that might effect the outcome of an election. It used to be the case in America that this was supposed to happen. One of the main responsibilities of a free press was supposed to be the education of the voting public. That was why it was given the unprecedented protection of the First Amendment of the United States Constitution—to guard against the abuses of government. Somewhere between 1788 and 1988, something went seriously wrong that needs to be set right. By 1988, in fact, the Founding Fathers had come to be identified by the President of the United States with a band of cut-throat guerillas in Central America, and any attempt by a journalist to think, write, or say otherwise was instantly deemed suspect and the journalist was likely to become a target of a team of psychological warfare specialists operating under the seal of the President and Vice President of the United States.

THE CARTER FACTOR

Although former President Jimmy Carter did not formally participate in the 1988 presidential election campaign, he did add some important new information to the "October Surprise" story. In its October 1988 issue, *Playboy* magazine published a letter from the former President dated February 24, 1988:

"We [the Carter Administration] had reports since late summer 1980 about Reagan campaign officials dealing with Iranians concerning de-layed release of the American hostages. I chose to ignore those reports. Later, as you know, former Iranian President Bani Sadr has given several interviews stating that such an agreement was made involving Bob McFarlane, George Bush, and perhaps [1980 Reagan-Bush campaign manager] Bill Casey. By this time the elections were over and the results could not be changed. I have never tried to obtain any evidence about these allegations, but have trusted that investigations and historical records would some day let the truth be known."[30]

President Carter made a similar statement on the nationwide Larry King program on June 15, 1988. In response to a question from a listener about the author's research on the "October Surprise" story, he said:

> "There were reports made to me before the [1980] election that this was going on. That the [fifty-two U.S] hostages would not be released [to me] and that weapon sales would be restored to Iran, either directly or through the Israelis. . . If Dukakis calls on me to help clarify a controversial issue where I was personally involved and know that the facts need to be revealed, I'll certainly do that—usually through the media, not out on the campaign trail."[31]

Surely the "October Surprise" story and details of what then President Carter knew about the 1980 Reagan-Bush campaign's efforts to delay the release of the fifty-two hostages would qualify as such a "controversial issue" with regard to which he was "personally involved." Yet, concerted efforts by former CIA officer David McMichael to persuade former President Carter to participate in a press conference before the 1988 election to reveal what he knew on this critical question, either in person or by letter, yielded no results. McMichael dealt with Mr. Carter's former press secretary, Jody Powell, between October 12 and 19, 1988, including sending an informed and impassioned letter to Mr. Carter dated October 13th, all to no avail.

The question, of course, is why former President Carter chose not to come forward, either before the 1988 presidential election or afterwards, with the details of what he knows. Part of the answer, as in the case of Democratic candidate Michael Dukakis, may again rest with the cunning Iranian government and their Shiite followers in southern Lebanon. On November 20, 1988, twelve days after the presidential election, Associated Press revealed that Iran had been holding President Carter's personal friend, a former pilot from his days as governor of Georgia, since 1981—for over nine years. The man, David Rabhan, was taken hostage in Iran in the last days of the Carter Administration and has been held captive ever since, making him by far the longest-held U.S. citizen. As in the parallel cases involving the U.S. press corps and Terry Anderson; and Governor Dukakis and hostage Alan Steen of Boston, President Carter may not have wanted to reveal information that might displease those who determined the fate of someone with whom he closely identified. It is not without reason that the Iranians are considered the shrewdest and most cunning bargainers on earth. They carefully selected just those hostages who would give them maximum, but invisible, influence on both the American political process and media, at the least cost.

It was also revealed ten days before the 1988 presidential election that former President Carter had written a letter, dated October 30, 1988, to the Ayatollah Khomeini, the man who controlled the fate of Mr. Rabhan, offering the Carter Presidential Center as a mediator in negotiations for the release of the nine U.S. hostages still held in Lebanon.

> "My hope is that the U.S. hostages in Lebanon may be released as soon as possible. Such a measure would remove a prime barrier to the resumption of friendly relations between Iran and the United States, which has importance for both countries. . . . In order to prevent this humanitarian act from appearing political in our country, *and in order to prevent a delay in the release of the hostages,* an as-neutral-as-possible U.S. channel should be used.[33] [author's emphasis added.]

In a postscript to his letter, former President Carter asked Khomeini to help secure the release of his friend, Mr. Rabhan, from prison in Iran.

On the same day as the date of President Carter's letter to Khomeini asking him to take action to prevent a delay in the release of the U.S. hostages held in Lebanon—October 30, 1988—hostage Terry Anderson's videotaped statement was released in Beirut, charging President Reagan and Vice President Bush with repeatedly intervening to delay his release.

CALLS FOR OFFICIAL ACTION

A number of calls for official and semi-official action have been made at the time of this writing with relation to charges that the 1980 Reagan-Bush campaign dealt secretly with Iran to delay the release of the fifty-two U.S. hostages until President Ronald Reagan's inauguration in January of 1981.

On August 7, 1987, then majority leader of the United States Senate, Senator Robert Byrd, called in a speech on the floor of the Senate for an investigation of the charges. His remarks were published in the *Congressional Record*:

> "Mr. President, the [Congressional Iran/Contra] Committee has worked hard at unravelling this sad tale of misjudgement and intrigue at the

highest levels of our Government. The investigation has also had the salutory effect of stimulating other important lines of inquiry on these matters. Many questions are still not fully answered. . . . Of particular note is a column by Flora Lewis of *The New York Times* [August 3, 1987] which indicates that the secret policy of arming the Ayatollah may even have begun early in the 1980's, and that this bribery and ransom strategy was on the minds of the inner circle of the President's advisers even before this [Reagan-Bush] administration took office. What other explanation is there for the allegation Flora Lewis notes, of a meeting between Mr. Allen, the first security adviser to the President, and a campaign official who apparently met with Iranian officials during that Presidential campaign and who may have been linked to Israeli shipments of weapons to the Ayatollah in the early 1980's. This opens up disturbing questions about the longevity of this ill-conceived arms-for-hostages strategy. It needs further investigation, in my judgment."[34]

As a result of Senate Majority Leader Robert Byrd's call for further investigation of the "October Surprise" allegations, Representative John Conyers, Chairman of the Criminal Investigations Subcommittee of the U.S. House of Representatives Committee on the Judiciary opened an informal investigation into charges that the 1980 Reagan-Bush campaign secretly negotiated with Iran to delay the release of the U.S. hostages for political gain. Conyers' subcommittee is where impeachment investigations begin, and he in fact oversaw hearings that resulted in the impeachment of a federal judge, Alcee L. Hastings, during President Reagan's second term in office.

Although Congressman John Conyers' legal counsel, Rutgers University Constitutional law professor Frank Askin, devoted some time to the investigation in 1988, he was without subpoena power and had no funding. On October 5, 1988, however, Mr. Askin announced that his investigation would nevertheless go forward. Based upon a review of documentation for the charges to date, Mr. Askin was able to say that, "While the evidence is not [yet] conclusive, it is substantial." To obtain conclusive evidence will, of course, require subpoena power and the authority to take sworn testimony from principals in the case, neither of which Mr. Askin has been granted.

What is needed at the time of this writing is for the House Judiciary Committee of the Congress, chaired by Representative Jack Brooks of Texas, to convene a hearing of the full committee to take testimony from witnesses under oath, with subpoena power and sufficient funding to undertake a thorough investigation of "October Surprise" allegations—which now include charges by alleged eyewitnesses of the presence of then vice-presidential candidate George Bush and Reagan-Bush campaign manger William Casey in Paris on October 19, 1980 for a meeting with Iranian officials. Should the House Judiciary Committee elect not to begin formal investigation in a full committee hearing, the Committee, under Brooks, has the power to grant subpoena power, authority to obtain sworn testimony, and funding to Representative John Conyers' Criminal Investigations Subcommittee to continue its ongoing investigation with resources needed to do the job right. A full, open Congressional investigation is now needed to complete and extend the work of the Congressional Iran/Contra Committees, which looked only superficially into "October Surprise" allegations because their mandate focused their attention on events that happened only in 1984 and after.

Following a cursory review of evidence of Republican and Republican-loyalist interference in the release of the fifty-two hostages in 1980, the Congressional Iran/Contra Committees tried literally to reduce the "October Surprise" story to a footnote in history. Its report contained the following footnote: "Reagan campaign aides were, in fact, approached by individuals who claimed to be Iranian intermediaries about potential release of hostages. . . . The [Iran/Contra] Committees *were told* [author's emphasis added] that the approaches were rejected and have no credible evidence to suggest that any discussions were held or agreements reached on delaying the release of the hostages or arranging an early arms-for-hostages deal."[35] The Congressional Iran/Contra Committees, however, merely took the word of former and active Administration principals, some of whom had either already pled guilty to having misled Congress or been charged with having misled Congress. In addition, thirteen Reagan-Bush Administration officials were allowed to read the Iran/Contra report of the Senate Intelligence Committee and to delete any portions they deemed "necessary."[36]

The Congressional Iran/Contra Committees also apparently ignored important testimony on the "October Surprise". According to self-proclaimed former CIA contract pilot Richard Brenneke, Brenneke told investigators from the Congressional Iran/Contra Committees about pre-1980-election events related to the inquiry and his arms flights to Iran in the early 1980's, but, he said, "They didn't want to know."[37] In an interview with radio journalist Jerry Bohnen of KTOK radio in Oklahoma City, Oklahoma, Brenneke again confirmed that he had discussed the 1980 connections to the Irangate affair with representatives of the Congressional Iran/Contra Committees: "Yes, we talked about this," he told Bohnen. "Basically, it didn't fall within the scope of what they wanted to do. . . .

They were very selective in what they decided to go after. . . . They kept looking for the twenty-four-carat gold witness with the smoking gun in his hand. . . . Can't we [the Congressional investigators] just look for the truth? I guess we can't. That's the bottom line."[38]

Twenty-year CIA contract agent William Herrmann, who claims to have discussed an arms-for-hostages proposal with Iran/Contra middlemen Manucher Gorbanifar and Cyrus Hashemi in Europe in 1984 on behalf of the Agency, was prevented from testifying to the Congressional committees investigating the Iran/Contra affair. Herrmann's repatriation to the United States from England, where he was in prison in 1986 for a counterfeiting operation he claims to have infiltrated on behalf of the FBI, was held up by top officials of the Reagan-Bush Administration to ensure that he could not tell Congress what he knew about the 1980 genesis of the later Iran arms sales. "It's fairly clear that the Americans don't want this man back in the country, and therefore accessible to the Senate inquiry while the Iran arms deal is being discussed," a senior British official told the London *Sunday Telegraph*.[39] Herrmann is a longtime associate of the deputy minister of the Iranian Revolutionary Guards, Hamid Nagashian, who told him in January 1981 that George Bush, William Casey, Richard Allen, Allen's deputy Dr. Fred Ikle, and Senator John Tower's then aide Robert McFarlane had met in Paris in October 1980 with top Iranian officials, including Nagashian.[40]

In addition to the unusual hold being placed on Mr. Herrmann's requested repatriation, which was due him under U.S. law, he was moved to Parkhurst high security prison in England, despite being a model "low-risk Category C prisoner," according to the *Telegraph*. Not surprisingly, the Reagan-Bush and Bush-Quayle Administrations have refused to grant Mr. Herrmann's repeated requests for furlough in the United States, where he was finally repatriated to federal prison in Loretto, Pennsylvania. According to John Pendleton, a spokesman for the U.S. Bureau of Prisons in Washington, D.C., Herrmann's furlough requests have been denied "due to the sensitivity and high publicity characteristics of his case."[41]

A 1987 memorandum from ABC News' European correspondent Pierre Salinger to his network headquarters noted that an associate of William Herrmann's, Swedish arms dealer Sven Klang, told Salinger that Senator Daniel Inouye, Co-Chairman of the Congressional Iran/Contra Committees, "is fully aware of Herrmann's story and is astounded that the Committee did not proceed on this matter."[42] *Newsweek* reporter Robert Parry questioned another member of the Congressional Iran/Contra Committees, Senator Mitchell, about why the Committee had not devoted serious time or energy to exploring the October 1980 links to the later Iran arms sales. His blunt answer was, "It was not our mandate."[43] According to Iran/Contra author Leslie Cockburn, "It's very distressing, the number of people they [the Congressional Iran/Contra Committees] did not talk to, in some cases intentionally"[44]—and, one might add, did not listen to or take seriously when they did receive their testimony. Given what is known from earlier chapters about the genesis of U.S. arms shipments to Iran, it is not surprising that, after months of hearings and hundreds of thousands of taxpayers' dollars, according to Committee Co-Chairman Senator Daniel Inouye, at the end of its investigations Congress still did not understand the *origins* of the administration's secret arms deliveries to Iran.

Likewise, the 1983–84 Congressional investigation into the theft of President Carter's debate briefing books was shut down when the first hints of what the 1980 Reagan-Bush campaign's "October Surprise" Group was really up to started to become clear. In January 1984 that investigation was suddenly suspended with a recommendation that a special prosecutor be appointed to continue the inquiry. But that was like putting the wolf in charge of the chicken coop. By law, a special prosecutor can only be appointed by the Attorney General of the United States, and Attorney General Ed Meese, having ordered the creation of the 1980 Reagan-Bush campaign's "October Surprise" Group himself, declined to appoint such a prosecutor.

Similarly, the mandate for Iran/Contra special prosecutor Lawrence Walsh's investigation into the secret Iran arms sales was drafted by the Department of Justice under the watchful eye of Attorney General Ed Meese. That mandate limits Walsh to investigate and bring criminal charges against defendants for actions taken only in 1984 and after. Once again, Attorney General Meese and the Reagan-Bush Administration slammed the door on any thorough and serious investigation of Irangate-related events dating back to 1980 and 1981.

In late September 1988, the Executive Board of the California State Democratic Party unanimously passed a resolution calling for an official investigation into now President George Bush's role in the "October Surprise" operations. Two weeks later, on October 7, 1988, the California Democratic Council (CDC) approved the Executive Board's resolution. In a press release dated October 8, 1988, CDC President Robert Farran stated, "These charges are serious. They imply a gross violation of law bordering on treason; thus the Vice President [now President George Bush] has an imperative to answer them."

In addition to formal hearings in the United States Congress, another forum where an official investigation of "October Surprise" allegations and evidence could take place would be as part of the formal investigation to fix responsibility for the Iran/Iraq War. When Iran and Iraq agreed to a cease-fire in their war on August 20, 1988, they agreed to cooperate with a future official tribunal charged with determining how the conflict began.

BRINGING THE "OCTOBER SURPRISE" HOME

On October 17, 1988, the "October Surprise" allegations directly touched the lives of some of the fifty-two Americans held hostage for 444 days until the moment of President Reagan's inauguration. On that date, attorney James H. Davis of Los Angeles executed a legal action on their behalf in a standing civil suit, *William Belk*, et al. v. *United States*, requesting additional time to file a petition to rehear the case based on new information from alleged eyewitnesses that then Reagan-Bush campaign manager William Casey and others may have acted to prolong their captivity, pain, and suffering.[45] In this already-existing case, the former hostages had sued the U.S. Government for depriving them, under the terms of the Algiers Accord which ended the hostage crisis, of their right to seek legal redress against the government of Iran for 444 days of pain, suffering, and financial loss. The legal action, taken on October 17, 1988, followed a review of evidence for the "October Surprise" allegations in documents provided by the author to plaintiffs' attorney, Mr. Davis, as well as his own subsequent investigations. On October 29, 1988, Mr. Davis appeared on the nationwide Michael Jackson radio program to discuss why the hostages had decided to go forward with their action. The judge in the case, however, declined the petition of the hostages requesting additional time to file a motion to rehear their case based on the new evidence. At the time of this writing, therefore, they must decide whether to appeal their existing case or to bring a new legal action.

UNTIE A YELLOW RIBBON

I had the honor of sharing an especially moving experience with one of the fifteen hostages in this lawsuit. His name is Charles ("Chuck") Scott, and he was the Pentagon's top officer stationed at the U.S. embassy in Tehran when it was seized on November 4, 1979. Mr. Scott had overseen Iran's purchases of U.S. military equipment, and so was particularly interested in evidence that the 1980 Reagan-Bush campaign may have agreed to exchange weapons to prolong this captivity. Chuck Scott, in fact, was one of the first to inform the author that "a deal was done" between Bush-loyal forces in the CIA and the Iranians in 1980, based on his sources inside the Central Intelligence Agency.

In the fall of 1987, Chuck agreed to meet me for dinner during his first trip in many years to the Monterey Peninsula, where I lived. Before joining his friends in the lobby, we had time for a drink and walked up to the lounge on the top floor of the Double Tree Hotel. As he relaxed in a comfortable chair and ordered a cocktail, the lights of Monterey Bay began glimmering in the distance through the picture window to our right. Chuck had started to tell me how, ironically, he had been the one to tell Iran's feared "Judge Blood," Ayatollah Khalkali, that the United States still owed Iran some $400 million in American military equipment purchased by the Shah of Iran before his fall from power—the very arms that President Carter had embargoed—when he suddenly stopped in mid-sentence. His eyes fixed on the lights in the distance and, after a long and obviously emotion-filled pause, he spoke.

"You know, I just realized—" he began.

"What?" I asked, watching his gaze as he looked out the window.

"Do you know what I'd dream of that kept me going during those agonizing days in Iran?" he asked.

"No. What?" I said.

"When things got really hard, I'd remember back to my days here in Monterey, and imagine this view. This very view of Monterey Bay. I prayed that someday I would be free again—to see *those* lights."

My throat tightened and tears welled up in my eyes. "Well," I managed, "Here you are!"

"Yes," he echoed. "Here I *am!*" Then he lightened up. "Hey!" he said, reaching for his coat. "Let's eat! I'm starved!"

As we left the lounge, I turned back to look at the lights, which gently sprinkled the arc of the moon-shaped bay like a well-loved Christmas tree. In that moment, for the first time, it struck me. Regardless of how Chuck Scott and the other hostages had been set free, they *were* free, and for that I would be forever and immensely grateful.

EPILOG

A KINDER, GENTLER NATION

President Reagan signed intelligence authorizations in 1984 and 1985 which were considered "licenses to kill," according to top government officials.[1] As we have seen, Oliver North and Amiram Nir's U.S.-Israeli covert operations were authorized by a still-secret "accord," never revealed to the Congressional intelligence committees as required by law, which may have also authorized political assassinations in the name of counterterrorism. We have seen that Vice President George Bush met with Amiram Nir in Israel in late July 1986, when he could have signed the accord with Israeli Prime Minister Peres, for whom Nir worked.

Author Seymour Hersh has charged Oliver North with being President Reagan's assassination planner.[2] We have reviewed reports that North boasted that anyone who leaked or threatened to reveal the administration's secret Iran initiative would be killed and that some of the North-Secord-Hakim team were reportedly involved in political assassinations under the umbrella of counterterrorism.[3] Given this context, it is instructive to note what has happened to many of the individuals who were reportedly involved in, or knew about, secret negotiations between Iran and the 1980 Reagan-Bush campaign and/or about secret U.S. arms deliveries to the Khomeini regime in the early 1980's.

- **DEAD: WILLIAM CASEY,** CIA Director, who reportedly attended meetings in Paris, France, on October 19 and 20, 1980, with Iranian officials and agents of French intelligence to arrange an arms-for-hostages-delay deal with Iran. The morning of his first scheduled under-oath testimony before the Senate Intelligence Committee on the secret Iran initiative he was struck by seizures in his CIA headquarters office in Langley, Virginia, and underwent speech-incapacitating left-brain surgery shortly thereafter. Had he lived to testify, according to life-long friend and counsel Milton Gould, Casey would have told the "entire truth." He died on May 6, 1987.

- **DEAD: AMIRAM NIR** died November 30, 1988, in a plane crash in Mexico. Nir, who resigned in March 1988, had been chief counterterrorism adviser to Israeli Prime Minister Shimon Peres. He was Oliver North's Israeli counterpart in the Nir-North covert operations covered by a still-secret "accord" reportedly signed by Peres and either President Reagan or, according to some U.S. government sources, by someone "at a lower level"—easily Vice President George Bush during his late July 1986 meeting with Nir in Jerusalem, when Nir briefed Bush on the Iran arms initiative. Informed sources suspect sabotage of Nir's plane.[4] When Oliver North sought to introduce the secret U.S.-Israel accord as part of the defense in his trial on conspiracy charges, the Reagan-Bush Administration refused to produce the document and the conspiracy charge was dropped. Nir died two months before the start of North's trial. The truth of the final entry in Michael Ledeen's book, *Perilous Statecraft*, may have something to do with his timely death: "Insofar as *anyone* may have something dramatically new to add to our knowledge of Iran/Contra, it is likely to be Amiram Nir."

- **DEAD: CYRUS HASHEMI** died in London on July 21, 1986, two days after being diagnosed as having a rare, virulent form of fast-acting cancer. According to Iranian-American arms dealer Houshang Lavi, with whom he worked on a major Iran-arms-related "sting" operation in late 1985 and early 1986, Hashemi was assassinated by U.S. government agents. According to self-proclaimed former CIA pilot Richard Brenneke, Hashemi had been a participant at the October 20, 1980, Paris meeting with 1980 Regan-Bush campaign manager William Casey, Iranian arms dealer Houshang Lavi, Iranian officials, and agents of French intelligence to work out the original arms-for-hostage-delay deal with Iran. Before his death, Hashemi was reported to have said that his 1981–82 U.S. arms sales to Iran had been "necessary" to obtain the release of the original fifty-two U.S. hostages, released moments after Reagan's inauguration in 1981, and had been approved by the CIA, which Casey headed. Hashemi was also the instigator of the arms-for-hostages proposal which resulted in the August 1985 TOW missile shipment to Iran.[5]

- **DEAD: THE AYATOLLAH MOHAMMED BEHESHTI,** who reportedly sent a personal representative, according to one source Jalal al-Din Farsi, to the pre-election Paris meeting of October 19, 1980 with 1980 Reagan-Bush campaign manager William Casey and, according to some reports, also vice-presidential candidate George Bush. Beheshti died in a bomb explosion at Islamic Republic Party headquarters in Iran on June 28, 1981.

- **DEAD: SADEGH GHOTBZADEH,** the foreign minister of Iran at the time of the U.S. embassy hostage crisis. According to the former U.S. chief of SAVAK (the Shah of Iran's secret police), a Republican-loyalist faction in the CIA prevailed upon Ghotbzadeh before the 1980 presidential election to persuade the Ayatollah Khomeini to delay the release of the fifty-two U.S. hostages until Ronald Reagan's inauguration, guaranteeing a Republican victory at the polls on November 4, 1980. Following revelations of his alleged involvement in planning a coup attempt against Khomeini in 1981, Khomeini ordered Ghotbzadeh tortured and executed. According to the former President of Iran, Abolhassan Bani Sadr, it was Secretary of State Alexander Haig's then aide, Michael Ledeen, who tipped off the Khomeini regime to the alleged coup attempt and sealed Ghotbzadeh's fate.

- **DEAD: WILLIAM BUCKLEY,** CIA station chief in Beirut, Lebanon. Depending on the report, died June 3, 1985, or some time in October 1985, in captivity in Lebanon. Buckley did not want to return to Beirut, fearing that his cover had already been blown and that he would be killed. According to Informant "Y," Buckley may have been involved in arrangements for the pre-1980-election Paris meeting among Iranian officials, 1980 Reagan-Bush campaign manager William Casey, and perhaps also vice-presidential candidate George Bush. According to Heinrich Rupp, who claims to have flown Casey to the Paris meeting of October 19, 1980, Rupp himself worked with Buckley in the Middle East and claims that Buckley was abandoned by the U.S. Government. Buckley's successor, another CIA Beirut station chief, was on board the sabotaged Pan American Flight 103, which crashed in Scotland on December 21, 1988, four days before Christmas. The key suspect is the leader of a PLO faction, Ahmed Jibril, a former bodyguard to the Ayatollah Khomeini.

- **DEAD:** U.S. Ambassador to Pakistan **ARNOLD RAPHEL,** in a sabotaged plane crash with Pakistani President Mohammed Zia ul-Haq on August 17, 1988. Raphel was not only fully briefed on the Reagan-Bush Administration's secret Iran initiative,[6] but was one of two or three top officials copied in highly classified documents inside the Carter Administration in October 1980 on the proposed arms-for-hostages exchange proposed by Iranian-American arms dealer Houshang Lavi. (Lavi, by his own admission, was also the "Iranian emissary" who offered an arms-for-hostages deal to 1980 Reagan-Bush campaign's foreign policy adviser Richard Allen; Allen's aide Laurence Silberman; and then aide to Senator John Tower, Robert McFarlane, in Washington, D.C., in early October 1980; and, according to some sources, also attended the follow-up meeting in Paris, France, with Reagan-Bush campaign manager William Casey on October 20, 1980, to make arrangements for implementing an arms-for-hostage-delay deal between the 1980 Reagan-Bush campaign and Iran.)

According to former Secretary of State to President Carter, Edmund Muskie, Raphel also "played an instrumental role in the release of the [fifty-two U.S.] hostages in Iran."[7]

- **DEAD:** Former Iranian President **MOHAMMED ALI RAJAI,** killed in a bomb blast in his office in Tehran.[8] Rajai visited the United Nations in mid October 1980 and left New York the same night that Informant "Y" claims vice-presidential candidate Bush and Reagan-Bush campaign manager William Casey flew to New York, October 18, 1980, before leaving for the October 19th Paris meeting with Iranian officials. They may well have met in New York prior to Rajai's departure on the night of October 18, 1980.

- **DEAD: RICHARD BEAL,** Special Assistant to President Reagan for National Security. Died in his thirties c. November 3, 1984, in Washington, D.C., of a heart attack. Beal had performed the sophisticated computerized "October Surprise" study before the 1980 election, which revealed that the Reagan-Bush campaign *had* to prevent President Carter from bringing the hostages home between October 18—the night William Casey and George Bush reportedly left for the secret Paris meeting with Iranian officials—and October 25, 1980, or lose the election. According to one of his former students, Beal's computer studies were funded by the CIA. As Special Assistant to the President for National Security, Beal had consolidated national-security-related information from the Pentagon and governmental and military intelligence agencies for the first time in U.S. history in a sophisticated computer used by the White House National Security Council. Oliver North had access to one of the computer terminals of this newly-integrated system.

- **DEAD: DONALD FORTIER,** deputy to national security advisers Robert McFarlane and John Poindexter, and the number-three man on the National Security Council, died on December 4, 1985 of liver cancer. Fortier was one of the few U.S. officials knowledgeable about the full genesis and details of the secret Iran initiative. In 1980, he and Robert McFarlane worked closely together as Congressional aides at the time McFarlane arranged the early October 1980 meeting among Reagan-Bush campaign foreign policy adviser Richard Allen, Laurence Silberman, himself (McFarlane), and Iranian emissary Houshang Lavi, at which Lavi proposed an arms-for-hostages deal with Iran. Fortier may therefore have been knowledgeable about the details of that critical meeting, and others.

- **DEAD: GLENN SOUHAM,** murdered after going into business with Adnan Khashoggi and Iranian arms dealer Cyrus Hashemi who (Hashemi) was also reportedly killed after stating that his 1981–82 U.S. arms sales to Iran were part of a deal to obtain the release of the original fifty-two hostages. Souham reportedly died while his father, a former top civilian NATO official, was in a meeting at the White House.

- **DEAD: MEHDI HASHEMI,** head of Khomeini's office for the export of militant Islamic fundamentalism to other countries, was executed in Iran on September 21, 1987. Iranian-Israeli agent Manucher Gorbanifar had arranged with Mehdi Hashemi for the release of Rev. Lawrence Jenco three days before Vice President George Bush's meeting with Prime Minister Peres's adviser Amiram Nir in Jerusalem on July 29, 1986. Gorbanifar and other loyalists of Khomeini's once designated successor, Ayatollah Montazeri, released the story of Robert McFarlane, North, and Nir's secret May 1986 trip to Tehran in revenge for Mehdi Hashemi's arrest, triggering the Iran/ Contra affair.

- **DEAD: ABBIE HOFFMAN,** social activist, who was found dead in his home on April 12, 1989. Press reports of Hoffman's death noted that he had been depressed about an automobile accident, which had occurred some months before. This accident happened just before Mr. Hoffman was to deliver his manuscript entitled ''An Election Held Hostage'' to *Playboy* magazine's offices in Chicago in the summer of 1988. The article, which was published in *Playboy*'s October, 1988 issue, is a summary of the ''October Surprise'' story.

- **ATTEMPTED ASSASSINATION: HASSAN SABRA,** chief editor of the Lebanese weekly *Al Shiraa*, which first published the story of McFarlane, North, and Nir's secret trip to Tehran of late May 1986, triggering the Iran/Contra scandal.

Sabra was shot on the same day that Mehdi Hashemi was executed in Tehran, September 21, 1987.

- **ATTEMPTED SUICIDE: ROBERT McFARLANE,** national security adviser to President Reagan, who claims to have obtained permission for the August 20, 1985, U.S. arms delivery to Iran by Israel. May have obtained permission instead from Acting President George Bush during the eight hours that Bush was Acting President, on July 13, 1985. McFarlane led the secret presidential mission to Tehran of late May 1986 carrying HAWK missile parts, a cake, and six pistols (the Bible wasn't delivered until October 1986, at another meeting in Europe, by Oliver North and George Cave), revelations of which triggered the Iran/Contra scandal. McFarlane arranged the early October 1980 meeting with "Iranian emissary" Houshang Lavi, 1980 Reagan-Bush foreign policy adviser Richard Allen, and Allen's aide Laurence Silberman in Washington, D.C., at which Lavi offered an arms-for-hostages deal with Iran; and reportedly also attended meetings in Paris and Zurich with Iranian officials before the 1980 presidential election.

- **ATTEMPTED ASSASSINATION & HEART ATTACK: HOUSHANG LAVI,** the "Iranian emissary" who claims to have offered an arms-for-hostages deal to the 1980 Reagan-Bush campaign, as well as to the 1980 John Anderson campaign and to the Carter Administration, in early October 1980. His approach to the Reagan-Bush camp, unlike that to the Anderson camp, was not reported by the Reagan-Bush campaign to President Carter's State Department. Lavi worked with Iranian arms dealer Cyrus Hashemi, now deceased, on a $2.5 billion Iran arms sales "sting" operation in late 1985 and early 1986. Mr. Lavi informed the author in June 1988 that there have been three attempts on his life. In addition to these, in January 1988, while trying to recover documents, which he says can "prove multi-billion-dollar U.S. arms deals" with Iran by a Belgian company with which he was associated in the early 1980's, Lavi reportedly collapsed from a heart attack in Munich, West Germany. He has recovered at the time of this writing and is going public with at least a portion of what he knows about the 1980 Reagan-Bush campaign's arms-for-hostage-delay negotiations with Iran before the 1980 presidential election and U.S. arms deliveries to the Khomeini regime during the very first years of the Reagan-Bush Administration.

- **ATTEMPTED ASSASSINATION: RICHARD BRENNEKE.** A former 18-year contract agent and pilot for the CIA, Brenneke claims to have met with Reagan-Bush campaign manager William Casey, Iranian arms dealer and banker Cyrus Hashemi, Houshang Lavi, later Iran/Contra middleman Manucher Gorbanifar, then Carter NSC aide Donald Gregg, French intelligence agents, and Iranian arms procurement officials of the radical Revolutionary Guards in Paris, France, on October 20, 1980, to work out arrangements for U.S. arms shipments to Iran in fulfillment of the Reagan-Bush campaign's secret pre-election arms-for-hostage-delay agreement with Iran. In 1986, Mr. Brenneke was shot at while sitting in his car in Portland, Oregon. The bullet narrowly missed his head. Beginning in August 1988, he began going public with his inside knowledge of the Reagan-Bush campaign's secret, pre-election negotiations with the Khomeini regime. Over Thanksgiving weekend in 1986, the FBI broke into the institute where Mr. Brenneke worked, the International Center for Development Policy in Washington, D.C., and ransacked its files.[9]

- **ATTACKED AND PROBABLY FRAMED: HEINRICH RUPP,** the former CIA pilot who claims to have flown Reagan-Bush campaign manager William Casey to Paris on the night of October 18, 1980. On July 18, 1984, Mr. Rupp was bound and gagged in a hotel room near the Denver airport. According to his attorney, and also his friend Richard Brenneke, Rupp was framed in 1987–88 for alleged bank fraud, tried, and sentenced to forty-one years in prison in September 1988 to prevent him from talking about the October 18, 1980 flight, at the Paris end of which Rupp claims to have seen then vice-presidential candidate George Bush. In September 1988, Brenneke testified at Rupp's sentencing hearing in Denver that Rupp was being framed for this reason. In early

October 1988, Mr. Rupp began going public with his knowledge of pre-1980-election events.

- **ATTEMPTED ASSASSINATION: GLENN McDUFFIE,** a thirty-year former employee of Westinghouse Corporation who was fired for alerting his superiors in 1982 that the company was shipping critical HAWK missile parts to Iran, parts which were to have gone to NATO for the defense of western Europe. During a break in his trial for wrongful dismissal, one of McDuffie's supervisors tried to run him down, he claims, in a car whose license plate was traced to an Iranian employee of Intergraph Corporation. According to McDuffie, there is reason to believe that Intergraph employees were involved in a drugs-for-arms operation between the United States, Mexico, and Iran in the 1980's.

- **MURDERED: CHARLES WHITE,** a former employee of Intergraph Corporation who, according to Glenn McDuffie, was knowledgeable about illegal drugs-for-arms operations being run out of the United States and Mexico to Iran. Mr. White was killed on November 9, 1984, in Huntsville, Alabama. According to McDuffie, CIA involvement in the murder has been covered up by the FBI.

- **ATTEMPTED MURDER: ANTHONY PARKER.** A former employee of an Intergraph Corporation contractee, Parker was knowledgeable, according to Glenn McDuffie, about illegal diversions of U.S. military equipment to Iran in the 1980's. Shortly after the murder of Charles White in Huntsville, Alabama, an attempt was also made on Parker's life, which McDuffie likewise claims has been covered up by the FBI.

- **THREATENED WITH LOSS OF LIFE: ROBERT JACKSON,** Petty Officer in the U.S. Navy. His life was threatened in 1985 when he tried to alert his superiors to the theft of military equipment from the U.S.S. *Kitty Hawk* and Miramar Naval Supply Depot and its attempted diversion to Iran.

- **THREATENED WITH LOSS OF LIFE: MANSUR RAFI-ZADEH,** former U.S. chief of SAVAK, the Shah of Iran's secret police. According to Mr. Rafizadeh, before publication of his book *Witness* in 1987, the CIA threatened his life if he published. One of the chapters in his book, "When the Hostages Didn't Come Home," details how Reagan-Bush-loyalist elements in the CIA prevailed upon then Iranian foreign minister Sadegh Ghotbzadeh to persuade the Ayatollah Khomeini to delay the release of the fifty-two U.S. hostages until Ronald Reagan's inauguration in January 1981.

A kinder, gentler nation, indeed.

REFERENCES

INTRODUCTION

1. *New York Times*, October 31, 1980.
2. *San Jose Mercury News*, March 12, 1988.
3. *The Nation*, August 1–8, 1987.
4. *Washington Post*, October 9, 1988.
5. *Los Angeles Times*, June 28, 1988, p. 8.
6. *Landslide*, by Jane Mayer and Doyle McManus, Houghton Mifflin Sons, Boston, 1988, p. 300.
7. *San Francisco Chronicle*, December 13, 1988, from *The New York Times*.

CHAPTER I
OCTOBER SURPRISE

1. *Behind the Scenes*, by Michael Deaver and Mickey Herskowitz, William Morrow Company, 1988, p. 99.
2. *Hidden Power*, by Roland Perry, Beaufort Books, Inc., New York, 1984, p. 124.
3. *Hidden Power*, by Roland Perry, Beaufort Books, Inc., New York, 1984, p. 124.
4. Interview with Abolhassan Bani Sadr, KPFK Radio, Los Angeles, California, by Ian Masters, September 12, 1988.
5. *Perilous Statecraft*, by Michael Ledeen, Charles Scribner Sons, New York, 1988, p. 24.
6. *The Nation*, August 27, 1988.
7. *Christian Science Monitor*, March 21, 1988.
   Playboy, October 1988, p. 150.
8. *Christian Science Monitor*, March 21, 1988.
9. *Interlock*, by Mark Hulbert, Richardson and Snyder, New York, 1982.
   The Crowned Cannibals, p. 42.
   The Rebel, by Donald Freed, November 22, 1985.
10. Interview by the author with Gene Wheaton, former U.S. Marine officer with 25 years of criminal investigative experience with the U.S. military, of December 26, 1988.

11. "Unauthorized Transfers of Nonpublic Information During the 1980 Presidential Election," Report Prepared by the Subcomittee on Human Resources of the Committee on Post Office and Civil Service, U.S. House of Representatives, May 17, 1984, Vol. I, p. 52. (In the text, and below, sometimes referred to as the "Albosta Report").

12. Interview with Pierre Blai, former graduate student of Richard Beal, KKUP Radio, November 9, 1988.

13. *Washington Star*, July 15, 1980.
    Washington Post, July 1, 1983.

14. *Miami Herald*, April 12, 1987.

15. "Unauthorized Transfers of Nonpublic Information During the 1980 Presidential Election," Report Prepared by the Subcommittee on Human Resources of the Committee on Post Office and Civil Service, U.S. House of Representatives, May 17, 1984, Vol. I, pp. 47–48. (Referred to in the text as "The Albosta Report").
    The Nation, July 4, 1987.
    New York Times, October 7, 1980.
    Miami Herald, April 12, 1987.
    San Jose Mercury News, April 12, 1987, p. 21A.

16. *Chicago Tribune*, March 15, 1987.
    Wall Street Journal, December 12, 1986, p. 54.
    Landslide, by Jane Mayer and Doyle McManus, Houghton Mifflin Company, Boston, 1988, p. 69.

17. Remarks by Prof. Ray Tanter to a luncheon gathering of University of California, Berkeley, professors, Winter 1987, communicated to the author by Prof. Peter Dale Scott of the University of California at Berkeley, July 23, 1988, Los Angeles, California.

18. "Unauthorized Transfers of Nonpublic Information During the 1980 Presidential Election," Report Prepared by the Subcommittee on Human Resources of the Committee on Post Office and Civil Service, U.S. House of Representatives, May 17, 1984, Vol. I, p. 49.
    The Nation, July 4, 1987.
    New York Times, July 8, 1983, p. 18.

19. *Hidden Power*, by Roland Perry, Beaufort Books, Inc., New York, 1984, p. 131.

20. "Unauthorized Transfers of Nonpublic Information During the 1980 Presidential Election," Report Prepared by the Subcommittee on Human Resources of the Committee on Post Office and Civil Service, U.S. House of Representatives, May 17, 1984, Vol. I, p. 47.
    The Nation, July 4, 1987.
    New York Times, July 6, 1983 and July 7, 1983.

21. "Unauthorized Transfers of Nonpublic Information During the 1980 Presidential Election," Report Prepared by the Subcommittee on Human Resources of the Committee on Post Office and Civil Service, U.S. House of Representatives, May 17, 1984, Vol. I, pp. 40–42 & 49.
    Washington Post, July 1, 1983.
    All Fall Down, by Gary Sick, Penguin Books, New York, 1985 & 1986, paperback ed., p. 371.

22. *Blue Smoke and Mirrors*, by Jack Germond and Jules Witcover, Viking, 1981, pp. 10–11.

23. "Unauthorized Transfers of Nonpublic Information During the 1980 Presidential Election," Report Prepared by the Subcommittee on Human Resources of the Committee on Post Office and Civil Service, U.S. House of Representatives, May 17, 1984, Vol. I, p. 54.

24. *The Nation*, July 4, 1987.

25. Interviews by the author with Michel ("Mickey") Smith, July 17, 1988 and August 10, 1988.

26. *New York Times*, July 7, 1983.

"Unauthorized Transfers of Nonpublic Information During the 1980 Presidential Election," Report Prepared by the Subcommittee on Human Resources of the Committee on Post Office and Civil Service, U.S. House of Representatives, May 17, 1984, Vol. I, p. 49.

27. *The Reagans: A Political Portrait*, by Peter Hannaford, p. 285.

28. *All Fall Down*, by Gary Sick, Penguin Books, New York, 1985 & 1986, paperback ed., p. 364.

29. "Unauthorized Transfers of Nonpublic Information During the 1980 Presidential Election," Report Prepared by the Subcommittee on Human Resources of the Committee on Post Office and Civil Service, U.S. House of Representatives, May 17, 1984, Vol. I, pp. 55–56.

30. "Unauthorized Transfers of Nonpublic Information During the 1980 Presidential Election," Report Prepared by the Subcommittee on Human Resources of the Committee on Post Office and Civil Service, U.S. House of Representatives, May 17, 1984, Vol. I, p. 37.

31. *Los Angeles Times*, July 9, 1983.

"Unauthorized Transfers of Nonpublic Information During the 1980 Presidential Election," Report Prepared by the Subcommittee on Human Resources of the Committee on Post Office and Civil Service, U.S. House of Representatives, May 17, 1984, Vol. I, pp. 55–56.

32. Interview with Bill Moushey of the *Pittsburgh Post-Gazette*, October 13, 1988.

33. Interview by the author with Mansur Rafizadeh, August 30, 1987.

34. Interview with Prof. Peter Dale Scott, June 23, 1988. Scott was a participant in the meeting with Prof. Tanter.

35. *Miami Herald*, October 11, 1986, April 12, 1987, August 9, 1987, September 28, 1987, and April 3, 1988.

Out of Control, by Leslie Cockburn, The Atlantic Monthly Press, New York, 1987, pp. 192–193 and p. 281 (Notes).

Washington Post, October 24, 1986 and November 29, 1986.

New York Times, November 24, 1986.

Wall Street Journal, November 28, 1986.

Playboy, October 1988, p. 152.

36. *Washington Post*, October 9, 1988, p. D1.

Boston Globe, October 23, 1988, p. A25.

The Oakland Tribune, October 19, 1988.

37. Interview by the author with Gary Sick, April 27, 1988.

38. *Newsday*, November 22, 1987, p. 30.

39. Interviews by the author with Houshang Lavi of June 14, 1988, July 13, 1988, and December 22, 1988.

40. *Out of Control*, pp. 192–193.
    Playboy, October 1988, p. 153.
41. *Out of Control*, p. 193.
42. Interview by the author with Houshang Lavi of June 14, 1988;
    Playboy, October 1988, p. 151.
43. *New York Times*, December 9, 1979.
44. Interview by the author with Houshang Lavi of December 22, 1988.
45. *Newsday*, April 3, 1988, p. 15; and personal communication with Brian Donovan of Newsday.
46. *Miami Herald*, April 6, 1988, p. 9D.
47. *Miami Herald*, April 6, 1988, p. 9D.
48. *Los Angeles Times*, November 16, 1986, by Alton Frye, editorial-opinions section.
    All Fall Down, paperback ed., p. 422.
49. *Playboy*, October 1988, p. 152.
    Interview with Richard Allen by *Der Spiegel*, communicated to the author on August 25, 1988.
50. Interview with Robert McFarlane by *Der Spiegel*, communicated to the author on August 25, 1988.
51. *Miami Herald*, April 12, 1987.
52. *America in Search of Itself*, by Theodore H. White, Harper and Row, New York, 1982 p. 397.
53. *New York Times Magazine*, January 22, 1989, p. 29.
54. *Newsday*, April 3, 1988, p. 15
    Los Angeles Times, July 9, 1983.
55. Letter to the editor of the *Miami Herald* by Judge Laurence L. Silberman, September 1, 1987.
56. *Newsday*, April 3, 1988, p. 15.
57. Interview by the author with Judge Laurence Silberman, January 27, 1989.
58. Letter to the editor of the *Miami Herald* by Judge Laurence L. Silberman, September 1, 1987
59. *Witness*, by Mansur Rafizadeh, William Morrow and Co., New York, 1987, p. 347.
60. Albosta Report, Vol. II, pp. 1123–1124.
61. *Veil*, by Bob Woodward, Pocket Books, New York, 1987, paperback ed., p. 8.
62. *San Francisco Chronicle*, February 9, 1989.
63. *San Francisco Chronicle*, February 9, 1989.
64. *Washington Post*, November 29, 1986.
    Time, December 8, 1986, p. 28.
65. Interview with Richard Allen and Robert McFarlane by *Der Spiegel*, communicated to the author on August 25, 1988.
66. *New York Times Magazine*, January 22, 1989, p. 29.
67. *Newsday*, April 3, 1988, p. 15.
68. *Newsweek*, December 8, 1986, p. 44.
69. Albosta Report, Vol. I, pp. 51–52, and Vol. II, p. 1491.
70. *Los Angeles Times*, February 27, 1987, p. 19.
    Perilous Statecraft, by Michael Ledeen, p. 278.

71. *Washington Post*, November 29, 1986, p. 1.
72. "The October Surprise," by Garry Emmons, 1988, p. 55, note: "R.S., February 25, 1988."
73. *London Observer*, November 30, 1980.
74. *New York Times*, May 26, 1988, by William Safire.
75. Interview by the author with Michel Smith, July 17, 1988, San Francisco, California.
76. *Witness*, by Mansur Rafizadeh, p. 347.
77. Albosta Report, Vol. II, pp. 1123–1124.
78. *Newsweek*, December 22, 1986, p. 22.
    Time, January 19, 1987, p. 26.
    San Francisco Examiner, February 28, 1987, p. A24.
79. Interview by the author with Houshang Lavi, June 14, 1988.
    Associated Press, June 13, 1987, in the *Huntsville Times*, p. A9.
80. *Parade* magazine, December 18, 1988, p. 1.
81. *San Francisco Chronicle*, December 17, 1988. p. 1.
82. Interviews by the author with Houshang Lavi, June 14, 1988 and December 22, 1988.
83. *Out of Control*, p. 192.
84. *Out of Control*, p. 281 (Notes).
85. Interview by the author with Houshang Lavi, June 14, 1988.
86. *Veil*, by Bob Woodward, Pocket Books, New York, 1987, paperback, ed., p. 102.
87. *New York Times*, October 3, 1980.
88. *Portrait of an Election*, Elizabeth Drew, Simon and Schuster, New York, 1981, p. 387.
89. *Penthouse*, November 1984, pp. 142 & 150.
90. Albosta Report, Vol. I, pp. 51–52.
91. *New York Times*, October 16, 1980.
    Interview by the author with Gary Sick, June 14, 1988.
    February 12, 1987, *Evening News*.
92. Albosta Report, Vol. I, p. 57;
    Miami Herald, April 3, 1988.
93. *All Fall Down*, paperback ed., p. 372.
94. Interview by the author with Houshang Lavi, June 14, 1988.
95. *Miami Herald*, April 3, 1988.
    Playboy, October 1988, p. 152.
96. Interview with former President Carter, Larry King radio program, June 15, 1988.
97. Interview with Houshang Lavi by Jonathan Silvers of *Playboy* magazine, April 21, 1988;
    Interviews by the author with Houshang Lavi of July 13, 1988 and December 22, 1988.
98. *New York Times*, October 30, 1980.
99. *New York Times*, October 30, 1980, p. A14.
100. *The Rebel*, November 22, 1983;
    All Fall Down, paperback ed., p. 373.
101. *Newsday*, April 3, 1988, p. 15.

102. Gannett News Services and the *Courier-Post* of Cherry Hill, New Jersey, December 19, 1980.

103. *Newsday*, April 3, 1988, p. 15.

104. Interview with Frank Askin, KABC radio, Los Angeles, California, by Frank Press, October 20, 1988.

105. Albosta Report, Vol. II, pp. 1160–1161.

106. Albosta Report, Vol. I, p. 119, and Vol. II, p. 1078.

107. Albosta Report, Vol. I., p. 119.

108. Interview by the author with Milton Graham, June 28, 1988.

109. Albosta Report, Vol. II, pp. 1165–1166.

110. *Washington Post*, July 1, 1983.

111. *Landslide*, by Jane Mayer and Doyle McManus, Houghton Mifflin Co., Boston, 1988, p. 70.

112. Los Angeles *Times*, July 8, 1983, p. 18;
Albosta Report, Vol. I, p. 119.

113. *Los Angeles Times*, July 8, 1983.

114. *New York Times*, May 26, 1988, by William Safire.

115. *Out of Control*, p. 191.

116. "Report of Independent Counsel (Jacob Stein) Concerning Edwin Meese III," Washington, D.C., September 20, 1984, U.S. Court of Appeals for the District of Columbia Circuit, #84–1.

117. Associated Press, March 1, 1984.

118. Associated Press, January 21, 1984, in the *Monterey Herald* (California) of the same date, p. 36.

119. Interview by the author with Mrs. Carol Preble, June 18, 1988.

120. Associated Press, January 21, 1984.
Interview by the author with Mr. James DeLisio, June 16, 1988.

121. Interview by the author with Mr. James DeLisio, June 16, 1988.

122. *Centre Daily Times*, June 11, 1984.

123. Associated Press, January 21, 1984.

124. Interview with Jody Powell, by Mark Ziolo, for "Other Americas Radio," August 1987.

CHAPTER II
QUIET DIPLOMACY

1. *Los Angeles Times*, July 8, 1983, p. 18.

2. *Hidden Power*, by Roland Perry, Beaufort Books, New York, 1984, p. 143.

3. *The Biggest Deal*, by Roy Assersohn, p. 194.
The Nation, July 4–11, 1987, p. 7.

4. Foreign Broadcast Information Service (FBIS), October 16, 1980, citing Kuwaiti publication *Al-Qabas*.

5. *All Fall Down*, by Gary Sick, Penguin Books, New York, 1985 & 1986, paperback ed., p. 370.

   FBIS, October 16, 1980.

   Wall Street Journal, March 5, 1987.

6. *Out of Control*, by Leslie Cockburn, Atlantic Monthly Press, New York, 1987, p. 192.

7. *Washington Post*, October 15, 1980, by Micheal Getler.

8. *All Fall Down*, by Gary Sick, Penguin Books, New York, 1985 & 1986, paperback ed., p. 370.

9. *All Fall Down*, by Gary Sick, Penguin Books, New York, 1985 & 1986, paperback ed., p. 422, Note 10.

   New York Times, November 22, 1986.

   Ma'ariv (Israel), November 23, 1986.

   Time, July 25, 1983, p. 27.

   ABC *Nightline*, December 18, 1986.

   Newsweek, December 8, 1986, p. 50, and January 8, 1987.

10. Interview by the author with Houshang Lavi, June 14, 1988.

11. *New York Times*, August 3, 1987, by Flora Lewis.

12. *Portrait of an Election*, by Elizabeth Drew, Simon and Schuster, New York, 1981, p. 316.

13. Memo for the Record, by Harold Saunders, Assistant Secretary of State (1980), October 21, 1980.

14. Memo for the Record, by Harold Saunders, Assistant Secretary of State (1980), October 21, 1980.

15. *Boston Globe*, October 23, 1988, p. A27.

16. *Wall Street Journal*, March 5, 1987.

17. *Playboy*, October 1988, p. 154.

18. *Los Angeles Times*, October 25, 1988, p. 18.

19. Interview with Abolhassan Bani Sadr, KABC Radio, Los Angeles, California, by Bill Press, October 20, 1988.

20. *Playboy*, October 1988, p. 154.

    Boston Globe, October 23, 1988, p. A27.

21. *Oakland Tribune*, October 19, 1988, by Jonathan Marshall.

22. Interview by the author with former U.S. hostage, William Belk, November 11, 1988.

23. *Los Angeles Times*, October 25, 1988, p. 18.

24. Interview by the author with Abolhassan Bani Sadr, January 1988, in response to correspondence to Mr. Bani Sadr by the author of December 21, 1988.

25. Interview by the author with Mansur Rafizadeh, August 4, 1988, transcript p. 16.

26. "Unauthorized Transfers of Nonpublic Information During the 1980 Presidential Election," Report Prepared by the Subcommittee on Human Resources of the Committee on Post Office and Civil Service, U.S. House of Representatives, May 17, 1984, Vol. II, pp. 1123–1124. (Referred to in the text as "The Albosta Report").

27. Interview by the author with Michel Smith, July 13, 1988.

28. *Out of Control*, by Leslie Cockburn, Atlantic Monthly Press, New York, 1987, p. 192.

29. *Playboy*, October 1988, p. 153.

30. *New York Times*, August 3, 1987, by Flora Lewis.

31. Interview by *Playboy* with Abolhassan Bani Sadr, April 10, 1988, transcript pp. 3–4.
32. Correspondence with the author, Abolhassan Bani Sadr, January 29, 1989.
33. Interview with Abolhassan Bani Sadr by KABC Radio, Los Angeles, California, by Bill Press, October 20, 1988.
34. Interview by *Playboy* with Abolhassan Bani Sadr, April 10, 1988.
35. Interview with Abolhaassan Bani Sadr by KABC Radio, Los Angeles, California, by Bill Press, October 20, 1988.
36. *Rocky Mountain News* (Denver, Colorado), October 2, 1988.
37. *In These Times*, October 12–18, 1988, p. 11.
38. *Rocky Mountain News*, October 2, 1988; October 9, 1988; September 24, 1988. Scripps-Howard News Service, October 5, 1988.
39. *Boston Globe*, October 23, 1988. p. A27.
40. Interview by the author with Michael F. Scott, attorney for Heinrich Rupp, October 19, 1988.
41. "Sixteen Hours on Adnan Khashoggi's Credit Card," by Kevin Sanders, October 1988, p. 12.
42. Testimony of Richard Brenneke, p. 64, Reporter's Transcript before the Hon. Jim Carrigan, U.S. District Court for the District of Colorado, Docket #88-CR-112, September 23, 1988, in U.S.A. v. Heinreich Rupp.
43. *In These Times*, October 12–18, 1988.
44. "Sixteen Hours on Adnan Khashoggi's Credit Card," by Kevin Sanders, October 1988.
45. Interview by the author with Informant "Y " September 25, 1988.
46. Interview by the author with Michael F. Scott, November 1988.
47. Portland *Oregonian*, October 20, 1988, p. E4.
48. Testimony of Richard Brenneke, Reporter's Transcript before the Hon. Jim Carrigan, U.S. District Court for the District of Colorado, Docket #88-CR-112, September 23, 1988, in U.S.A. v. Heinreich Rupp.
49. *New York Times*, February 2, 1987, p. 4.
50. Interview by the author with Richard Brenneke, August 26, 1988.
   New York Times, February 2, 1987.
51. *New Republic*, June 13, 1988, p. 14.
   Interview by the author with Richard Brenneke, August 26, 1988.
52. Portland *Oregonian*, October 20, 1988, p. E6.
53. *In These Times*, October 12–18, 1988, p. 13.
54. ABC TV, *World News Tonight*, April 7, 1988.
55. *In These Times*, October 12–18, 1988, p. 11.
56. *In These Times*, January 25–31, 1989, p. 3.
57. *In These Times*, January 25–31, 1989.
58. Portland *Oregonian*, October 20, 1988, p. E3.
   Interview by the author with Richard Brenneke, August 26, 1988.
59. Portland *Oregonian*, October 20, 1988, p. E3.
60. Testimony of Richard Brenneke, p. 8, Reporter's Transcript before the Hon. Jim Carrigan, U.S. District Court for the District of Colorado, Docket #88-CR-112, September 23, 1988, in U.S.A. v. Heinreich Rupp.

61. Testimony of Richard Brenneke, p. 56, Reporter's Transcript before the Hon. Jim Carrigan, U.S. District Court for the District of Colorado, Docket #88-CR-112, September 23, 1988, in U.S.A. v. Heinreich Rupp.

In These Times, October 12–18, 1988, p. 11.

62. Interview by the author with Informant "Y," October 8, 1988.

63. Testimony of Richard Brenneke, p. 12, Reporter's Transcript before the Hon. Jim Carrigan, U.S. District Court for the District of Colorado, Docket #88-CR-112, September 23, 1988, in U.S.A. v. Heinreich Rupp.

64. Testimony of Richard Brenneke, p. 13, Reporter's Transcript before the Hon. Jim Carrigan, U.S. District Court for the District of Colorado, Docket #88-CR-112, September 23, 1988, in U.S.A. v. Heinreich Rupp.

65. *In These Times*, October 12–18, 1988, p. 11.

66. Testimony of Richard Brenneke, pp. 13–14, Reporter's Transcript before the Hon. Jim Carrigan, U.S. District Court for the District of Colorado, Docket #88-CR-112, September 23, 1988, in U.S.A. v. Heinreich Rupp.

67. Testimony of Richard Brenneke, p. 42, Reporter's Transcript before the Hon. Jim Carrigan, U.S. District Court for the District of Colorado, Docket #88-CR-112, September 23, 1988, in U.S.A. v. Heinreich Rupp.

68. Testimony of Richard Brenneke, p. 14, Reporter's Transcript before the Hon. Jim Carrigan, U.S. District Court for the District of Colorado, Docket #88-CR-112, September 23, 1988, in U.S.A. v. Heinreich Rupp.

69. Interview by the author with Informant "Y," October 8, 1988.

70. *Rocky Mountain News*, September, 24, 1988; and October 2, 1988; and October 9, 1988.

Scripps-Howard News Service, October 5, 1988, in *San Francisco Examiner* of the same date, p. 1.

71. Interview by the author with Richard Brenneke, October 11, 1988.

72. Portland *Oregonian*, December 2, 1986.

73. Interview by the author with Richard Brenneke, August 26, 1988.

74. *Boston Globe*, October 23, 1988, p. A27.

Interview by the author with Richard Brenneke, October 11, 1988.

75. Interview by the author with Richard Brenneke, September 25, 1988.

76. KGIL Radio, Carold Hemingway Show, Los Angeles, interview with Richard Brenneke, October 7, 1988.

77. Personal communication from Martin Kilian of *Der Spiegel*, January 2, 1988, based on *Der Spiegel*'s interview with Richard Brenneke.

78. KGIL Radio, Carol Hemingway Show, Los Angeles, Interview with Richard Brenneke, October 7, 1988.

Boston Globe, October 23, 1988, p. A27.

79. "October Surprise" radio program, produced by The Other Americas Radio, Santa Barbara, California, June 1988, including an interview with Mansur Rafizadeh.

80. *In These Times*, October 12–18, 1988, p. 12.

81. *In These Times*, October 12–18, 1988, p. 12.

82. Interview by the author with Richard Brenneke, October 18, 1988.

83. *In These Times*, October 12–18, 1988, p. 11.

84. *Boston Globe*, October 23, 1988, p. A27.

In These Times, October 12–18, 1988, p. 11.

85. Interview with Richard Brenneke, KTOK Radio, Oklahoma City, Oklahoma, by Jerry Bohnen, October 6, 1988, transcript, p. 12.

86. Interview by the author with Informant ''Y,'' September 25, 1988.

87. Interview by the author with Richard Brenneke, October 18, 1988.

88. Portland *Oregonian*, October 20, 1988, p. E6.

89. *Boston Globe*, October 23, 1988.

90. Interview by the author with Richard Brenneke, December 18, 1988.

91. *Boston Globe*, October 23, 1988, p. A27.

92. *Boston Globe*, October 23, 1988, p. A27.

93. *Boston Globe*, October 23, 1988, p. A27.

94. Personal communication with Martin Kilian of *Der Spiegel*, based on conversation with the *Boston Globe*.

95. *Boston Globe*, October 23, 1988.
    Correspondence with the author by KGO listeners, July–August 1987.
    Personal communication with Ray Talliferro, October 1988.

96. Personal communication with Martin Kilian of *Der Spiegel*, September 15, 1988, based on *Der Spiegel*'s interview with Richard Brenneke.

97. *Washington Post*, November 29, 1986, p. 1.

98. *Landslide*, by Jane Mayer and Doyle McManus, Houghton Mifflin Company, Boston, 1988, p. 39.

99. *Executive Intelligence Review*, January 30, 1987, p. 63.

100. *Landslide*, by Jane Mayer and Doyle McManus, Houghton Mifflin Company, Boston, 1988, p. 142.
    Wall Street Journal, January 17, 1984, p. 12.
    The Spotlight, September 29, 1986.
    The Spotlight, April 6, 1987, p. 3.

101. *Witness*, by Mansur Rafizadeh, William Morrow and Company, Inc., New York, 1987, p. 192.

102. Interview by the author with Mansur Rafizadeh, August 30, 1987.
    Playboy, October 1988, p. 154.

103. *All the President's Men* (the film).

104. Interview by the author with Michel Smith, July 17, 1988.

105. *The Campaign for President*, by Jonathan Moore, Auburn House, 1985, pp. 210–215.

106. *Newsweek*, February 2, 1987, p. 24.
    San Jose Mercury News, February 25, 1987, p. 20A.

107. *San Jose Mercury News*, October 27, 1988, p. 1.
    San Jose Mercury News, October 28, 1988, p. 22A.

108. *Los Angeles Weekly,*, October 14–20, 1988.

109. *Los Angeles Herald Examiner*, July 25, 1988, p. A11.
    Jack Anderson, November 10, 1988.

110. Associated Press, December 11, 1988.

111. Jack Anderson, November 10, 1988.

112. Interview by the author with Informant ''Y,'' September 13, 1988.

113. *Perilous Statecraft,* by Michael Ledeen, Charles Scribner Sons, New York, 1988, p. 259.

114. *Perilous Statecraft*, by Michael Ledeen, Charles Scribner Sons, New York, 1988, p. 214.

115. *Perilous Statecraft*, by Michael Ledeen, Charles Scribner Sons, New York, 1988, p. 4.

116. Interview by the author with Richard Brenneke, December 18, 1988.

117. *Boston Globe*, October 23, 1988.

118. *Boston Globe*, October 23, 1988.

119. "Sixteen Hours on Adnan Khashoggi's Credit Card," by Kevin Sanders, October 1988.

120. *Boston Globe*, October 23, 1988.

121. Interview by the author with Informant "Y," November 1, 1988.

122. Interview by the author with Richard Brenneke, October 14, 1988.

123. *Perilous Statecraft*, by Michael Ledeen, Charles Scribner Sons, New York, 1988, p. 224.

124. *Veil*, by Bob Woodward, Pocket Books, New York, 1987, paperback ed.

125. Personal communication with David McMichael, November 1988, based on Mr. McMichael's interview with former CIA director Stansfield Turner.

126. *Minute* (France), "A Bomb Under Bush," October 19, 1988.

127. Interview by the author with Informant "Y," December 15, 1988.

128. Personal communication with Ray Talliferro, KGO radio host, November 1988.
     Boston Globe, October 23, 1988.

129. New York *Daily News*, August 27, 1988, p. 20.

130. *Miami Herald*, April 12, 1987, in *San Jose Mercury News* of the same date, p. 21A.

131. Associated Press, April 12, 1987, in the *Huntsville Times* (Alabama), p. A12.

132. Interview by the author with Informant "Y," November 16, 1988.

133. *The Nation*, July 4–11, 1987.
     Oakland Tribune, October 18, 1988.

134. *The Hidden Election*, by Thomas Ferguson, ed., Pantheon, 1982, pp. 223–224.
     The Secret Life of Ronald Reagan, by Donald Freed, p. 140.
     Earth News, December 17, 1976.

135. Portland *Oregonian*, October 20, 1988, p. E4.

136. Personal communication with Martin Kilian of *Der Spiegel*.

137. Portland *Oregonian*, October 20, 1988, p. E4.

138. Personal communication with Ben Bradlee, Jr. of the *Boston Globe*, October 18, 1988.

139. *Boston Globe*, October 23, 1988, p. A27.

140. *New York Times*, May 1, 1988, p. 39.

141. *San Diego Newsline*, September 6, 1988, p. 5.

142. *Los Angeles Weekly*, October 14–20, 1988.

143. *Reagan's Ruling Class*, by Ronald Brownstein, ed. by Nina Easton, Pantheon, 1983, p. 622.

144. *In These Times*, October 12–18, 1988, p. 11.
     Personal communication with David Armstrong, October 13, 1988.

145. "Unauthorized Transfers of Nonpublic Information During the 1980 Presidential Election," Report Prepared by the Subcommittee on Human Resources of the Com-

mittee on Post Office and Civil Service, U.S. House of Representatives, May 17, 1984, Vol. II, pp. 1123–1124.

146. *Boston Globe*, October 23, 1988.

147. Portland *Oregonian*, October 20, 1988, p. E4.

148. Portland *Oregonian*, October 20, 1988, p. E4.

149. Portland *Oregonian*, October 20, 1988, p. E4.

150. Public address by former Lt. Col. James "Bo" Gritz, Santa Barbara, California, 1989.

Taped interview with Mr. Gritz by journalist Lars Hansson, January 4, 1989.

CHAPTER III
THE PLO CONNECTION

1. *Time*, December 26, 1988, p. 19.
New York Times, December 15, 1988, p. A7.

2. *Time*, December 26, 1988, p. 19.
New York Times, December 15, 1988, p. A7.

3. *New York Times*, December 15, 1988, p. A7.

4. *The Reign of the Ayatollahs*, by Shaul Bakhash, Basic Books, Inc. Publishers, New York, 1984, p. 109. Note: The former President of Iran, Mr. Abolhassan Bani Sadr, appointed a man named "Abu Sharif" to head the Iranian Revolutionary Guards in May 1980. Although Mr. Bani Sadr denies that this is the same "Abu Sharif" who later became chief adviser and spokesman to PLO Chairman Yassar Arafat, both men trained in Lebanon, both men were close to the Iranian Revolutionary Guards, and both men had the same name. If they are not the same individual, the "Abu Sharif" who headed Khomeini's Revolutionary Guards in May 1980 (whose birth name was Abbas Zamani) clearly identified with Mr. Bassam Abu Sharif of the PLO.

5. *Playboy*, September 1988, pp. 57–58.

6. *San Francisco Chronicle*, July 26, 1988.

7. *Playboy*, September 1988, pp. 57–58.

8. *San Jose Mercury News*, December 16, 1988, p. 1.

9. *San Jose Mercury News*, December 16, 1988, p. 6A.

10. *Ft. Lauderdale News & Sun-Sentinel*, Robert Fabricio, December 1988.

11. *San Jose Mercury News*, December 16, 1988, p. 6A.

12. *San Jose Mercury News*, December 16, 1988, p. 1.

13. *The Reign of the Ayatollahs*, by Shaul Bakhash, Basic Books, Inc., Publishers, New York, 1984, pp. 63 & 109 (see Note in Ref. 4.)

14. *The Reign of the Ayatollahs*, by Shaul Bakhash, Basic Books, Inc., Publishers, New York, 1984, p. 63.

15. *San Francsico Examiner*, August 19, 1984, p. 1.

16. *San Francisco Examiner*, August 19, 1984, p. 1.

17. Associated Press, July 26, 1988, p. 2A, in the *Huntsville Times*.

18. Interviews by the author with Informant "Y" of September 6, 1988, September 15, 1988, and February 8, 1989.

19. Interview by the author with Informant "Y" of September 10, 1988.

Interview by the author with Will Herrmann (who claims as his source Revolutionary Guards official Hamid Nagashian, in a conversation of January 20, 1981), March 22, 1989.

20. *San Francsico Examiner*, August 19, 1984, p. A19.

21. Associated Press, July 26, 1988, p. 2A, in the *Huntsville Times*.

22. *San Francisco Chronicle*, July 26, 1988, p. A14.

23. *Landslide*, by Jane Mayer and Doyle McManus, Houghton Mifflin Company, Boston, 1988, pp. 122–123.

24. *Landslide*, by Jane Mayer and Doyle McManus, Houghton Mifflin Company, Boston, 1988, p. 239.

25. *San Francisco Chronicle*, January 5, 1989.

26. *Perilous Statecraft*, by Micheal Ledeen, Charles Scribner Sons, New York, 1988, p. 28.

Landslide, by Jane Mayer and Doyle McManus, Houghton Mifflin Company, Boston, 1988, p. 48.

The Iranian Triangle, by Samuel Segev, The Free Press (a division of Macmillan, Inc.), New York, 1988, p. 257.

27. *San Jose Mercury News*, January 15, 1989, p. 4A.

28. *San Francisco Chronicle*, December 31, 1988, back page.

29. *New Solidarity*, December 5, 1983.

30. *Washington Post*, January 4, 1989.

San Francisco Chronicle, December 29, 1988, back page.

31. *San Francisco Chronicle*, December 31, 1988, back page.

San Francisco Chronicle, February 2, 1989, p. A18.

CBS News, February 1, 1989.

San Francisco Chronicle, February 7, 1989.

London *Sunday Times*, March 26, 1989, in *San Francisco Chronicle*, March 27, 1989, p. A13.

32. Jack Anderson, November 25, 1988.

33. *San Jose Mercury News*, January 15, 1989, p. 14A.

34. *Perilous Statecraft*, by Michael Ledeen, Charles Scribner Sons, New York, 1988, p. 182.

35. *Perilous Statecraft*, by Michael Ledeen, Charles Scribner Sons, New York, 1988, p. 107.

36. *La Repubblica* (Italy), January 25, 1987.

37. *Landslide*, by Jane Mayer and Doyle McManus, Houghton Mifflin Company, Boston, 1988, p. 145.

38. *Landslide*, by Jane Mayer and Doyle McManus, Houghton Mifflin Company, Boston, 1988, p. 262.

CHAPTER IV
IN LIKE A BURGLAR

1. *Hidden Power*, Roland Perry, Beaufort Books, Inc., New York, 1984, p.162.
2. *Veil*, Bob Woodward, Pocket Books, New York, 1987, paperback ed., p. 3.
3. *Christian Science Monitor*, March 21, 1988.
4. KABC Radio, Los Angeles, Bill Press interview with Abolhassan Bani Sadr, October 20, 1988.
5. *New Perspectives Quarterly*, interview with Abolhassan Bani Sadr, p. 43.
6. KPFK Radio, Ian Masters interview with Abolhassan Bani Sadr, September 12, 1988.
7. *New Perspectives Quarterly*, interview with Abolhassan Bani Sadr, p. 43.
8. *Veil*, Bob Woodward, Pocket Books, New York, 1987, paperback edition, p. 1.
9. Foreign Broadcast Information Service (FBIS), October 16, 1980.
10. *All Fall Down*, Gary Sick, Penguin Books, New York, 1985 & 1986, paperback edition, p. 370.
11. *Veil*, Bob Woodward, Pocket Books, New York, 1987, paperback edition, p. 20.
    Wall Street Journal, March 5, 1987.
12. *Veil*, Bob Woodward, Pocket Books, New York, 1987, paperback edition, p. 22.
13. *Newsday*, November 22, 1987, p. 32.
    Washington Post, November 29, 1986, in *San Francisco Chronicle*.
14. *Miami Herald*, August 9, 1987.
15. *The Iranian Triangle*, by Samuel Segev, The Free Press (a division of Macmillan, Inc.), New York, 1988, p. 9.
16. *Wall Street Journal*, August 8, 1985.
17. *Washington Post*, November 29, 1986, p. 1.
18. *Ma'ariv* (Israel), May 15, 1986.
    San Francisco Examiner-Chronicle, November 30, 1986, p. A14.
    San Jose Mercury News, January 22, 1987.
19. *London Observer*, November 30, 1986.
20. *The Washington Report on Middle East Affairs*, April 1988.
    Perilous Statecraft, by Michael Ledeen, Charles Scribner Sons, New York, 1988, p. 109.
21. *Newsweek*, December 22, 1986, p. 22.
    Washington Times, December 3, 1986.
    Los Angeles Times, January 12, 1987.
    New York Times, January 19, 1987.
    Ha'aretz (Israel), December 5, 1986.
    Time, January 19, 1987, p. 26.
    Washington Post, January 31, 1987, in *San Francisco Chronicle*.
    San Francisco Examiner, March 1, 1987, "This World," p. 20.
    San Jose Mercury News, January 22, 1987.
    Monterey (California) *Herald*, February 2, 1987, from Associated Press.
22. *Witness*, by Mansur Rafizadeh, William Morrow Company, Inc., New York, 1987, p. 371.

23. *San Francisco Examiner*, April 25, 1987, p. A10.

   Perilous Statecraft, by Michael Ledeen, Charles Scribner Sons, New York, 1988, p. 218.

   Washington Post, January 6, 1987.

   Davar (Israel), November 24, 1986.

   Los Angeles Times, December 28, 1986.

   Jack Anderson, January 7, 1987.

24. *Washington Times*, December 17, 1986.

25. *San Francisco Examiner*, April 25, 1987, p. A10.

26. *San Jose Mercury News*, June 13, 1987, p. 21A, from the *Los Angeles Times*.

27. *Executive Intelligence Review*, September 13, 1985, p. 27.

28. *San Jose Mercury News*, June 13, 1987, p. 21A.

   Personal notes of Oliver North, cited in *U.S. News & World Report*, March 21, 1988, p. 26.

29. *San Jose Mercury News*, June 13, 1987, p. 21A.

   Interview by the author with Houshang Lavi, June 14, 1988.

30. Foreign Broadcast Information Service (FBIS), November 5, 1980.

31. *New York Times*, August 3, 1987.

32. *New Perspectives Quarterly*, p. 44.

CHAPTER V
ONCE UPON A PERFECT TIMING

1. *Witness*, by Mansur Rafizadeh, William Morrow Company, New York, 1987, p. 347.

2. *Revolution*, by Martin Anderson, Harcourt Brace Jovanovich Publishers, San Diego, New York and London, 1988, pp. 302–303.

3. (That Gorbanifar was on the agenda on 1/21/81.)

4. *Caveat*, by Alexander Haig, Macmillan, 1984, p. 79.

5. *New York Times*, October 30, 1980, pp. 1 & A14.

6. *New Perspectives Quarterly*, pp. 43–44.

7. Foreign Broadcast Information Service (FBIS) October 16, 1980.

8. *Playboy*, October 1988.

9. *The Agency*, by John Ranelagh, Simon & Schuster, 1986, p. 659.

10. Interview by the author with Captain Gary Sick, December 22, 1988.

11. Foreign Broadcast Information Service (FBIS), October 16, 1980.

12. Foreign Broadcast Information Service (FBIS), October 16, 1980.

13. *South* magazine, April 1982, p. 10.

14. CBS News, September 29, 1980, from *Ma'ariv* (Israel) of the same date.

15. *Jerusalem Post*, August 23, 1981.

   New York Times, August 22, 1981.

   Time, July 25, 1983, p. 27.

ABC *Nightline*, December 18, 1986.

Newsweek, December 8, 1986, p. 50.

16. *Intelligence/Parapolitics*, 86:VII, pp. 12–13.

17. *Los Angeles Times*, November 22, 1986.

Los Angeles Times, January 25, 1987.

Time, July 25, 1983, p. 27.

18. *All Fall Down*, by Gary Sick, Penguin Books, New York, 1985 and 1986, paperback edition, p. 417, Note 11. Mr. Sick confirmed to the author that Note 11 refers to Mr. Cyrus Hashemi.

19. *Washington Post*, April 13, 1987.

20. *San Francisco Chronicle*, November 28, 1986.

21. *Washington Post*, April 13, 1987.

CHAPTER VI
THE SMOKING GUNS

1. *Witness*, by Mansur Rafizadeh, William Morrow Company, Inc., New York, 1987, p. 347.

2. *Witness*, by Mansur Rafizadeh, William Morrow Company Inc., New York, 1987, p. 347.

3. "October Surprise," including interview with Mansur Rafizadeh, Other Americas Radio, Santa Barbara, California, June 1988.

4. *New York Times*, August 3, 1987.

5. KPFK Radio, Los Angeles, California, September 12, 1988, interview by Ian Masters with Abolhassan Bani Sadr.

6. *New York Times*, November 25, 1986.

7. *Time*, December 22, 1986.

8. *Business Week*, November 19, 1986.

9. *Intelligence/Parapolitics*, VII:86, p. 13.

10. *Dimikratikos Logos* (Greece), November 29, 1986.

11. *Wall Street Journal*, January 27, 1988, p. 46.

12. *San Francisco Chronicle*, December 2, 1988.

13. *Washington Post*, December 4, 1988.

Perilous Statecraft, by Michael Ledeen, Charles Scribner Sons, New York, 1988, pp. 190–192.

Time, July 25, 1983, p. 26.

14. Orange County *Register*, October 5, 1988.

15. L. Fletcher Prouty, personal communication, Washington, D.C., August 1988.

16. *World Almanac and Book of Facts*, 1979 to 1986.

17. Interview by the author with Richard Brenneke, Washington, D.C., August 23, 1988.

18. *Washington Times*, December 17, 1986.

19. *San Jose Mercury News*, June 13, 1987, p. 21A.

San Francisco Examiner, April 25, 1987, p. A10.

20. Interview with Richard Brenneke, Jerry Bohnen, KTOK Radio, October 6, 1988.

21. Interview by the author with Richard Brenneke, August 26, 1988.

22. *San Jose Mercury News*, June 13, 1987, p. 21A.

23. Personal communication with Martin Kilian of *Der Spiegel*, March 12, 1989.

24. *The Nation*, October 24, 1987. NOTE: *The Nation* incorrectly quotes Mr. Bani Sadr as having said that Manucher Gorbanifar may have attended the early October 1980 meeting at the L'Enfant Plaza Hotel in Washington, D.C. Mr. Bani Sadr has clarified in a letter to the author that he intended to be quoted as saying, rather, that Mr. Sabati may have been a participant at the Paris meeting(s) of c. October 19–20, 1980.

25. *Newsweek*, December 22, 1986, p. 22.

Landslide, by Jane Mayer and Doyle McManus, Houghton Mifflin Company, Boston, 1988, p. 117.

Time, January 19, 1987, p. 26.

Los Angeles Times, December 28, 1986.

26. *Perilous Statecraft*, by Michael Ledeen, Charles Scribner Sons, New York, 1988, p. 109; p. 123, Footnote 4; and p. 237.

Landslide, by Jane Mayer and Doyle McManus, Houghton Mifflin Company, Boston, 1988, p. 117.

Washington Post, January 31, 1987, in *San Francisco Chronicle*.

Associated Press, February 2, 1987.

San Jose Mercury News, January 22, 1987.

San Francisco Examiner, "This World," March 1, 1987, p. 20.

27. *The Washington Report on Middle East Affairs*, April 1988.

London Observer, November 30, 1986.

28. *Washington Report on Middle East Affairs*, April 1988.

Perilous Statecraft, by Michael Ledeen, Charles Scribner Sons, New York, 1988, p. 109.

29. *Perilous Statecraft*, by Michael Ledeen, Charles Scribner Sons, New York, 1988, p. 110.

30. *South* magazine, May 1987.

31. Interviews by the author with Houshang Lavi of June 14, 1988 and December 17, 1988.

Washington Post, October 9, 1988.

32. *Newsday*, April 3, 1988, p. 15.

33. Interview by the author with Houshang Lavi, December 22, 1988.

34. *Newsday*, November 22, 1987.

35. Interview by the author with Houshang Lavi, December 22, 1988.

36. *Washington Post*, August 16, 1987.

37. *Newsday*, November 22, 1987, p. 30.

38. Affidavit of Ahmad Tabatabai, April 1987, p. 1, in 83 CIV. 2071 (R.J.D.), U.S. District Court, Eastern District of New York.

39. *New Perspective Quarterly*, p. 44.

40. *Newsday*, November 22, 1987, p. 31.

41. Letter to the author from a former employee of Albert Hakim's Stanford Technology Corporation office in Tehran in the mid-1970's. Correspondent wishes to remain anonymous.

42. *Jerusalem Post*, August 2, 1981.

43. IDF Radio, Tel Aviv, September 28, 1980.
   CBS News, September 29, 1980, from *Ma'ariv* (Israel) of the same day.

44. *Washington Post*, January 27, 1988.

45. *Perilous Statecraft*, by Michael Ledeen, Charles Scribner Sons, New York, 1988, p. 137.

46. *Newsweek*, October 5, 1987, p. 66 (referring to *Veil*, by Bob Woodward, 1987).
   New York Times, January 6, 1987, p. 6.

47. *Miami Herald*, August 9, 1987.

48. Congressional Iran/Contra Committee Report, testimony by Duane Clarridge, August 4, 1987.

49. *Wall Street Journal*, November 28, 1986, pp. 3–4.
   Perilous Statecraft, by Michael Ledeen, Charles Scribner Sons, New York, 1988, p. 99.
   Washington Post, May 1982, interview with Ariel Sharon.

50. *Boston Globe*, December 4, 1986.

51. *Washington Post*, December 4, 1988.

52. *Miami Herald*, August 9, 1987.

53. *Miami Herald*, June 5, 1983.

54. *The Chronology*, National Security Archive, Warner Books, 1987, paperback ed., p. 7.
   Washington Post, May 8, 1983.
   San Francisco Chronicle, November 22, 1987.

55. *San Francisco Examiner*, November 20, 1987.
   U.S. News & World Report, March 21, 1988.

56. *Miami Herald*, June 5, 1983.

57. *New York Times*, March 14, 1988, with reference to *Secret Warriors*, by Stephen Emerson, G. P. Putnam's Sons, New York, 1988.

58. *Los Angeles Times*, January 26, 1988.

59. *Garrison State*, by Steve Goldfield, Palestine Focus Publications, San Francisco, California, 1985, p. 15.
   San Francisco Chronicle, December 5, 1986, p. 16, citing the forthcoming book *Israel's World War* by Hallahmi Haifa.
   Los Angeles Times, January 11, 1987.

60. NBC TV, April 23, 1984.

61. *McNeil-Lehrer Television Hour*, interview with Richard Allen, November 7, 1986, transcript.

62. *Newsweek*, December 8, 1986.

63. *Washington Post*, November 29, 1986.
   Miami Herald, August 9, 1987.

64. *Miami Herald*, December 7, 1986.
   The Chronology, National Security Archive, Warner Books, New York, 1987, p. 6.
   Los Angeles Times, January 11, 1987.

65. *Washington Post*, November 29, 1986.
    Newsweek, December 8, 1986.
66. *New York Times*, January 29, 1981.
67. *South* magazine, April 1982.
68. *Washington Post*, August 16, 1987.
69. *Newsday*, November 22, 1987, p. 31.
70. *Newsday*, November 22, 1987, p. 31.
71. *Wall Street Journal*, November 28, 1986.
    Wall Street Journal, December 12, 1986, p. 54.
72. Congressional Iran/Contra Committee Report, testimony of Duane Clarridge, August 4, 1987.
    Washington Times, December 16, 1986, p. 10A.
73. *Dimikratikos Logos* (Greece), November 29, 1986.
    In These Times, January 21–27, 1987, p.9.
74. *Perilous Statecraft*, by Michael Ledeen, Charles Scribner Sons, New York, 1988, p. 96.
75. *Washington Post*, November 29, 1986.
76. *Los Angeles Times*, May 5, 1986.
    Washington Report on Middle East Affairs, January 1987, p. 10.
77. *International Herald Tribune*, March 9, 1982.
    New York Times, March 9, 1982 and November 23, 1986.
    Wall Street Journal, November 28, 1986.
    San Jose Mercury News, April 12, 1987, p. 21.
    Jack Anderson, April 30, 1986.
    Senate Intelligence Committee, Iran/Contra Report, January 29, 1987, in the *New York Times*, January 30, 1987, p. 6.
    Congressional Iran/Contra Committee, testimony of Adm. John Poindexter, November 21, 1986.
    NBC Television, "The Arms, the Men and the Money," January 6, 1987.
    Miami Herald, April 12, 1987.
    Washington Post, November 29, 1986.
    Los Angeles Times, January 25, 1987.
    Aerospace Daily, August 18, 1982.
78. Abolhassan Bani Sadr, correspondence with the author, January 16, 1988 and March 26, 1988.
79. "October Surprise," interview with Mansur Rafizadeh, Other Americas Radio, Santa Barbara, California, June 1988.
80. *Sunday Times* of London, July 26, 1981.
    Jerusalem Post, July 23, 1981, and July 27, 1981.
    Cyprus Weekly, July 24, 1981.
    National Public Radio, July 26, 1981, and July 27, 1981.
    Houston Post, column by Jody Powell, January 14, 1987.
81. *New York Times*, July 26, 1981.
    San Francisco Examiner, July 27, 1981.

The Chronology, National Security Archive, Warner Books, New York, 1987, p. 8.

Washington Post, August 16, 1987.

Newsday, November 22, 1987, p. 32.

International Herald Tribune, March 23, 1982.

Boston Globe, July 27, 1981.

82. *Executive Intelligence Review*, September 13, 1985, p. 29.

83. *The Chronology*, National Security Archive, Warner Books, New York, 1987, p. 3.

84. Congressional Iran/Contra Committee Report. p. 159.

85. *Executive Intelligence Review*, November 27, 1987, p. 61.

86. *South* magazine, May 1987.

Mujahed, #159, July 7, 1983.

San Francisco Examiner, November 30, 1986.

87. *Intelligence/Parapolitics*, VII: 86, pp.12–13.

88. *The Washington Report on Middle East Affairs*, April 1988.

London Observer, November 30, 1986.

89. *Engelab-e Eslami dar Hejrat*, (Islamic Revolution), Collected Reprints, Abolhassan Bani Sadr, ed., pp. 23–24.

90. *The Iranian Triangle*, by Samuel Segev, The Free Press (a division of Macmillan, Inc.) New York, 1988, p. 3.

91. BBC TV, *Panorama*, February 1, 1982.

92. *The Israeli Connection*, by Benjamin Beit-Hallahmi, p. 13.

BBC TV, *Panaroma*, February 1, 1982.

93. *Ma'ariv* (Israel), November 23, 1986.

94. The *Israeli Connection*, by Benjamin Beit-Hallahmi, p. 13.

95. *Executive Intelligence Review*, September 13, 1985, p. 29.

96. *The Chronology*, National Security Archive, Warner Books, New York, 1987, p. 15.

Evans and Novak, May 21, 1982.

97. *The Chronology*, National Security Archive, Warner Books, New York, 1987, p. 19.

Wall Street Journal, December 12, 1986, p. 54.

U.S. News & World Report, March 9, 1987, p. 16.

98. *Time*, July 25, 1983, p. 27.

99. *San Francisco Chronicle*, December 29, 1988.

100. *Jerusalem Post*, February 3, 1982.

NBC Television, January 6, 1987.

101. *The Iranian Triangle*, by Samuel Segev, The Free Press (a division of Macmillan, Inc.), New York, 1988, p. 6.

102. *The Iranian Triangle*, by Samuel Segev, The Free Press (a division of Macmillan, Inc.), New York, 1988, pp. 10–11.

CHAPTER VII
A NEAT IDEA

1. ABC News, *Nightline*, "Spy Ring Scandal," August 25, 1988, with Alexander Haig and Stanislav Levchenko.

CHAPTER VIII
"PROJECT DEMOCRACY"

1. Correspondence of Glenn McDuffie to the FBI, September 1, 1985.
2. *Huntsville Times*, April 19, 1984.
3. Correspondence of Glenn McDuffie to the FBI, January 28, 1985.
4. *Miami Herald*, June 5, 1983.
5. *South* magazine, May 1987.
6. *New York Times*, October 30, 1980, pp. 1 and A14.
7. *San Jose Mercury News*, November 19, 1987, p. 11A.
   San Francisco Examiner, November 20, 1987
8. *Huntsville Times*, September 6, 1985, p. A3.
9. *Huntsville Times*, September 6, 1985, p. A3.
10. Correspondence of Glenn McDuffie to Judge MacKinnon, February 6, 1987.
    Correspondence of Glenn McDuffie to Representative Lee Hamilton, November 21, 1986.
11. Correspondence of Glenn McDuffie to Senator David Boren, February 20, 1987.
    Correspondence of Glenn McDuffie to Representative William Gray, February 26, 1987.
    Correspondence of Glenn McDuffie to the Attorney General of the United States, May 8, 1984.
    Correspondence of Glenn McDuffie to the Nashville, Tennessee, FBI, October 5, 1984.
    Correspondence of Glenn McDuffie to FBI Director William Webster, October 14, 1983.
12. *Wall Street Journal*, April 13, 1987, p. 7.
13. Correspondence of Glenn McDuffie to the Attorney General of the United States, April 13, 1987, p. 7.
14. *Witness*, by Mansur Rafizadeh, William Morrow and Co., New York, 1987, p. 375.
15. *New York Times*, December 31, 1986.
16. Jack Anderson, January 17, 1987.
    Correspondence of Glenn McDuffie to Senator David Boren, February 20, 1987.
17. *San Francisco Chronicle*, June 15, 1988.
18. *Taking the Stand: The Testimony of Lt. Col. Oliver North*, Pocket Books, pp. 90 and 92–94.

Landslide, by Jane Mayer and Doyle McManus, Houghton Mifflin Co., Boston, 1988, p. 166.

Perilous Statecraft, by Michael Ledeen, p. 160. Charles Scribner Sons, New York, 1988, p. 160.

19. *Newsday*, November 22, 1987;

    San Francisco Chronicle, January 3, 1987, p. 6, from the *London Daily Telegraph* and *London Independent*.

20. Report of the Vice President's Involvement in the Iran/Contra Scandal, by William Loiry, 1988.

21. *Washington Post*, November 29, 1986.

22. Report on the Vice President's Involvement in the Iran/Contra Scandal, by William Loiry, 1988.

23. Report on the Vice President's Involvement in the Iran/Contra Scandal, by William Loiry, 1988.

24. Report on the Vice President's Involvement in the Iran/Contra Scandal, by William Loiry, 1988.

25. Civil Action #386-87C, U.S. Court of Claims, Washington, D.C., June 1987.

26. *New York Times*, August 3, 1987.

    Etelaat (Tehran), July 23, 1987.

27. *The Independent* (London), cited in the *Washington Post*, December 2, 1987, p. 2.

28. *Executive Intelligence Review*, November 13, 1987, p. 53.

29. *Newsweek*, April 16, 1988, p. 32.

30. *Newsweek*, April 16, 1988, p. 32.

31. *Washington Post*, December 1, 1987, p. A30.

    Washington Post, December 2, 1987, p. A1 & A14.

    Washington Post, December 8, 1987.

32. *Washington Post*, December 2, 1987, p. A1 & A14.

33. *San Francisco Chronicle*, December 8, 1987, p. A17.

    Jack Anderson, January 21, 1987.

34. *Executive Intelligence Review*, November 20, 1987.

35. *Middle East Perspective*, October 1981.

    Boston Globe, August 21 & 22, 1981.

    New York Times, August 22, 1981.

36. BBC Television, *Panorama*, February 1, 1982.

37. *The Iranian Triangle*, by Samuel Segev, The Free Press, New York, 1988, p. 3.

38. Civil Action 386–87C, U.S. Court of Claims, Washington, D.C., June 1987.

39. *Fanning the Flames*, by Ken Timmerman, German ed., 1988, p. 138.

40. *In These Times*, July 10–16, 1987.

    New York Times, February 2, 1987, pp. 1 & 4.

41. *In These Times*, July 10–16, 1987.

    San Jose Mercury News, February 20, 1987, from the *Orlando Sentinel*.

42. *Executive Intelligence Review*, September 13, 1985, p. 26.

43. *Executive Intelligence Review*, September 13, 1985, p. 28.

    New York Times, February 2, 1987, pp. 1 & 4.

44. *Executive Intelligence Review*, September 13, 1985, pp. 26–29.

45. *In These Times*, July 10–16, 1987.
46. *Huntsville Times*, November 30, 1986.
47. Report on the Vice President's Involvement in the Iran/Contra Affair, by William Loiry, 1988.
48. *Washington Times*, March 11, 1985.
    Executive Intelligence Review, November 13, 1987, p. 53.
    Washington Times, March 11, 1985.
    Newsweek, March 9, 1987.
49. *Le Quotidien de Paris*, January 6, 1986.
    La Presse de La Manche, February 18, 1986.
    Liberation, November 22, 1986.
    Associated Press, November 2, 1987.
    San Francisco Chronicle, November 5, 1987, p. A24.
    Le Monde (France), November 4, 1987.
    Le Figaro (France), November 4, 1987.
50. *Engelab-e Eslami dar Hejrat*, Abolhassan Bani Sadr, ed., Collected Reprints, p. 66.
51. *New Federalist*, November 13, 1987, pp. 1 & 12.
52. *New Federalist*, November 13, 1987, pp. 1 & 12.
53. *Washington Post*, November 29, 1986.
54. Interview by the author with Gene Wheaton, December 26, 1988.
55. *San Jose Mercury News*, September 3, 1988, p. 18A.
    Miami Herald, July 11, 1987.
    Washington Post, May 15, 1987.
    "Larry King Live," July 31, 1987.
56. Interview by the author with Gene Wheaton, December 26, 1988.
57. Memo for the Record, by Assistant Secretary of State Harold Saunders, October 15, 1980.
58. *The Octopus Eagle*, by "Michael Fredericks" (Hans Bihn), Loiry Publishing House, 1987. pp. 89–89.
    New York Times, February 2, 1987.
59. *Perilous Statecraft*, by Michael Ledeen, Charles Scribner Sons, New York, 1988, p. 290.
60. *Los Angeles Herald*, December 16, 1984, p. A5.
    New York Times, January 8, 1987, p. 25.
61. *Dimikratikos Logos*, November 29, 1986.
62. *Revolution*, by Martin Anderson, Harcourt Brace Jovanovich, San Diego, 1988.
    Associated Press, in the *Huntsville Times*, December 3, 1986.
63. *Interlock*, by Mark Hulbert, Richarson and Snyder, New York, 1982, p. 111.
64. *L'Expresso*, November 30, 1986.
65. *Executive Intelligence Review*, September 18, 1987, pp. 46–47.
66. *New York Times*, December 1, 1986.
67. Affidavit of Ahmad Tabatabai, April, 1987, in 83 CIV. 2071 (RJD), U.S. District Court, Eastern District of New York.
68. *Executive Intelligence Review*, September 25, 1987, p. 45.
    Executive Intelligence Review, October 23, 1987, p. 48.

69. *San Francisco Chronicle*, March 14, 1988.
    U.S. News & World Report, March 21, 1988, pp. 24–32.
70. *Executive Intelligence Review*, September 18, 1987, p. 47.
71. *Los Angeles Herald Examiner*, December 16, 1984.
    Executive Intelligence Review, September 18, 1987, p. 46.
72. "Persian Drugs," by Jonathan Marshall, *City Paper*, Washington, D.C., 1987.
73. *Perilous Statecraft*, by Michael Ledeen, p. 110.
    Senate Intelligence Committee Iran/Contra Report, January 29, 1987.
74. *Executive Intelligence Review*, September 25, 1987, p. 45.
75. *Perilous Statecraft*, by Michael Ledeen, p. 110.
76. *Executive Intelligence Review*, October 23, 1987, p. 45.
77. *The Brotherhood*, by Stephen Knight, Panther (a division of Granada Publishing), 1985.
78. *Perilous Statecraft*, by Michael Ledeen, p. 173.
    Landslide, by Jane Mayer and Doyle McManus, p. 314.
79. *Newsweek*, March 2, 1987, p. 24.
80. *Newsweek*, February 2, 1987, p. 23.
81. *Newsweek*, February 2, 1987, p. 23.
82. *La Repubblica*, January 25, 1987.
83. *La Repubblica*, January 25, 1987.
84. Interview by the author with Houshang Lavi, June 14, 1988.
    Interview by Jonathan Silvers with Houshang Lavi, April 21, 1988.
85. *Perilous Statecraft*, by Michael Ledeen, p. 251.
86. *Executive Intelligence Review*, April 15, 1988.
87. "Persian Drugs," by Jonathan Marshall, *City Paper*, Washington, D.C., 1987.
88. *All Fall Down*, by Gary Sick, Penguin Books, New York, 1985 and 1986, paperback edition, p. 366.
89. *Executive Intelligence Review*, October 9, 1987, p. 46.
90. *Paris Match*, October 22, 1987.
91. *Executive Intelligence Review*, October 23, 1987, p. 48.
92. *Executive Intelligence Review*, October 30, 1987, p. 55.
    New York Times, January 6, 1987, p. 5.
93. *Executive Intelligence Review*, October 23, 1987, p. 44.
    Executive Intelligence Review, October 9, 1987, p. 46.
94. *San Francisco Chronicle*, March 14, 1988.
    U.S. News & World Report, March 21, 1988, p. 24–32.
    U.S. New & World Report, March 13, 1988.
95. *Inside the Shadow Government*, The Christic Institute, 1988, p. 121.
96. *Executive Intelligence Review*, October 9, 1987, p. 46.
97. *Executive Intelligence Review*, April 15, 1988.
    Executive Intelligence Review, November 20, 1987, p. 37.
98. *Executive Intelligence Review*, October 23, 1987, p. 46.
99. "60 Minutes," November 29, 1987.
100. *Washington Post*, June 16, 1988, in *San Francisco Chronicle*.

101. *Executive Intelligence Review*, November 20, 1987, p. 34.
102. Interview with Informant "Y," September 13, 1988.
103. KFI Radio, Los Angeles, September 17, 1988, interview with Informant "Y" on the "Bill Moran Show."
    Interview with *Press* (Copenhagen), January 26, 1989.
104. *San Francisco Chronicle*, December 16, 1988.
    New York Times, December 15, 1988.
105. *Executive Intelligence Review*, November 20, 1987, p. 37.
106. *Wall Street Journal*, October 10, 1987.
107. *Dagens Nyhether* (Stockholm), June 16, 1986.
108. *Executive Intelligence Review*, October 23, 1987, p. 46.
109. *Executive Intelligence Review*, November 20, 1987, p. 28.
110. *Executive Intelligence Review*, November 20, 1987, p. 37.
111. *Executive Intelligence Review*, November 20, 1987, p. 30.
112. *Executive Intelligence Review*, November 20, 1987, p. 30–31 & 37.
113. "Persian Drugs," by Jonathan Marshall, *City Paper*, Washington, D.C., 1987.
114. *New York Times*, February 14, 1985.
115. *New York Times*, November 9, 1986.
    Los Angeles Times, November 17, 1986.
116. Report on the Vice President's Involvement in the Iran/Contra Scandal, by William Loiry, 1988.
117. Jack Anderson, *San Francisco Chronicle*, May 17, 1988.
118. *Engelab-e Eslami dar Hejrat*, Abolhassan Bani Sadr, Collected Reprints, p. 66.
119. *San Francisco Examiner*, November 15, 1986.
120. *San Jose Mercury News*, November 20, 1987, from the *Boston Globe*.
121. Abolhassan Bani Sadr, correspondence with the author of January 16, 1988 and March 26, 1988;
122. *Time*, July 25, 1983, p. 27.
    Time, January 19, 1987, p. 27.
123. *Landslide*, by Jane Mayer and Doyle McManus, p. 143.
124. *New York Times*, November 25, 1986.
125. *San Francisco Chronicle*, March 9, 1988.
    San Francisco Chronicle, March 10, 1988.
    Newsweek, July 4, 1988, p. 23.
    Wall Street Journal, November 28, 1986.
126. *San Francisco Chronicle*, February 23, 1988.
127. *San Francisco Chronicle*, July 14, 1988.
128. *Newsweek*, July 4, 1988, p. 23.
129. *San Francisco Chronicle*, April 15, 1988.
130. *Far Eastern Economic Review* (Hong Kong), cited in *San Francisco Chronicle*.
131. The Information Bulletin of the Committee for Peace and Democracy In Iran, October 1988, p. 3.
132. *Christian Science Monitor*, August 6, 1981.
133. *San Francisco Examiner*, February 28, 1987.

134. *San Francisco Chronicle*, October 24, 1988, from Associated Press.

135. *San Jose Mercury News*, June 18, 1988, from Associated Press.

136. *Time*, December 8, 1986, p. 54.

137. *New Solidarity*, December 1, 1986, p. 3.

138. *San Francisco Chronicle*, October 22, 1988, pp. 1 & A14.

139. *San Jose Mercury News*, July 26, 1988, p. 1.

140. *San Francisco Examiner*, November 27, 1988, p. A25, from Associated Press.

141. *Dimikratikos Logos*, November 29, 1986, in *Huntsville Times*, November 30, 1986, from Associated Press.

142. *Time*, July 25, 1983, p. 26.

143. *San Francisco Examiner-Chronicle*, January 1, 1989, Warren Hinkle.

144. *Landslide*, by Jane Mayer and Doyle McManus, p. 306.

145. *Landslide*, p. 314.

146. *Landslide*, p. 306.
    Time, February 2, 1987, p. 22.

147. *Los Angeles Times*, June 28, 1988.

CHAPTER IX
NAME OF THE ROSE

1. *In God's Name*, by David Yallop, Bantam Books, New York, 1984, p. 115.
   In These Times, September, 1982.

2. *In God's Name*, by David Yallop, Bantam Books, New York, 1984, pgs. 5–6.

3. *In God's Name*, by David Yallop, Bantam Books, New York, 1984, p. 114.

4. *In God's Name*, by David Yallop, Bantam Books, New York, 1984, p. 115.

5. *In God's Name*, by David Yallop, Bantam Books, New York, 1984, p. 5.

6. *In God's Name*, by David Yallop, Bantam Books, New York, 1984, p. 116.

7. *Old Nazis, The New Right and the Reagan Administration*, by Russ Bellant, Political Research Associates, Boston, 1988, p. 22.

8. *In God's Name*, by David Yallop, Bantam Books, New York, 1988, p. 112.

9. *New York Times*, June 4, 1981, p. 7.
   In These Times, September 1982.

10. *St. Peter's Banker: Michele Sindona*, by Luigi de Fonzo, Watts, 1983, p. 230.

11. *St. Peter's Banker*, by Luigi De Fonzo, 1983, p. 230. (See ref. #10, above).

12. *San Francisco Examiner*, February 28, 1987, p. A3.
    The Brotherhood, by Stephen Knight, Panther Books, 1985, paperback, ed., p. 273. Previously published by Granada Publishing, London, 1983.

13. *In God's Name*, by David Yallop, Bantam Books, New York, 1984, p. 274.

14. *San Francisco Examiner*, February 28, 1987, p. A3.

15. *Wall Street Journal*, August 8, 1985.

16. Interview by the author with informant "Y," September 20, 1988.

17. *In These Times*, September 1982.
   Executive Intelligence Review, August 24, 1982.
18. *Executive Intelligence Review*, August 24, 1982.
19. *In These Times*, September 1982.
20. *Landslide*, by Jane Mayer and Doyle McManus, Houghton Mifflin Company, Boston, 1988, p. 325.
21. *The Brotherhood*, by Stephen Knight, Panther Books, 1985, p. 278.
22. *Executive Intelligence Review*, August 24, 1982.
23. *In These Times*, September 1982.
   Executive Intelligence Review, August 24, 1982 and November 20, 1984.
24. *Europa*, January 18, 1982.
   In These Times, September 1982.
25. *San Francisco Examiner*, February 1, 1987, p. A14.
26. *Los Angeles Herald Examiner*, December 16, 1984.
   Executive Intelligence Review, September 18, 1987, p. 46.
27. *San Francisco Examiner*, February 28, 1987, p. A3.
28. *Executive Intelligence Review*, October 23, 1987, p. 45.
29. *Sunday Times* of London, July 26, 1981.
   Jerusalem Post, July 23, 1981.
   New York Times, July 26, 1981.
30. *Perilous Statecraft*, by Michael Ledeen, Charles Scribner Sons, New York, 1988, p. 28.
31. *Perilous Statecraft*, by Michael Ledeen, Charles Scribner Sons, New York, 1988, p. 96.
32. *Newsweek*, December 8, 1986.
   Miami Herald, August 9, 1987.
   Washington Post, December 29, 1986.
   Wall Street Journal, December 12, 1986, p. 54.
33. *Perilous Statecraft*, by Michael Ledeen, Charles Scribner Sons, New York, 1988, p. 96.
34. *In These Times*, January 21–27, 1987, p. 9.
35. *Perilous Statecraft*, by Michael Ledeen, Charles Scribner Sons, New York, 1988, p. 96.
36. *The Messianic Legacy*, by Michael Baigent, et al., H. Holt & Company, 1987, p. 314.
37. *Baltimore Sun*, January 18, 1987.
38. *San Jose Mercury News*, June 13, 1987, p. 21A.
39. *New York Times*, December 24, 1982.
40. *Perilous Statecraft*, by Michael Ledeen, Charles Scribner Sons, New York, 1988., p. 178.
41. *Executive Intelligence Review*, August 24, 1982.
   In These Times, September 1982.
42. *New York Times*, February 2, 1987.
43. *New York Times*, February 2, 1987.
44. *Perilous Statecraft*, by Michael Ledeen, Charles Scribner Sons, New York, 1988, p. 290.

45. *Executive Intelligence Review*, September 18, 1987, pp. 46–47.
46. *Dimikratikos Logos* (Greece), November 29, 1986.
47. Interview by the author with Informant "Y," September 13, 1988.
48. *New Solidarity*, August 24, 1984.
49. *Old Nazis, The New Right and the Reagan Administration*, by Russ Bellant, Political Research Associates, Boston, 1988, p. 22.
50. *In These Times*, September 1982.
    San Francisco Examiner, February 28, 1987, p. A3.
51. *New York Times*, March 6, 1986.
52. *Lords of the Reich*, p. 42.
53. *New Solidarity*, August 24, 1984.
54. *Boston Globe*, October 18, 1987, p. A18.
    In God's Name, by David Yallop, Bantam Books, New York, 1984, p. 116.
55. *The Senator Must Die*, by Robert D. Morrow, Roundtable Publishing, Inc., Santa Monica, California, 1988, regarding the assassination of Senator Robert Kennedy.
    Jack Anderson, November 17, 1988, regarding the assassination of President John F. Kennedy.
56. Interview by the author with informant "Y," September 6, 1988.
57. Interview by the author with informant "Y," September 13, 1988.
58. *Fanning the Flames*, by Ken Timmerman, German ed., 1988, p. 138.
59. *San Francisco Examiner*, February 1, 1987, p. A14.
60. *Landslide*, by Jane Mayer and Doyle McManus, Houghton Mifflin Company, Boston, 1988, p. 143.
61. *Washington Post*, May 23, 1976.
62. *Executive Intelligence Review*, September 18, 1987, pp. 46–47.
63. *Los Angeles Herald Examiner*, December 16, 1984.
    Executive Intelligence Review, September 18, 1987, p. 46.
    "Persian Drugs," by Jonathan Marshall, *City Paper*, Washington, D.C., 1987.
    Newsweek, December 22, 1986.
    Perilous Statecraft, by Michael Ledeen, Charles Scribner Sons, New York, 1988, p. 110.
    Senate Intelligence Committee Iran/Contra Report, January 29, 1987.
64. *New York Times*, January 31, 1987.
65. *Veil*, by Bob Woodward, Pocket Books, New York, 1987, paperback ed., p. 211.
66. *Contract on America*, by David Scheim, Shapolsky Publishers, p. 317.
67. *Veil*, by Bob Woodward, Pocket Books, New York, 1987, paperback ed., pp. 132–133.
68. *Reagan's Ruling Class*, by Ronald Brownstein, ed. by Nina, Easton, Pantheon, 1983, p. 622.
69. *Boston Globe*, October 18, 1987, p. A18.
    In God's Name, by David Yallop, Bantam Books, New York, 1984, p. 116.
70. *San Francisco Examiner*, June 28, 1987.
    Landslide, by Jane Mayer and Doyle McManus, Houghton Mifflin Company, Boston, 1988, p. 167.

71. *Landslide*, by Jane Mayer and Doyle McManus, Houghton Mifflin Company, Boston, 1988, p. 368.
72. Jack Anderson, January 24, 1986.
73. *San Francisco Chronicle*, February 9, 1987.
74. *Landslide*, by Jane Mayer and Doyle McManus, Houghton Mifflin Company, Boston, 1988, p. 58.
75. Congressional Iran/Contra Committee Report, Testimony of Duane "Dewey" Clarridge, August 4, 1987.
76. *In God's Name*, by David Yallop, Bantam Books, New York, 1984, p. 116.
77. *Executive Intelligence Review*, August 24, 1982.
78. Interview by the author with Informant "Y," September 13, 1988.
    KFI Radio, Los Angeles, California, "The Bill Moran Show," interview with Informant "Y," September 17, 1988.
79. *Playboy*, October, 1988, "An Election Held Hostage."
80. Communication from Jonathan Silvers, and notes of teleconversation by *Playboy* informant with Peter Moore, Spring 1988.
81. Interview by the author with Raji Samghabadi, *Time* magazine, September 1987.
82. Interview by the author with Mansur Rafizadeh, August 30, 1987.
83. *Witness*, by Mansur Rafizadeh, William Morrow Company, New York, 1987.
84. Interview by the author with Informant "Y," September 13, 1988.
85. *Executive Intelligence Review*, December 12, 1986, pp. 35–36 & 38, citing CIA Cables #4504464 and #4632503.
86. Unpublished chapter from *The Fish is Red*, by Warren Hinkle and William Turner, 1981.
87. *Los Angeles Weekly*, October 10–14, 1988.
88. *In God's Name*, by David Yallop, Bantam Books, New York, 1984, p. 116.
89. *In God's Name*, by David Yallop, Bantam Books, New York, 1984, p. 116.
90. *Los Angeles Weekly*, October 14–20, 1988.
91. *San Francisco Chronicle*, November 23, 1988.
92. *"60 Minutes,"* November 29, 1987.
93. *Dallas Morning News*, from UPI, December 10, 1981, quoting from The Investigative Reporter, "Who Is trying to Kill Persident Reagan?", by Jack Anderson.
94. White House correspondent Sarah McClendon, personal communication with the author, July 16, 1987.
95. *Looking Forward: The George Bush Story*, by George H. Bush and Herbert Gold, Bantam Books, 1988 paperback ed., pp. 216–219.

CHAPTER X
SOUND OF SILENCE

1. ABC *Nightline*, December 18, 1986.
2. *Witness*, by Mansur Rafizadeh, William Morrow Company, New York, 1987, p. 347.
3. *Playboy*, "An Election Held Hostage," October 1988.

4. *Foreign Policy*, Fall 1988, Number 72, "Iran/Contra: The Untold Story," by Robert Parry and Peter Kornbluh, pp. 3–30.

5. *Los Angeles Weekly*, October 14-20, 1988.

6. *Landslide*, by Jane Mayer and Doyle McManus, Houghton Mifflin Company, Boston, 1988, p. 279.

7. *Los Angeles Times*, September 11, 1988.

8. *Hidden Power*, by Roland Perry, Beaufort Books, Inc., New York, 1984, p. 166.

9. *New York Times*, October 5, 1988, p. A17.
   San Francisco Chronicle, October 5, 1988, p. A17.
   San Francisco Chronicle, October 6, 1988.
   Orange County *Register*, October 5, 1988, p. A22.

10. ABC *Nightline*, November 3, 1988, Show #1944.
    Los Angeles Times, October 31, 1988.
    Boston Globe, November 1, 1988.

11. ABC *Nightline*, November 3, 1988, Show #1944.
    San Jose Mercury News, November 4, 1988, p. 8A.

12. KPFK Radio, Los Angeles, California, Ian Masters program, September 12, 1988.

13. *San Francisco Chronicle*, October 6, 1988.

14. *Iran Times International*, August 19, 1988, p. 5, from Engelabe-e Ešlami dar Hejrat, Abolhassan Bani Sadr, ed.

15. *Iran Times International*, August 19, 1988, p. 5, from Engelab-e Eslami dar Hejrat, Abolhassan Bani Sadr, ed.

16. *The Nation* (Israel), Hesh Kestin, ed., September 30, 1988.
    San Francisco Chronicle, October 3, 1988, p. A12.
    Depth, September 30, 1988, in Orange County *Register*, October 5, 1988, p. A22.

17. *Newsweek*, November 7, 1988, p. 71.

18. Interview with the author by WCVB Television, Channel 5, Boston, at the Communuity Church of Boston, September 29, 1988.

19. *Minute* (France), "A Bomb Under Bush," October 19, 1988.

20. KGO Radio, San Francisco, California, October 19, 1988.

21. *New York Times*, November 22, 1988.

22. *San Jose Mercury News*, October 21, 1988, p. 25A.

23. *Boston Globe*, October 23, 1988.

24. *San Jose Mercury News*, November 16, 1988, p. 1.
    Boston Globe, October 2, 1988, p. 32.

25. *San Jose Mercury News*, September 13, 1988, p. 9A.

26. *San Jose Mercury News*, November 21, 1988.

27. *Los Angeles Herald Examiner*, October 5, 1988, p. A5.
    ABC *Nightline*, November 3, 1988.

28. *Fort Wayne Sentinel*, 1977.

29. *Legal Times*, December 19, 1988.

30. *Playboy* magazine, October 1988, "An Election Held Hostage," p. 74.

31. Larry King Radio, June 15, 1988, interview with former President Carter.

32. *San Francisco Examiner*, November 20, 1988, p. A13, from Associated Press.
33. *San Francisco Examiner*, November 20, 1988, p. A13.
34. Congressional Record: Senate, August 7, 1987, pp. S11585–S11587.
35. Congressional Iran/Contra Committee Report, p. 162.
36. *Time*, January 19, 1987, p. 16.
37. Telephone conversation with Richard Brenneke, December 18, 1988.
38. Jerry Bohnen, interview with Richard Brenneke, KTOK Radio, Oklahoma City, Oklahoma, October 6, 1988, transcript pp. 15 & 17.
39. *Sunday Telegraph* (London), December 28, 1986, pp. 1–2.
40. Letter to the author from William Herrmann, March 29, 1989.
41. Pittsburgh *Post-Gazette*, January 25, 1989, p. 7.
42. Memorandum from ABC News European correspondent Pierre Salinger to Roone Arledge et al., September 8, 1987.
43. Conversation with *Newsweek* reporter Robert Parry, August 22, 1988, Washington, D.C.
44. *San Francisco Examiner*, November 20, 1987.
45. Appellants' Application for Order Enlarging Time to File Petition for Rehearing, U.S. Court of Appeals for the Federal Circuit (Washington, D.C.), in BELK et al. vs. U.S., Case Number 87-1631, executed October 17, 1988. Filed by mail October 22, 1988. (Action in suit filed by 13 of the 52 U.S. embassy hostages).

EPILOGUE
A KINDER, GENTLER NATION

1. *Washington Post*, October 5, 1988.
2. *San Jose Mercury News*, February 28, 1987, Seymour Hersh.
3. *Los Angeles Times*, December 17, 1986.
4. *Strategic Investment*, December 12, 1988.
5. *San Francisco Chronicle*, January 6, 1987;
   New York Times, January 6, 1987, p. 6.
6. *Perilous Statecraft*, by Michael Ledeen, Charles Scribners Sons, New York, 1988, p. 214.
7. *Washington Post*, August 23, 1988.
8. *New York Times*, August 31, 1981.
9. *New York Times*, January 8, 1987.